OXFORD MEDIEVAL TEXTS

General Editors
C. N. L. BROOKE   D. E. GREENWAY
M. WINTERBOTTOM

ALCUIN
THE BISHOPS, KINGS, AND
SAINTS OF YORK

ALCUIN

THE BISHOPS, KINGS, AND SAINTS OF YORK

EDITED BY

PETER GODMAN

Fellow of Pembroke College, Oxford

CLARENDON PRESS · OXFORD

1982

THE UNITED LIBRARY

GARRETT/SEABURY SEMINARIES

Oxford University Press, Walton Street, Oxford OX2 6DP

London Glasgow New York Toronto
Delhi Bombay Calcutta Madras Karachi
Kuala Lumpur Singapore Hong Kong Tokyo
Nairobi Dar es Salaam Cape Town
Melbourne Auckland

and associates in
Beirut Berlin Ibadan Mexico City Nicosia

Published in the United States by
Oxford University Press, New York

© *Peter Godman 1982*

British Library Cataloguing in Publication Data
Alcuin
    The bishops, kings and saints of York.
    I. Title   *II. Godman, Peter*
    871'.03   *PA6202.A/*
    ISBN 0-19-822262-9

Library of Congress Cataloging in Publication Data
Alcuin, 735–804.
    The bishops, kings, and saints of York.

    (Oxford medieval texts)
    Text in Latin and English; commentary in English.
    Bibliography: p.
    Includes indexes.
    1. York (North Yorkshire)—History—Poetry.
2. England—Church history—Anglo-Saxon period,
449–1066—Poetry. 3. Northumbria (Kingdom)—
History—Poetry. I. Godman, Peter. II. Title.
III. Series.
PA8245.D4E5   *1983*   *874'.03*   *82–8205*
ISBN 0-19-822262-9

Typeset by Joshua Associates, Oxford,
Printed in Great Britain
at the University Press, Oxford
by Eric Buckley
Printer to the University

IN MEMORY OF
COLIN MACLEOD

Was man sich und dem Leser als erzählende
Dichtung zumutete, zeigt Alcuins annalenartige
Kirchengeschichte von York . . .

(CURTIUS)

Wenn ein Buch und ein Kopf zusammenstossen
und es klingt hohl, liegt das allemal im Buch?

(LICHTENBERG)

PREFACE

WHEN J.-K. Huysmans described the literary tastes of his anti-hero, des Esseintes, he singled out those Latin poets who, in the eyes of an orthodox public, seemed most obscure and boring. Commodian and Orientius, Dracontius and Tatwine could engage des Esseintes's perverse attention. But at Alcuin and the authors of his time even des Esseintes seems to have drawn the line: 'son attirance diminuait . . . peu ravi, en somme, par la pesante masse des latinistes carlovingiens, les Alcuin et les Éginhard . . .' (*A Rebours*, Garnier–Flammarion, p. 93).

Scholarly opinion, almost paradoxically, shares des Esseintes's view of Alcuin as an imaginative writer. 'Paradoxically' because Alcuin's name is generally the first among authors of the Carolingian period that springs to mind and to print, and yet there is little interest in him as a literary figure. This paradox can be partly explained by recent scholarship on Alcuin which, in its variety and high quality, creates an illusion of issues settled and of comprehensiveness achieved. The present state of edition and interpretation of Alcuin's major poetical work provides a measure of the neglect which this area of his writing has received.

A century has passed since the last published edition of Alcuin's poem on York, and it marks no dramatic textual improvement over the *editio princeps* of 1691. The poem on York is one of our chief literary sources for eighth-century Northumbrian history and for Alcuin's biography; it occupies a significant place in the development of Anglo-Latin and Carolingian literature; its interest as a witness to early medieval scholarship is recognized, but there exists no sustained attempt at interpretation of any one of these aspects of Alcuin's work. The Latinity of the author often regarded as the principal agent of Charlemagne's linguistic reforms has never been studied, nor has his cultural background, as reflected in this text, been systematically examined in its Insular and Carolingian contexts. There would thus seem

to be room for a fresh appraisal of Alcuin's work, but sympa-
thetic revaluation is unlikely to lead to artificial enthusiasm.
Anglo-Latin and Carolingian poetry contain few masterpieces,
and Alcuin's poem on York is not among their number.

No illusion of issues settled and of comprehensiveness
achieved will be created by the present edition. I have
attempted, imperfectly, to provide some of the philological,
literary, and historical material with which to interpret this
poem, the interest of which reaches beyond more than one
specialized discipline. I hope that others will correct and
extend what I have seen. There are problems posed by
Alcuin's text, such as the list of authors in the York library
of his youth, which seem to me ultimately insoluble, and in
discussing them I have chosen to stress the limitations of our
evidence. Older and more experienced scholars may think
otherwise. Of some aspects of Alcuin's writing, such as his
hagiography, I have deliberately provided a summary
account, knowing that other research was in progress else-
where. By reason of these limitations of scope and defi-
ciencies of execution, the present edition is intended to be
nothing more than an *editio minor*.

This book, written chiefly in the years 1979–81, has been
generously supported by a number of institutions, scholars,
and friends. My first debt is to Corpus Christi College, Cam-
bridge, which made a home for me when I went there to
read Medieval Latin after school in New Zealand. The Jebb
Studentship in the University of Cambridge during 1978–9
facilitated the travel to foreign libraries upon which parts of
this edition are based. To Christ Church, Oxford, which
appointed me to a Research Lectureship in 1979, and to
Pembroke College, Oxford, which elected me to a Tutorial
Fellowship in 1980, I owe the congenial environment in
which my work was completed.

The staffs of a number of libraries in Munich, Reims,
Paris, Oxford, Cambridge, and London have greatly assisted
my research and, in particular, I should like to thank the
Director and staff of the Warburg Institute in the University
of London, *locus amoenus*. Inquiries about specific words
have been answered with courtesy and despatch by the
editorial staffs of the *Dictionary of Medieval Latin from*

British Sources, the *Mittellateinisches Wörterbuch* and the *Thesaurus Linguae Latinae*. A grant from the British Academy defrayed the costs of preparing successive drafts of a complicated manuscript. Special thanks are due to Mrs Dorothy Tanfield for the meticulous care with which she has typed my work.

Since I was an undergraduate, I have talked about Alcuin with Professor Donald Bullough and Professor Dieter Schaller. Their kindly interest and welcome advice have made me feel that this subject is worth doing and that this book might perhaps be worth writing. Dr Michael Winterbottom has been my prop and stay. Professor Christopher Brooke and Dr Diana Greenway, as editors of the Oxford Medieval Texts, provided valuable criticism and tactful support. My work has benefited from the comments of Professor Julian Brown and Dr Michael Lapidge, who examined the Cambridge dissertation upon which this edition draws; and Dr Lapidge has been so kind as to read through a draft of the Introduction and Commentary. My friend Mr Michael Reeve made excellent suggestions for change and improvement of parts of the manuscript, which I have gratefully adopted. A number of scholars have answered queries or provided me with offprints of their work, and these debts are specified in my notes. Here I should like to thank my colleagues in Oxford, particularly the early medieval historians, who have made the perilous transition from another place so stimulating, and to acknowledge those scholars who have generously discussed with me points of detail and of interpretation, especially Mr P. Dronke, Professor H. Gneuss, Mme M.-P. Laffitte, Dr V. Law, Mr C. Leach, Dr J. Marenbon, Mr and Mrs P. Meyvaert, Professor F. Munari, Mr M. Parkes, Mr D. Phillips, Professor G. Rigg, Dr G. Silagi, and Mr N. Wright. The errors which remain are my own, and no one thanked in this preface will doubt my capacity for independent misjudgement.

Oxford   P. G.
St. Bartholomew's Day, 1981

CONTENTS

CONTENTS

ABBREVIATIONS
(INTRODUCTION AND COMMENTARY)

AASSOSB	*Acta Sanctorum Ordinis Sancti Benedicti.*
ASE	*Anglo-Saxon England*, edd. P. Clemoes *et al.*
Bischoff, *Mittelalterliche Studien*	B. Bischoff, *Mittelalterliche Studien.* 2 vols. Stuttgart, 1966, 1967.
Blaise, *Vocabulaire latin*	A. Blaise (rev. A. Dumas), *Le vocabulaire latin des principaux thèmes liturgiques.* Turnhout, 1966.
Blumenshine	G. B. Blumenshine (ed.), *Liber Alcuini Contra Haeresim Felicis.* Edition with an Introduction, Studi e Testi 85. Città del Vaticano, 1980.
Bullough	D. A. Bullough, 'Hagiography as Patriotism: Alcuin's York Poem and the Early Northumbrian *Vitae Sanctorum*'. In *Hagiographie, Cultures, et Sociétés*, Centre de recherche sur l'antiquité tardive et le haut moyen âge, Université de Paris (Paris, 1981), pp. 339–59.
Brunhölzl, *Geschichte*	F. Brunhölzl, *Geschichte der lateinischen Literatur des Mittelalters*, i. Munich, 1975.
CCSL	*Corpus Christianorum. Series Latina.*
CLA	*Codices Latini Antiquiores*, ed. E. A. Lowe. 11 vols. and Suppl. Oxford, 1934–71, ii^2 (1972).
CSEL	*Corpus Scriptorum Ecclesiasticorum Latinorum*
Colgrave–Mynors	Bede's *Ecclesiastical History of the English People*, edd. B. Colgrave and R. A. B. Mynors (OMT). Oxford, 1969.
Comp. Lit.	*Comparative Literature.*
Cramp, *Anglian and Viking York*	R. Cramp, *Anglian and Viking York.* Borthwick Papers 33. York, 1968.
Curtius	E. R. Curtius, *European Literature and the Latin Middle Ages*, translated by W. R. Trask. New York, 1953.
Deutsches Archiv	*Deutsches Archiv für Erforschung des Mittelalters.*
Druhan, *Syntax*	D. R. Druhan, S.J., *The Syntax of Bede's Historia Ecclesiastica.* The Catholic University of America, Studies in Medieval and Renaissance Latin, 8. Washington, 1938.

EHR	*English Historical Review*
Ebvracvm	*An Inventory of the Historical Monuments in the City of York*, i. *Ebvracvm. Roman York.* Royal Commission on Historical Monuments, 1962.
Fm. St.	*Frühmittelalterliche Studien.*
Famulus Christi	*Famulus Christi. Essays in Commemoration of the Thirteenth Centenary of the Birth of the Venerable Bede*, ed. G. Bonner. London, 1976.
Farmer, *Dictionary*	D. H. Farmer, *The Oxford Dictionary of Saints.* Oxford, 1978.
HE	Bede's *Historia Ecclesiastica Gentis Anglorum.*
Haddan and Stubbs	A. W. Haddan and W. Stubbs, *Councils and Ecclesiastical Documents Relating to Great Britain and Ireland.* 3 vols. Oxford, 1869-78.
History of York Minster	*A History of York Minster*, edd. G. E. Aylmer and R. Cant. Oxford, 1977.
Karl der Grosse	*Karl der Grosse. Lebenswerk und Nachleben*, i. *Persönlichkeit und Geschichte*, ed. H. Beumann; ii. *Das Geistige Leben*, ed. B. Bischoff. Düsseldorf, 1965.
Klopsch, *Einführung*	P. Klopsch, *Einführung in die Dichtungslehren des lateinischen Mittelalters.* Darmstadt, 1980.
Latham, *Dictionary*	R. E. Latham, *A Dictionary of Medieval Latin from British Sources.* 2 vols. Oxford, 1975- .
Leumann-Hofmann-Szantyr	M. Leumann, J. B. Hofmann, A. Szantyr, *Lateinische Grammatik.* 2 vols. Munich, 1977.
Levison, *England and the Continent*	W. Levison, *England and the Continent in the Eighth Century.* Oxford, 1946.
Löfstedt, *Kommentar*	E. Löfstedt, *Philologischer Kommentar zur Peregrinatio Aetheriae.* Uppsala, 1911.
Löfstedt, *Late Latin*	id., *Late Latin.* Oslo, 1959.
Löfstedt, *Syntactica*	id., *Syntactica. Studien und Beiträge zur historischen Syntax des Lateins* i², ii. Lund, 1956.
Löfstedt, *Vermischte Studien*	id., *Vermischte Studien zur lateinischen Sprachkunde und Syntax.* Lund, 1936.
MÆ	*Medium Ævum*
MGH AA	*Monumenta Germaniae Historica: Auctores Antiquissimi*

Epp.	*Epistolae*
PLAC	*Poetae Latini Ævi Carolini*
SrM	*Scriptores rerum Merowingicarum*
SS	*Scriptores*
Mlat. Jb.	*Mittellateinisches Jahrbuch*
Mlat. Wb.	*Mittellateinisches Wörterbuch*
Monumenta Alcuiniana	*Monumenta Alcuiniana*, ed. P. Jaffé, W. Wattenbach, and E. Dümmler. *Bibliotheca rerum Germanicarum*, vi. Berlin, 1873.
Neues Archiv	*Neues Archiv der Gesellschaft für ältere deutsche Geschichtskunde.*
Niermeyer, *Lexicon*	J. F. Niermeyer, *Mediae Latinitatis Lexicon Minus.* Leiden, 1976.
Norberg, *Beiträge*	D. Norberg, *Beiträge zur spätlateinischen Syntax.* Uppsala, 1944.
Norberg, *Introduction*	id., *Introduction à l'étude de la versification latine médiévale.* Uppsala, 1958.
Norberg, *Syntaktische Forschungen*	id., *Syntaktische Forschungen auf dem Gebiete des Spätlateins und des frühen Mittelalters.* Stockholm, 1943.
OCT	Oxford Classical Texts.
OMT	Oxford Medieval Texts.
PBA	*Proceedings of the British Academy.*
PL	J.-P. Migne, *Patrologia Latina.*
Plummer, i, ii	C. Plummer, *Venerabilis Bedae Opera Historica.* 2 vols. Oxford 1896.
RS	Rolls Series.
SCH	*Studies in Church History.*
SM	*Studi medievali.*
Salway	P. Salway, *Roman Britain.* Oxford, 1981.
Schaller–Könsgen	D. Schaller and E. Könsgen, *Initia Carminum Latinorum Saeculo Undecimo Antiquiorum. Bibliographisches Repertorium für die lateinische Dichtung der Antike und des früheren Mittelalters.* Göttingen, 1977.
Soldier and Civilian	R. M. Butler, *Soldier and Civilian in Roman Yorkshire.* Leicester, 1971.
Spoleto ... Settimane	*Settimane di Studio del Centro Italiano di Studi sull'alto medioevo* (Spoleto).
Stenton	F. M. Stenton, *Anglo-Saxon England*[3]. Oxford, 1971.

TLL	*Thesaurus Linguae Latinae.*
Tangl, *Epp.*	M. Tangl, *Die Briefe des heiligen Bonifatius und Lullus. MGH, Epistolae Selectae*, i. Berlin, 1916.
Taylor i, ii, iii	H. M. and J. Taylor, *Anglo-Saxon Architecture.* 3 vols. Cambridge, 1965–78.
Wallace-Hadrill, *Early Germanic Kingship*	J. M. Wallace-Hadrill, *Early Germanic Kingship in England and on the Continent.* Oxford, 1971.
Wallace-Hadrill, *Early Medieval History*	id., *Early Medieval History.* Oxford, 1975.
Wallach, *Alcuin and Charlemagne*	L. Wallach, *Alcuin and Charlemagne. Studies in Carolingian History and Literature*, Cornell Studies in Classical Philology, 30. 2 Ithaca, 1959.
Whitelock	D. Whitelock, *English Historical Documents*, c.*500–1042*, i². London and New York, 1979.
Y. Arch. Jnl.	*Yorkshire Archaeological Journal.*
Z.f.r.Ph.	*Zeitschrift für romanische Philologie.*

SELECT BIBLIOGRAPHY
AND TEXTUAL REFERENCES[1]

A. MANUSCRIPTS CITED[2]

ANTWERP
Museum Plantin-Moretus, M. 17. 4, lxviii, n. 1

BAMBERG
Staatsbibliothek, B. II. 10 (Misc. Patr. 17), lxv, n. 5; lxviii and n. 1;
lxxi, n. 2

(EAST) BERLIN
Staatsbibliothek der Stiftung Preussischer Kulturbesitz,
Diez. B. Sant. 66, lxxiii, n. 2
lat. fol. 877, lxiii, n. 2

CAMBRIDGE
Corpus Christi College, 173, lxx and n. 2
Trinity College, 1130 (0.2.26) $[T, T^1, T^2]$, cxi; cxv–cxx; cxxii–
cxxviii; cxxxi; 184
University Library, Kk. 5. 16, 1600 ff.

CUES
Hospitalbibliothek MS. 171, lxix–lxx and n. 1

DURHAM
Dean and Chapter Library, B. II. 30, 1546

DÜSSELDORF
Heinrich-Heine-Institut, B. 215, 1546
     "   "   "   C. 118, 1546
Staatsarchiv, Fragm. 20, 1546
     "   MS. 2. 4. No. 2, 1543

FLORENCE
Biblioteca Medicea Laurenziana, pl. XLV. 15, 1556

HAUZENSTEIN
Graf Walderdorff Sammlung [*C.L.A.* viii 1052], lxiii, n. 2

KASSEL
Landesbibliothek MS. Theol. fol. 21, 1541

---

[1] For a bibliography of Alcuin's life and work, see the Introduction, pp.
xxxiii–ix.

[2] Only extant manuscripts are listed here. Sigla employed in this edition are
listed in square brackets beside the manuscript to which they refer. (See further
pp. cxxxi–cxxxii). *C.L.A.* numbers are noted in the case of manuscripts in private
collections. References in bold type are to the Introduction (Roman numerals)
and Commentary (Arabic numerals).

LENINGRAD
  National Public (Saltykov-Shchedrin) Library,
  F. V. i. 3, 1541
  Q. V. xiv. 1, lxx and n. 7

LEIDEN
  Universiteitsbibliotheek Voss. lat. F. 4, 1545

LONDON
  British Library, Add. 4277, cxvi, n. 4
  ”   ”   Harley 2793, cxi and n. 5

MAESEYCK
  Eglise Ste-Cathérine, Trésors SN, lxiii, n. 2

MILAN
  Biblioteca Ambrosiana, C. 74 sup., lxxi and n. 2

MUNICH
  Hauptstaatsarchiv, Raritäten-Selektion 108, lxiii, n. 2

PARIS
  Bibliothèque nationale, lat. 8051, 1554
  ”   ”   lat. 9347, lxxi and n. 2, cxxix and n. 3

REIMS
  Bibliothèque municipale, 426 [R, r], cxi, cxiii, n. 1, cxx–cxxviii,
    cxxxi, 1436-7, 1437, 1438-5, 1441-5, 1446

SPANGENBERG
  Pfarrbibliothek SN, 1557

VATICAN
  Biblioteca Apostolica Vaticana, Pal. lat. 235, lxx and n. 6
  ”   ”   ”   Reg. lat. 226, 1447
  ”   ”   ”   Reg. lat. 2078, cxxix and n. 4

WEINHEIM (?)
  E. Fischer Sammlung SN. [C.L.A. ix 1370], lxiii, n. 2; 1549

B. PRINTED PRIMARY SOURCES[1]

Alcuin   *Carmina*, ed. E. Dümmler, *MGH PLAC* i, pp. 113,
[Alc.]   160–351, 631-3; ii, pp. 690-3; ed. K. Strecker
              iv. 2, pp. 904–10, 1128; vi, p. 159.

              Poem on York, see pp. cxxxi–ii.

---

[1] Sections B and C list texts quoted in or relevant to this edition, with the exception of those which appear in the list of Abbreviations (Introduction and Commentary). Relevant works of major authors are listed in full (see under Alcuin). The abbreviation in square brackets indicates the form in which each author/text is referred to in apparatus ii or apparatus iii. The edition which first appears in this list is the one quoted in app. ii or app. iii.

De Orthographia, ed. A. Marsili. Pisa, 1952.

De Rhetorica et de Virtutibus, ed. C. Halm, *Rhetores latini minores* (Leipzig, 1863), pp. 525-50; (with translation) W. S. Howell, *The Rhetoric of Alcuin and Charlemagne*. Princeton, 1941.

Disputatio, edd. W. Suchier and L. W. Daly, *Disputatio regalis et nobilissimi iuvenis Pippini cum Albino scholastico*; in *Altercatio Hadriani Augusti et Epicteti philosophi*. Illinois Studies in Language and Literature 24, nos. 1-2. Urbana, 1939.

Epistolae, ed. E. Dümmler, *MGH Epp.* iv, pp. 1-481; v, pp. 643-5; Colin Chase, *Two Alcuin Letter-Books*. Toronto Medieval Latin Texts 5. Toronto, 1975.

Hagiographica:
    Vita Richarii confessoris Centulensis, ed. B. Krusch, *MGH SrM* iv, pp. 381-401.
    Vita Vedastis episcopi Atrebatensis, ed. B. Krusch, *MGH SrM* iii, pp. 414-27; iv, p. 770; vii, pp. 819-20.
    Vita Willibrordi archiepiscopi Traiectensis (prose), ed. W. Levison, *MGH SrM* vii, pp. 81-141, 856-8; (metrical), ed. E. Dümmler, *MGH PLAC* i, pp. 207-20; A. Poncelet, *AASSOSB, Novembris* iii (Brussels, 1910), pp. 435-57.

Propositiones ad acuendos iuvenes, ed. M. Folkerts, *Denkschriften der österreichischen Akademie der Wissenschaften*, Mathematisch-naturwissenschaftliche Klasse 116, 6. Abhandlung (Vienna, 1978), pp. 15-78.

Opera cetera, PL c, ci.

Translations: S. Allott, *Alcuin of York* (York, 1974); H. Kusch, *Einführung in das lateinische Mittelalter*, i (Berlin, 1957); H. Waddell, *Mediaeval Latin Lyrics* (London, 1933), pp. 78 ff.; id., *More Latin Lyrics* (London, 1976), pp. 146 ff.; *Son Well-Beloved: Six Poems by Alcuin, Translated by the Benedictines of Stanbrook* (Worcester, 1967).

Aldhelm
[Aldh.]

Opera, ed. R. Ehwald, *MGH AA* xv. Berlin, 1919.

Translation: M. Lapidge and M. Herren, *Aldhelm: The Prose Works*. Ipswich and Totowa, 1979.

'Annales   T. Arnold (ed.), *Symeonis monachi Dunelmensis*
  Eboracenses'   *Opera omnia*, ii (*R.S.*) (London, 1885), pp. 31–
  [*'Ann. Ebor.'*] 66.

Arator   *De Actibus Apostolorum*, ed. A. P. McKinlay,
  [Arat.]   *CSEL* lxxii. Vienna, 1951.

Augustine   *Epistolae* 1–123, ed. A. Goldbacher, *CSEL* xxxiv.
                    Prague, Vienna, and Leipzig, 1895.

Avitus, Alcimus   *Poemata*, ed. R. Peiper, *MGH AA* vi. 2 (Berlin,
  [Avit.]   1883), pp. 201–94.

Æthelwulf   *De Abbatibus*, ed. A. Campbell (Oxford, 1967).
  [Æthelw.]   ed. E. Dümmler, *MGH PLAC* i, pp. 583–604.

Bede   *Carmina*. *Bedae Venerabilis liber hymnorum,
                    rhythmi, variae preces*, ed. J. Fraipont, *CCSL*
                    cxxii (Turnhout, 1955), pp. 405–70.

                    De Arte Metrica, ed. C. B. Kendall, *Bedae Venera-
                    bilis Opera* i, Opera didascalia, *CCSL* cxxiii. *A*
                    (Turnhout, 1975), pp. 59–141.

                    De Orthographia, ed. C. W. Jones, ibid., pp. 1–
                    57.

                    Epistola ad Ecgbertum, ed. Plummer i, pp. 405–23.

                    HE, edd. Colgrave–Mynors; Plummer i, pp. 1–363.

                    Historia Abbatum, ed. Plummer i, pp. 364–87.

                    Vita S. Cuthberti (prose), ed. B. Colgrave, *Two
                    Lives of St. Cuthbert*. Cambridge, 1940; (metrical),
                    ed. W. Jaager, *Bedas metrische 'Vita Sancti Cuth-
                    berti'*, *Palaestra* 198. Leipzig, 1935.

Boniface   *Ænigmata*, ed. Fr. Glorie, *Ænigmata Bonifatii:
  [Bonif.]   Ænigmata 'Laureshamensia'*, *CCSL* cxxxiii (Turn-
                    hout, 1968), pp. 273–343; *MGH PLAC* i, pp. 3–23.

                    Epistolae, ed. Tangl, *Epp.*

Calendarium   A. Wilmart (ed.), 'Un témoin anglo-saxon du calen-
  Eboracense   drier métrique de York', *Revue bénédictine* 46
  metricum   (1934), pp. 41–69; U. Westerbergh, *Beneventan
  [*Cal. Ebor. metr.*] Ninth Century Poetry* (Stockholm, 1957), pp.
                    74–90.

Carmina   E. Dümmler (ed.), *MGH PLAC* ii, pp. 637–48.
  Salisburgensia
  [*Carm. Salisb.*]

Cicero   *De Oratore*, ed. A. S. Wilkins. Oxford, 1892.

Continuations to Colgrave–Mynors (ed.), pp. 572–6.
  Bede's *HE*
  [*HE Contin.*]

Dracontius [Drac.]	*Carmina*, ed. F. Vollmer, *MGH AA* xiv (Berlin, 1905), pp. 22-113.
Eddius Stephanus	*Vita Wilfridi*, ed. B. Colgrave, *Eddius Stephanus' Life of Bishop Wilfrid.* Cambridge, 1927.
Einhard	*Vita Karoli Magni*, ed. L. Halphen, *Vie de Charlemagne.* Paris, 1923.
Epitaphia Civitatis Papiae [*Epitaph. Civ. Pap.*]	E. Dümmler (ed.), *MGH PLAC* i, pp. 101-5.
Ermoldus Nigellus [Ermold.]	*Carmina*, ed. E. Dümmler, *MGH PLAC* ii, pp. 1-93.
	E. Faral (ed.), *Poème sur Louis le Pieux et épîtres au roi Pépin.* Paris, 1932.
Felix	*Life of St. Guthlac*, ed. B. Colgrave. Cambridge, 1959.
Florus of Lyons [Flor. Lugd.]	*Carmina*, ed. E. Dümmler, *MGH PLAC* ii, pp. 507-66.
Fortunatus, Venantius [Ven. Fort.]	*Carmina*, ed. F. Leo, *MGH AA* iv. 1. Berlin, 1881.
Gildas [Gild.]	*De Excidio Britonum*, ed. M. Winterbottom, *Gildas: The Ruin of Britain and Other Documents.* London and Chichester, 1968.
Heiric of Auxerre [Heiric]	*Carmina*, ed. L. Traube, *MGH PLAC* iii, pp. 427-517.
Helpidius Rusticius	*Carmen de Iesu Christi Beneficiis*, ed. F. Corsaro. Catania, 1953.
'Hibernicus Exul' ['Hib. Exul']	*Carmina*, ed. F. Dümmler, *MGH PLAC* i, pp. 395-413.
Horace [Hor.]	*Opera*, ed.[5] F. Klingner. Leipzig, 1970.
Hrabanus Maurus [Hrab. Maur.]	*Carmina*, ed. E. Dümmler, *MGH PLAC* ii, pp. 117, 154-244.
Isidore of Seville [Isid.]	*Etymologiae*, ed. W. M. Lindsay, *OCT.* 2 vols. Oxford, 1911.
[ps.-Isid.]	*Versus in Bibliotheca*, ed. A. Ortéga, *Helmantica* 12 (1961), pp. 261-99.
Jerome	*De Viris Illustribus*, ed. C. A. Bernoulli. Freiburg-im-Breisgau and Leipzig, 1895.
John of Fulda [Joh. Fuld.]	*Versus*, ed. E. Dümmler, *MGH PLAC* i, p. 392.

Joseph Scottus [Joseph Scott.]   *Carmina*, ed. E. Dümmler, *MGH PLAC* i, pp. 149–59.

Juvencus [Juvenc.]   *Evangelia*, ed. J. Huemer, *CSEL* xxiv. Prague, Vienna, and Leipzig, 1891.

'Karolus Magnus et Leo Papa' ['Karolus Magnus']   E. Dümmler (ed.), *MGH PLAC* i, pp. 366–79; H. Beumann, F. Brunhölzl, and H. Winkelmann, *Karolus Magnus et Leo Papa. Ein Paderborner Epos vom Jahre 799*. Paderborn, 1966.

Lactantius (attrib.) ['Lactant.']   *De Ave Phoenice*, ed. M. C. Fitzpatrick. Philadelphia, 1933.

Licentius   *Carmen* (*See* Augustine, *Epistola* xxv, ed. Goldbacher, pp. 89–95).

Lucan   *Bellum Civile*, ed. A. E. Housman. Oxford, 1926.

Lul   *Epistolae*, ed. Tangl, *Epp.*

Milo of Saint-Amand [Milo]   *Carmina*, ed. L. Traube, *MGH PLAC* iii, pp. 557–675.

Miracula Nynie Episcopi   K. Strecker (ed.), *MGH PLAC* iv. 3, pp. 943–62.

Moduin   *Egloga*, ed. E. Dümmler, *MGH PLAC* i, pp. 382–91; 569–73.

Navigatio S. Brendani   G. Orlandi (ed.), Testi e documenti per lo studio dell'antichità. Milan, 1960; C. Selmer (ed.), University of Notre Dame Publications in Medieval Studies 16. Notre Dame, 1959.

Ovid   *Heroides*, ed. A. Palmer. Oxford, 1908.

Paulinus of Aquileia [Paulin. Aquil.]   *Carmina*, ed. D. Norberg, *L'Œuvre poétique de Paulin d'Aquilée*. Kungl. Vitterhets Historie och Antikvitets Akademiens Handlingar, Filologiskfilosofiska serien 18. Stockholm, 1979.

Paulinus of Nola [Paul. Nol.]   *Carmina*, ed. W. V. Hartel, *CSEL* xxix, xxx. Vienna, 1894.

Paulus Diaconus [Paul. Diac.]   *Carmina*, ed. K. Neff, *Die Gedichte des Paulus Diaconus*. Quellen und Untersuchungen zur lateinischen Philologie des Mittelalters 3. 4. Munich, 1908.

'Poeta Saxo' [Poet. Saxo]   '*Annales*', ed. P. v. Winterfeld, *MGH PLAC* iv, pp. 1–71, 1129.

Prosper of Aquitaine [Prosper]   *De Ingratis*, ed. C. T. Huegelmeyer. Washington, 1962.

Epigrammata ex sententiis Augustini. PL li, cols. 497–532.

Epigrammata in obtrectatorem Augustini. PL li. cols. 149-52.

Prosper (attrib.) [Ps.-Prosper] *Carmen de Providentia Dei*, ed. M. McHugh. Washington, 1964.

Prudentius [Prud.] *Carmina*, ed. M. P. Cunningham, *CCSL* cxxvi. Turnhout, 1966.

Publilius Optatia-nus Porfyrius [Publ. Optat. Porf.] *Carmina*, i, ii, ed. J. Polara. Turin, 1973.

Quintilian *Institutio Oratoria*, ed. M. Winterbottom, OCT. 2 vols. Oxford, 1970.

Regula Sancti Benedicti [*Reg. S. Ben.*] A. de Vogüé and J. Neufville (ed.). 7 vols. Paris, 1972-7.

The Seafarer I. L. Gordon (ed.), Norwich, 1960.

Caelius Sedulius [Sedul.] *Carmina*, ed. J. Huemer, *CSEL* x. Vienna, 1885.

Statius [Stat.] *Thebaid*, ed.[2] A. Klotz and Th. C. Klinnert. Leipzig, 1973.

Achilleid, ed. O. A. W. Dilke. Cambridge, 1954.

Silvae, ed. F. Vollmer. Leipzig, 1898.

Sylloge of Canterbury [*Syll. Epig. Cantab.*] A. Silvagni (ed.), 'La Silloge di Cambridge', *Rivista di archaeologia christiana* 20 (1943), pp. 49-112.

'Symeon of Durham' See 'Annales Eboracenses'.

Theodulf of Orléans *Carmina*, ed. E. Dümmler, *MGH PLAC* i, pp. 445-581, 629-30.

Versus de Verona, Versum de Mediolano Civitate [*Laud. Veron. civ., Laud. Medio. civ.*] G. B. Pighi (ed.), Università di Bologna, Studi di filologia classica 8. Bologna, 1969.

Virgil [Virg.] *Opera*, ed. R. A. B. Mynors, OCT. Oxford, 1969.

Vita Alcuini [*Vit. Alc.*] W. Arndt (ed.), *MGH SS* xv 1 (Hannover, 1887), pp. 182-97; *Monumenta Alcuiniana*, pp. 1-34.

Vita Gregorii Magni B. Colgrave (ed.), *The Earliest Life of Gregory the Great, by an Anonymous Monk of Whitby*. Kansas, 1968.

Vulgate R. Weber *et al.* (ed.), *Biblia Sacra iuxta vulgatam versionem*. 2 vols. Stuttgart, 1975.

Walahfrid Strabo   *Carmina*, ed. E. Dümmler, *MGH PLAC* ii, pp. 259–
[Walahfr.]   423.

Waltharius   K. Strecker (ed.), *MGH PLAC* vi. 1, pp. 24–85.
[*Walthar.*]

Widukind of   *Res gestae Saxonicae*, ed. H. E. Lohmann (rev.
   Corvey   P. Hirsch), *MGH, Scriptores rerum Germanicarum
[Widukind]   in usum scholarum*. Hannover, 1935.

C. SECONDARY WORKS

(i) *Literary Histories, Bibliographical Handbooks, etc.*

Bolton, W. F.   *A History of Anglo-Latin Literature 597–740*,
                       i. Princeton, 1967.

Courcelle, P.   *Histoire littéraire des grandes invasions german-
                       iques*[3]. Paris, 1964.

Curtius, E. R.   'Die Musen im Mittalalter', *Z.f.r.Ph.* 59 (1939
                       pp. 129–88; ibid. 63 (1943), pp. 256–68.

                       'Dichtung und Rhetorik im Mittelalter', *Deutsche
                       Vierteljahrschrift* (1938), pp. 435–73.

Ebert, A.   *Allgemeine Geschichte der Literatur des Mittel-
                       alters im Abendlande bis zum Beginne des XI.
                       Jahrhunderts*. 3 vols. Leipzig, 1874–87.

Ermini, F.   *Storia della letteratura latina medievale dalle
                       origini alla fine del secolo VII*. Spoleto, 1960.

Ghellinck, J. de   *Littérature latine au moyen âge*. 2 vols. Brussels,
                       1939.

Gröber, G.   *Übersicht über die lateinische Literatur von der
                       Mitte des 6. Jahrhunderts bis 1350*; in *Grundriss
                       der romanischen Philologie*, i. 1 (Strasburg, 1902),
                       pp. 97–432.

Langosch, K.   *Profile des lateinischen Mittelalters*. Darmstadt,
                       1965.

Raby, F. J. E.   *A History of Christian Latin Poetry from the
                       Beginning to the Close of the Middle Ages*[2].
                       Oxford, 1953.

                       *A History of Secular Latin Poetry in the Middle
                       Ages*[2]. 2 vols. Oxford, 1957.

Schumann, O.   *Lateinisches Hexameter-Lexikon*. 4 vols. Munich,
                       1979–81.

Szövérffy, J.   *Weltliche Dichtungen des lateinischen Mittelalters*,
                       i. Berlin, 1970.

(ii) *Literary and Philological Studies*

Bischof, Br.
'Die Abhängigkeit der bukolischen Dichtung des Moduinus, Bischof von Autun, von jener des T. Calpurnius Siculus und des M. Aurelius Olympius Nemesianus.' In *Serta Philologica Aenipontana* i, Innsbrucker Beiträge zur Kulturwissenschaft 7-8, ed. R. Muth (Innsbruck, 1962), pp. 387-423.

Bischoff, B.
'Das Thema des Poeta Saxo.' In *Speculum historiale: Festschrift Johannes Spörl* (Munich, 1975), pp. 198-203.

'Caritas-Lieder.' In B. Bischoff, *Mittelalterliche Studien*, ii, pp. 56-77.

'Theodulf und der Ire Cadac-Andreas', ibid., pp. 19-25.

Bittner, F.
'Studien zum Herrscherlob in der mittellateinischen Dichtung', Diss. phil. Würzburg. Volkach, 1962.

Boas, M.
Alcuin und Cato. Leiden, 1937.

Bulst, W.
'Alchuuines *Ecloga de Cuculo*', *Zeitschrift für deutsches Altertum*, 86 (1955), pp. 193-6.

Burghardt, H.-D.
'Philologische Untersuchungen zu den Gedichten Alkuins', Diss. phil. Heidelberg, 1960.

Campbell, A.
'Some Linguistic Features of Early Anglo-Latin Verse and its Use of Classical Models', *Transactions of the Philological Society* (1953), pp. 1-20.

Dronke, U. and P.
Barbara et Antiquissima Carmina. Barcelona, 1979.

Ebenbauer, A.
Carmen historicum. Untersuchungen zur historischen Dichtung im karolingischen Europa i. Philologica Germanica 4. Vienna, 1978.

Friederichs, H.
'Die Gelehrten um Karl den Grossen in ihren Schriften, Briefen, und Gedichten', Diss. hist. Berlin, 1931.

Georgi, A.
Das lateinische und deutsche Preisgedicht des Mittelalters. Berlin, 1969.

Godman, P.
'The Authenticity of *O mea cella* and Alcuin's Poetic Style', *SM* (3ª Ser.) 20. 2 (1979), pp. 555-63.

'The Anglo-Latin *opus geminatum* from Aldhelm to Alcuin, *M.Æ.* 50.2 (1981), pp. 215-29.

Henshaw, M.
'The Latinity of the Poems of Hrabanus Maurus,' Ph.D. dissertation. University of Chicago, 1933.

Herzog, R.
Die Bibelepik der lateinischen Spätantike, i. Theorie und Geschichte der Literatur und der schönen Künste, 37. Munich, 1975.

Huemer, J.   *De Sedulii Poetae Vita et Scriptis Commentatio.*
                     Vienna, 1878.

Kamphausen, H. J.   *Traum und Vision in der lateinischen Poesie der
                     Karolingerzeit.* Lateinische Sprache und Literatur
                     des Mittelalters, 4. Berlin and Frankfurt, 1975.

Lapidge, M.   'The Authorship of the Adonic Verses Ad Fido-
                     lium attributed to Columbanus', *SM* (3ª Ser.)
                     18. 2 (1977), pp. 249–314.

                     'Aldhelm's Latin Poetry and Old English Verse',
                     Comp. Lit. 31. 3 (1979), pp. 209–31.

Manitius, M.   'Poetarum posteriorum loci expressi ad Fortuna-
                     tum', *MGH AA* iv. 2 (Berlin, 1855), pp. 137–44.

                     'Zu Aldhelm und Beda', *Sitzungsberichte der
                     philologisch-historischen Classe der kaiserlichen
                     Akademie der Wissenschaften zu Wien*, 112 (1886),
                     pp. 535–634.

                     'Beiträge zur Geschichte frühchristlicher Dichter
                     im Mittelalter' i, ibid. 117. 12 (1889) 2–6; ii,
                     ibid. 121. 7 (1890) 2–5.

Önnerfors, A.   *Mediaevalia—Aufsätze und Abhandlungen*, Latein-
                     ische Sprache und Literatur des Mittelalters 6.
                     Frankfurt, Bern, and Las Vegas, 1977.

Roberts, M.   'Alcuin's Life of St Willibrord and its Literary
                     Antecedents.' Unpublished M.A. thesis, University
                     of Illinois at Urbana-Champaign, 1974.

                     'The Hexameter Paraphrase in Late Antiquity:
                     Origins and Applications to Biblical Texts.'
                     Unpublished Ph.D. dissertation. University of
                     Illinois at Urbana-Champaign, 1978.

Schaller, D.   'Philologische Untersuchungen zu den Gedichten
                     Theodulfs von Orléans', Diss. phil. Heidelberg, 1956.

                     'Die karolingischen Figurengedichte des Cod. Bern.
                     212.' In *Medium Ævum Vivum. Festschrift für
                     W. Bulst*, edd. H. R. Jauss and D. Schaller (Heidel-
                     berg, 1960), pp. 23–47.

                     'Philologische Untersuchungen zu den Gedichten
                     Theodulfs von Orléans', *Deutsches Archiv*, 18
                     (1962), pp. 13–91.

                     'Vortrags- und Zirkulardichtung am Hof Karls des
                     Grossen', *Mlat. Jb.* 6 (1970), pp. 14–36.

                     'Lateinische Tierdichtung in frühkarolingischer
                     Zeit.' In *Das Tier in der Dichtung*, ed. U. Schwab
                     (Heidelberg, 1970), pp. 91–113.

'Der junge "Rabe" am Hof Karls des Grossen.' In *Festschrift B. Bischoff*, edd. J. Autenrieth and F. Brunhölzl (Stuttgart, 1971), pp. 123–41.

'Das Aachener Epos für Karl den Kaiser', *Fm. St.* 10 (1976), pp. 134–68.

'Alkuin.' Article in *Die deutsche Literatur des Mittelalters, Verfasserlexikon*, i. 1, edd. K. Ruh *et al.* (Berlin, 1977), cols. 241–53.

'Interpretationsprobleme im Aachener Karlsepos', *Rheinische Vierteljahrsblätter*, 41 (1977), pp. 160–79.

Steinen, W. von den   'Karl und die Dichter.' In *Karl der Grosse* ii, pp. 63–94.

Thraede, K.   'Epos.' Article in *Reallexikon für Antike und Christentum*, v, cols. 983–1042.

Traube, L.   *Karolingische Dichtungen, Schriften zur germanischen Philologie*, i. Berlin, 1888.

Vinay, G.   *Alto medioevo latino: conversazioni e no* Naples, 1978.

(iii) *Manuscript Transmission, Cultural History*

Alexander, J. J. G.   *Insular Manuscripts, 6th to the 9th Century.* London, 1978.

Becker, G.   *Catalogi bibliothecarum antiqui.* Bonn, 1885.

Berschin, W.   *Griechisch-lateinisches Mittelalter.* Munich, 1980.

Bischoff, B.   *Mittelalterliche Studien. Ausgewählte Aufsätze zur Schriftkunde und Literaturgeschichte.* 2 vols. Stuttgart, 1966, 1967.

Sammelhandschrift Diez. B. Sant. 66—Grammatici Latini et Catalogus Librorum. Codices selecti phototypice impressi, 42. Graz, 1973.

'Panorama der Handschriftenüberlieferung aus der Zeit Karls der Grossen.' In *Karl der Grosse*, ii, pp. 233–54.

'Die Hofbibliothek Karls des Grossen.' Ibid., pp. 42–52.

'Die Bibliothek im Dienste der Schule.' In *Spoleto . . . Settimane 19, La Scuola nell'Occidente Latino dell'Alto Medioevo* (Spoleto, 1971), pp. 385–415.

Brown, T. J.   'An Historical Introduction to the Use of Classical Latin Authors in the British Isles from the Fifth to the Eleventh Century.' In *Spoleto . . . Settimane. 22, La Cultura Antica nell'Occidente Latino dal VII. all'XI. Secolo* (Spoleto, 1974), pp. 239–93.

Brunhölzl, F.   'Der Bildungsauftrag der Hofschule.' In *Karl der Grosse*, ii, pp. 28-41.

Bullough, D. A.   'Alcuino e la tradizione culturale insulare.' In *Spoleto . . . Settimane* 20, *I Problemi dell'Occidente nel Secolo VIII* (Spoleto, 1972), pp. 571-600.

'Roman Books and Carolingian *renovatio*.' In *Renaissance and Renewal in Christian History*, SCH 14 (Oxford, 1977), pp. 23-50.

Carey, F. M.   'The Scriptorium of Reims during the Archbishopric of Hincmar (845-882).' In *Classical and Medieval Studies in Honour of Edward Kennard Rand* (New York, 1938), pp. 41-60.

Dolbeau, F.   'La tradition textuelle du poème d'Alcuin sur les saints de York', *Mlat. Jb.* 17 (1982, forthcoming).

Dümmler, E.   'Die handschriftliche Überlieferung der lateinischen Dichtungen aus der Zeit der Karolinger', *Neues Archiv* 5 (1879), pp. 89-159, 241-322.

Glauche, G.   *Schullektüre im Mittelalter. Entstehung und Wandlungen des Lektürekanons bis 1200.* Münchener Beiträge zur Mediävistik und Renaissance-Forschung 5. Munich, 1970.

Gneuss, H.   'A Preliminary List of Manuscripts written or owned in England up to 1100', *ASE* 9 (1981), pp. 1-60.

Godman, P.   'Mabillon, Ruinart, Gale, et l'*Eboracum* d'Alcuin', *Revue Mabillon* 59 (1978), pp. 254-60.

'The Textual Tradition of Alcuin's Poem on York', *Mlat. Jb.* 15 (1980), pp. 33-50.

Herren, M. W. (ed.)   *Insular Latin Studies. Papers on Latin Texts and Manuscripts of the British Isles: 550-1066* Toronto, 1981.

Jacobsen, P. C.   *Flodoard von Reims. Sein Leben und seine Dichtung 'De Triumphis Christi'.* Mittellateinische Studien und Texte 10. Leiden and Cologne, 1974.

Laistner, M. L. W.   *A Hand-List of Bede Manuscripts.* Ithaca, 1943.

Thought and Letters in Western Europe, 500-900[2] London, 1957.

Langosch, K.   'Überlieferungsgeschichte der mittellateinischen Literatur.' In *Geschichte der Textüberlieferung der antiken und mittelalterlichen Literatur* ii, edd. G. Ineichen *et al.* (Zürich, 1964), pp. 9-186.

Lapidge, M.   (Appendix to) R. W. Hunt, 'Manuscript Evidence for Knowledge of the Poems of Venantius Fortunatus in Late Anglo-Saxon England', *ASE* 8 (1979), pp. 287–95.

Law, V.   *The Insular Latin Grammarians*. Woodbridge, 1982.

Marenbon, J.   *From the Circle of Alcuin to the School of Auxerre*. Cambridge, 1980.

Ogilvy, J. D. A.   *Books known to the English, 597–1066²*. Cambridge, Mass., 1967.

Riché, P.   *Éducation et Culture dans l'Occident barbare*. Paris, 1962.

Roger, M.   *L'enseignement des lettres classiques d'Ausone à Alcuin*. Paris, 1905.

Traube, L.   *Vorlesungen und Abhandlungen*. 3 vols. Munich, 1920.

(iv) *Political and Ecclesiastical History*

Anton, H. H.   *Fürstenspiegel und Herrscherethos in der Karolingerzeit*. Bonner Historische Forschungen 32. Bonn, 1967.

Bullough, D. A.   *The Age of Charlemagne²*. London, 1973.

Campbell, J.   'Bede.' In *Latin Historians*, ed. T. A. Dorey (London, 1966), pp. 159–90.

    'The First Century of Christianity in England', *Ampleforth Journal*, 76 (1971), pp. 12–29.

Clemoes, P. and K. Hughes (edd.)   *England before the Norman Conquest. Studies in Primary Sources presented to Dorothy Whitelock*. Cambridge, 1971.

Colgrave, B.   'The Earliest Saints' Lives written in England', *PBA* 44 (1958), pp. 35–90.

Dinzelbacher, P.   *Vision und Visionsliteratur im Mittelalter*. Dusseldorf, 1981.

Fichtenau, H.   *Das Karolingische Imperium: soziale und geistige Problematik eines Grossreiches*. Zurich, 1949.

Fleckenstein, J.   'Karl der Grosse und sein Hof.' In *Karl der Grosse*, i, pp. 24–50.

Godfrey, J.   *The Church in Anglo-Saxon England*. Cambridge, 1962.

Gransden, A.   *Historical Writing in England c.550–c.1307*. London, 1974.

Hauck, A.   *Kirchengeschichte Deutschlands*, i. Leipzig, 1952.

Hoffmann, E.   *Die heiligen Könige bei den Angelsachsen und skandinavischen Völkern*. Quellen und Forschungen zur Geschichte Schleswig-Holsteins 69. Neumünster, 1975.

Hunter Blair, P.   'The Origins of Northumbria', *Archaeologia Aeliana* (Ser. 4) 25 (1947), pp. 1–57.

'Some Observations on the *Historia Regum* attributed to Symeon of Durham.' In *Celt and Saxon*, edd. K. Jackson *et al.* (Cambridge, 1964), pp. 63–118.

The World of Bede. London, 1970.

Northumbria in the days of Bede. London, 1976.

'From Bede to Alcuin.' In *Famulus Christi*, pp. 239–60.

John, E.   *Orbis Britanniae.* Leicester, 1966.

Jones, C. W.   *Saints' Lives and Chronicles in Early England.* Ithaca, 1947.

Levison, W.   *Aus rheinischer und fränkischer Frühzeit.* Düsseldorf, 1946.

Mayr-Harting, H.   *The Coming of Christianity to Anglo-Saxon England.* London, 1972.

Stenton, F. M.   *Preparatory to Anglo-Saxon England.* Oxford, 1970.

Thompson, A. H.   *Bede: His Life, Times, and Writings.* Oxford, 1935.

Ullmann, W.   *The Carolingian Renaissance and the Idea of Kingship.* London, 1969.

Vollrath-Reichelt, H.   *Königsgedanke und Königtum bei den Angelsachsen.* Kölner Historische Abhandlungen 19. Cologne and Vienna, 1971.

Wattenbach, W., W. Levison, and H. Löwe   *Deutschlands Geschichtsquellen im Mittelalter*, ii, *Vorzeit und Karolinger.* Weimar, 1952.

Whitelock, D.   *From Bede to Alfred. Studies in Early Anglo-Saxon Literature and History.* Variorum Reprints. London, 1980.

(v) *History of York (City and Minster)*

Addyman, P. V.   'York and Canterbury as Ecclesiastical Centres.' In *European Towns. Their Archaeology and Early History*, ed. M. W. Barley (London, 1977), pp. 499–509.

Harrison, K.   'The Saxon Cathedral at York', *Y. Arch. Jnl.* 39 (1956–8), pp. 436–44.

'The Pre-Conquest Churches of York: with an

appendix on eighth-century Northumbrian annals', ibid. 40 (1967), pp. 232–49.

Phillips, D. 'Excavations at York Minster, 1967–73.' In *Friends of York Minster 46th Annual Report* (1975), pp. 19–27.

'Excavation Techniques in Church Archaeology.' In *The Archaeological Study of Medieval Churches*, edd. P. V. Addyman and R. Morris, CBA Research Reports 13 (London, 1976), pp. 54–60.

'York Minster: The Excavations.' In N. Pevsner, *The Buildings of England. Yorkshire East Riding* (Revised edn.), forthcoming. (With N. Hutchinson.)

Ramm, H. G. 'The Growth and Development of the City to the Norman Conquest.' In *The Noble City of York*, ed. A. Stacpoole (York, 1971), pp. 225–54.

Reynolds, S. *An Introduction to the History of English Medieval Towns.* Oxford, 1977.

(vi) *Archaeology, Numismatics, Magic*

Clapham, A. W. *English Romanesque Architecture before the Conquest.* Oxford, 1930.

Collingwood, W. G. *Northumbrian Crosses of the pre-Norman Age.* London, 1927.

Grierson, P. *Dark Age Numismatics.* Variorum Reprints. London, 1979.

Hope-Taylor, B. *Under York Minster. Archaeological Discoveries 1966–1971.* York, 1971.

Page, R. I. 'Anglo-Saxon Runes and Magic', *Journal of the British Archaeological Association* (Ser. 3) 27 (1964), pp. 14–31.

Storms, G. *Anglo-Saxon Magic.* The Hague, 1948.

Sutherland, C. H. V. *English Coinage 600–1900.* London, 1973.

Taylor, H. M. 'The Position of the Altar in Early Anglo-Saxon Churches', *The Antiquaries Journal*, 53 (1973), pp. 52–8.

INTRODUCTION

i. *Alcuin: The Reputation and the Research*

ALCUIN'S many-sided activity in England and on the Continent has guaranteed his reputation both as a scholar and as an architect of Charlemagne's political, religious, and cultural reforms.[1]

A rich tradition of historical scholarship, that has no exponent more lucid than Wilhelm Levison[2] and none more emphatic than Liutpold Wallach,[3] stresses Alcuin's importance at the court of Charlemagne. Alcuin's hagiographical, philosophical, and theological writings are discussed in a number of recent studies.[4] His didactic treatises, from the programmatical *Disputatio de Vera Philosophia*[5] to his rhetorical, orthographical, and even mathematical tracts,[6]

---

[1] The subject of D. A. Bullough's Ford Lectures in English History, delivered before the University of Oxford, Hilary Term 1980, under the title *Alcuin: The Achievement and the Reputation* (forthcoming). A valuable recent survey of this subject is provided by C. Leonardi, 'Le ambizioni di una cultura unitaria: Alcuino e l'Accademia palatina', *Spoleto . . . Settimane*, 27, 1981, pp. 459-96.

[2] id., *England and the Continent*. See further Wallace-Hadrill, *Early Germanic Kingship*, especially chapters IV and V.

[3] id., *Alcuin and Charlemagne* and *Diplomatic Studies in Latin and Greek Documents from the Carolingian Age* (Ithaca and London, 1977).

[4] Most recently by I. Deug-Su, 'L'opera agiografica di Alcuino . . .' *SM* (3ª Ser.) 21. 1 (1980), pp. 47-96 (on Alcuin's *Vita S. Willibrordi*) and ibid. (3ª Ser.) 21. 2 (1980), pp. 665-706 (on Alcuin's *Vita Vedastis*); Sibylle Mähl, *Quadriga Virtutum: Die Kardinaltugenden in der Geistesgeschichte der Karolingerzeit*, Beihefte zum Archiv für Kulturgeschichte 9 (Cologne and Vienna, 1969), Part II. D; V. Serralda, *La Philosophie de la Personne chez Alcuin* (Paris, 1978); C. Ineichen-Eder, 'Theologisches und philosophisches Lehrmaterial aus dem Alcuin-Kreise', *Deutsches Archiv* 34 (1978), pp. 192-201; J. Marenbon, *From the Circle of Alcuin to the School of Auxerre* (Cambridge, 1981), especially chapter 2; W. Heil, *Alcuinstudien* i (Düsseldorf, 1970) and 'Der Adoptianismus, Alkuin und Spanien', *Karl der Grosse*, ii, pp. 95-155.

[5] See F. Brunhölzl, 'Der Bildungsauftrag der Hofschule', in *Karl der Grosse*, ii, pp. 28-41, and P. Courcelle, *La Consolation de Philosophie dans la Tradition littéraire* (Paris, 1967), pp. 33-47.

[6] For the *De Rhetorica et de Virtutibus*, see W. S. Howell, *The Rhetoric of Alcuin and Charlemagne* (Princeton, 1941; repr. New York, 1965). Editions of the *De Orthographia* are listed below, p. cxi, n. 4. It is discussed by R. Wright, 'Late Latin and Early Romance: Alcuin's *De Orthographia* and the Council of Tours (813 AD)', *Papers of the Liverpool Latin Seminar* 3 (1981), pp. 343-61

have been re-examined, and a book is devoted to his work on the liturgy.[1] The splendid studies of Bonifatius Fischer have illuminated Alcuin's role in Carolingian reform of the Bible.[2] His letters, placed on a firm textual foundation by Th. Sickel and Ernst Dümmler,[3] have been investigated as a sociological source[4] and have been edited anew from the excerpts of two medieval letter collections.[5]

It would be otiose to multiply bibliographical evidence of recent interest in Alcuin's life and work. At no time since the Middle Ages has there been such varied and documented concern with virtually every aspect of Alcuin's writing— every aspect, that is, except his poetry. Alcuin the scholar overshadows Alcuin the poet, and orthodox views of his verse are plainly expressed in the judgement of F. J. E. Raby: 'a great teacher, if a mediocre poet'.[6]

Less plain are the grounds for this judgement. No critical study of Alcuin's poetry exists, nor is there any adequate

and C. Dionisotti, 'On Bede, Grammars, and Greek' *Revue bénédictine* 92 (1982), pp. 129-41. The *Propositiones ad acuendos iuvenes* ascribed to Alcuin are edited and discussed by M. Folkerts, 'Die älteste mathematische Aufgabensammlung in lateinischer Sprache: Die Alkuin zugeschriebenen *Propositiones ad acuendos iuvenes*. Überlieferung, Inhalt, kritische Edition', *Denkschriften der österreichischen Akademie der Wissenschaften*, mathematisch–naturwissenschaftliche Klasse 116, 6. Abhandlung (Vienna, 1978), pp. 15-78. There is a useful edition of Alcuin's *Disputatio cum Pippino* by W. Suchier and L. W. Daly in *Altercatio Hadriani Augusti et Epicteti philosophi*, Illinois Studies in Language and Literature 24, nos. 1-2 (Urbana, 1939).

[1] G. Ellard, S.J., *Master Alcuin, Liturgist. A Partner of Our Piety* (Chicago, 1956).

[2] *Die Alkuin-Bibel*, Aus der Geschichte der lateinischen Bibel 1 (Freiburg-im-Breisgau, 1957); 'Bibeltext und Bibelreform unter Karl dem Grossen', *Karl der Grosse*, ii, pp. 156-216; and *Die Bibel von Moutier-Grandval, British Library Additional MS. 10,546* (facs.), edd. B. Fischer *et al.* (Bern, 1971), especially pp. 49-98.

[3] Th. Sickel, 'Alcuinstudien', *Sitzungsberichte der königlichen Akademie der Wissenschaften*, philologisch–historische Klasse 79 (Vienna, 1875), pp. 461-550 and E. Dümmler, *MGH Epp.* iv.

[4] W. Edelstein, *eruditio und sapientia. Untersuchungen zu Alcuins Briefen* (Freiburg, 1965).

[5] *Two Alcuin Letter-Books*, ed. C. Chase, Toronto Medieval Latin Texts 5 (Toronto, 1975).

[6] *The Oxford Book of Medieval Latin Verse* (Oxford, 1959), p. 466, *sub* no. 48. Cf. '. . . his poems by their number, extent and influence, if not by their merit, occupy the first place, "though real inspiration is rare" ', W. Levison, *England and the Continent*, p. 163. The quotation is from M. L. W. Laistner, *Thought and Letters in Western Europe, A.D. 500 to 900*[2] (London, 1957), p. 192.

account of the literary context in which his verse may be set.[1] The only survey of early Anglo-Latin literature ends with Bede, Alcuin's immediate predecessor; and it is less than a conspicuous success.[2] The standard literary histories of Medieval Latin, on the other hand, offer a panorama of the entire Middle Ages. They have no time to linger over a single poet: an entire millennium is grist to their mill. There is, in consequence, a contrast between the close and sympathetic attention paid to most of Alcuin's writing by recent scholarship and its comparative neglect of his poetry.

In this area the last century has seen little progress in the critical edition and interpretation of Alcuin's work.[3] Even his major narrative poem on York, the importance of which is signalled by historians and philologists alike,[4] has attracted scant notice. And yet this poem, known generally by the title *Versus de [Patribus Regibus] et Sanctis Euboricensis Ecclesiae*,[5] has a significant place among the primary sources for Northumbrian history and for Alcuin's career, as will emerge from an account of its author's life.

ii. *The Life of Alcuin and its Sources*

Alcuin's life is among the most richly documented of any intellectual's of the eighth century.[6]

---

[1] A study of the authenticity of the canon of Alcuin's poetry is presented by H. D. Burghardt, 'Philologische Untersuchungen zu den Gedichten Alkuins', diss. phil. (Heidelberg, 1960).

[2] W. F. Bolton, *A History of Anglo-Latin Literature, 597–1066* (Princeton, 1967): 'Die Geschichte der anglolateinischen . . . Literatur ist nach wie vor zu schreiben' (D. Schaller, review of Bolton, op. cit., *Anglia*, 90/2 (1972), p. 207).

[3] The major exception is K. Strecker's edition of the rhythmical poetry attributed to Alcuin (*MGH PLAC* iv. 3, pp. 903–10).

[4] Cf. Wallace-Hadrill, *Early Germanic Kingship*, p. 87, Brunhölzl, *Geschichte*, pp. 268–9.

[5] On the authority for this title, see comm, pp. 2–3ᵃ.

[6] Biographies: F. Lorentz, *Alkuins Leben* (Halle, 1829 (translated by J. M. Slee as *The Life of Alcuin* (London, 1937)); K. Werner, *Alcuin und sein Jahrhundert* (Paderborn, 1876); C. J. B. Gaskoin, *Alcuin, His Life and Work* (London, 1904; repr. New York, 1966); G. F. Browne, *Alcuin of York* (London, 1908); A. Kleinclausz, *Alcuin*, Annales de l'Université de Lyon iii. 15 (Paris, 1948); E. S. Duckett, *Alcuin, Friend of Charlemagne: his World and his Work* (New York, 1951). The best short account of Alcuin's career is by E. Dümmler, 'Zur Lebensgeschichte Alchuins', *Neues Archiv*, 18 (1893), pp. 51–70. See further id., 'Alchuinstudien', *Sitzungsberichte der königlichen Preussischen Akademie der Wissenschaften*, phil.-hist. Klasse (Berlin, 1891), pp. 495–523; D. Schaller,

Born in Northumbria in the second quarter of the eighth century,[1] possibly of noble family,[2] Alcuin spent his early years in the cathedral community of York.[3] There his teacher, patron, and friend was Ælberht, the future bishop (767–73) and archbishop (773–8), whom he succeeded as master at the school of York in 767.[4] Ælberht travelled to Rome and to Francia, and Alcuin accompanied the bibliophile prelate on his continental journeys.[5] By 778–80, the date of a poetic epistle which he addressed to friends abroad after returning to England,[6] Alcuin's contacts among the lay and ecclesiastical aristocracy of Carolingian Europe were already appreciable. Although widely travelled and well connected, Alcuin derived his standing until middle age chiefly from his office at York and from the patronage of his teacher and friends. Alcuin's official position in the Church counted for little. He was never to advance beyond the deacon's orders which he had taken during his youth in Northumbria.

In 781 came the turning-point in Alcuin's career. Returning from Rome, where he had been sent on behalf of Ælberht's successor Eanbald to receive the archbishop's *pallium* from Pope Hadrian I, Alcuin met Charlemagne at Parma, probably on 15 March 781.[7] (This was not their

'Alkuin (Alchuine)', in *Die deutsche Literatur des Mittelalters. Verfasserlexikon*, edd. K. Ruh *et al.* i. 1 (Berlin and New York, 1978), cols. 241–53; and W. Heil, 'Alcuin', in *Theologische Realenzyklopädie* ii. 1/2 (Berlin, 1977), pp. 266–76.

[1] See comm. to vv. 1635–6. The traditional date of *c.*735 is discussed by Dümmler, *Neues Archiv* 18 (1893), pp. 53–4. It is a mystery to me why S. Allott, *Alcuin of York* (York, 1974), pp. iii and v, gives Alcuin's date of birth as '*c.*732'.

[2] See comm. to vv. 754–5.   [3] See vv. 1651–3, with app. iii ad loc.

[4] See vv. 1526 ff., especially vv. 1533–5 with app. iii ad loc.

[5] See *Carmen* ii. 7–10 (*MGH PLAC* i, p. 206), *Ep.* 172 (*MGH Ep.* iv, p. 285, 3–4), and *Ep.* 271 (ibid., p. 429, 1–2, with nn. 5 and 6). At least one of these journeys (to Rome) was made before 767. See vv. 1454–9 with comm. and app. iii ad vv. 1450 ff. On the (improbable) conjecture that Charlemagne sent Alcuin as an envoy to Pope Hadrian in 773, see M. Papetti, 'Intorno ai viaggi di Alcuino in Italia', *Sophia*, 3 (1935), pp. 216–18 and Levison, *England and the Continent*, p. 154, n. 3.

[6] *Carmen* iv (*MGH PLAC* i, pp. 220–3). On the date and genre of this poem, see D. Schaller, 'Vortrags- und Zirkulardichtung am Hof Karls des Grossen', *Mlat. Jb.* 6 (1970), p. 19 and n. 18.

[7] Not Pavia, as recorded by Brunhölzl, *Geschichte*, p. 268. For the meeting with Charlemagne, see *Vita Alcuini*, c. IX (Arndt, p. 198 [= *Monumenta Alcuiniana*, c. VI, p. 17]).

first encounter.[1]) Invited to join the Frankish court and to assist Charlemagne in his educational and cultural reforms, Alcuin left England either in 781 or early in 782. In later life, he was to regard this move as the due fulfilment of an earlier prophecy.[2]

Alcuin remained on the Continent until the end of his life, with the exception of two return visits to England, in 786 and 790-3. His activities on both of these occasions point to his new-found eminence. In 786 he accompanied the papal legates, on their first visitation to England since the Augustinian mission, to the Northern synod and the court of King Offa.[3] During his stay of 790-3 the 'York Annals' embedded in Symeon of Durham's *Historia Regum* record Charlemagne's despatch to England of a translation of the proceedings of the Council of Nicaea (787), to which Alcuin replied with a letter.[4] Now the companion of papal legates and the counsellor of kings, Alcuin derived much of his standing from the influence he had come to enjoy over Charlemagne. And that influence derived in turn from two qualities displayed by Alcuin with a flair unrivalled among his contemporaries: practical erudition and didactic efficiency.[5]

At Charlemagne's courts, itinerant between 782 and 793 but settled at Aachen in 794,[6] Alcuin was at the centre of that international élite of scholars and poets in whose work is celebrated the first brilliant·phase of the Carolingian *renovatio*.[7] Already abbot of St.-Loup at Troyes and of

[1] *Vita Alcuini*, c. IX; see Dümmler, *MGH PLAC* i, p. 160, n. 9.

[2] Perhaps made by the Northumbrian anchorite Echa. See v. 1393 with app. iii and comm. ad loc.

[3] The legatine report is printed in *MGH Epp.* iv. 3, pp. 19-29. For a concise appraisal of this mission, see Stenton, pp. 215-16.

[4] lv, *s.a.* 792 (Arnold, *Symeonis Monachi Opera Omnia*, ii, pp. 53-4 (transl. in Whitelock, p. 272)). On these annals see P. Hunter Blair, 'Some Observations on the *Historia Regum* attributed to Symeon of Durham', in *Celt and Saxon: Studies in the Early British Border*, edd. K. Jackson *et al.* (Cambridge, 1963; revised 1964), pp. 63-118 and M. Lapidge, 'Byrhtferth of Ramsey and the Early Sections of the *Historia Regum* Attributed to Symeon of Durham', *ASE* 10 (1981), pp. 72-122. See further pp. lvi-lvii, lxix.

[5] Cf. Einhard, *Vita Karoli Magni*, XXV.

[6] See J. Fleckenstein, 'Karl der Grosse und sein Hof', in *Karl der Grosse*, i, pp. 24-50, on the successive 'phases' of Charlemagne's courts.

[7] Bibliography on this subject is immense. Volumes i and ii of the *Karl der Grosse* symposium are fundamental. See too Levison, *England and the Continent*, pp. 132 ff.; W. Ullmann, *The Carolingian Renaissance and the Idea of Kingship*

Ferrières, in 796 he acquired the abbacy of St. Martin's at Tours.[1] Although he was to travel back to the court after that date, his last years were spent in increasing retirement at St. Martin's. Alcuin died on 19 May 804.[2] His career marks the final and most fertile point of contact between Anglo-Saxon and continental scholarship in the eighth century.[3]

Our primary sources for Alcuin's life and work are of unequal value. Analysis of them begins with the conspectus of Alcuin's career which survives in the anonymous *Vita Alcuini*.

Composed between 823 and 829, probably at Ferrières, under the inspiration of Alcuin's pupil Sigulf, this local portrait sets Alcuin chiefly in his retirement at Tours. Its anonymous author, influenced by hagiographical models common in the ninth century, was scarcely more interested in his subject's work on dialectic, grammar, or orthography than in the story that Alcuin commented on Psalm 118 with a golden pen.[4] He provides corroborative, sometimes plausible, evidence for material attested elsewhere, but little which is of independent authority. The richest body of evidence for Alcuin's life and work is provided not in the *Vita Alcuini*, but in Alcuin's own poems and letters.

Alcuin's letters tell us most about the last decade of his career. For his earlier years they are less revealing. If we wish to know what Alcuin was doing in 793, his letters are highly informative.[5] If we wish to know what he was doing in 783, they tell us next to nothing. From a total of more than three hundred extant letters, little more than one-eighth antedates the last ten years of his life.[6] A mere handful was written

(London, 1969), pp. 1–20; H. Fichtenau, *Das Karolingische Imperium* (Zürich, 1949), pp. 56 ff. For outstanding studies of the court circle of poets see the items listed under Schaller and Bischoff (Select Bibliography C. ii, pp. xxvi and xxv).

[1] See J. Chélini, 'Alcuin, Charlemagne, et Saint-Martin de Tours' *Revue d'histoire de l'Église de France*, 47 (1961), pp. 19–50 and F. J. Felten, *Äbte und Laienäbte im Frankreich* (Stuttgart, 1980), pp. 234 ff.

[2] *Testimonia* are conveniently assembled by Levison, *England and the Continent*, p. 155, n. 1.

[3] See Levison, op. cit., especially p. 155.

[4] c. XXI (Arndt, pp. 194–5 [= *Monumenta Alcuiniana* c. XII, p. 28]).

[5] *MGH Epp.* iv, *Epp.* 15–40, pp. 40–83.

[6] Ibid., *Epp.* 1–2, 4–38, pp. 18–19, 29–81.

before 790, and their dating is largely conjectural.[1] Alcuin's letters provide an invaluable testimony to his middle and old age. But they tell us very little about his boyhood, youth, or early manhood.

The chief autobiographical sources for the earliest period of Alcuin's life are the few poems which antedate 781/2. Of these, *Carmen* iv provides evidence of Alcuin's continental connections before he left England,[2] while *Carmen* ii adds little to the information which can be derived from elsewhere.[3] It is in the *Versus de . . . Sanctis Euboricensis Ecclesiae* that we find a description of Alcuin's teachers, a sketch of the authors available to him at York, and an outline of developments which took place in Northumbria within his own living memory, from *c.*732 (the close of Bede's *HE*) to *c.*782.[4] The poem on York is therefore of special interest as an autobiographical witness to Alcuin's early career. It is also one of the rare sources for fifty years of Northumbrian history in which our only other literary evidence is provided by the 'Northern recension' of the Anglo-Saxon Chronicle,[5] by the *Continuations* to Bede's *HE* and by the cryptic entries of the 'York Annals'. Much of the authority of this poem as an autobiographical and historical source depends upon its date and character.

iii. *The Date and Character of Alcuin's Poem on York*

The 1658 hexameters of Alcuin's *Versus de . . . Sanctis Euboricensis Ecclesiae* celebrate the political, ecclesiastical, and intellectual history of his native Northumbria, with its spiritual centre at York.[6] Two-thirds of his poem draws on Bede's *HE* and prose and metrical lives of St. Cuthbert;[7] the rest describes events of Alcuin's own lifetime. His interest is trained on the propagation of the faith in Northumbria,

---

[1] *MGH Epp.* 1-2, 4-6, pp. 18-19, 29-31.   [2] See p. xxxvi, n. 6 above.
[3] See ibid., n. 5 above.   [4] vv. 1215-1658.
[5] On this 'recension', see D. Whitelock, *The Anglo-Saxon Chronicle* (Norwich, 1961), p. xiv and *The Peterborough Chronicle*, Early English Manuscripts in Facsimile, 4 (Copenhagen, 1954), pp. 29 ff.
[6] The *MGH* text has 1657 lines. On the 'new' verse, see comm. to v. 578.
[7] vv. 19-1205. Alcuin states his debt to Bede at lines 685 ff., 741 ff., 781 ff., and 1207 ff. See further pp. xlvii-lviii, lxviii-lxix, lxxv-lxxvii, lxxxiv-lxxxix below.

on the kingdom's defence and extension, and on the moral example provided by the miraculous deeds of the Northern bishops, saints, and anchorites. Alcuin refashions Bede's text to these ends, and his work culminates in an account of the school and archbishops of York during his youth.

The central themes of Alcuin's poem may be represented by a brief synopsis:[1]

vv. 1–18	Invocation of Christ and the saints; plea for divine inspiration; statement of theme.
vv. 19–45	The Roman foundation of York; its site and amenities; the withdrawal of the Romans and inept rule by the Britons; Pictish incursions.
vv. 46–78	The Saxons are enlisted against the Picts; they turn against their allies and assume power in accordance with God's will.
vv. 79–89	Pope Gregory the Great's initiative in the conversion of the English.
vv. 90–133	A heavenly messenger prophesies Edwin's successes; his restoration and excellent rule; his marriage.
vv. 134–233	The mission of Paulinus; conversion of Edwin; rejection of paganism by Coifi the high priest; foundation of the Church of York; its elevation to be chief city of the realm; death of Edwin.
vv. 234–506	Accession of Oswald and revenge for Edwin's death; defeat of Cadwallon; benefactions to the church; the prophecy of Aidan and the posthumous miracles of Oswald.
vv. 507–74	Oswiu's initial difficulties as king; his victory over Penda; security for Northumbria and conversion of Mercia; military successes of Oswiu.

[1] For fuller discussion, see pp. xlvii–lx. A chronological table of the bishops, archbishops, and kings of Northumbria in Alcuin's lifetime is provided in the Appendix (pp. 136–7).

vv. 575-645	Accession of Ecgfrith; life and attainments of Wilfrid I.
vv. 646-750	The career of Cuthbert; a summary of Bede's Lives of the Saint.
vv. 751-846	Reign of Ecgfrith; miracles of Æthelthryth and of the *thegn* Imma; defeat and death of Ecgfrith; accession of Aldfrith.
vv. 847-75	Bosa's ecclesiastical reforms.
vv. 876-1007	Vision of Dryhthelm.
vv. 1008-77	Activities of the Anglo-Saxon missionaries on the Continent and in Ireland.
vv. 1077-1215	Return to the theme of the Northumbrian kings and bishops; miracles of John of Beverley.
vv. 1216-50	Endowments of the church by Wilfrid II; his reign as bishop.
vv. 1251-87	Admirable episcopacy of Egbert; his régime; his harmony with the king; elevation of York to archiepiscopal status.
vv. 1288-1318	Death of Bede; account of his life and works; his miracle.
vv. 1319-87	The anchorite Balthere; his spiritual achievements.
vv. 1388-93	The hermit Echa.
vv. 1394-1596	The life and teaching of archbishop Ælberht; his endowments to the church and construction of Sancta Sophia; his books; lament for his death.
vv. 1597-1648	A prophecy and a vision of the community of York in heaven as witnessed in Alcuin's youth.
vv. 1649-58	Final prayer and conclusion.

Alcuin's longest narrative poem, the *Versus de . . . Sanctis Euboricensis Ecclesiae* are comparable to the metrical Life of St. Willibrord,[1] which Alcuin wrote in commemoration of

---

[1] See further, pp. xliii–xliv, lxxviii.

his kinsman, the apostle of the Frisians and founder of the monastery of Echternach.[1] The remainder of Alcuin's poetry is of a lyrical, dedicatory, and panegyrical character.[2] With the exception of *Carmen* ii and *Carmen* iv,[3] it derives from the last twenty-two years of his life (782–804), when he was largely absent from his homeland. The extant Latin verse of one of Anglo-Saxon England's most eminent poets was written chiefly on the Continent.

Alcuin's *Versus de . . . Sanctis Euboricensis Ecclesiae* are commonly regarded as his earliest composition in verse. The poem is generally attributed to the period before his departure for Charlemagne's court and is often assigned, more specifically, to the years 780–2. The problem of dating this text has special interest, given the sparseness of primary evidence for Northumbrian history in the half-century before 782 and the lack of reliable biographical material for the early years of Alcuin's career. If a date before 782 is accepted, it would establish the poem on York as a historical and autobiographical source of singular authority.

The received dating of this text is founded on internal evidence. External evidence is wanting. The transmission history of the *Versus de . . . Sanctis Euboricensis Ecclesiae* provides no clues as to their date of composition.[4] Recent scholarship has followed Alcuin's nineteenth-century editor, Wilhelm Wattenbach, who assigned the poem to the years 780–2 on the grounds that there is nothing in it to indicate that its author was separated from the clergy of the church at York.[5]

It is true that there is nothing in Alcuin's poem to prove that he was separated from the clergy of the church of York. However, it is also true that there is nothing in the text to prove that he was not separated from them. The pride in the institutions and traditions of York displayed in Alcuin's *Versus de . . . Sanctis Euboricensis Ecclesiae* remains equally prominent in a number of letters and in a poem which he

---

[1] On Willibrord see comm. to vv. 1037–43.

[2] See the classification by Schaller (art. cit., p. xxxv, n. 6 above), col. 245.

[3] See above, p. xxxvi, nn. 5, 6.   [4] See pp. cxiii–cxxix below.

[5] *Monumenta Alcuiniana*, p. 80. Cf. Dümmler, *MGH PLAC* i, p. 162; Brunhölzl, *Geschichte*, pp. 268–69: 'Es stammt *ohne Zweifel* noch aus den Jahren, da Alkuin in York lehrte' (my italics).

wrote between 793 and 801, on the Continent.[1] The regional interest of the poem on York has therefore been used too simply as evidence for its date of composition: Alcuin's concern for his *patria* was not restricted to any one period of his literary output, but continued throughout his life, including the years after 781/2 spent abroad.

At vv. 1408 ff. of his poem on York Alcuin addresses the *Euboricae . . . iuventus.*[2] This suggests that his poem was intended for an audience at York, but does not demonstrate that he was there when he wrote it. Moreover, the unambiguous evidence for Alcuin's travel abroad in the years 780-1 and of his subsequent departure from England casts further doubt upon Wattenbach's hypothesis that Alcuin composed his most complex, ambitious, and lengthy poetical work in the eventful months following the death of Ælberht. Nothing in the text disproves the (counter-)hypothesis that Alcuin's *Versus de . . . Sanctis Euboricensis Ecclesiae*, like *Carmen* lix, which is addressed in the same manner to the young men of York,[3] were written after 781/2 and from the Continent. Since Alcuin returned to England both in 786 and in 790-3, there is every reason to believe that he maintained personal as well as written contact with his circle at York (where he spent Lent of 793) after the move to Charlemagne's court. This leads in turn to the second counter-hypothesis, that one of these return visits to England in 786 or 790-3 prompted Alcuin to compose or finally to revise his poem on York, a hypothesis that is supported by the evidence of this work's nearest analogues, earliest diffusion, and historical background.

In style, scale, and content, none of Alcuin's poems is so closely related to the *Versus de . . . Sanctis Euboricensis Ecclesiae* as his metrical Life of St. Willibrord. Like the poem on York, much of which is a re-working in verse of the text of Bede, the *Vita S. Willibrordi metrica* is designed as a poetical counterpart to Alcuin's prose *Vita.* The metrical Life observes and extends the conventions of the *opus*

---

[1] *Carm.* lix (*MGH PLAC* i, p. 273) and *MGH Epp.* iv, nos. 16, 17, 18, 30, 42, 43, 44, 46, 47, 48, 108, 109, 114, 115, 116, 125, 226, 232, 233.

[2] p. 110.

[3] 'Moenibus Euboricae habitans tu sacra iuventus' (*MGH PLAC* i, p. 273, v. 8).

geminatum, by which the poem on York is also influenced.[1]
Alcuin's only other large-scale narrative poem, the *Vita S.
Willibrordi metrica* reveals similar hagiographical and histori-
cal interests to those displayed in the *Versus de . . . Sanctis
Euboricensis Ecclesiae*. These affinities of scale and content,
reinforced by a large number of verbal parallels,[2] are too
close and too numerous to be referred to mere similarity of
genre. The verse Life of St. Willibrord was issued, together
with Alcuin's prose work, no earlier than 785 and perhaps as
late as 797.[3] If Alcuin wrote the two poems at the same time,
then the date of the metrical Life of St. Willibrord lends
support to the hypothesis that Alcuin composed his poem on
York after 781/2.

The poem known as the *Miracula S. Nyniae* was written,
probably at Whithorn, by a pupil of Alcuin's after his depar-
ture for the Continent.[4] It draws on many of the same
sources (especially Aldhelm and Bede) as the *Versus de . . .
Sanctis Euboricensis Ecclesiae*, but never plainly borrows
from Alcuin's poem. If the *Versus de . . . Sanctis Eubori-
censis Ecclesiae* were composed by Alcuin in York before his
departure for the Continent in 781/2, it is curious that they
made no positive impact on Anglo-Latin verse written during
his lifetime, by one of his own pupils, such as the *Miracula
S. Nyniae*.

Not until the composition of Æthelwulf's *De Abbatibus*,
in the first quarter of the ninth century is an Anglo-Latin
poem clearly indebted, both in style and in substance, to
Alcuin's *Versus de . . . Sanctis Euboricensis Ecclesiae*.[5] This

---

[1] See pp. lxxviii-lxxxviii below.

[2] The evidence, assembled in app. iii, is listed on p. 143.

[3] See Levison, *MGH SrM* vii, p. 85. A dating to 796-7 has been proposed by
I. Deug-Su, *SM* (3ª Ser.) 2. 1 (1980), p. 61.

[4] Ed. K. Strecker, *MGH PLAC* iv. 3 (Berlin, 1896), pp. 943-62. The *Miracula
S. Nyniae* are referred to by Alcuin at *Ep.* 273 (*MGH Epp.* iv, p. 431, 32-7) and
possibly at *Carmen* lix. 14 (*MGH PLAC* i, p. 273, with n. 1 ad loc.). On the poem
as a whole, see Strecker, 'Zu den Quellen für das Leben des heiligen Ninian',
Neues Archiv, 43 (1920-2), pp. 1-26; W. Levison, 'An Eighth-Century Poem on
St. Ninian', *Antiquity*, 14 (1940), pp. 280-91; W. W. MacQueen, 'Miracula Nynie
Episcopi', *Transactions of the Dumfriesshire and Galloway Natural History and
Antiquarian Society* (Ser. 4) 38 (1959-61), pp. 21-57.

[5] Ed. A. Campbell (Oxford, 1967); Dümmler, *MGH PLAC* i, pp. 583-604.
The poem is dated by Campbell (p. xxiii) to 803-21. See L. Traube, *Karolingische
Dichtungen*, Schriften zur germanischen Philologie, i (Berlin, 1888), especially

corresponds to what can be reconstructed of the York poem's influence on continental literature written during or soon after Alcuin's lifetime. The first extant work of Carolingian Latin poetry to display substantial affinities with the *Versus de . . . Sanctis Euboricensis Ecclesiae* is '*Karolus Magnus et Leo Papa*', of the first decade of the ninth century.[1] There is no doubt that Alcuin's poem circulated on the Continent, but in England, even allowing for the fragmentary state of our evidence due to Viking devastation in the ninth century, the diffusion of this text seems to have been extremely limited and relatively late.

These facts from philology and literary history in support of the hypothesis that Alcuin issued the *Versus de . . . Sanctis Euboricensis Ecclesiae* later in his career are reinforced by the political background of the work.

At vv. 388-91 Alcuin describes and praises the benefactions of Offa, king of Mercia (757-96), to the shrine of Oswald.[2] How are we to account for this emphasized reference to Offa of Mercia in Alcuin's account of the seventh-century saints and kings of Northumbria?

In the elevation of York to the status of a major episcopal see in 735 and, especially, in the harmony between Archbishop Egbert (*c.*732-66) and his brother king Eadberht (737-58) Alcuin saw the coming of a 'Golden Age' of the Northern Church which Bede in his *HE* had set in the time of Theodore.[3] The learning of the school of York, and the example of the career of his own teacher, Archbishop Ælberht, gave Alcuin further reason for pride.[4]

But if the spiritual and ecclesiastical history of Northumbria in Alcuin's youth was a story of success, its later political history was a dismal chronicle of unrest.[5] The 'Golden Age'

---

pp. 24-5; Kamphausen, *Traum und Vision in der lateinischen Poesie der Karolingerzeit*, Lateinische Sprache und Literatur des Mittelalters 4 (Bern and Frankfurt, 1975), pp. 86 ff.; and D. A. Howlett, 'The Provenance, Date, and Structure of *de Abbatibus*', *Archaeologia Aeliana* (Ser. 5) 3 (1975), pp. 121-30.

[1] Dating following Schaller 'Das Aachener Epos für Karl den Kaiser', *Fm. St.* 10 (1976), pp. 134 ff. For the stylistic affinities of this poem with Alcuin's, see app. iii and pp. lxxxix-xci below.

[2] See p. lx below.   [3] See vv. 1251 ff. and p. lvi.   [4] See vv. 1395 ff.

[5] Cf. Stenton, pp. 92-3. A different view of the political history of this period is set out in P. H. Sawyer's *From Roman Britain to Norman England* (London, 1978), pp. 107-8.

in which Egbert and Eadberht ruled over Church and king-
dom, depicted in the *Versus de . . . Sanctis Euboricensis
Ecclesiae* (vv. 1277-87), must be seen in full contrast to the
political turbulence of Alcuin's manhood. A usurper of non-
royal birth, Æthelwald 'Moll' seized power in 759, and was
not expelled until 765. A rebellion of 774 cost King Alhred
his throne; and after four or five years Æthelred the son of
Æthelwald 'Moll', who had replaced him, was also driven into
exile. His two successors reigned for no more than a decade
between them, and Æthelred, again king of Northumbria
from 789 to 796, was considered by Alcuin in an unfavour-
able light.[1] The years in which the *Versus de . . . Sanctis
Euboricensis Ecclesiae* were written, following either the
accepted hypothesis of 780-2 or my own suggestion of a
date of composition or revision as late as the 790s, repre-
sented a nadir of Northumbrian kingship.

In these circumstances, Alcuin's reference to the benefac-
tions made by Offa to the shrine of Oswald can be seen as a
pointed turning away from the Northumbrian tyrants and
usurpers of his own times to the powerful monarch of neigh-
bouring Mercia. There Offa had secured a political stability
which Alcuin's own strife-torn *patria* lacked. It is significant
that the only contemporary king apart from Eadberht of
Northumbria whom Alcuin praises in the *Versus de . . .
Sanctis Euboricensis Ecclesiae* is Offa of Mercia—a power-
ful overlord, like Alcuin's heroes Edwin, Oswald, and Oswiu.[2]

An act of calculated deference to the Mercian king would
appear most natural when Offa's relations with Northumbria
were most harmonious. In 792 Offa married a daughter to
King Æthelred of Northumbria—and in that year Alcuin
was, as we have noted, back in England. Is the allusion to
Offa's gifts to the shrine of one of the leading Northumbrian
royal saints a sign of the *rapprochement* between Mercia and
Alcuin's homeland in the early 790s and a tribute to the in-
fluence of the great Mercian king[3] with whom Alcuin enjoyed

---

[1] *MGH Epp.* iv, *Ep.* 9 (dated 793), p. 35, 7-10.

[2] See below, pp. xlix-li.

[3] On Offa's influence, see Stenton, p. 212; id., 'The Supremacy of the Mercian
Kings', in *Preparatory to Anglo-Saxon England, being the Collected Papers of
Frank Merry Stenton*, ed. Doris Mary Stenton (Oxford, 1970), especially pp. 60-1;
and Wallace-Hadrill, *Early Germanic Kingship*, pp. 111-12.

friendly relations?[1] This would be in keeping with the other evidence of the poem's stylistic affinities and influence, which points to a date of final composition and 'publication' after Alcuin had left England in 781/2, perhaps as late as 792/3.

The poem on York remains a privileged witness to the Northumbrian history of Alcuin's youth and early manhood and it continues to be a rare source for his own biography, but it would be rash to assume that it is a documentary account of even the events of his lifetime. The genre of Alcuin's work is influenced by panegyric, and fond reminiscence is one of his motives for writing.[2] A properly critical view of this text's value as a historical and biographical source will take these factors into account. This leads us to the ecclesiastical and political background of the Northumbria Alcuin describes in his poem on York.

iv. *The Political and Ecclesiastical Background*

In a letter to Æthelred, king of Northumbria, written after the Vikings had sacked the monastery of Lindisfarne in 793, Alcuin stated with urgency the ties that ought to bind his fellow Northumbrians to one another: 'by a double bond of kinship we are fellow citizens of one city in Christ: that is, as sons of Mother Church and as natives of one fatherland.'[3] This perspective, uniting the Northumbrian *patria* and the church of York, is embodied in Alcuin's *Versus de . . . Sanctis Euboricensis Ecclesiae*. Alcuin's vision of the political and ecclesiastical development of Northumbria, from the Roman foundation of York until the final quarter of the eighth century, can be recovered by examining this poem in the light of the views implied by his use of Bede and expressed in his letters.

The *Versus de . . . Sanctis Euboricensis Ecclesiae* open

[1] *MGH Epp.* iv, *Epp.* 7 (p. 33); 9 (p. 35); 61 (pp. 104–5); 62 (pp. 105–6); 82 (pp. 124–5); 85 (p. 128); 87 (p. 131); 100 (pp. 144–6); 101 (pp. 146–7); 102 (pp. 148–9); 122 (p. 180); and Wallace-Hadrill, *Early Germanic Kingship*, p. 116.

[2] See below, pp. lxv–lxvi.

[3] *Ep.* 16 (*MGH Epp.* iv, p. 42): 'Duplici enim germanitate concives sumus unius civitatis in Christo: id est, matris ecclesiae filii et unius patriae indigene' (my repunctuation).

with a firm regional emphasis. Patriotism, centred on York and Northumbria, is a major theme of Alcuin's work. It shaped his sense of relevance. After dwelling on the achievements of the Anglo-Saxon missionaries in Ireland and on the Continent later in his poem (vv. 1008-77), Alcuin was to draw back, on the grounds that it was time to revert to his central theme of the kings and bishops of York (vv. 1077 ff.). In this regional emphasis, stated at the beginning and sustained in the course of the poem, Alcuin differs from Bede, who sees Northumbria, his native land, partly in the perspective of Canterbury.[1]

For Bede's description of the *situs Britanniae* at *HE* i. 1 Alcuin substitutes an *ekphrasis* on York (vv. 19-37). The opening of his poem has been compared with the eighth-century encomia on Milan (of *c.*740) and Verona (of *c.*796),[2] but the resemblance is superficial. The Italian urban encomia deal with the foundation, amenities, and rulers of the cities that are their subjects. Brevity is of their essence. They celebrate a place, but do not set out a developed view of its past. *Ekphrasis*, not history, is what they are chiefly about. For Alcuin, by contrast, a description of York serves only as the preface to a narrative of Northumbrian history which he adapted and extended from Bede.

From Bede and from Gildas[3] Alcuin took over a dismissive view of the Britons as a corrupt and slothful race, justly conquered by the Saxons. His pride in the toughness of his own people, apparent in the play on Isidore's etymology of the name *Saxones* at v. 48, is also reflected in letters that Alcuin wrote in 793, using the example of the martial valour of the pagan Anglo-Saxon forefathers to spur on their Christian descendants at a time of Viking incursion.[4] To Bede's account of the Britons' defeat and subjection, presented in a similar moral light and influenced by Gildas, Alcuin goes on to add and to emphasize (vv. 58-60) the

[1] See Wallace-Hadrill, *Early Medieval History*, p. 104.

[2] See app. ii to v. 19. For the comparison, and for the conjecture that Alcuin may have been inspired by a lost Italian urban encomium, see Bullough, pp. 340, 354-5.

[3] Whose *De Excidio Britonum* Alcuin knew at first hand. See app. iii to vv. 41-5 and app. ii to vv. 23, 38 ff., 41 ff., 49, 62 ff. and comm. to vv. 71-9.

[4] See vv. 46-8, with app. iii ad loc.

themes of love of liberty and of the *patria*.[1] There is nothing nostalgic about these lines: they are highly charged. Set against the background of internal dissension and external threat to his native Northumbria in the 780s and 790s, Alcuin's poem, like his letters, assumes at its outset a tone of stern admonition.[2]

The conversion of Northumbria, to which Alcuin turns at vv. 78 ff., is presented in terms of the personal initiative of three central figures: Pope Gregory the Great, King Edwin, and (arch)bishop Paulinus of York.[3] Scant attention is paid to the chronology provided by Bede's *HE*, and no mention is made of Augustine of Canterbury or Æthelberht of Kent. Alcuin's view is strictly Northumbrian and Romanist. Like the anonymous author of the Whitby *Vita S. Gregorii Magni* (704-14),[4] he is chiefly interested in Edwin of Northumbria and Gregory the Great, and less preoccupied with Paulinus of York. Paulinus is depicted as the agent of Rome; his acquisition of the archbishop's *pallium* is seen (vv. 205-10) as the simple fulfilment of Gregory's plans; the conversion of Edwin is the first fruit of an initiative that began with Northumbria's great benefactor in Rome (vv. 78 ff.). York's first bishop, in Alcuin's poem, is subordinated to the *cultus* of Rome and of Gregory the Great.

Bede depicted a trio of kingly virtue in the early books of the *HE*.[5] Alcuin shared and amplified Bede's admiration for the first member of this trio, Edwin of Northumbria (vv. 90 ff.). For Bede, Edwin was an excellent ruler. For Alcuin, he was the supreme example of Anglo-Saxon kingship (vv. 231-3). Predictably, the *Versus de . . . Sanctis Euboricensis Ecclesiae* emphasize the importance of Edwin's conversion. But they lay stress too on his generosity, his mercy, his

[1] Signalled by Dümmler, *MGH PLAC* i, p. 171, n. 1.

[2] See pp. lii-liii and lix. For the language of Alcuin's admonitions, see Godman, 'Alcuin's Poetic Style and the Authenticity of *O mea cella*' *SM* (3ª ser.) 20. 2 (1979), pp. 581 ff.

[3] The archbishop's *pallium* was conferred on Paulinus in 634, but he had fled Northumbria long before that date. See Stenton, p. 115, and B. Colgrave, *The Earliest Life of Gregory the Great, by an Anonymous Monk of Whitby* (Lawrence, Kansas, 1968), pp. 156-7.

[4] Colgrave ed. cit., p. 48, and see p. lxxvi below.

[5] See Wallace-Hadrill, *Early Germanic Kingship*, chapter IV, especially pp. 86 ff.

justice (vv. 124 ff.) and, rhetorically, on the extent of his hegemony (vv. 119–23).[1] Edwin, in Alcuin's poem, emerges as a model of warrior-kingship.

Oswald, the second member of this kingly trio, is presented in a different light. Oswald is depicted as the instrument of divine vengeance for Edwin's murder, as a benefactor of the Church,[2] and as a hero for his victory over Cadwallon. But the living Oswald has a far smaller part in Alcuin's poem than does his reputation after death. What impressed Alcuin, like Bede, about Oswald was his combination of kingship and sanctity. It is the miracles Oswald performed after death that are prominent in the *Versus de . . . Sanctis Euboricensis Ecclesiae*: his career in life is reduced almost to a prelude to his posthumous deeds. Its significance is presented in terms of the activity of divine power in the material world. Bishop Aidan, for example, enters Alcuin's account of Oswald only to make his celebrated prophecy that the royal saint's hand, because of his humility, would survive uncorrupted after death (vv. 291 ff.). Each of the miracles producing conversions, moral reform, and acts of wondrous healing recorded by Alcuin at vv. 300–498 serves to emphasize Oswald's role in the propagation of the faith. More space is devoted to Oswald's royal and saintly attributes, unique among early Northumbrian kings, than to any other figure in the *Versus de . . . Sanctis Euboricensis Ecclesiae*.

From Oswald Alcuin passes directly to Oswiu (vv. 503–6). This transition is noteworthy for what it omits. The third member of Bede's trio of royal virtue, Oswine, king of Deira—portrayed by Bede as a *rex humilis*, a protector of the Church, and a saintly ruler[3]—is never referred to in Alcuin's account. This omission is also one of the main reasons why Aidan plays such an insignificant role in the poem, being mentioned only in connection with Oswald. Aidan was too much bound up with the memory of Oswine. And Oswine himself never appears in the poem on York because his murder, described and censured by Bede,[4] casts little credit upon Oswiu, who was one of Alcuin's heroes.

---

[1] See comm. to v. 123. [2] See comm. to vv. 275–83.
[3] *HE* iii. 14; see Wallace-Hadrill, *Early Germanic Kingship*, pp. 85–7.
[4] *HE* iii. 14.

To Alcuin, Oswiu shared with Edwin and Oswald the regal attributes of munificence, justice, and equitability. But the essential common feature in his portrayal of all three kings is a stress on their role as father of the *patria* and defender of the faith. Thus Oswiu's victory over the Mercian Penda, described and emphasized by epic hyperbole,[1] is seen as the proper outcome of a just war which brought the Mercians into the Christian fold and preserved the Northumbrians against the heathen (vv. 556-64).

Throughout the poem Alcuin makes little or no room for the Irish influence in the Northumbrian church. His standpoint is strictly Romanist. The four Irish bishops who held the Northern see in the thirty years after the flight of Paulinus (633-64) are ignored even more pointedly than is Aidan earlier in the *Versus . . . de Sanctis Euboricensis Ecclesiae*. Even Chad, bishop Wilfrid's rival claimant to the Northumbrian episcopate, is never mentioned.[2] To read the *Versus de . . . Sanctis Euboricensis Ecclesiae* it is as if the synod of Whitby (664) had not needed to be held, and indeed Alcuin never refers to it. A logical consequence of these unstated but firm anti-Irish sentiments was Alcuin's sympathy for the ardent Romanist bishop, Wilfrid I of York.

Alcuin's account of Wilfrid (vv. 577 ff.) betrays a noteworthy bias by its deliberate omissions and silences. Bede is known for a certain reserve about the controversies provoked by Wilfrid's turbulent career; Eddius Stephanus for partisan advocacy of his patron's cause.[3] Alcuin differs from both of these writers. He omits anything which might conceivably

---

[1] vv. 525 ff.

[2] J. Campbell, 'Bede', in *Latin Historians*, ed. T. A. Dorey (London and Edinburgh, 1966), p. 189, n. 76 points out that Eddius claims that Wilfrid was made bishop of all Northumbria but that Chad supplanted him when he was abroad, while Bede implies that Northumbria was divided between them. The metrical Calendar of York (see p. lxiv, below) omits Chad from its otherwise complete list of bishops of York up to Wilfrid II (718-32).

[3] The troubled history of these years, and the value of Eddius' and Bede's accounts, has been admirably discussed by E. John, 'The Social and Political Problems of the Early English Church', in *Agricultural History Review*, 18th Supplement (1970), ed. J. Thirsk, pp. 39-63. See further D. P. Kirby, 'Northumbria in the Time of Wilfrid', in *Saint Wilfrid at Hexham*, ed. Kirby (Newcastle upon Tyne, 1974), pp. 1-34; and G. Isenberg, 'Die Würdigung Wilfrieds von York in der Historia Ecclesiastica Gentis Anglorum Bedas und der Vita Wilfridi des Eddius', diss. hist. (Münster, 1978).

present Wilfrid in an unfavourable light. He says nothing about the strife between the bishop and King Ecgfrith, about Wilfrid's expulsion from his see, or the division of the Northumbrian diocese. Instead Alcuin selects and combines (vv. 606 ff.) material from *HE* v. 19, referring to events that took place in 704, into a narrative of events that occurred in or before 672, deriving from the fourth book of Bede's history. This is one of the few points at which Alcuin departs radically from the narrative sequence of the *HE* and his object in doing so is plain. Wilfrid figures in Alcuin's poem on York as a missionary renowned for his work among the pagan Saxons and Frisians. There is no hint that much of that work was done in forced exile. The most controversial bishop of the early Northumbrian church is represented in the *Versus de . . . Sanctis Euboricensis Ecclesiae* as a straightforward figure of uncontested sanctity. Alcuin whitewashes Wilfrid's career.[1]

With the appearance of St. Cuthbert in his poem Alcuin's perspective changes: from kings and bishops in a Romanized context to an ascetic saint trained within an originally Celtic tradition. Cuthbert was bishop of Lindisfarne, never bishop of York. There are several churchmen of eminence in the North whom Alcuin never mentions, such as Chad, or on whom he touches only fleetingly, such as Aidan. But Cuthbert he could not exclude.

This fact lends a different emphasis to the anti-Irish sentiments detectable earlier in the *Versus de . . . Sanctis Euboricensis Ecclesiae*. Alcuin's York was in Romanist Deira, and it would be easy to allege that his poem retains traces of a thinly-veiled antagonism to the Irish traditions of neighbouring Bernicia.[2] However, the inclusion and lengthy celebration of Cuthbert in his poem indicate that this was the kind of regionalism which Alcuin sought to overcome. His *Versus de . . . Sanctis Euboricensis Ecclesiae* identify Cuthbert with the whole of Northumbria; the centre of the saint's cult is made to seem far less important than its diffusion. It would

---

[1] Cf. comm. to vv. 1467-8.

[2] On the early history of Bernicia see B. Hope-Taylor, *Yeavering. An Anglo-British Centre of Early Northumbria*, Department of the Environment Archaeological Reports 7 (London, 1977), pp. 276 ff.

be tendentious to argue from this an attempt by York's leading eighth-century advocate to check the rival pretensions of Lindisfarne. When Lindisfarne is mentioned in Alcuin's letters its special associations and importance are acknowledged, but it is firmly set in the context of the entire northern see.[1] In his *Versus de . . . Sanctis Euboricensis Ecclesiae* Alcuin was following a tradition begun by Bede at Wearmouth-Jarrow:[2] of celebrating the career of the outstanding northern saint in comparatively recent times, and of assimilating his cult to the Northumbrian *patria* as a whole. In these circumstances, the hypothesis that St. Cuthbert and Lindisfarne were intended to be to the English what St. Martin and Tours were to the Franks[3] is unnecessary. Alcuin's taste in saints was similar to his taste in kings. Like Bede,[4] he admired expansionists: men capable, spiritually or politically, of uniting both halves of Northumbria. The earlier Irish influence in the northern see goes unmentioned in the *Versus de . . . Sanctis Euboricensis Ecclesiae* not only because it ran counter to Alcuin's Romanist sympathies but also because it was divisive. For Alcuin (as for Bede), Lindisfarne was part of Northumbria in the same way as were Wearmouth-Jarrow and York, and St. Cuthbert was a central figure in the spiritual traditions of a united Northumbrian church.

By the stage in the poem at which he turned to Cuthbert, kingship had already ceased to be one of Alcuin's chief concerns. Ecgfrith (670–85) and Aldfrith (685–704/5) are the last Northumbrian kings he mentions before dealing with events of his own lifetime. About Ecgfrith (vv. 751 ff.) we learn that he was a warrior-king whose expedition against the Irish was unprovoked and unjust. Of his quarrels with Wilfrid

---

[1] 'ecclesia sancti Cuthberti . . . locus cunctis in Britannia venerabilior . . . ubi primum post discessum sancti Paulini ab Euborica christiana religio in nostra gente sumpsit initium', *Ep.* 16 (*MGH Epp.* iv, pp. 42–3); and cf. *Ep.* 17 (ibid., p. 57). These passages are discussed by Bullough, pp. 345–6 and R. A. Markus, *Bede and the Tradition of Ecclesiastical Historiography* (Jarrow Lecture, 1965), pp. 12 ff.

[2] *Vita S. Cuthberti metrica* 26–9 (Jaager, p. 60).

[3] Wallace-Hadrill, *Early Medieval History*, p. 91. At *Vita S. Cuthberti metrica*, 11–29 (Jaager, pp. 59–60), Bede lists the patron saints of the Christian peoples, beginning with Rome and SS. Peter and Paul and ending with St. Cuthbert. Here, if anywhere, one might expect a comparison between St. Martin and St. Cuthbert, had this been in Bede's mind. Martin, significantly, is never mentioned.

[4] Wallace-Hadrill, *Early Medieval History*, p. 90.

we hear nothing: one could not be sure from Alcuin's account that they were even contemporaries. There is no hint of Eddius Stephanus' contention that Ecgfrith's success coincided with his friendship with Wilfrid and his failure with the bishop's opposition. Alcuin's sensitivity about Wilfrid colours his portrayal of Ecgfrith. Ecgfrith's career serves simply as a frame for an account of his queen Æthelthryth's chastity[1] and of the *thegn* captured in battle whom chains could not bind.[2] What mattered to Alcuin were the visible signs of divine intervention that touched the queen or the king's subjects rather than Ecgfrith himself. Similarly, the cultivated Aldfrith, *rex et magister* (the very combination of qualities praised by Alcuin in his panegyrics on Charlemagne), is given only the briefest of notices (vv. 843-6). It is on the achievements of kings as propagators of the faith and as defenders of the Church and kingdom that attention is focused in the *Versus de . . . Sanctis Euboricensis Ecclesiae*: their other successes have second place. In Alcuin's perspective, which made some room, but not much, for political history, Edwin, Oswald, and Oswiu, royal heroes of the seventh century, took the limelight.

Unlike the Irish bishops who held office in Northumbria after Paulinus, the monks of Whitby who became bishops of York were not regarded as a threat by Alcuin. He pays general tribute to the ecclesiastical reforms of Bosa (678-86, 691-c.705), who became bishop after Wilfrid's first expulsion from Northumbria and who ruled the diocese of York until his death except for the five years (686-91) of Wilfrid's restoration (vv. 847-75). The saintly John of Beverley, another former monk of Hexham, who succeeded Bosa, is singled out for special and lengthy praise (vv. 1084-1215). Between his accounts of these bishops is placed a brief narrative (vv. 1008 ff.) of the missionary activities abroad of the Anglo-Saxons that leads to a momentary enlargement of Alcuin's purview, from the specific affairs of Northumbria to the wider achievements of his compatriots.

Alcuin lays particular stress on the miraculous, as providing examples of divine intervention in the affairs of the Northumbrian kingdom and illustrations of the pressing need

[1] *HE* iv. 19(17), 20(18) [= vv. 751-85].   [2] Ibid. iv. 22(20) [= vv. 786-835].

for moral reform. Visions, in particular, play an important role in the *Versus de . . . Sanctis Euboricensis Ecclesiae*, from the heavenly messenger who prophesies Edwin's delivery from his enemies and his kingdom to come (vv. 90-107, 145 ff.) to the experience of Dryhthelm related at vv. 876-1007. Alcuin follows Bede's account of Dryhthelm's vision with scrupulous fidelity. His approach is cautionary, and his emphasis is on corporate salvation (vv. 876-8). Both Bede and St. Boniface in a famous letter[1] write about visions to remind their audience of the nearness of Heaven and Hell. To their tradition Alcuin in his account of Dryhthelm gives a further, ascetic emphasis. He repeats from Bede[2] Dryhthelm's resolve to give up the pleasures of the flesh (vv. 895-9). But the renunciation is hardly an act of repentance. Far from being sinful, Dryhthelm's life and conduct before the vision were positively commendable (v. 884). His story is more than an admonitory tale for wrong-doers: it advocates the superiority of ascetic and celibate over marital life. In the next section of his poem, describing the ascetics Echa and Balthere, Alcuin was to develop this theme further. Dryhthelm's vision urges a renunciation of the world which Echa and Balthere, like Cuthbert, had made.

To describe in full the spiritual history of his *patria* Alcuin goes beyond the *HE*. At vv. 1215 ff. he ceases to draw on Bede and writes about contemporary events. From Bede Alcuin had gained two approaches to the history of Northumbria: the one stressed Romanist tradition in the North and considered the kings of the seventh and eighth centuries in its light; the other, centred upon St. Cuthbert, emphasized moral reform, world renunciation, and asceticism. To this second approach, and to the history of the York episcopate, Alcuin turned when he began to describe his own times.

Alcuin's interest in the bishops and archbishops of his own lifetime lay partly in the moral example they provided and partly in the benefactions they made to the church at York. Wilfrid II (718-32), by virtue of his munificence (vv. 1222 ff.), is presented as a fitting precursor to Egbert. And Egbert, whose reign saw the confirmation of York's full metropolitan

[1] Ed. Tangl, *Ep.* 10 (pp. 8 ff.).   [2] *HE* v. 12.

status in 735 (v. 1280),[1] directed the Northumbrian see in perfect harmony with his brother, the warrior-king Eadberht (vv. 1277-87). This concord between the secular and spiritual rulers of Northumbria during his youth represented to Alcuin an ideal of ecclesiastical and political order.[2] By it he took the measure of earlier history and, in particular, of the relations between Wilfrid I and Ecgfrith,[3] whose reigns hardly provided an edifying example of royal and episcopal collaboration. In Egbert, possibly the only bishop or archbishop of royal birth in the early history of the Northumbrian see, Alcuin identified an architect of the growing ascendancy of the church at York.[4] It is significant that his commemoratory lines on Bede (vv. 1288-1318), whom he revered as 'magister', as 'nostrae cathegita terrae',[5] and to whom he deferred as the major source for his own work, are deliberately placed within an account of Egbert's reign and draw attention to Bede's background at Jarrow (vv. 1293-5). Here, perhaps even more than in his treatment of St. Cuthbert, one can see how far regionalism was from Alcuin's mind. The outstanding achievements of all Northumbria could be seen as a unity in the reign of Bede's protégé, Archbishop Egbert of York.[6]

The best traditions of the northern Church were not confined to the (arch-)episcopate, and at vv. 1319 ff. Alcuin turns to the anchorites Balthere and Echa, whose deaths are recorded in the 'York Annals'[7] and whose names are listed among the *nomina anchoritarum* in the Lindisfarne portion of the Durham *Liber Vitae*.[8] Neither Balthere nor Echa lived at York. Balthere 'fought with the hosts of the air' at a place described by Alcuin as the very opposite of a *locus amoenus* and identified by the later Middle Ages with the Bass Rock.[9]

---

[1] See the comm. to this verse.　　　　　　　　　[2] See p. xlv above.

[3] See pp. lii, liv above.　　　　　　　　[4] See further p. lxii.

[5] 'Magister' at v. 1547; 'nostrae cathegita terrae' *Carm*. ix. 175 (*MGH PLAC* i, p. 233), *Carm*. lxxii. 5 (ibid., p. 294).

[6] For Bede's *Letter to Egbert* see Plummer i, pp. 405-23, and cf. Boniface, ed. Tangl *Ep*. 75, pp. 156 ff., *Ep*. 91, pp. 206 ff.

[7] See app. iii to vv. 1319 ff., vv. 1388 ff.

[8] See J. Stevenson, *Liber Vitae Ecclesiae Dunelmensis*, Surtees Society 13 (London, 1841), p. 6, facsimile, with introduction by A. Hamilton Thompson (Surtees Society 136), f. 15.

[9] See vv. 1325 ff., with comm. ad loc. For an identification of these sites and for valuable discussion of the role of both anchorites in Alcuin's poem, see Bullough, pp. 349-54.

The earliest annalistic compilations note his death in 756 at Tyningham in East Lothian.[1] Echa died in 767 at a place identified as Crayke.[2] Until the 'York Annals' are convincingly dated and located it will remain unclear whether Alcuin referred to them for knowledge of the two anchorites or whether he and an annalist, writing at or near York, were drawing upon oral information and their personal experience. The inclusion of Balthere and Echa in the poem on York linked Alcuin's times to Cuthbert's, laying stress on a continuous tradition of ascetic spirituality and of prophecy (v. 1393), and setting it in the context of the *patria* as a whole. Balthere and Echa showed that the asceticism of Lindisfarne lived on in the Northumbria of Alcuin's own times.

The *Versus de . . . Sanctis Euboricensis Ecclesiae* commemorate the learning of the school at York and the career of Alcuin's teacher, Archbishop Ælberht. A substantial part of the poem is given over to a description of Ælberht and, especially, to a prolonged lament for his death (vv. 1563-96). To the Roman foundation and occupation of York are devoted nineteen lines of Alcuin's poem: the death of Ælberht alone receives thirty-four![3] The subjects upon which Alcuin naturally chose to dwell were his teacher, Archbishop Ælberht, and the school of York in which he himself had taught.[4]

The *Versus de . . . Sanctis Euboricensis Ecclesiae* do not end with the death of Ælberht, even though Alcuin says himself (vv. 1597-8) that he had thought of concluding them there. The lament for the archbishop is offset by hope, by a vision of reunion in the other world which seems to hold a place specially appropriated to the community of York (vv. 1623-5).[5] Alcuin's account of Northumbrian history, which began in Roman York, ends in Heaven.

Alcuin defers to Bede, explicitly and at length, in a number

---

[1] Bullough, p. 349 and n. 42.

[2] *Cric* in the 'York Annals'; cf. app. iii to v. 1388. The identification is Arnold's op. cit. (p. 43).

[3] See further *SM* (3ª Ser.) 20. 2 (1979), pp. 579 ff.

[4] See pp. lx-lxxv below.

[5] In a letter of *c.*795 (*MGH Epp.* iv, *Ep.* 42, p. 86) to the community at York Alcuin recalls a similar vision (see app. iii to vv. 1623-5).

of passages in the *Versus de... Sanctis Euboricensis Ecclesiae.*[1] In his specified debts to the Ecclesiastical History Ludwig Traube saw a total dependence,[2] and others have regarded Alcuin as an unoriginal compiler of others' ideas.[3] Although he draws extensively on Bede's work, Alcuin offers a distinctive and substantially independent view of Northumbrian history. His poem on York is neither wholly original nor merely imitative: it is the work of an independent intelligence.

Alcuin's *Versus de . . . Sanctis Euboricensis Ecclesiae* are a celebration of a united Northumbrian *patria*, centred on York and once (vv. 1008 ff.) including the whole Anglo-Saxon people. Among the poem's heroes are the seventh-century kings who not only defended the fatherland and promoted the faith but also lived in harmony with their bishops. Considering his own times, Alcuin took pride in a continuous tradition of asceticism and learning, and in his master Ælberht.

Alcuin's *Versus de . . . Sanctis Euboricensis Ecclesiae* are also a reflection of York's rise to the status of a major episcopal see, a rise welcomed with approval by Bede in his letter to Archbishop Egbert,[4] whose own *Dialogus Ecclesiasticae Institutionis* is a treatise on the organization of the Church and the role of its bishops. The papal legation to England of 786, which Alcuin accompanied, drew up a document emphasizing the value of harmony between royal and episcopal power, the sanctity of the king's person, and the authority of Pope Gregory.[5] The same subjects figure prominently in Alcuin's poem on York. In 793 Alcuin wrote to Offa, answering a query about the authority of the two metropolitans by reference to Bede's work. In this letter, Alcuin drew his evidence from *HE* i. 17 and 18, where Bede records Pope Honorius's gift of the *pallium* to the two archbishops, one of them being Paulinus of York.[6] The place and

---

[1] See p. lxxxviii, n. 1.

[2] 'Alchuine hatte Beda hinter sich und konnte ihn für den grössten theil fast wörtlich benutzen', *Karolingische Dichtungen*, p. 24.

[3] 'He created nothing, he originated nothing, he added nothing to what had gone before', Gaskoin, *Alcuin, His Life and Work* (London, 1904), p. 246.

[4] Ed. cit., p. lvi, n. 6.   [5] Ed. Dümmler, *MGH Epp.* iv, pp. 20-9.

[6] The letter is reprinted from Lehmann's edition by Levison, *England and the Continent*, pp. 245-6.

organization of the Church, matters which concerned Alcuin in his practical life and on which both Bede and Egbert had written, are reflected in the Northumbrian patriotism of his poem on York.

Alcuin's apparent optimism at the end of the *Versus de . . . Sanctis Euboricensis Ecclesiae* about the state of affairs he saw around him is deceptive. The turbulence of Northumbrian politics in the 780s and 790s lends his work a tone of pointed remonstrance. The rapid succession of corrupt and violent rulers which he traced from the reign of Ælfwald (778/9-88)[1] had committed crimes that in the past had cost kings their kingdoms and nations their *patria*.[2] The royal virtues, which Alcuin identified with the fortunes of the people, needed urgent reconsideration: such is the theme of a succession of his letters from the early 790s.[3] That is why the unsatisfactory kings of eighth-century Northumbria, with the single exception of Archbishop Egbert's brother, Eadberht, are excluded from the *Versus de . . . Sanctis Euboricensis Ecclesiae*. Looking back to the past, Alcuin saw in kings such as Edwin, Oswald, and Oswiu the qualities needed in his own day: qualities of justice, valour, and piety linked to co-operation with the Church.[4] The failure of contemporary kings provided a further reason why, in recounting the history of Northumbria, Alcuin laid special emphasis on the intellectual and spiritual traditions of the contemporary Church. With the influence of the ancient centres of Bamburgh and Lindisfarne on the wane, the renascent archbishopric of York could offer a moral primacy for a united Northumbria which Northumbrian kings were no longer

[1] '. . . A diebus Aelfwaldi regis fornicationes adulteria et incestus inundaverunt super terram . . .' *MGH Epp.* iv, *Ep.* 16 (of 793), p. 43; and see Appendix (p. 137). Ælfwald's sons, Œlf and Œlfwine, were forcibly abducted from York and murdered in 791, a year in which Alcuin may have been there to witness these events ('*Ann. Ebor.*' *s.a.* [= Symeon, *Hist. Reg.* lv], Arnold, p. 53).

[2] *MGH Epp.* iv, *Ep.* 16.

[3] See Wallace-Hadrill, *Early Germanic Kingship*, pp. 105, 118-19.

[4] 'Nichil melius patriam defendit quam principum equitas et pietas et servorum Dei intercessiones' *MGH Epp.* iv, *Ep.* 16, p. 44. Cf. Alcuin's cautionary words to Eanbald II, archbishop of York, in 801: 'Tu ipse vidisti, quomodo perierunt reges, principes, qui adversati sunt antecessoribus tuis et ecclesiae Christi', *MGH Epp.* iv, *Ep.* 232, p. 377, 31-2. See further H. H. Anton, *Fürstenspiegel und Herrscherethos in der Karolingerzeit*, Bonner Historische Forschungen 35 (Bonn, 1968), pp. 84 ff.

capable of providing. Alcuin's view of kingship was increasingly theocratic.[1] At a time of violent upheaval in his native land, he saw hope for stability partly in the influence of Offa,[2] partly in the example of the past, and, above all, in the continuous traditions of a successful Church. It was a message to which kings might attend.[3] Set against the political and ecclesiastical background of Northumbria in the late eighth century, Alcuin's *Versus de . . . Sanctis Euboricensis Ecclesiae* go beyond historical panegyric to appeal in time of crisis for unity from his fellow citizens in one *patria* and one Church.

v. *The School of York and the Sources and Audience of Alcuin's Poem*

Political circumstance as well as personal loyalty determined that the primary audience of Alcuin's *Versus de . . . Sanctis Euboricensis Ecclesiae* should be the cathedral community of York.[4] In particular, Alcuin's poem was addressed to and commemorated the Minster school in which he had been educated and had taught.[5]

The most enduring monument to the Minster and school of Alcuin's day remains his own poem on York. No material trace of the Anglo-Saxon buildings has yet been uncovered. Recent excavations, completed by Mr Derek Phillips and soon to be published by the Royal Commission on Historical Monuments,[6] have uncovered nothing of Edwin's church or of the basilica constructed by archbishop Ælberht with the assistance of Alcuin and his contemporary, the future archbishop Eanbald I, and consecrated to Sancta Sophia ten days before Ælberht's death in 780.[7] As a result of extensive excavations undertaken in connection with the consolidation of the towers in the years 1967–72, the earliest foundations of York Minster have now conclusively been proved to be

[1] See comm. to v. 1479.　　　　[2] See pp. xlv–xlvii above.
[3] See comm. to v. 1479.　　　　[4] See pp. xlii–xliii above.
[5] See vv. 1408–11, 1649–58.
[6] I wish to thank Dr B. Heywood and Mr D. Phillips, who allowed me to see this report before publication. See further p. lxi, n. 1 below.
[7] vv. 1518–20. See further comm. to vv. 79 ff., 197 ff., 220–2, 275–83, 1218, 1396, 1488 ff., 1507 ff., 1512, 1513, 1515–17.

the work of Thomas of Bayeux, the first Norman archbishop
(1070-1100).[1] For the construction of Sancta Sophia and the
splendour of Ælberht's endowments to York Minster,
Alcuin's poem is our only source.

Hardly less obscure are the origins of the school attached
to the Minster.[2] Traditions of learning and education are
commonly supposed to have existed at York under the pre-
decessors of Archbishop Egbert, but the evidence for them
is slight. Paulinus' foundation of an enduring school in 627
is the stuff of legend.[3] Some have favoured the initiative of
Wilfrid I.[4] Chapter xxi of Eddius' Life of Wilfrid suggests,
but does not describe, the household instruction offered by
this ecclesiastical magnate,[5] without specifying that it took
place at York (rather than at Ripon or Hexham, Wilfrid's
other sees); and it is difficult to envisage how, in his turbu-
lent career, which involved so much foreign travel, Wilfrid
might have commanded the leisure necessary to establish a
major school at York.[6] Moreover, Alcuin, in his *Versus de . . .
Sanctis Euboricensis Ecclesiae*, never associates Wilfrid with
that school; and he is not inclined to minimize the antiquity
of the see or the achievements of its bishops. Bede's allusion
to a number of 'young men, mostly laymen' in the retinue
of John of Beverley[7] proves little about formal instruction
in Alcuin's native city during the early eighth century. Not
until the reigns of the archbishops of Alcuin's own lifetime,
Egbert and Ælberht, is there firm evidence for a school at
York.

[1] For an account of the results of these works and the difficulties involved in
them see D. Phillips, 'Excavations of York Minster, 1967-73', in *Friends of York
Minster 46th Annual Report* (1975), pp. 19-27; id., 'Excavation Techniques in
Church Archaeology', in *The Archaeological Study of Medieval Churches*, edd.
P. V. Addyman and R. Morris, CBA Research Reports 13 (London, 1976), pp.
54-60; and id. and N. Hutchinson, 'York Minster: The Excavations', in N. Pevsner,
The Buildings of England: Yorkshire: East Riding ii (revised edn., forthcoming).

[2] The best short sketch is by C. B. L. Barr, 'The Minster Library', in *History of
York Minster*, pp. 487-538.

[3] S. M. Toyne, *St. Peter's School and Alcuin*, York Minster Historical Tracts 6
(London, 1928) (unpaginated).

[4] G. F. Browne, *Alcuin of York* (London, 1908), p. 69; and recently R. M. T.
Hill in *History of York Minster*, pp. 9 ff.

[5] 'Principes quoque saeculares, viri nobiles filios suos ad erudiendum sibi
dederunt, ut aut Deo servirent, si eligerent, aut adultos, si maluissent, regi armatos
commendaret', ed. B. Colgrave (Cambridge, 1927), p. 44.

[6] Cf. Stenton, p. 184.   [7] *HE* v. 6; Hill, art. cit., p. 10.

The impulse to renewal, if not the actual foundation, of the school at York is often attributed to Archbishop Egbert.[1] This is possible, but far from certain. One of the two extant accounts of Egbert's teaching is transmitted in a continental source written some sixty years after his death by an author whose reliability may be questioned.[2] Alcuin himself in the poem on York, our second and most important source for the development of this school, hardly describes Egbert as a teacher. Rather, he celebrates Egbert's success as an administrator.[3] The one surviving work certainly attributable to Egbert—his *Dialogus Ecclesiasticae Institutionis*—corroborates this picture. I see no reason for preferring the tradition of the *Vita Alcuini* to what Alcuin tells us himself. The man who made the school at York what it represented to Alcuin was not Egbert, but his successor Ælberht.[4] It is fair to assume that Archbishop Egbert created the conditions in which it might flourish and that, a protégé of Bede, he transmitted something of Bede's teaching to those in his charge; but the presiding intellect of the school, the creator of its library, and the most significant figure in Alcuin's intellectual development seems to have been his teacher, Archbishop Ælberht.

Detailed evidence of the size and character of the cathedral school in Ælberht's reign is not provided by our sources: the picture of an establishment 'staffed with a faculty numbering about one hundred and fifty canons' we owe to the imagination of Virgil R. Stallbaumer, O.S.B.[5] Knowledge of Ælberht's school and its activity derives largely from the example of Alcuin's career and the testimony of his *Versus de . . . Sanctis Euboricensis Ecclesiae.*

---

[1] e.g. J. Godfrey, *The Church in Anglo-Saxon England* (Cambridge, 1962), p. 213. The foundation of the library is ascribed to Egbert by William of Malmesbury, *Gesta Regum, RS* 90 (London, 1847), p. 68 and *Gesta Pontificum, RS* 52 (London, 1870), p. 246 and repeated by later writers, e.g. J. Leland, *Commentarii de Scriptoribus Britannicis* (London, 1709), p. 121.

[2] See above, p. xxxviii and comm. to vv. 1259-60.

[3] vv. 1251 ff. Other aspects of Alcuin's portrayal of Egbert are discussed on pp. xlv-xlvi, lv-lvi, lxiii-lxiv.

[4] 1397 ff. Cf. P. Hunter Blair, 'From Bede to Alcuin' in *Famulus Christi*, pp. 254-5.

[5] 'The York Cathedral School', *American Benedictine Review*, 22 (1971), pp. 293 and 296. See further comm. to v. 1218.

Ælberht, we know from Alcuin, was a collector and an organizer, both of books and of men. His teaching and patronage gave the school of York an eminence which, by the final quarter of the eighth century, even the school of Wearmouth-Jarrow seems to have lacked. Unlike Bede, and partly by virtue of his noble birth and powerful connections, Ælberht was not only a teacher but also an effective administrator. This practical emphasis is significant. The milieu in which Alcuin was trained was less a monastic community of reflective scholarship than the cathedral church of a major episcopal see on the rise. Educated in a city the metropolitan status of which had been reaffirmed as recently as 735, the pupil of a school organized with deliberation and flair, Alcuin, trained in the York of Ælberht, was naturally impelled to commemorative poetry.[1]

There survive only scant remnants of the intellectual activity of the community commemorated by Alcuin in his poem on York. Few, if any, extant manuscripts have been convincingly assigned to the York of the later eighth century.[2] Other written sources are rare. Although Bede's *Epistola ad Ecgbertum* provides valuable evidence of the state of the Northumbrian see in 734 and of the provisions made for its future promotion, his letter was not written in York.[3] Egbert's *Dialogus Ecclesiasticae Institutionis*—a collection, in dialogue form, of practices of canon law designed to help an ecclesiastical community in its relations with secular society—attests administrative and legal practice at York in

---

[1] Cf. pp. xlvii–lx.

[2] Three fragmentary manuscripts—E. Berlin, Staatsbibliothek Preussischer Kulturbesitz lat. fol. 877 and Hauzenstein, Graf Walderdorff Sammlung (Calendar and Sacramentary: *CLA* viii. 1052, p. 9; T. Brandis *et al.*, *Zimilien. Abendländische Handschriften* (Wiesbaden, 1975), no. 12; and G. Kotzor, *Abhandlungen der Bayerischen Akademie der Wissenschaften, Philologisch-Historische Klasse. NF* 88/1-2 (1981) i, pp. 261 ff.); Munich, Hauptstaatsarchiv, Raritäten-Selekt. 108 (Calendar: *CLA* ix. 1236, p. 3); Weinheim (?), E. Fischer Sammlung S.N. (Justinus, *Epitome: CLA* ix. 1370, p. 38)—have been attributed, unconvincingly, to York in the second half of the eighth century. See Bullough, *Spoleto . . . Settimane* 20 (1972), pp. 574-5 and comm. to v. 1549. A single illuminated manuscript of the early eighth century has been ascribed to York on highly speculative grounds: Maeseyck, Église Ste Cathérine, Trésors S.N., ff. 1-5 (Gospel book, fragmentary: *CLA* x. 1558, p. 34; A. Grabar and C. Nordenfalk, *Early Medieval Painting* (Skira, 1957), p. 120; J. J. G. Alexander, *Insular Manuscripts, 6th to the 9th Century* (London, 1978), n. 22.)

[3] Discussed by Hill, *Famulus Christi*, pp. 102 ff.

Alcuin's youth and early manhood.[1] From Archbishop
Ælberht there survives a letter addressed to the missionary
Lul, that ends with six metrical lines.[2] Alcuin refers to being
trained by Ælberht in versification,[3] and three quotations in
the archbishop's verse *post scriptum* are illustrative of the
literary training his pupil received at the school of York.
Once Ælberht cites Bede, once he cites Caelius Sedulius, and
once he quotes a line which may have been taken from
Lucan, Dracontius, Venantius Fortunatus, or an Anglo-
Saxon collection of papal epitaphs and inscriptions.[4] These
quotations from Bede, Alcuin's intellectual debt to whom
was all-pervasive,[5] from Caelius Sedulius, a representative of
the Christian Latin tradition which, chiefly through the late-
antique Biblical epic, exercised a powerful influence in
eighth-century Northumbria,[6] and from a source of un-
decided origin indicating a real, but often indeterminable,
debt to the Latin classics and their later imitators, point to
authors mentioned, by name or obliquely, in Alcuin's sketch
of the archbishop's library at York.[7] These hints of Ælberht's
reading, preserved in his only surviving work, and supported
by the evidence of Alcuin's poem, should not be ignored.

The correspondence of Anglo-Saxon missionaries on the
Continent with Egbert and Ælberht, requesting copies of the
works of Bede,[8] further illustrates the strong interest in his
writings in later eighth-century York. The 'York Annals',
contemporary with Alcuin, preserve a record of events kept
by an annalist probably working at or near Alcuin's native
city;[9] while a metrical calendar bears witness to the saints and
martyrs venerated at York towards the end of the eighth
century.[10] From Alcuin himself survive a number of letters

[1] Ed. Haddan and Stubbs iii, pp. 403-13. Cf. vv. 1259-60, with comm. ad
loc. The authenticity of the Penitential and Pontifical once attributed to Egbert
has been either disproved or brought into question.
[2] Ed. Tangl, *Ep.* 124, p. 262.   [3] vv. 1438-9, with comm. ad loc.
[4] v. 4: cf. Bede, *Vit. S. Cuthb. metr.* 135; v. 6: cf. Caelius Sedulius, *Carm.
pasch.* i. 368; v. 3: cf. Lucan, *Bell. civ.* ii. 389; Dracontius, *de Laud. Dei* iii. 20;
Ven. Fort. iii. 22. 5; and the *syllogae* discussed by Wallach, *Alcuin and Charle-
magne*, pp. 261 ff.   [5] See p. lxviii, and pp. lxxxiv-lxxxviii below.
[6] See below, pp. lxxx-lxxxii, lxxxvi-lxxxvii.
[7] vv. 1547, 1551, 1553, 1554.   [8] See comm. to vv. 1533-5.
[9] See pp. xxxvii and n. 4, xxxix, lvi and n. 7, lvii and nn. 1, 2 above.
[10] Recorded in the comm. ad loc. For editions of this text see the Biblio-
graphy, B, p. xx.

and poems relating to England in general and to York in particular,[1] but only two brief compositions in verse date with strong probability from the years he spent there,[2] and their number does not include the *Versus de . . . Sanctis Euboricensis Ecclesiae*.[3] The florilegium compiled by Alcuin and containing the *Miracula S. Nyniae*[4] was assembled after he had left York in 781/2.[5] The literary evidence that can be dated and attributed with any probability to what has been described as 'the principal centre of English scholarship'[6] in the later eighth century is severely limited.

The fragmentary state of the evidence for texts read and written at York in Alcuin's lifetime will affect our interpretation of the picture of Ælberht's school drawn in the *Versus de . . . Sanctis Euboricensis Ecclesiae*. The little we know makes it difficult to verify the claims made by Alcuin, either by reference to extant manuscripts containing the texts he appears to cite, or by comparison with works composed at York, or by analogy with his own writings.

Virtually all of Alcuin's surviving works were written after he had gone to Charlemagne's court in 781/2. They naturally reflect something of Alcuin's learning in England, but to distinguish what he brought to the Continent from what he acquired during his years in Charlemagne's entourage is a speculative task. Moreover, special problems are posed by the *Versus de . . . Sanctis Euboricensis Ecclesiae* and, in particular, by the outline of 'York books' at vv. 1536-62.[7]

The first of these problems lies in the character of Alcuin's description. He displays the names of the best authorities, and suggests a store of learning both varied and profound

---

[1] Listed at p. xliii, n. 1.   [2] See p. xxxix.
[3] See pp. xliii–xlvii.   [4] See p. xliv and n. 4 above.
[5] The best-known manuscript of this florilegium is the tenth-century continental MS. Bamberg, Staatsbibliothek B. II. 10 (Misc. Patr. 17). For a description and analysis of its contents see F. Leitschuh, *Katalog der Handschriften der königlichen Bibliothek zu Bamberg*, i. 1. 3 (Bamberg, 1903), no. 17, pp. 363-6; F. Vollmer, *MGH AA* xiv (Berlin, 1905), pp. xiv–xvi; and K. Strecker, *MGH PLAC* iv. 2, pp. 452-4. A study of this florilegium, incorporating his recent discoveries about its textual transmission, is being prepared by D. A. Bullough. Preliminary accounts include R. Constantinescu, 'Alcuin et les *Libelli Precum* de l'époque carolingienne', *Revue d'histoire de la Spiritualité*, 50 (1974), pp. 17-56; and M. Lapidge, in *ASE* 8 (1979), pp. 294-5. Brief remarks below, pp. lxviii and n. 1.
[6] Stenton, p. 188.   [7] pp. 122-6.

(vv. 1536-40, 1558-62); but one can easily overrate the list of forty-one authors in his poem on York. It resembles less a catalogue than a learned advertisement. Its purpose is to impress rather than to inform.[1] A general reference to a great figure in the list of authors is no guarantee that all of his writings were to be found at York in Alcuin's day.[2] It is possible that a considered principle of selection lay behind Alcuin's mention of some writers and exclusion of others, but brevity and metre also dictated which names he might and might not include.[3]

These problems are compounded by the circumstances of the poem's composition. Alcuin's recollections of Ælberht's library may not be wholly innocent of romantic nostalgia or generous pride, particularly if he wrote or revised the *Versus de . . . Sanctis Euboricensis Ecclesiae* after he had left York.[4] Nor would a later dating of the poem allow one to claim that, in writing or revising it after spending some years in the literary circle of Charlemagne's entourage, Alcuin drew exclusively on books he had read at the school of Ælberht. The poem remains our chief surviving witness to what Alcuin asserts York was able to offer in the later eighth century, but the sparseness of relevant external evidence and the problematical character of the text itself do not permit us to equate its sources with what Alcuin had learnt in Ælberht's library.

From this it follows that there can be no hard-and-fast method of assessing which texts cited by Alcuin in his poem might have been made accessible to him by his training at York. Only a scale of probability can be constructed, the co-ordinates of which are few and inexact.

Three criteria seem relevant to this problem: the mention of an author's name in the sketch of Ælberht's library at vv. 1536 ff.; quotation from that author's text both by Alcuin and by Bede, the principal Northumbrian writer in the

---

[1] Cf. P. Riché, *Éducation et Culture dans l'Occident barbare, VIe-VIIIe siècles* (Paris, 1962), p. 433: 'Il s'agit moins . . . de souvenirs, que de la présentation d'un modèle d'école.' While accepting a date of composition in 781-2, Riché also suggests that the work was 'destinée à encourager les lettrés carolingiens qui, à cette époque, réorganisaient les écoles franques'.

[2] Cf. Laistner, *Intellectual Heritage*, p. 118.

[3] vv. 1558-62.

[4] See pp. xliii-xlvii.

generation before Alcuin who also had links with York; and the existence of an eighth-century manuscript of Northumbrian origin of the work in question. If Alcuin quotes from a major poet such as Lucan, who was also known to Bede,[1] then it is possible that a text of the *Bellum civile* was available in Ælberht's York, as v. 1554 would imply. If Alcuin cites extensively from an author of late Antique Biblical epic, whose name is listed among those poets he claims were available in Ælberht's library and whose works, also quoted by Bede, survive in an eighth-century manuscript of Northumbrian origin,[2] then possibility hardens into probability. But even the coincidence of these three criteria falls short of firm proof that Alcuin first became familiar with any given text at York.

The identification of verbal borrowings, often subjective and ambiguous, is indispensable in attempting to establish this point; and authors whose works Alcuin cites, without mentioning their names, may have had their place among Ælberht's books. Nor does infrequent quotation from a poem necessarily prove limited acquaintance with it. It is possible to be familiar with a text, and to cite from it rarely. The study of verbal borrowings, if made in a purely quantitative manner, can be insensitive to the reality of this semi-passive knowledge. Although Prudentius and Alcimus Avitus are included in Alcuin's list of authors, his use of the one in this poem is slight and his use of the other appears even slighter.[3] Prosper of Aquitaine's name is listed by Alcuin at v. 1552, but only his *Carmen de Ingratis* and *De Providentia Dei*[4] attributed to him are cited by Alcuin, although excerpts

[1] Bede cites Lucan, *Bell. civ.* i. 1–3, 10–12 at *De Arte Metrica*, i. 11. 62–9 (Kendall, p. 115).

[2] As in the case of Paulinus of Nola (see p. lxx and nn. 4–7).

[3] Both names are recorded at v. 1552. Cf. Index of Quotations and Allusions, pp. 151 and 145 respectively. Note that the reading 'Alcimus' at v. 1552 rests on Froben's emendation. On Aldhelm and Alcimus Avitus and Prudentius, see Ehwald, *MGH AA* xv, p. 432 (on v. 1912) and p. 458 (on v. 2631). Bede cites Prudentius in his *De Arte Metrica* i. 14. 63–6 (Kendall, p. 125) and echoes are discerned in the metrical *Life of Cuthbert* by Jaager (p. 94, on v. 478; p. 112, on v. 709), who records one borrowing from Alcimus Avitus in the work (pp. 62–3, on v. 61). See further Manitius, 'Zu Aldhelm und Beda', *Sitzungsberichte der phil.-hist. Classe der Kaiserlichen Akademie der Wissenschaften* 112 (Vienna, 1886), pp. 571–2, 579, 619, 623.

[4] See Index of Quotations and Allusions, p. 151.

from Prosper's Epigrams are included among the Christian Latin poems in the florilegium compiled by Alcuin.[1] The influence of Lactantius, if he is the author of the *De Ave Phoenice*, is not pronounced.[2] All these poets share a number of recurrent expressions—some liturgical reminiscences, others mere clichés—which make it difficult to ascribe commonplace features of Alcuin's verse to any one of them. The absence of specific and extensive borrowings from an author listed in the *Versus de . . . Sanctis Euboricensis Ecclesiae* does not necessarily point to rhetorical exaggeration on Alcuin's part. His poetical sketch of the York library is not a catalogue of his sources. Can this sketch, according to the three criteria described above, be considered broadly representative of Alcuin's reading at the school of Ælberht?

Long tracts of Alcuin's poem closely follow Bede's *HE*,[3] possibly in a text of the 'M-type'.[4] The thorough knowledge of the prose and metrical Lives of St. Cuthbert displayed in Alcuin's poem is accompanied by some acquaintance with Bede's minor verse.[5] Second only to Bede's influence ranks that of Aldhelm, every one of whose metrical works was known to Alcuin. Alcuin's debts to Aldhelm range from dozens of verbal echoes[6] to one outright plagiarism (v. 1449). A mere list of borrowings cannot do justice to the influence of these two writers on Alcuin's text, an influence which will receive separate analysis in this Introduction.[7] It is,

---

[1] Alcuin's excerpts from Prosper's *Epigrams* occur on fol. 152^V of Bamberg Staatsbibliothek B. II. 10 (Misc. Patr. 17) (see p. lxv, n. 5 above). Bede quotes extensively from them in both the *De Arte Metrica* and the metrical Life of St. Cuthbert. Aldhelm's borrowings from Prosper are listed by Ehwald, *MGH AA* xv, p. 545. See further Manitius, 'Zu Aldhelm und Beda' (art. cit. p. lxvii, n. 3), pp. 573-4 and 621. The MS. Antwerp, Museum Plantin-Moretus M. 17. 14 (*s*. ix *in.*) represents a copy of an eighth-century Northumbrian MS. containing both Prosper's *Epigrammata* and Caelius Sedulius, *Carmen paschale* (this work is discussed further at·p. lxx). See J. J. G. Alexander, *Insular Manuscripts, 6th to 9th Century* (London, 1978), no. 65.

[2] See comm. to v. 1325 ff. There is no clear evidence that the poem was known in Anglo-Saxon England until the ninth century, when the most important witness is vernacular. See *The Phoenix*, ed. N. F. Blake (Manchester, 1964), pp. 17-24. On the authorship of this poem see M. C. Fitzpatrick, *Lactanti 'de ave Phoenice'* (Philadelphia, 1933), pp. 31-7; E. Rapisarda, *Il Carme 'de ave Phoenice' di Lattanzio*[3] (Catania, 1959), pp. 93-113.

[3] e.g. vv. 876-1007 [= *HE* v. 12].   [4] See comm. to vv. 1600 ff.
[5] See Index of Quotations and Allusions, p. 145.
[6] Ibid., pp. 143-4.   [7] See pp. lxxvi-lxxvii, lxxxii-lxxxviii.

however, noteworthy that when Alcuin set about composing a large-scale poem in celebration of his *patria* he turned first to Bede and Aldhelm: to both of the leading figures in previous Anglo-Latin literature.

In the early part of the *Versus de . . . Sanctis Euboricensis Ecclesiae* Alcuin draws on Gildas,[1] while in the later portion of the poem, dealing with the events of his own lifetime, he includes information also to be found in the 'York Annals'.[2] Many of the bishops, saints, and martyrs recorded in the metrical Calendar of York are commemorated by Alcuin.[3] He cites too from the poetry of St. Boniface,[4] and shares common sources with Felix's Life of St. Guthlac[5] and similar concerns with earlier Northumbrian hagiography.[6] In these respects, Alcuin's poem on York represents the first major work of imaginative writing whose primary debts are to a literary culture that, in source and inspiration, was neither exclusively Northumbrian nor Southumbrian, but fully Anglo-Latin.

The Anglo-Latin writers upon whom Alcuin drew in the *Versus de . . . Sanctis Euboricensis Ecclesiae* were heirs to a tradition of late Antique and early Medieval Latin poetry which, by the end of the eighth century, had formed a definable 'school canon'.[7] At vv. 1551-3 of his poem Alcuin lists the names of many of the authors whose writings made up this canon.

The late Antique poets whom Alcuin knew and cited in similar proportions are Caelius Sedulius, Arator, and Juvencus.[8] Familiar to both Bede and Aldhelm, the works of these three writers formed a core of Biblical epic poetry which enjoyed a wide circulation in early Anglo-Saxon England. The Cues, Hospitalbibliothek MS. 171 (? Northumbria,

---

[1] See the references listed p. xlviii, n. 3.

[2] See pp. lvi–lvii and comm. to vv. 1319 ff., 1388 ff.

[3] Noted in the comm. throughout.

[4] See Index of Quotations and Allusions, p. 147.

[5] See comm. to vv. 1327 ff.   [6] See p. lxxvi.

[7] See G. Glauche, *Schullektüre im Mittelalter. Entstehung und Wandlungen des Lektürekanons bis 1200 nach den Quellen dargestellt*, Münchener Beiträge zur Mediävistik und Renaissance-Forschung 5 (Munich, 1970), especially pp. 10–11; and R. Herzog, *Die Bibelepik der lateinischen Spätantike*, i (Munich, 1975), pp. xxiii–xxxiii.

[8] Index of Quotations and Allusions, pp. 151, 144–5, 149.

s. vii[2]),[1] containing a bifolium of Juvencus, and the Cambridge, Corpus Christi College MS. 173 (Kentish, *s.* viii[1]),[2] containing Caelius Sedulius' *Carmen paschale*, are the scattered remnants of a tradition of late antique Biblical epic that was diffused both north and south of the Humber, on which Alcuin drew extensively and at key points in his work.[3]

Alcuin's knowledge of the entire poetic corpus of Paulinus of Nola compares favourably with his use of any other late Antique poet. Before Alcuin, Paulinus seems to have been known most extensively in the North: Aldhelm does not cite him at any length,[4] but Bede quotes Paulinus repeatedly in the *De Arte Metrica*, the commentary on Luke, the metrical Life of St. Cuthbert and, especially, his *Vita S. Felicis*, which is based on the *Natalicia*.[5] The early Insular tradition of Paulinus' text is represented in Vatican, Pal. lat. 235 (Northumbria, *ss.* vii–viii)[6] and in its contemporary, MS. Leningrad, National Public Library (lat. Q. V. xiv. 1 (Northumbria).[7] It therefore seems probable that, in drawing on Paulinus, Alcuin was using an author whose works were readily available in Northumbria, if not elsewhere.

Verbal borrowings alone are, exceptionally, enough to show Alcuin's familiarity with the eleven-book collection of Venantius Fortunatus's occasional verse and with his metrical Life of St. Martin.[8] Whole passages of the *Versus de . . . Sanctis Euboricensis Ecclesiae* are directly modelled on the

---

[1] *CLA* viii. 1172, p. 42. The dating of this and of the following three MSS. is T. J. Brown's. Lowe assigns this MS. to *s.* vii *ex.*

[2] *CLA* ii.[2] 123, p. 3. Dated *s.* viii by Lowe.

[3] Cf. vv. 1 ff.

[4] See Ehwald, *MGH AA* xv, p. 545 and M. Manitius, 'Zu Aldhelm und Beda', *Sitzungsberichte der phil.–hist. Classe der kaiserlichen Akademie der Wissenschaften*, 112 (Vienna, 1886), p. 571.

[5] The evidence is summarized by T. W. Mackay, 'Bede's Hagiographical Method: His knowledge and Use of Paulinus of Nola', *Famulus Christi*, pp. 77-9. Still fundamental for the study of Paulinus' influence is E. Chatelain, 'Notice sur les manuscrits des poésies de S. Paulin de Nole, suivie d'observations sur le texte', *Bibliothèque des Écoles françaises d'Athènes et de Rome*, 14 (Paris, 1880), especially pp. 1-30.

[6] *CLA* i. 87, p. 26. This manuscript is dated *s.* viii by B. Bischoff, *Lorsch im Spiegel seiner Handschriften* (Munich, 1974), pp. 78, 108.

[7] *CLA*, xi. 1622, p. 12. Dated *s.* viii[2/4] by Lowe. See further Brown in C. D. Verey, T. J. Brown, and E. Coatsworth, *The Durham Gospels*, Early English Manuscripts in Facsimile 20 (Copenhagen, 1980), pp. 48-9.

[8] Index of Quotations and Allusions, p. 148.

Vita S. Martini and there can be little doubt that Alcuin's use of Fortunatus (whose name he cites at v. 1553) is far more extensive than Bede's.[1] Alcuin's verbal debts to Venantius Fortunatus are of the same order as his debts to Paulinus and to the three authors of late antique Biblical epic discussed above. The absence of any Insular manuscript of Fortunatus's verse antedating the tenth century therefore casts little doubt upon Alcuin's knowledge of Fortunatus's text. It points only to a vicissitude of manuscript transmission which, in the absence of other external evidence, prevents one from being certain that Alcuin read Fortunatus's works at York.

The group of late Antique and early Medieval Latin poets whom Alcuin lists at vv. 1551-3 and from whom he quotes repeatedly—Caelius Sedulius, Arator, Juvencus, Paulinus of Nola, and Venantius Fortunatus—form a coherent whole. They correspond to texts contained in a number of composite manuscripts of the early ninth century, such as Milan, Biblioteca Ambrosiana, C. 74 sup. and Paris, Bibliothèque nationale, lat. 9347, which are among our major witnesses to a poetical 'school canon'.[2] The list of poets in the '*Versus Isidori*' X, attributed to Isidore of Seville, and in Venantius Fortunatus's *Vita S. Martini* i. 14-25 point to the earlier circulation of a similar body of texts.[3] This argument is not affected by Alcuin's minimal acquaintance with Christian Latin poets such as 'Cyprianus Gallus', Commodian, and 'Proba', marginal to the canon; while the absence from Alcuin's list (and sources) of poets known to Venantius Fortunatus, such as Paulinus of Périgueux, the author of a metrical paraphrase of Sulpicius Severus's Life of St. Martin, may simply reflect the popularity in the later eighth century of Fortunatus's own version of the same text. In substance

---

[1] For a brief account of the circulation of Venantius Fortunatus's poetry in early Anglo-Saxon England, see M. Lapidge, *ASE* 8 (1979), pp. 289-95.

[2] Descriptions in Glauche, *Schullektüre*, pp. 31-2. The Milan manuscript shares with Alcuin's list Venantius Fortunatus (occasional poetry and *Vita S. Martini*), Arator, Paulinus of Nola (*Natalicia*), Prosper, Juvencus; the Paris manuscript contains Caelius Sedulius, Juvencus, Prosper, Arator, and Fortunatus (occasional poetry). The same authors, together with Bede and Aldhelm, are among those excerpted for the Bamberg florilegium (Vollmer, p. xvi).

[3] See app. ii to vv. 1551-4 and Glauche, *Schullektüre*, pp. 5, 7, and cf. pp. 23 ff.

and in some detail it therefore seems probable that at *Versus de . . . Sanctis Euboricensis Ecclesiae* 1551-3 Alcuin referred to, and knew well, a 'school canon' of late Antique and early Medieval Latin poetry in one of the forms it had assumed since the time of Venantius Fortunatus, and in which it circulated in early Anglo-Saxon England and was available at York.

Alcuin's knowledge of Classical Latin poetry was chiefly confined to the epic, as v. 1554 implies. The influence of Virgil, from the entire *Aeneid* to the *Georgics* and *Eclogues*, is all-pervasive in the *Versus de . . . Sanctis Euboricensis Ecclesiae*.[1] Alcuin's debts to Lucan are smaller, but by no means unimportant. In at least one place where the *textus receptus* requires emendation[2] the allusion is plainly to Lucan, and a number of other echoes are not to be ignored.[3] Borrowings from Statius are rarer.[4] Allusions to Ovid and to Horace, which some have found in the *Versus de . . . Sanctis Euboricensis Ecclesiae*,[5] can be paralleled with greater precision from Christian and early Medieval Latin sources. Many had become proverbs or mere clichés by the late eighth century.[6] At most, Alcuin's acquaintance with Ovid and Horace was slight and at second hand.[7]

The sum total of Alcuin's acquaintance with Classical Latin poetry is thus modest indeed: overwhelmingly Virgilian, with elements of 'Silver Age' epic, it amounts to no more than a strictly limited choice. In the reading of Bede and of Aldhelm, Lucan figures infrequently and Statius hardly at all, but extensive use is made of Virgil.[8] If Alcuin's quotation

[1] See Index of Quotations and Allusions, pp. 152-4. Alcuin's use of Virgil has been studied by D. F. Long, *Studies in Honour of Basil L. Gildersleeve* (Baltimore, 1902), pp. 377-86 and E. M. Sanford, *Classical Journal*, 26 (1925), pp. 526-33.

[2] v. 184 with comm. ad loc.

[3] Index of Quotations and Allusions, p. 150.

[4] Ibid., p. 152.

[5] Manitius, *Neues Archiv*, 11 (1886), pp. 558-61; Dümmler, *MGH PLAC* ii, pp. 690-3; J. D. A. Ogilvy, *Books known to the English, 597-1066²*, Medieval Academy of America (Cambridge, Mass., 1967), p. 211.

[6] See comm. to v. 785.

[7] Cf. Schaller, *Verfasserlexikon*, i, col. 246.

[8] The view that Bede derived his knowledge of Virgil from grammarians (P. Hunter Blair, *Famulus Christi*, pp. 244-50) is convincingly rebutted by N. Wright, 'Bede and Virgil', *Romanobarbarica*, 6 (1981), pp. 145-62.

of Classical Latin poetry in his *Versus de . . . Sanctis Eubori-censis Ecclesiae* is representative of Ælberht's library, then at York, as at other English centres, the pre-eminence of Virgil, exploited as a grammatical as well as a literary source, is further evidence for the maintenance of a curriculum of strictly orthodox range.[1] With the possible exception of Statius, no Latin poet cited by name or echoed verbally in Alcuin's poem points to the rich variety of classical texts available in the exceptional library of Charlemagne.[2]

A number of works that occupied an important place in Alcuin's general culture are also referred to in the *Versus de . . . Sanctis Euboricensis Ecclesiae*. The Bible, Isidore, and collections of inscriptional texts[3] all leave their mark on the poem. The possibility that the Latin traditions upon which Alcuin drew explicitly were supplemented at certain points by vernacular poetry of which he was incidentally aware may not be pressed.[4] The poem on York is the product of a distinctively latinate and Insular culture, the principal areas of which may now be distinguished as follows:[5]

Insular Latin Authors	Bede, *HE, Vitae S. Cuthberti, Opera poetica minora*
	Aldhelm, *Opera poetica*
	Gildas, *De Excidio Britonum*
	Boniface, *Carmina*

---

[1] See comm. to vv. 1558-62.

[2] Bischoff, 'Die Bibliothek im Dienste der Schule', *Spoleto . . . Settimane*, 19. 1 (1971), pp. 387-8; id., *Karl der Grosse* ii, pp. 57 ff. and *Sammelhandschrift Diez B. Sant. 66. Grammatici Latini et Catalogus Librorum . . .* , Codices Selecti Phototypice Impressi 42 (Graz, 1973), introduction. On the unusual range of this library on the Continent see Glauche, *Schullektüre*, p. 22.

[3] The importance of such collections as the *Sylloge Epigraphica Cantabrigiensis* is stressed by Wallach, *Alcuin and Charlemagne*, pp. 261 ff. See further M. Lapidge, 'Some Remnants of Bede's Lost *Liber Epigrammatum*', *EHR* 90 (1975), especially p. 801; and J. Higgitt, 'The Dedication Inscription at Jarrow and its Context', *The Antiquaries Journal*, 59 (1979), pp. 343-74.

[4] See comm. and app. iii to v. 1325. For a different view of this question see W. F. Bolton, *Alcuin and Beowulf. An Eighth-Century View* (London, 1979).

[5] If Alcuin's use of a work or an author is doubtful, then the title or name in question is placed within square brackets.

Late Antique Biblical Epic	Arator, *De Actibus Apostolorum*, [*Ep. ad Parthenium*] Caelius Sedulius, *Carmen Paschale* Juvencus, *Historia Evangeliorum* Prudentius, *Psychomachia*, [*Hamartigena, Apotheosis*] Alcimus Avitus, *Poemata*
Late Antique Christian Latin Poetry	Paulinus of Nola, *Opera Poetica* Prosper of Aquitaine, *Carmen de Ingratis, De Providentia Dei* (attrib.) Licentius, *Carmen*[1] [Publilius Optatianus Porfyrius, *Carmina*] ['Lactantius', *De Ave Phoenice*] Venantius Fortunatus, *Carmina, Vita S. Martini metrica*
Classical Epic and other Poetry	Virgil, *Aeneid, Georgics, Eclogues* Lucan, *Bellum civile* Statius, *Thebaid, Achilleid, Silvae*
	Scripture Isidore, *Etymologiae*
Epigraphical Sources	*Sylloge Epigraphica Cantabrigiensis*

The breadth of Alcuin's reading is neither great nor unusual among poets of his time. His familiarity with a wide range of late Antique texts, his sound knowledge of Venantius Fortunatus's poetical works, and his thorough acquaintance with Virgil were matched by European writers of the same period,[2] and in certain areas he was left far behind. Prudentius, who appears at the margins of Alcuin's

[1] See app. ii to vv. 1412, 1590-1.
[2] Two of the best critical editions that enable one to assess these questions are K. Neff, *Die Gedichte des Paulus Diaconus*, Quellen und Untersuchungen zur lateinischen Philologie des Mittelalters 3. 4 (Munich, 1908) and D. Norberg, *L'œuvre poétique de Paulin d'Aquilée*, Kungl. Vitterhets Historie och Antikvitets Akademiens Handlingar, Filologisk–Filosofiska serien 18 (Stockholm, 1979). On Theodulf, see Schaller, 'Philologische Untersuchungen zu den Gedichten Theodulfs von Orleans', diss. phil. Heidelberg, 1956.

learning, or Ovid, who scarcely figures in his work, played a significant part in the reading of a number of Alcuin's continental contemporaries, notably Theodulf of Orléans. It is Alcuin's reliance upon the chief Latin authors of his native land that truly sets his *Versus de . . . Sanctis Eubori-censis Ecclesiae* apart from the work of continental poets and links it with Northumbrian Latin literature composed during or shortly after his lifetime, such as the anonymous *Miracula S. Nyniae* and Æthelwulf's *De Abbatibus*.[1] Probability indicates that Alcuin knew in England sources of his poem such as Virgil, a number of late Antique epic poets, Paulinus of Nola, and Venantius Fortunatus. His extensive use of Bede and Aldhelm enables one to go further. Where Alcuin first studied these two authors is not a matter for doubt. What distinguished Alcuin's background as a poet from that of fellow writers at Charlemagne's court and linked it with Latin verse in the Northumbria of his own times is that detailed knowledge of the works of Bede and Aldhelm which he acquired at school in Ælberht's York.

vi. *Anglo-Latin Literature before 800 and the Poetry of Alcuin*

At the centre of Alcuin's literary culture, acquired at York and reflected in the sources of his *Versus de . . . Sanctis Euboricensis Ecclesiae*, stand Bede and Aldhelm, the two principal writers of early Anglo-Latin. What light does Anglo-Latin literature before 800 cast on Alcuin's background as a poet and, especially, on his poem on York?[2]

By the final quarter of the eighth century, from which dates most of Alcuin's poetry, the Latin literature of Anglo-Saxon England reached back only a century. Its first masterpiece is a work of prose: Bede's *HE*. In founding his poem on York on the history of his own people, written by the leading Northumbrian scholar and counsellor to Archbishop Egbert,

---

[1] The sources of the *Miracula S. Nyniae* are examined exhaustively by Strecker, *MGH PLAC* iv. 3, pp. 944–62. On the *De Abbatibus* see Dümmler, ibid. i, pp. 583 ff. and Campbell, *Æthelwulf 'de Abbatibus'*, pp. xliv–xlvii.

[2] For a bibliographical survey of early Anglo-Latin literature see M. Lapidge in *Insular Latin Studies. Papers on Latin Texts and Manuscripts of the British Isles: 550–1066* (Toronto, 1981), pp. 45–82.

Alcuin chose not only the outstanding model of previous Anglo-Latin prose but also the one most immediate to him.

History intermingled with works of clerical biography and of hagiography. Four of these works are especially relevant to an understanding of Anglo-Latin literature in the time of Alcuin: the anonymous Whitby *Vita Gregorii Magni*, Bede's Lives of St. Cuthbert, the same author's *Historia Abbatum*, and Eddius Stephanus's Life of Wilfrid.

Eddius Stephanus's Life of Wilfrid is a justificatory biography of the bishop, written by one of his fervent supporters.[1] Bede's *Historia Abbatum* (725-31)[2] is a less plainly partisan work. It presents a collective *vita* of the abbots of Wearmouth-Jarrow, stressing the corporate achievements of their exemplary community and the saintliness of its individual members. The anonymous author of the *Vita Gregorii Magni*, writing at Whitby between 704 and 714[3] with great ingenuity and little knowledge of his subject, admired Edwin of Northumbria as much as he revered Gregory the Great. Bishop and ascetic unite in the central figure of Bede's Lives of St. Cuthbert.

This cluster of works from the north of England in the eighth century betrays a number of regional preoccupations: in the Whitby Life of Gregory is found an emphasis on Romanist tradition expressed in the cult of Gregory the Great; the *Historia Abbatum* is concerned with the development of a spiritual community; and the interest in episcopal power and the northern see in Eddius's Life of Wilfrid is matched in Bede's *Vitae* by an ideal of the asceticism Cuthbert had represented. These local interests of early Northumbrian hagiography and biography are reflected in Alcuin's poem on York.[4]

Exemplary and often polemical, much Anglo-Latin prose

---

[1] Ed. cit., p. lxi, n. 5.   [2] Ed. Plummer, i, pp. 364-87.

[3] Ed. B. Colgrave, *The Earliest Life of Gregory the Great, by an Anonymous Monk of Whitby* (Lawrence, Kansas, 1968). For a valuable study of this life, see O. Limone in *SM* (3ª ser.) 19 (1978), pp. 37-68.

[4] See pp. xlix-lv above and Bullough, pp. 339 ff. For surveys of early Anglo-Latin hagiography see B. Colgrave, 'The earliest Saints' Lives written in England', *PBA* 44 (1958), pp. 35-60; C. W. Jones, *Saints' Lives and Chronicles in Early England* (repr. New York, 1968); A. Thacker, 'The Social and Continental Background to Early Anglo-Saxon Hagiography' (unpublished D.Phil. thesis; Oxford, 1976).

before Alcuin lives one life with verse. Bede's *Vitae S. Cuthberti* provide one example of this point; for another we must look to the South, to Aldhelm's *De Virginitate*, which enjoyed such widespread influence in Anglo-Saxon England, both during and after the eighth century.[1] Aldhelm's was a moral-didactic treatise; Bede's was hagiography. Aldhelm's metrical *De Virginitate* was conceived as a verse counterpart to his prose tract; Bede's prose Life of Cuthbert was designed to complement his metrical *Vita*. The practice of these two writers would influence Alcuin when he came to adapt prose works by Bede.

In their edifying purpose the minor works of Anglo-Latin poetry are comparable to the narrative verse of Bede and Aldhelm. In oblique form the *aenigmata* or riddles present facts about the natural or spiritual world;[2] the hymns, prayers, and other religious poems celebrate sacred themes;[3] while inscriptional and commemorative pieces express a practical, generally didactic, design.[4] In verse, the arduous medium of an acquired language, Anglo-Latin authors offered a statement of what they considered instructive and true. Their works, in style and conception, are all sententious.[5]

Poetry of an admonitory and metaphorical character, written to complement prose on historical, hagiographical, or moral–didactic themes, thus figures as one of the central currents in Anglo-Latin literature before 800. Its unity derives partly from the dominance of two leading writers and partly from its limited range. Bede and Aldhelm between them command barely half the genres in which Alcuin wrote, and the variety of his poetical works[6]—from inscriptions to panegyrics and from verse-epistles to hymns—reflects the varied circumstances of their production. It is chiefly in Alcuin's longer poems that these currents in early Anglo-Latin reach their point of confluence.

[1] The difficulty of dating this work is discussed by Lapidge, *Aldhelm: The Prose Works* (Ipswich and Totowa, N.J., 1979), pp. 14–15. For its diffusion see ibid., pp. 2–3.

[2] The *aenigmata* of Aldhelm are edited by Ehwald, *MGH AA* xv, pp. 97–149; the principal collections of other early Anglo-Latin *aenigmata* are published in *CCSL* cxxxiii, lcxxxiiia (Turnhout, 1968).

[3] Bede's *Hymni* and *Preces* are edited in *CCSL* cxxii, pp. 407 ff.

[4] For Aldhelm's *Carmina Ecclesiastica* see Ehwald, pp. 11–32.

[5] See further pp. lxxxii–lxxxviii below.   [6] See p. xlii and n. 2 above.

All three of Alcuin's longer poems were written as verse counterparts to works in prose. The metrical Life of St. Willibrord was intended to be one half of a composition, the other half of which was formed by Alcuin's *Vita S. Willibrordi prosaica*. *Carmen* ix, Alcuin's elegiac epistle on the destruction of Lindisfarne by the Vikings in 793,[1] refashions the central themes of a number of consolatory letters which he sent to England soon after that date.[2] In a manner frequently oblique and invariably edifying both poems sum up the subject-matter of the prose works to which they are matched. These formal and stylistic features of Alcuin's *Carmen* ix and *Vita S. Willibrordi metrica* are amply displayed in his poem on York. In tracing the historical factors which influenced Alcuin's choice of literary form when he set out in this poem to write a counterpart to Bede's *HE* and Lives of St. Cuthbert, some of the links between the major works of early Anglo-Latin literature and its classical background become clearer.

vii. *The Rise of the* opus geminatum *and the Form of Alcuin's Poem on York*

Behind Alcuin's use of Bede lay the traditions of a literary form whose most influential exponent for the early Middle Ages was the fifth-century poet, Caelius Sedulius.[3] The form which Sedulius initiated and to which Alcuin was indebted is the *opus geminatum*: a work of two paired parts, the one in prose, the other in verse.[4] Its

---

[1] The poem is translated by H. Waddell, *More Latin Lyrics* (London, 1976), pp. 160–75. Cf. Alcuin, *Ep.* 20 (*MGH Epp.* iv, pp. 56–8). For discussion and further examples see *SM* (3ª Ser.) 20. 2 (1979), pp. 581 ff.

[2] Ibid., pp. 564 ff.

[3] All references are to the *CSEL* edition of J. Huemer (Vienna, 1885). The best study of Caelius Sedulius's biography remains that of Huemer, *De Sedulii poetae vita et scriptis commentatio* (Vienna, 1878).

[4] Aldhelm, *De Virg. metr.*, vv. 2868 and 2870 (Ehwald, p. 469) uses the term *opus geminum*. The first use of *opus geminatum* as a technical term occurs at Bede, *HE* v., 18, a reference to be discussed below. However, Caelius Sedulius's allusion (second *Epistola ad Macedonium* [Huemer, *Sedulius*, p. 171. 5–6]) to 'quod placuerit [i.e., the *Carmen paschale*] ideo geminari volueris' is in keeping with literary and grammatical usage of the verb from which this term developed. See *TLL* vi. 2. II. B. 2, col. 1745. Valuable studies which take the *opus geminatum* into account are: E. R. Curtius, 'Dichtung und Rhetorik im Mittelalter',

origins are to be found in the rhetorical practice of Antiquity.[1] The practice of *conversio* or paraphrase in Roman rhetorical training was a vital factor in the rise of the *opus geminatum*. *Conversio,* the exercise of turning poetry into prose and vice versa, is first mentioned in Latin by Cicero at *De Oratore*, i. 34. 154-5.[2] There, in a criticism of paraphrase as one of the *progymnasmata* or preparatory exercises in composition, Cicero provides a valuable description of the school task of turning a poem or a speech into carefully chosen words of the opposite medium. His reservations were not shared by Quintilian, whose earliest remarks on paraphrase appear in the context of a discussion of the elementary exercises with which *grammatici* should educate the young.

At *Institutio Oratoria,* i. 9. 2-4 Quintilian lays stress on the difficulty of paraphrase: it is not just a useful tool for beginners; it can tax even an expert.[3] Verse, according to Quintilian, should be turned into prose by resolving the metre of the original, substituting prosaic for poetic vocabulary and abbreviating and embellishing the prose version without substantially altering the sense of its verse model. Prominent in Quintilian's account is a criterion of fidelity to the text paraphrased which was to be echoed in the late Antique poets studied by Alcuin.

Deutsche Vierteljahrsschrift für Literaturwissenschaft und Geistesgeschichte, 16 (1938), pp. 437-75; P. Klopsch, 'Prosa und Vers in der mittellateinischen Literatur', *Mlat. Jb.* 3 (1966), pp. 9-24; M. L. Roberts, 'Alcuin's Life of St. Willibrord and its Literary Antecedents' (M.A. thesis, University of Illinois at Urbana-Champaign, 1974); R. Herzog, *Die Bibelepik der lateinischen Spätantike,* i (Munich, 1975); and D. Kartschoke, *Bibeldichtung: Studien zur Geschichte der Bibelparaphrase von Juvencus bis Otfrid von Weissenburg* (Munich, 1975). The best account of the relation between Roman rhetoric and late Antique Biblical epic is M. L. Roberts, 'The Hexameter Paraphrase in Late Antiquity: Origins and Applications to Biblical Texts' (Ph.D. dissertation, University of Illinois at Urbana-Champaign, 1978). Ernst Walter, 'Opus Geminum, Untersuchungen zu einem Formtyp in der mittellateinischen Literatur' (diss. phil. Erlangen–Nürnberg, 1973) and V. Schupp, *Studien zu Williram von Ebersberg* (Bern and Munich, 1978), pp. 113-70 present useful surveys of the development of this form up to the twelfth century. For a study of the origins and early history of the *opus geminatum* see Godman, 'The Anglo-Latin *opus geminatum*: from Aldhelm to Alcuin', *MÆ* 50. 2 (1981), pp. 215-29, upon which these pages draw.

[1] Discussion of medieval texts is confined to those which demonstrably influenced Alcuin. Fuller bibliography and discussion are to be found in the article cited above.   [2] Ed. A. S. Wilkins (Oxford, 1892), pp. 148-9.

[3] Ed. M. Winterbottom (Oxford, 1970), p. 58.

A similar emphasis is to be found in Quintilian's description of exercises which he recommends at *Institutio Oratoria*, x. 5. 4–11[1] to advanced students in order to provide fullness and fluency of expression. Applicable both to one's own writings and to those of other people, the techniques of paraphrase outlined by Quintilian are discussed and practised in a range of ancient sources from the Younger Pliny to Suetonius and St. Augustine.[2]

The reception into Christian Latin literature of the paraphrastic methods long established in Roman rhetorical practice is marked by the *Evangelia* of Juvencus.[3] Composed between 329 and 330, this verse paraphrase of parts of the Bible (chiefly the Gospel according to St. Matthew) was intended, experimentally, as a stylistic elaboration of Scripture.[4] To the educated classes Juvencus set out to make the subject-matter of Scripture attractive by re-expressing it, without altering its content, in the special charm of verse. His fidelity to the Biblical original, demanded by its unique authority as a text, also reflects the criteria set out in Quintilian's account of paraphrase. The experiment was a success. Juvencus is the only poet whom St. Jerome included in his *De Viris Illustribus.*[5]

Juvencus' example was followed and extended in the mid fifth century by Caelius Sedulius, in a work of two parts known as the *Carmen* and *Opus paschale*. The *Carmen paschale* treated of divine miracles recounted in the Four Gospels, with an introductory book devoted to miracles selected from the Old Testament. In two letters to his patron Macedonius, intended as prefaces to the *Carmen* and *Opus paschale*, Caelius Sedulius set out what he took to be the character and purpose of his work.[6] Among the reasons for

[1] Winterbottom, pp. 607–8.
[2] See *MÆ* 50 (1981), p. 217.
[3] Ed. Huemer, *CSEL* xxiv (Vienna, 1891).
[4] iv. 804–5 (Huemer, pp. 145–6).
[5] Ch. lxxxiv. ed. C. A. Bernoulli (Freiburg-im-Breisgau and Leipzig, 1895), p. 45. See further *MÆ* 50 (1981), p. 218.
[6] 'cur autem metrica voluerim haec ratione componere, non differam breviter expedire. raro . . . divinae munera potestatis stilo quisquam huius modulationis aptavit et multi sunt quos studiorum saecularium disciplina per poeticas magis delicias et carminum voluptates oblectat. ni quicquid rhetoricae facundiae perlegunt, neglegentius adsequuntur, quoniam illud haud diligunt; quod autem

versifying Scripture which he gave to Macedonius in the
first of these letters was a wish to provide in Christian poetry
the pleasures of secular verse without the drawbacks of its
profane subject-matter. Sedulius drew attention to the
mnemonic value of his paraphrase.[1] He made free with his
text, both by omissions and by extended verse commentary
upon it. The result, in the *Carmen paschale*, is a disconnected
series of single episodes.

In writing the *Opus paschale*, a prose counterpart to his
earlier poem, Caelius Sedulius did more than adopt tech-
niques of *conversio* described by Quintilian.[2] By producing
a work of two paired parts, the one in prose and the other
in verse, Sedulius created the literary form which came to
be known as the *opus geminatum*. In the second Letter to
Macedonius prefatory to his prose work Caelius Sedulius
emphasized that there was no difference, save one of style,
between his *Carmen* and *Opus paschale*.[3] Quintilian's state-
ment that prose could fill the deficiencies and restrain the
stylistic excesses of verse[4] was echoed by Sedulius' profession
that his second work supplied what was lacking in the first
and by his allusions, perhaps not wholly sincere, to a fear of
being criticized on the score of fidelity to his original. The
two parts of his composition, in subject and arrangement,
were identical.[5] He claimed not to be altering the *Carmen*'s
account but merely to be expanding it stylistically.

---

versuum *viderint* blandimento *mellitum, tanta cordis aviditate suscipiunt ut* in alta
memoria *saepius haec iterando* constituant et reponant' (Huemer, pp. 4–5).

[1] For the *voluptas* of poetry cf. Quintilian, *Inst. Orat.* x. 1. 28; for the
mnemonic value of paraphrase cf. Cicero, *De Oratore* i. 34, 157.

[2] *Inst. Orat.* x. 5. 8–11 (Winterbottom, pp. 608–9).

[3] 'Praecepisti, reuerende mi domine, paschalis carminis textum, quod officium
purae deuotionis simpliciter exsecutus uobis obtuli perlegendum, in rhetoricum
me transferre sermonem. utrum quod placuerit, *ideo geminari uolueris*, an quod
offenderit (ut potius arbitror) *stilo* censueris *liberiore describi*, sub dubio uideor
fluctuare iudicio . . . siquidem multa pro metricae necessitatis angustia priori
commentario nequaquam uidentur inserta, quae postmodum linguae resolutio
magis est adsecuta, dederimus hinc aliquam forsitan obtrectatoribus uiam, dicent-
que nonnulli *fidem translationis* esse corruptam, quia certa uidelicet sunt in
oratione quae non habentur in carmine . . . *nostri prorsus ab sese libelli non dis-
crepant, sed quae defuerant primis addita sunt secundis, nec impares argumento
uel ordine, sed stilo uidentur et oratione dissimiles . . .*' (Huemer, pp. 171–3).

[4] *Inst. Orat.* x. 5. 4–5 (Winterbottom, pp. 607–8).

[5] Cf. Quintilian i. 9. 2–4 (Winterbottom, p. 58).

This is not strictly accurate. In his *Opus paschale* Caelius Sedulius adopts the presentation and order of the *Carmen*, but greatly extends its doctrinal exposition and Biblical allusion. The marked differences between the two parts of his work appear to have been grasped by his later audience, which opted for one or the other part of it. Only four manuscripts contain both the *Carmen* and the *Opus paschale*. The poem is transmitted in approximately five times as many manuscripts as the prose *Opus*.[1] To Anglo-Latin writers from Aldhelm to Alcuin, Caelius Sedulius bequeathed a general statement of what the relation between the prose and verse parts of an *opus geminatum* might be. That its form imposed tight restrictions or that its conventions were inflexible was not to be inferred from his work.

Bede pointed out the debt of Aldhelm's *De Virginitate* to Caelius Sedulius in terms which reveal that he considered the parts of an *opus geminatum* as two halves of a single whole rather than as the distinct *libelli* which they had remained for Sedulius.[2] The same point of view is taken by Aldhelm. In his prose work, which he wrote before the verse, he applies to his *opus geminatum* a metaphor of building which represents its two parts as a unity, neither of which was complete without the other.[3] At the beginning and end of the *Carmen de Virginitate* he refers explicitly to his intention that they should be read together.[4] Although Aldhelm imitates Sedulius in his choice of form, refers to him by

---

[1] For the codices see Huemer, pp. iiii–xxv and J. Claudel, 'Un nouveau manuscrit de l'*Opus Paschale* de Sedulius', *Revue philologique*, 28 (1904), pp. 283–92.

[2] *HE* v. 18: 'Scripsit et de virginitate *librum eximium*, quem *in exemplum Sedulii geminato opere*, et versibus exametris et prosa composuit.'

[3] 'Porro quemadmodum intactae virginitatis gloriam rethoricis relatibus favorabiliter venerari nitebar, sic identidem . . . heroicis exametrorum versibus eiusdem praeconium pudicitiae subtiliter comere Christo cooperante conabor et, *velut iactis iam rethoricis fundamentis et constructis prosae parietibus, cum tegulis trochaicis et dactilicis metrorum imbricibus firmissimum culmen* caelesti confisus suffragio *imponam*' (c. LX, Ehwald, p. 321).

[4]   Da pius auxilium . . .
    ut prius ex prosa laudabat littera castos,
    sic modo heroica stipulentur carmina laudem . . .
               (vv. 17, 19–20, Ehwald, p. 353).
    Nunc in fine precor prosam metrumque legentes
    Hoc opus ut cuncti rimentur mente benigna.
               (vv. 2867–8, Ehwald, p. 469; and cf. vv. 2219–21, p. 444.)

name, and cites the *Carmen paschale*,[1] he displays a marked, and perhaps considered, reluctance to refer to the conventions of the *opus geminatum* as described by Sedulius. The grounds for Aldhelm's reticence are to be found in the structure of the verse and prose versions of his *De Virginitate*.

The prose *De Virginitate* has two principal themes: the place and praise of women who, although technically no longer virgins, 'become' virgins by becoming nuns, and virgins as *athletae Christi*. In the later part of Aldhelm's prose work the celebration of *athletae Christi* assumes the greatest importance; the fact that the *athletae* are also virgins slips into oblivion.[2] This second theme of Aldhelm's prose is amplified in his metrical *De Virginitate*. There mention of virginity is often made in no more than a perfunctory aside, as an instance of the miraculous virtue distinguishing the *athletae Christi*. Aldhelm assumes his audience's foreknowledge of the prose, for without that assumption the title of his poem would barely be justified. The relation between the verse and the prose parts of the work, despite Aldhelm's own claims and Bede's flattering notice, is even looser than that between the *Carmen* and *Opus paschale* of Sedulius. This is most striking towards the end of the metrical *De Virginitate* (vv. 2446-761), in the passage dealing with the eight vices. The relation between the prose and most of the metrical *De Virginitate* might be thought tenuously to conform to Sedulius's declaration that the only difference between the two parts of an *opus geminatum* should be one of style. Aldhelm's virtuoso piece on the eight vices could not, and so constrained his silence.

These essential differences between the prose and metrical *De Virginitate* suggest why the two were always copied separately, never as a single work, in the extant manuscript tradition.[3] Aldhelm implied that the poetry and the prose formed a unified whole, but his practice does not conform to this implication. It was perhaps for this reason that he hesitated to formulate rules for his *opus geminatum*. Aldhelm's reluctance to be explicit about this form must

---

[1] Ehwald, pp. 544-6.

[2] Cf., for example, c. xxv (Ehwald, pp. 257-60).

[3] See Ehwald, pp. 329 ff.

be borne in mind when one considers his immense influence upon subsequent Anglo-Latin tradition.[1]

The Continent too had an important part to play in the development of paraphrastic techniques in England. Among the continental works read by Alcuin and exploited in his *Versus de . . . Sanctis Euboricensis Ecclesiae* the most important in this connection was Venantius Fortunatus's *Vita S. Martini metrica.*[2] Fortunatus's metrical version of Sulpicius Severus's Life of St. Martin set a precedent, followed by Alcuin, for composing a verse counterpart to a prose work written by someone else. Biographical details of Martin's life and work recorded by Sulpicius Severus are abbreviated or omitted by Fortunatus, who concentrates instead on miracles or on episodes which emphasize the saint's virtue. In Venantius Fortunatus, as in Aldhelm, liberty in handling his prose source inspired reticence about his intentions as paraphrast.

More immediate in time and place was the example provided for Alcuin by Bede. In Northumbria, between 700 and 705, Bede composed a prose version of Paulinus of Nola's *Carmina Natalicia* on the life of St. Felix. In his preface[3] Bede emphasizes the general usefulness of prose, based upon its familiar accessibility and entailing clarity of style. His motive in writing was to provide an attractive and easily understandable version of Paulinus of Nola's poems for the more 'general reader'. Bede abandons the ancient theory of verse's charm to which Sedulius had subscribed. For Bede poetry is almost the recherché form. His view of its complexity was to be borne out by the frequently oblique and sometimes obscure style of his own metrical Life of St. Cuthbert.

The *Vita S. Cuthberti metrica*, written by Bede between

---

[1] Cf. *MÆ* 50 (1981), p. 229, n. 39. [2] pp. lxx-lxxi.

[3] 'Felicissimum beati Felicis triumphum, quem in Nola Campaniae civitate, Domino adiuvante, promeruit, Paulinus eiusdem civitatis episcopus, versibus hexametris pulcherrime ac plenissime descripsit; qui quia metricis potius quam simplicibus sunt habiles lectoribus, placuit nobis *ob plurimorum utilitatem* eandem sancti confessoris historiam *planioribus dilucidare sermonibus* eiusque imitari industriam, qui Martyrium beati Cassiani de metrico opere Prudentii *in commune apertumque omnibus eloquium transtulit*' (J. A. Giles, *Venerabilis Bedae Opera*, iv (London, 1843), p. 174. A new, and much-needed, edition of this text is being prepared by T. W. Mackay [*Famulus Christi*, p. 77]).

705 and 716 together with his prose work of *c*.721,[1] represents the first application of the *opus geminatum* to a hagiographical subject in Anglo-Latin literature. In a clear-cut moralistic manner Bede's poem sums up the principal events of Cuthbert's career, displaying at every turn of its sententious style a penchant for metaphor and a distaste for the particular.[2] Bede also announced his intention, in the preface to the metrical Life, of complementing it with a later prose *Vita*, in language which recalls criteria invoked in Caelius Sedulius's second *Epistola ad Macedonium*[3] and which implies the familiarity of this convention.

Some years later, in the preface to his prose Life of St. Cuthbert, Bede was to give the Anglo-Latin *opus geminatum* a new articulateness about source. His critical and historical standards[4] entailed literary criteria, above all, of clarity, which Bede had also advocated in his *Vita S. Felicis*.[5] Laying stress on the completeness of his work, he judged the unity of its two parts in aesthetic terms.[6]

Aldhelm's implication of the unity of the two parts of his *opus geminatum* and Bede's statement of the unity of his are echoed and carried into effect by Alcuin. The two parts of his *Vita S. Willibrordi* were presented to Beornrad, archbishop of Sens and abbot of Echternach, at the same time and as a single whole. Alcuin's first innovation over his predecessors lay, therefore, in the simultaneous appearance of the two books of his *opus geminatum*.

[1] On the date of the two versions of the Life of St. Cuthbert, see Jaager, *Palaestra*, 198, pp. 4-6; B. Colgrave, *PBA* 44 (1958), p. 42; and Bolton, *A History of Anglo-Latin Literature*, pp. 138-40.

[2] See, for example, vv. 95-119 (Jaager, pp. 65-7) and cf. Alcuin, vv. 690-1.

[3] See the passage cited at comm. to vv. 685-7 and cf. p. lxxxi n. 3 above, especially 'integrare non plena' and 'quae defuerant primis addita sunt secundis'.

[4] '. . . nec tandem ea quae scripseram sine subtili examinatione testium indubiorum passim transcribenda quibusdam dare praesumpsi, quin potius primo diligenter exordium, progressum et terminum gloriosissimae conversationis ac vitae illius ab his qui noverant investigans. Quorum etiam nomina in ipso libro aliquotiens ob certum cognitae veritatis indicium apponenda iudicavi . . .' (Colgrave, p. 144).

[5] '. . . ablatis omnibus scrupulorum ambagibus ad puram, certam veritatis indaginem simplicibus explicitam sermonibus commendare membranulis . . . curavi' (ibid.).

[6] 'Si non deliberato ac perfecto operi nova interserere, vel supradicere minus congruum atque indecorum esse constaret' (ibid.).

In the preface to his prose Life Alcuin defined clearly the purpose of his *opus geminatum*.[1] The prose *Vita* was intended to be read aloud in church, section by section; and to its conclusion he added a substantial homily for the feast-day of St. Willibrord. Alcuin's preface goes on to contrast the stately pace of prose ('gradientem') with the speed of verse ('currentem'); and similar terms are used in the metrical *Vita*.[2] His language accurately implies that the verse Life is less full than the prose: it is cursory and it abbreviates (a tendency detected earlier in Venantius Fortunatus's metrical Life of St. Martin). Alcuin feels free to rearrange and even to truncate his earlier prose account. Like Bede in the *Vita S. Cuthberti metrica*, Alcuin is less concerned with details of the saint's life than with his moral qualities and divine mission, describing these by preference in a firmly positive style that cultivates the metaphor and the abstract noun. The didactic value of his poem, intended to be 'ruminated'[3] by students, is clear. The *Vita S. Willibrordi metrica* was to be used in private study as an edifying model of versification. Committed to memory, it served as a means of inculcating Latin vocabulary and poetic style.

A continuity can be traced in the works read and used by Alcuin, and in his own writings, through the parallel development of prose and verse. Between Caelius Sedulius's *Carmen paschale* in the mid fifth century and *c.*800 all the major works of Latin narrative poetry cited by Alcuin are of a

---

[1] '. . . tuis parui, pater sancte, praeceptis et duos digessi libellos, unum prosaico sermone gradientem, qui puplice fratribus in ecclesia, si dignum tuae videatur sapientiae, legi potuisset; alterum Piereo pede currentem, qui in secreto cubili inter scolasticos tuos tantummodo ruminari debuisset' (Levison, p. 113).

[2] Cf. *Vit. S. Willibr. metr.* xiii. 1-7:

> Plurima perque suum fecit miracula servum,
> quae nunc non libuit versu percurrere cuncta,
> sed strictim quaedam properanti tangere plectro,
> et gestis titulos paucos praefigere musis,
> ad prosamque meum lectorem mittere primam:
> illic inveniet iam plenius omnia gesta
> pontificis magni . . .

The reference at v. 5 to sending the reader back to his prose Life as 'prosam . . . primam' demonstrates that it is the earlier and fuller work on which the verse account is based.

[3] On the term *ruminari*, borrowed from the vocabulary of meditation on Scripture, see J. Leclercq, *Initiation aux auteurs monastiques du Moyen Age: l'amour des lettres et le désir de Dieu*[2] (Paris, 1963), pp. 72-3.

hagiographical or moral–didactic character, and all of them were written as verse counterparts to prose. From the Roman school exercise of paraphrase through the late Antique Biblical epic and, in particular, the work of Caelius Sedulius had grown the medieval *opus geminatum*, a form in which both the large-scale poems in early Anglo-Latin were composed. In Venantius Fortunatus, and before him in Juvencus, Alcuin saw respectable precedents for a metrical version of a prose work written by a different author, in a style, language, and manner hardly distinguishable from those employed in the *opus geminatum*.

Flexible but clear conventions had emerged in this tradition before Alcuin. Verse, to whose complexity Bede refers, was seen as a suitable vehicle for formulating the moral significance of a prose statement in lofty style. Learnt in the classroom, poetry retained a practical value in clerical education which is affirmed in Alcuin's metrical Life of St. Willibrord. Emphasis upon the brevity of verse accompanied this view of its elevation and utility. Although no author of an *opus geminatum* felt shackled by the criterion of fidelity expressed by Quintilian in his account of *conversio* and reiterated by Caelius Sedulius in his Letters to Macedonius, this standard lived on in the ideal of unity repeatedly invoked in the 'double works' and paraphrases of the early Middle Ages read by Alcuin. Finally, the writing of Bede, particularly his Lives of St. Cuthbert, had imported into this form a critical and quasi-historical attention to source.

Each of these conventions influenced Alcuin's understanding and choice of literary form in the *Versus de . . . Sanctis Euboricensis Ecclesiae*. His tendency to abbreviate, rearrange, and omit from the *HE* and Lives of St. Cuthbert[1] reflects the practice of earlier authors, while his stress on the moral utility of his poem (vv. 787–8) finds parallels in the history and hagiography of Bede. Alcuin gives prominence to the ideal of brevity[2] and even goes so far as to formulate a *ius brevitatis* to which verbs such as *currere, tangere,* and *properare* in his *Vita S. Willibrordi metrica* more vaguely refer.[3] This in turn led him to compare his verse narrative

---

[1] See pp. lxviii–ix, especially pp. lii–liii.
[2] See comm. to vv. 289–90. [3] v. 1206 and p. lxxxvi, n. 2 above.

with the *HE* in a systematic and critical manner, signalling omissions, pointing to digressions, and cautioning himself against gratuitous repetition of Bede's work.[1]

Alcuin's attention to his prose source is not only a mark of his reverence for Bede; it also reflects an increasing articulateness on the subject of this literary form, which we have traced both in his predecessors and in his own Life of St. Willibrord. By refashioning inherited material from the body of sources described earlier[2] Alcuin produced in the *Versus de . . . Sanctis Euboricensis Ecclesiae* the first major narrative poem on a historical subject in the extant Latin literature of the medieval West. A measure of the originality of his work will appear in an account of its genre and influence.

viii. *The Genre and Influence of Alcuin's Poem on York*

For the form and content of the *Versus de . . . Sanctis Euboricensis Ecclesiae* we have been able to specify a number of sources and analogues in Latin literature before Alcuin. In poetry, however, we have not found a true parallel to Alcuin's historical narrative. What was new about his poem on York, and what impact did it make on later literature? The following pages attempt to define the genre and to describe the influence of the *Versus de . . . Sanctis Euboricensis Ecclesiae* by comparing them with the large-scale narrative verse known to Alcuin, and with the work of other Carolingian poets.

The terms in which Alcuin himself describes the *Versus de . . . Sanctis Euboricensis Ecclesiae* reveal little about their genre. What view of narrative verse can Alcuin have formed from the large-scale poems that were among his chief sources?

With a single exception, none of the narrative poems known to Alcuin was on a profane subject. The Christian epics of late Antiquity dealt with Biblical themes. Bede and Fortunatus composed saints' lives in verse. Aldhelm wrote of the exploits of virgins as *athletae Christi*, and about the eight vices. Among the sources available to Alcuin, only Virgil's *Aeneid* was a political poem which combined a message for the present with a glorification of the past.

---

[1] vv. 741–6, 781–5, 1207–9.   [2] pp. lxvii–lxxv.

The *Versus de . . . Sanctis Euboricensis Ecclesiae* have
affinities with each of these types of narrative verse, but can
be identified with none of them. The poem treats of saints
and bishops, and celebrates the traditions of the northern
Church. But its subject is also 'reges et proelia',[1] and it
makes a forceful statement about the kind of kingship Alcuin
admired in the historical past and wished for in his own
times.[2] The model of Bede's *HE* accounts for much in this
respect, as we have seen; but Virgil too influenced both the
style and the conception of Alcuin's work. For his account
of the historical destiny of his fatherland, with its spiritual
and political capital at York, one of Alcuin's most important
models in Latin narrative poetry was the *Aeneid*, an epic
about the *patria* whose centre and symbol was Rome.

The principal literary influences on Alcuin's work thus
fall into two broad classes. The moral–didactic and hagio-
graphical verse of Aldhelm and Venantius Fortunatus and the
late Antique Biblical epic find echoes in the spiritual and
ecclesiastical themes of Alcuin's poem on York. They place
it in a line of direct descent from the Christian Latin poetry
of the early Middle Ages. But Alcuin goes further than this.
Drawing upon Bede and Virgil, he gained models for a large-
scale narrative poem on the history of his *patria*. These
historical and national interests of Alcuin's work, embracing
his own times, were applied by the earliest authors of
Carolingian epic to the heroic exploits of the emperors
of their day.[3] In this sense the *Versus de . . . Sanctis Eubori-
censis Ecclesiae* represent a point of transition from the
dominantly moral–didactic and hagiographical traditions of
large-scale Latin narrative poetry written between the sixth
and eighth centuries to the increasingly secular character of
epic in the early Carolingian period.[4]

With two major poems of the early ninth century—the
one traditionally known as '*Karolus Magnus et Leo Papa*',
which has recently been shown to be the third book of an

---

[1] Virgil, *Eclogue*, vii. 3.

[2] Wallace-Hadrill, *Early Germanic Kingship*, p. 87, and pp. xlvii–lx above.

[3] Discussed below.

[4] A recent bibliographical survey of early Carolingian epic is provided by A.
Ebenbauer, *Carmen historicum. Untersuchungen zur historischen Dichtung im
karolingischen Europa*, i, Philologica Germanica 4 (Vienna, 1978).

epic probably composed in the first decade of the ninth century,[1] and the other Ermoldus Nigellus's *In honorem Hludowici Pii* of 826/8, an account in four books of the achievements of Louis the Pious[2]—Alcuin's poem on York shares a composite character. The *Versus de . . . Sanctis Euboricensis Ecclesiae* are lent epic colouring by Alcuin's use of Virgilian similes and of hyperbole,[3] while the encomia on kings and bishops which introduce his accounts of their historical deeds are inspired by the example of Venantius Fortunatus.[4] Like Alcuin's poem, both early Carolingian epics owe primary debts to Virgil's *Aeneid*, displayed in a variety of verbal echoes and in a number of borrowed epic similes. Hardly less considerable is their use of Venantius Fortunatus's poetry, and especially of his panegyrics. These epic and panegyrical sources, keenly imitated and imperfectly controlled, affected not only the two poems' style but also their form and structure.

In the description of isolated incidents and as encomium, both the *In honorem Hludowici Pii* and '*Karolus Magnus et Leo Papa*' achieve an intermittent power which they lack as connected narrative. Long passages of panegyric, which list the moral qualities of Charlemagne and Louis the Pious, break up their accounts of successive events; and in the alternation of description and encomium there emerge short vignettes and full-scale eulogies, but nothing more sustained.[5]

Reproduced and expanded in the four books of Ermoldus Nigellus's *In honorem Hludowici Pii*, the episodic structure

[1] On the poem's genre and dating, see Schaller, *Fm. St.* 10 (1976), pp. 134 ff. The most recent edition is by H. Beumann, F. Brunhölzl, and H. Winkelmann, *Karolus Magnus et Leo Papa. Ein Paderborner Epos vom Jahre 799* (Paderborn, 1966). Most aspects of this edition have been critically reviewed by Schaller, art. cit., and 'Interpretationsprobleme im Aachener Karlsepos', *Rheinische Vierteljahrsblätter* 41 (1977), pp. 160 ff. The earlier edition of Dümmler (*MGH PLAC* i, pp. 366 ff.) is still indispensable. A good systematic guide to the older bibliography is in *Repertorium fontium historiae medii aevi*, iii (Rome, 1970), p. 132.

[2] Ed. Dümmler, *MGH PLAC* ii, pp. 4–79 and E. Faral, *Poème sur Louis le Pieux et Épîtres au Roi Pépin*, Les Classiques de l'Histoire de France au Moyen Age 14 (Paris, 1964), pp. 2–201. Full bibliography in Ebenbauer, *Carmen historicum*, pp. 101–49.

[3] See comm. to vv. 178 ff.   [4] See comm. to v. 1397.

[5] On the panegyrical character of these poems see F. Bittner, *Studien zum Herrscherlob in der mittellateinischen Dichtung*, diss. phil., Würzburg (Volkach, 1962) pp. 48 ff.

of 'Karolus Magnus et Leo Papa' prevents either poem from achieving sustained narrative on a single theme.[1] This in turn makes them susceptible to classification according to their component parts: the hybrid terminology of modern criticism reflects the composite character of the literature which it describes.[2] The essential characteristics of epic in this period cannot be strictly delimited. They lie partly in aspects of poetic form, and partly in common sources and content. Epic, to early Carolingian poets, amounted to politically motivated narrative poetry on secular subjects, closely linked with panegyric and taking much of its inspiration from Virgil and from contemporary events. The uneasy shifts from encomium to narrative in 'Karolus Magnus et Leo Papa' and in Ermoldus's poem are the signs of a (not wholly successful) attempt to create an independent epic narrative; an attempt which takes its initial impetus from Alcuin's metrical version of Bede.[3] The first step towards renewal of the genre of national, historical epic was taken for the early Middle Ages in Alcuin's *Versus de . . . Sanctis Euboricensis Ecclesiae*, through the originally paraphrastic techniques of the *opus geminatum*, as a verse counterpart to prose.

What impact did the poem on York have on poetry other than the early Carolingian epic? In England, we are confronted with major discontinuities. The later development of Anglo-Latin literature, severely disrupted by Viking invasion in the ninth century, was hardly influenced by Alcuin's poem. The only exception is the Northumbrian Æthelwulf's *De Abbatibus*, a work on the lives of the abbots of a monastic community, possibly of Bywell in Northumberland, written

---

[1] Cf. the accounts of the chase at *Karolus Magnus* 137 ff. (discussed by M. Thiébaux, *Romance Philology*, 22 (1968), pp. 288-9) and Ermoldus iv. 484 ff. These two passages are analysed in my 'Latin Poetry under Charles the Bald and Carolingian Poetry', in *Charles the Bald: Court and Kingdom*, edd. M. Gibson and J. Nelson (Oxford, 1981), pp. 229-301.

[2] Cf. E. R. Curtius on 'zeitgeschichtliches panegyrisches Epos', in *Gesammelte Aufsätze zur romanischen Philologie* (Bern and Munich, 1970), pp. 125-6 and P. Dronke on 'Karolus Magnus et Leo Papa' in id., *Barbara et Antiquissima Carmina* (Barcelona, 1977), p. 76, n. 99.

[3] The most perceptive analysis of this question remains the work of A. Ebert, in 'Die literarische Bewegung zur Zeit Karls der Grossen', *Deutsche Rundschau*, 11 (1877), expecially pp. 402-4, and *Allgemeine Geschichte der Literatur des Abendlandes im Mittelalter bis zum Beginne des XI. Jahrhunderts*, ii (Leipzig, 1880), pp. 27 ff.

between 803 and 821.[1] Æthelwulf, who borrows repeatedly from Alcuin,[2] derived from him the inspiration for a panegyric on his teachers and church. Two visions are recounted in the *De Abbatibus*,[3] and the second, experienced by Æthelwulf himself, ends with a revelation of his teacher Hygelac in Heaven, just as Alcuin's poem on York concludes in a vision of the other world that holds a special place for his own community.

The *De Abbatibus*, our only testimony to the influence of Alcuin's *Versus de . . . Sanctis Euboricensis Ecclesiae* in England, suggests that the poem on York did little to change the previous character of Anglo-Latin literature. At a time when the Viking threat to the north of England was growing more urgent, when Hiberno-Latin authors were turning to literature which offered a vision of escape from their own turbulent times, such as the *Navigatio S. Brendani*,[4] the Northumbrian Æthelwulf produced, under the influence of Alcuin, spiritual poetry with the same kind of regional interest that had been established in biography and hagiography from the north of England since the early eighth century.[5] In Alcuin's homeland, the *Versus de . . . Sanctis Euboricensis Ecclesiae* were read as a verse chronicle of local, ecclesiastical history.

On the Continent, the impact of Alcuin's poem on York was both greater and more durable. One of the writers who provides the firmest evidence of Alcuin's lasting impact is an anonymous Saxon poet, writing between the years 888 and 891, perhaps at Corvey, a five-book account of the deeds of Charlemagne.[6]

[1] Dating after Campbell, p. xxiii, location after Howlett, *Archaeologia Aeliana* (Ser. 5) 3 (1975), pp. 122-4.

[2] Borrowings listed on p. 145.

[3] xi (Campbell, pp. 26-32); xxii (Campbell, pp. 54-62; cf. Alcuin, *Versus* . . . 1602 ff.).

[4] The philological evidence of G. Orlandi points convincingly to a date of composition at the beginning of the ninth century, and in Ireland (*Navigatio S. Brendani*, Testi e documenti per lo studio dell'antichità 38 (Milan, 1968), especially pp. 131-60—as against C. Selmer, *Navigatio S. Brendani Abbatis* . . . University of Notre Dame Publications in Medieval Studies 16 (Notre Dame, 1959) pp. xxix ff.

[5] See pp. lxxvi-lxxvii.

[6] The best study of the 'Poeta Saxo' 's *Annales* is by B. Bischoff, 'Das Thema des Poeta Saxo', *Speculum Historiale: Festschrift Johannes Spörl* (Munich, 1968),

The chief sources of the 'Poeta Saxo' 's *Annales* are the annalistic compilation wrongly attributed to Einhard, the annals of Fulda, and Einhard's own *Gesta Karoli Magni*, of which he produced a metrical paraphrase.[1] Bernhard Bischoff has convincingly emphasized the Saxon poet's interest in Charlemagne not only as a great historical figure, but also as the one responsible for the conversion of his own people.[2] In the 'Poeta Saxo' 's decision to versify the prose sources for Charlemagne's career can be detected the influence of Alcuin.[3]

The 'Poeta Saxo' reproduced Alcuin's two-fold concern with the progress of conversion in his *patria* and with the rulers who achieved it. Charlemagne in his *Annales* takes the place of the seventh-century Northumbrian *bretwaldas* in Alcuin's poem; for the north of England is substituted Carolingian Saxony, and instead of the *HE* 'Poeta Saxo' draws on biographical and annalistic sources. On the basis of Carolingian prose writing he does what Alcuin had done with Anglo-Latin texts. The model for a historical poem on a major scale, designed as a verse counterpart to prose, 'Poeta Saxo' derived from the *Versus de . . . Sanctis Euboricensis Ecclesiae*. The true beneficiary of the Anglo-Saxon Alcuin's poem on York was a Saxon poet, writing at the end of the ninth century about the conversion of his people and the achievements of Alcuin's patron.

ix. *Language, Style, Metre, and Prosody*

The Latinity of Alcuin, an Anglo-Saxon writing an acquired language, is deeply influenced by the Latinity of his principal sources. A measure of Alcuin's literary scholarship, as of his skill and fluency, is provided by his language, style, metre, and prosody, the distinctive features of which are outlined

pp. 198-203. For an account of its sources, see J. Bohne, 'Der Poeta Saxo in historiographischer Tradition des 8.-10. Jahrhunderts' (diss. hist. Frankfurt am Main, 1965). Further bibliography in Schaller-Könsgen, p. li.

[1] See, especially, Bohne (diss. cit.), pp. 17-104; M. Lintzel in *Neues Archiv*, 44 (1921), pp. 1 ff., ibid., 49 (1932), pp. 183 ff.; and K. Strecker, ibid., 43 (1922), pp. 490 ff.

[2] 'Das Thema des Poeta Saxo' (art. cit.), p. 199.

[3] Parallels between the two works and references to common sources are listed on p. 151.

below. Many of them find parallels in the usage of other late Latin and early Medieval Latin poets; some distinguish Alcuin's practice from that of Classical Latin authors of the 'Golden Age'.[1] The following pages illustrate its chief points of correspondence to and divergence from Classical and early Medieval Latin usage.[2]

(i) *Grammar and Syntax*

(*a*) *Gender and Number.* There are few departures from Classical usage in the poem on York. *Prora*, if that reading is secure at v. 28, is neut. acc. pl., although Alcuin elsewhere construes the noun as feminine as in CL (see app. iii ad loc.). Substantival use of adjectives is frequent (see (*c*) 1, 2): adjectival use of substantives is normally eschewed.

(*b*) *The Cases.* Alcuin's usage is in general correct. The following aspects of case-usage in his poem on York deserve comment.

(i) *Nominative*	*nominativus pendens*: e.g. v. 937.	
	nominative used as vocative: e.g. v. 1 (with comm. ad loc.).	
(ii) *Accusative*	accusative of direction towards sometimes replaces *in* + acc.: e.g. v. 324.	
	intrare is regularly used with the acc. (comm. to v. 114).	
(iii) *Genitive*	the genitive of definition is frequent (see comm. to v. 707) and sometimes replaces the attributive adjective (v. 25).	
	the subjective genitive, instead of the corresponding possessive of the personal pronoun, is regularly employed (e.g. vv. 34, 961).	
	one unusual use of the genitive of quality: 'pulveris . . . pannum' (v. 345).	

---

[1] Discussed above, pp. lxxii–lxxiii. Features of Alcuin's language are discussed by Burghardt, 'Philologische Untersuchungen...' (diss. cit., p. xxv, n. 1), pp. 35 ff. Philological studies of Alcuin's sources relevant to this problem include Druhan, *Syntax.* M. Henshaw, 'The Latinity of the Poems of Hrabanus Maurus' (Ph.D. diss., University of Chicago, 1933) discusses Alcuin's close imitator and chief pupil.

[2] A number of common and classical features are recorded below. A list of anomalies would make Alcuin's usage appear more unusual than it is.

the genitive of the adjectival form of a place-name is twice used in ellipsis ('Euboricae [ecclesiae]' v. 220, and v. 1218).

'nominis unius . . . vocatus' (v. 1046).

(iv) *Dative* the dative of advantage and the 'ethical' dative are frequent (e.g. vv. 55, 474).

the dative of the pronominal adjective is formed both in -*i* and in -*o*: e.g. 'uni' (v. 858), 'soli' (v. 661), 'toto' (v. 79), 'alio' (v. 1211), 'nullo' (v. 530).

'iure' (v. 530): dative in -*e, metri causa*.

(v) *Ablative* the ablative of comparison is preferred to the construction with the conjunction *quam* (v. 1354).

the ablatives of accompaniment and manner are frequent and at times unusual (v. 474).

the frequent occurrence of the ablative absolute, with both the present and past participles, conforms to classical usage.

the ablative of extent of time is used with *in* (v. 670), without *in* (vv. 215, 499), and with *sub* (v. 588).

'erexit honore' replaces *erexit in honorem* (v. 644).

one instance (v. 1096) of *quis*, the poetic abl. pl. of the relative pronoun.

(vi) *Locative* occurs only once: *humi* (v. 331).

(c) *The Adjective and the Adverb*

1. In conformity to Biblical usage, *apostolicus* is used as a substantive at v. 1280 (see comm. ad loc.) but as an adjective at vv. 651, 1355.

2. *Daemoniacus* is used as an adjective at v. 704 but as a substantive at v. 731.

3. *Expers* takes both the genitive (v. 658) and the ablative (v. 1193).

4. The comparative is once formed with *magis* (v. 770).

5. The comparative is often used for the positive *metri causa* (e.g. v. 339).

6. The formation of the adverb is regular.

7. *Istic* = *illic* (v. 339), *qua* = *ubi* (e.g. v. 315), *nimium* and *satis* = *valde* (e.g. vv. 349, 556).

8. *Noctu* occurs once (v. 1066); *nocte* is much more common.

9. At v. 490 the adverbial form *aeternum* is the *lectio difficilior*.

10. *olim* = 'just/recently' (v. 146, with comm. ad loc.).

11. *cras* = 'on the next day' (v. 1204).

(*d*) *The Pronoun*. Special emphasis is given, for purposes of stress or contrast, to the personal pronoun. *Ego* occurs six times and is once reïnforced by *ipse* (v. 639); *tu* and *vos* are frequent. Reduplicated *sese* is frequent; the forms *temet* and *tibimet* recur. As is common in early Medieval Latin, the personal pronoun often replaces the possessive adjective (see under (*b*) iii above); *suus* supplants *eius*; and *proprius* is used in lieu of the reflexive adjective pronoun *suus*. *Ille* is Alcuin's preferred demonstrative pronoun but retains an intensive force, chiefly in quotations (v. 155; but cf. v. 232). *Hic*, generally avoided in the nom. sing. and pl., is often supplanted by *praedictus* and *praefatus* and once (v. 1530) by *praesens*. *Ipse* and *iste* are used now as intensives (vv. 165, 247) and now as synonyms for one another and for *ille*. *Idem* is rare. *Talis* is used both in a defining sense (v. 233) and as a synonym for the demonstrative pronoun (vv. 631, 828). The distinctions between *aliquis, qui, quis, quisque, quisquis,* and *quisquam* are blurred (vv. 7, 322, 865, 924, 939, 1051). The 'fossilized' form of *quisque* recurs (v. 145, with comm. ad loc.). *Nullus* is occasionally used as a substantive, replacing *nemo* (v. 405). *Cuncti* for *omnes* is frequent. *Alius* and *alter* are interchangeable; 'alii atque alii' (= 'more and more') occurs once (v. 1072). *Unus* in the indefinite, not numerical, meaning of 'one' is frequent.

(*e*) *Prepositions*. The following uses require mention:

a/ab	'praecisam a' (v. 302); 'rediens a morte' (v. 893); 'surrexi a morte' (v. 897); 'ab aequore fessus' (v. 29); 'ab origine claram' (v. 132); 'alter ab his' (v. 1066).
de	= *e/ex* occurs very frequently (cf. vv. 72, 88, 90,

etc.) and is used elliptically in this sense at
vv. 341, 398 ('tulerat de pulvere').

= *a/ab*: 'praecisae de' (v. 440; cf. *a/ab* above),
'nece de praesente . . . salvavit' (v. 587).

= *e*: 'de more' (v. 1155).

in 'largus in' + acc. (v. 116); 'in nocte dieque'
(v. 211); 'in populos sparsit' (v. 212); 'fiunt . . .
in languentes dona salutis' (vv. 375-6); 'usus in
armis' (v. 522); 'dans in pessum' (v. 528); 'multis
in annis' (v. 1040); 'in libris . . . studiosior'
(v. 1049).

iuxta once (v. 315) a preposition.

per instrumental or explanatory (vv. 64, 117).

post as in CL, sometimes = *postea* (vv. 426, 687).

propter 'in comparison with' (v. 981).

sub 'statuit sub nomine Petri' (v. 307); 'domuit sub
marte' (v. 752); 'nocte sub ipsa' (v. 891; cf.
v. 147); 'sub tempore pacis' (v. 1082); 'sub
Tartara' (v. 1357); 'dubia sub morte' (v. 1617).

super 'super hostem cachinnum' (v. 941); 'caras super
omnia gazas' (v. 1526).

usque both a preposition (vv. 684, 1021, 1061) and an
adverb (v. 375).

(*f*) *The Verb.* There are few departures from normal usage.
The (regular) forms 'eructuat' (v. 991) and 'lavatus' (v. 188)
occur *metri causa.* The active form 'epulare' (v. 343) for the
deponent appears once. *Simplex pro composito* is well
attested, e.g. 'duci' = *adduci* (v. 328); 'manere' = *permanere*
(v. 369); 'tangere' = *contingere* (v. 387); 'ciens' = *acciens*
(v. 540), 'scisci' = *ascisci* (v. 1154). *Compositum pro simplici*
occurs, e.g. 'persensit' = *sensit* (v. 332).

(*g*) *Nominal Forms of the Verb*

(i) *The Infinitive*

1. The accusative with the infinitive (e.g. v. 699) alternates
with *quod/quid* (e.g. v. 787) with verbs of speech, command,
feeling, understanding, and recollection.

2. Noteworthy uses of the infinitive with verbs expressing
intention or action include 'prandere sedebant' (v. 1170),
'causa . . . fuerat . . . convertere' (68-9).

3. With impersonal verbs, and with verbs of command and advice, *ut* + subjunctive is used less frequently than an infinitive.

4. The archaic passive infinitive is only once attested, in the deponent 'tutarier' (v. 532).

5. The infinitive is regularly construed with *facio*; cf. v. 369.

(ii) *The Gerund*

1. The accusative of the gerund expresses purpose with and even (v. 493) without *ad*.

2. The genitive of the gerund is used with concrete nouns, often with overtones of purpose, e.g. 'tecta manendi' (v. 707). In a number of instances it is construed with an object in the accusative (v. 1481).

3. The ablative of the gerund is used as the equivalent of a present participle, to indicate concomitance (v. 890) and, with an object in the accusative, to indicate agency (v. 21). It occurs once with *dignus* (v. 788).

(iii) *The Supine*

1. As in CL, the supine occurs after verbs of motion (v. 449) to express purpose.

2. The ablative of the supine is found with *dignus* (v. 881).

(iv) *The Participles*. A distinctive trait of Alcuin's Latinity is its exploitation of a large number of participles.

1. The predicative use of the present participle where the gerund with instrumental force would be expected is frequent.

2. The present participle with a future or final sense is well attested.

3. The present participle may denote action prior or subsequent to that of the main verb (e.g. vv. 527, 863).

4. The perfect participle is regularly used as attribute (e.g. v. 478).

5. 'manens' (v. 650) and 'positus' (v. 930) replace the non-existent present participle of *esse*.

6. Both the attributive and the predicative use of the future participle are attested (vv. 91, 1618).

(h) *Independent Clauses*

1. There are no instances of the absolute use of transitive verbs.

2. Alcuin displays great freedom in his use of tense. The present and the future or future perfect, the perfect and the imperfect, are interchanged constantly. Metre most frequently dictates Alcuin's substitutions of the pluperfect for the perfect (cf. vv. 533, 534, 536 ('legit . . . venerat . . . poposcit'). The imperfect with aorist meaning and the perfect vie as the most common tense of narration.

3. The sequence of tenses is observed with temporal conjunctions (cf. vv. 226-7) and with dependent clauses (vv. 672-3).

4. Most questions are introduced by interrogative adverbs or the pronouns *quis/quid*. *Num, numquid,* and *nonne* do not occur. *An* introduces both direct and reported questions (comm. to v. 177).

5. The enclitic *-que* occurs 220 times as against 210 instances of *et*. *Et* and *atque* occur in the same verse (e.g. v. 625). *Vel* and *seu* for *et* are standard (e.g. vv. 176, 310, 1303, 1456). *Aut* is weakened to a mere equivalent of *vel* (v. 690) and may co-ordinate with *non* (v. 1479). *Sic* is found in a consecutive sense equivalent to *deinde* (v. 1070).

6. In final clauses with *ut, quo magis, quo,* and *ne,* in concessive clauses with *cum, licet,* etc., and in some reported questions, the subjunctive is scrupulously observed. The dubitative subjunctive occurs (v. 61).

7. *Non* is used with prohibitions in the future tense (v. 1351).

8. The use of periphrastic constructions is frequent, e.g. v. 74 'servaturus . . . fuisset', v. 964 'fuimus stantes'.

9. *Foret, fieret,* and *esset* are used as synonyms (vv. 24, 25, 27).

10. *Fore* for *esse* occurs twice (vv. 308, 820).

(i) Subordinate Clauses

1. Alcuin's use of relative clauses generally corresponds to classical usage. The subjunctive is used in clauses of purpose or definition; otherwise the indicative is observed.

2. *Ante quam* and *prius quam* take the imperfect or pluperfect subjunctive (vv. 705, 1519). *Dum,* meaning 'while', generally takes the indicative. Once (v. 124) it is reinforced by *interea*. Used in narrative, it rarely expresses reason or proviso. *Donec* means 'until' rather than 'as long as' and always takes the indicative. *Quousque* and *ubi* take the indicative. The iterative use of *ubi* is not attested.

3. *Quamvis* replaces *quamquam*; (e.g v. 821). *Licet* is used with a subjunctive. *Quasi* replaces *tamqu* for *(sic)ut* (v. 954).

4. The extensive occurrence of *c* by two factors: its temporal use i and its causal use (more slightly) tive and the subjunctive are er concessive clauses with *cum* (vv. 4 5. *Quod* is rarely used in the cau is taken by *quapropter, quia, quoniam* (with the indicative), and *cum*. In indirect statements, especially after *verba sentiendi et declarandi, quod* is normal; *quia* is not used in this manner. *Quomodo* and *qualiter* are used in indirect statements with the subjunctive.

6. In final and consecutive clauses, Alcuin's usage is regular. There are no examples of *ut non* for *ne*.

7. Conditional sentences of fact take the indicative in both the protasis and the apodosis; unreal conditions observe the future perfect or the subjunctive (e.g. v. 176). The distinction is not always firm (v. 377).

(*j*) *Negation.* The variety of Alcuin's negatives is considerable.

Nec is most often used in double negative constructions: 'nec non' (v. 392); 'nec mora quin' + indicative (v. 491); 'nec . . . negabat' (v. 1166); 'nec non et' (v. 681); 'nec non ceu' (v. 941). It combines with *vel* (vv. 44, 45) to mean 'neither . . . nor'. 'Nec solum' is attested at v. 83. *Nec* is used, with special emphasis, as an equivalent of *ne . . . quidem*: 'non . . . effugies, *nec* si tenearis' (v. 1351). *Neque* occurs only once (v. 1480).

Non combines readily with *nec*, but is used most frequently in direct negations (v. 589).

Ni regularly takes the subjunctive (vv. 129, 478, 745). *Nisi quod* + indicative = 'except that'.

(ii) *Vocabulary*

1. Most words of Greek origin employed by Alcuin had long been absorbed into early Medieval Latin usage: *anachoreta* (v. 1389); *baptisma* (v. 195 *et passim*); *basilica* (v. 1507); *capsa* (v. 409); *Castalidus* (v. 1438); *catholicus* (vv. 139,

1399); *chelydrus* (v. 776); *chrisma* (v. 717); *coenobium* (v. 381); *cymba* (vv. 1322, 1657); *daemon* (v. 395 *et passim*); *diadema* (vv. 575, 1281); *dogma* (v. 655); *draco* (v. 665); *ecclesia* (v. 80 *et passim*); *emporium* (v. 24); *episcopus* (v. 157 *et passim*); *ergastulum* (v. 679), *exenium* (v. 56); *heremita* (v. 663); *heremus* (vv. 1389, 1475); *mandra* (v. 1121); *metropolis* (v. 204, with comm. ad loc.); *nummisma* (v. 868); *obrizum* (v. 1504); *oroma* (v. 93); *orphanus* (vv. 1402, 1577); *paralysis* (v. 325); *paschalis* (v. 194 *et passim*); *patriarcha* (v. 1567); *phalanx* (v. 257 *et passim*); *Pierius* (v. 1319); *scamma* (v. 315); *scolasticus* (v. 462); *sophia* (v. 1414 etc.); *sophista* (v. 845); *theoricus* (v. 1025); *toxicus* (v. 665); *trophaeum* (v. 248); *tyrannus* (v. 1356); *zona* (v. 1442). The majority of these words had already been accepted into Classical Latin; others become common in Christian Latin. *Sophista* seems to have gained a fresh currency with Alcuin (see v. 845, app. iii). Only *Castalidus*, presumably on analogy with *Castalides* (Κασταλίς) and *Castalius*, appears to be an Alcuinian coinage (if it is not a copyist's error).

2. A distinctive feature of Alcuin's vocabulary is its fondness for compound adjectives and nouns: *altithronus* (vv. 632, 1134); *armipotens* (v. 125); *belliger* (v. 227 *et passim*); *bellipotens* (vv. 1327, 1490); *caelicola* (v. 694); *christicola* (v. 282); *flammiger* (vv. 590, 631); *flammivomus* (vv. 916, 945); *floriger* (v. 31 *et passim*), *fructifer* (v. 652); *frugifer* (v. 601); *horrisonus* (v. 547); *lucifluus* (v. 1540); *mellifluus* (vv. 87, 1411); *mirificus* (v. 432); *mortifer* (v. 665); *multimodus* (v. 1329); *omnipotens* (v. 234 *et passim*); *rorifluus* (v. 749); *ruricola* (v. 437); *salutifer* (v. 190 *et passim*); *undivagus* (v. 1376); *veridicus* (vv. 713, 1436); *versificus* (vv. 1312, 1408). This use of compound nouns and adjectives derives from the elevated style of late Antique Latin epic poetry. It has nothing to do with the Germanic *kenning*.[1] Although Alcuin cultivates compound formations, none of the more playful and neologistic usages to be found in his lyric poetry (e.g. *Carmen* iv. 7, 'vaccipotens') figure in the poem on York.

[1] *Pace* H. Reuschel, *Beiträge zur Geschichte der deutschen Sprache und Literatur*, 62 (1938), pp. 143-55 and W. F. Bolton, *Alcuin and Beowulf. An Eighth-Century View* (London 1979), pp. 67 ff.

3. Alcuin exploits noun formations terminating in -*or*: *amator* (v. 2 *et passim*); *auctor* (vv. 167, 1554); *bellator* (v. 659); *cultor* (v. 81 *et passim*); *dator* (v. 3); *defensor* (vv. 1400, 1430); *doctor* (v. 139 *et passim*); *factor* (v. 2); *fautor* (v. 1399); *genitor* (v. 1415); *interventor* (v. 1358); *lector* (vv. 379, 1558); *ministrator* (v. 1521); *occisor* (v. 519); *pastor* (v. 725 *et passim*); *praeceptor* (v. 1399); *rector* (v. 130 *et passim*); *renovator* (v. 2); *servator* (v. 134); *solator* (v. 1402); *tutator* (v. 267); *vastator* (v. 519); *viator* (v. 314 *et passim*); *victor* (vv. 258, 546). A number of these nouns had been commonplace for centuries (e.g. *amator, viator, victor*); others are rarer and are employed by Alcuin in a specialized sense. *Renovator*, for example, appears before 800 only in a small number of late Antique texts and in inscriptions.[1] *Interventor* is also uncommon.[2] *Defensor*, used of a bishop, preserves something of its ancient administrative meaning (comm. to v. 1430). *Ministrator* rarely occurs in Medieval Latin before this poem.[3] Alcuin had a modest role in enlarging and invigorating the technical vocabulary of spirituality and ecclesiastical office (cf. 5 below).

4. Nouns terminating in -*men* are favoured: *conamen* (v. 1187); *medicamen* (v. 434); *moderamen* (v. 217 *et passim*); *molimen* (v. 1499); *refluamen* (v. 1435); *reg(i)men* (v. 843 *et passim*); *specimen* (v. 390 *et passim*), *spiramen* (v. 619); *tegmen* (v. 739); *tutamen* (v. 1121); *velamen* (vv. 278, 334); *volumen* (v. 1307 etc.). Although none of these words is new or employed in a novel sense, their frequency is noteworthy.

5. Discrimination in the sense and form of words is evident: *aequor* is used to mean 'plain' at v. 1185; elsewhere, in both sing. and pl., it means 'sea'. The distinction between *decor* (e.g. v. 221) and *decus* (e.g. v. 26) is preserved. Both *honos* (v. 1596) and *honor* (v. 662 *et passim*) are attested. In accordance with CL usage *dies* meaning 'day' (as opposed to night) is masculine (e.g. v. 142); used to mean a unit of time

---

[1] e.g. Augustine, *Fid. et Symb.* ix. 20; (CSEL xxxi, p. 27, 4-5); Ps.-Tertullian, *Carm. adv. Marc.* i. 39 (CCSL 2, p. 1422).

[2] See *TLL* vii. 1. 2301. 3, 54 ff. Alcuin's knowledge of this word probably derived from Paul Nol. *Carm.* xxvi. 195.

[3] Adamnan, *De locis sanctis*, ii. 30. 9, ed. D. Meehan, *Scriptores latini Hiberniae*, iii (Dublin, 1958), p. 100 uses the term. I have found no instance of its application to a bishop in pre-800 ML. Alcuin's source for the word was probably patristic (cf. *TLL* viii. 1016. 67-75).

it is feminine (e.g. v. 145). Alcuin points to the difference between sound and speech: 'nullis . . . verba loquelis' (v. 1101). *Fanum* and *templum* are distinct (comm. to v. 170). The alternatives *queat* for *possit* (v. 6) and *mars* (v. 752) and *duellum* (v. 42 *et passim*) for *bellum* are used indistinguishably. The common synonyms *sacerdos, praesul,* and *episcopus* (meaning 'bishop', 'archbishop', and 'pope'), and *caballus* (v. 1186) and *equus* are employed. Technical terms, such as *vicedom(i)nus* (v. 1218), occur.

(iii) *Style*

Alcuin's style—now ornate and epical, now starkly paraphrastic—combines considerable variety with frequent clumsiness.

(a) *Sense-Unit, Sentence, and Verbal Effect*

1. At the simplest level, Alcuin's narrative style consists of short sentences of between 2 and 5 lines, with simple coordination or subordination. Interruptions of grammar and of syntax mark a parenthesis as often as they introduce a new sentence (e.g. v. 384; see further (iv) 6 and comm. to v. 50).

2. At the most formal and elevated level, particularly in speeches (e.g. vv. 243 ff.) and invocations (vv. 1 ff.), Alcuin's style is elaborate. A brief analysis of vv. 1-7 will isolate features to be found elsewhere in the poem: asyndeton at vv. 1-2; anaphora at vv. 4 ('da . . . da') and 6-7 ('lingua . . . dicere'/'dicere lingua', 'de te'/'te sine'), antithesis at v. 5 ('stolidum vivaci').

Hyperbaton is found throughout the text; at times it is violent (e.g. vv. 363-5). Word-play, ranging from the simplest *annominatio* (e.g. v. 11 'regi regalia', v. 648 'signis insignis') to etymological puns (v. 48 and v. 1545 ('Fulgentius . . . coruscant')), is marked. The principal source of epic similes is Virgil's *Aeneid* (cf. vv. 178 ff., with comm. ad loc.). Recurrent metaphors derive chiefly from Scripture and from Christian Latin sources. Mixed metaphors are not uncommon (vv. 1569-70). Pleonasms (e.g. v. 714 'praescius ante videbat') and explanatory periphrases (v. 279 'auri brateolis', vv. 337-8 'loci spatium . . . /unius') recur.

3. Even in lengthier passages of heightened narrative the

repetition of conjunctions is often heavy and monotonous (cf. vv. 24, 25, 26 'ut', 'et', 'et'). In passages which closely summarize Bede the prosaic multiplication of subordinate clauses has a leaden effect. Cf. the accumulation of reported questions at vv. 685–740. This is the poetry of cross-reference.

4. Direct speech is Alcuin's principal means of narrative variation; cf. vv. 906 ff.

(b) Symmetry, Homoeoteleuton, Alliteration

1. *Symmetry*. The use of patterns of symmetry, commended by Bede in his *De Arte Metrica*, is marked in Alcuin. The poem on York has several examples of the 'golden line', e.g. v. 264, where it serves to lay stress on Oswald's splendid victory over the Mercians:

> claraque magnifico cessit victoria regi.

Chiastic patterns also occur, e.g. v. 219:

> ecclesiasque suis fundavit in urbibus amplas.

Symmetrical patterns with initial verbs,

> irrorans stolidum vivaci flumine pectus (v. 5),

are matched by patterns with the verb in second position:

> assiduis superans hostilia castra triumphis (v. 119).

2. *Homoeoteleuton* of nouns and adjectives in agreement, especially between an adjective in the third strong caesura and a final noun, is frequent:

> quae fere continu*is* Pictorum pressa duell*is* (v. 42).

Examples of the adjective placed before the fourth weak caesura to achieve homoeoteleuton with a final noun are less common:

> fertilitate sui mult*os* habitura colon*os* (v. 34).

Occasionally homoeoteleuton is attained by placing nouns and adjectives on either side of the fifth foot:

> Hinc Romana manus turbat*is* undique sceptr*is* (v. 38).

Examples of internal rhyme without agreement are rarer:

> iustitiae cult*or*, verus pietatis amat*or* (v. 138).

Although leonine rhyme is attested at vv. 633–4, 913–14 *et passim*, sustained internal rhyme is not a feature of Alcuin's poem on York or of his poetry in general.[1]

3. *Alliteration*, a marked feature of Latin,[2] is cultivated in the works of Virgil exploited by Alcuin.[3] Alcuin employs initial, medial, and final alliteration, and he does not hesitate to combine alliteration on three or even four words with alliterative pairs within a single line. The effect is to reinforce the predominantly dactylic rhythm of his verse, especially in swift-moving passages of heightened narrative, such as vv. 236-52:

Qui subito veniens *ex*ternis *ex*sul ab oris,
*f*irmiter *in*victae *F*idei con*f*isus *in* armis,
agmina *p*arva rapit *p*roperans et *p*ergit in hostem
vastantem patriam *f*erro *f*lammisque cremantem
milibus *in*numeris, *s*poliis *nim*iumque *s*uperbum.
Sed pius Osuualdus *n*umero *n*on territus ullo
alloquitur *p*ropriam constanti *p*ectore turmam:
'O quibus est semper bellorum *v*ivida *v*irtus,
nunc, precor, in*v*ictas *a*nimis *a*dsumite *v*ires,
*a*uxiliumque Dei cunctis praestantius *a*rmis
*p*oscite corde *p*io; *p*recibus *p*rosternite *v*estros
*v*ultus ante crucem, quam *v*ertice montis in isto
erexi, rutilat *C*hristi quae *c*lara trophaeo,
*q*uae *q*uoque *n*unc *n*obis praestabit ab hoste triumphum.'
Tunc clamor *p*opuli fertur super astra *p*recantis
et *c*ruce sic *c*oram *D*ominumque *D*eumque *p*otentem
*pop*litibus flexis *ex*ercitus *o*mnis *a*dorat.

<hr/>

[1] See further K. Strecker, 'Studien zu karolingischen Dichtern V. Leoninische Hexameter und Pentameter im 9. Jh.', *Neues Archiv*, 44 (1922), especially p. 220.

[2] From the extensive bibliography on this subject I refer to the two surveys by Leumann–Hofmann–Szantyr, *Lateinische Grammatik* ii. 2, pp. 700 ff. and J. Marouzeau, *Traité de stylistique appliquée au latin* (Paris, 1935), pp. 42-7. An analytical bibliography (to 1939) is presented in A. Cordier's useful book *L'allitération latine. Le procédé dans l'Énéide de Virgile*, Publications de la Faculté des lettres de l'Université de Lille 3 (Paris, 1939), pp. 2-18. Discussions of Alcuin's alliteration and Old English verse are to be found in J. D. A. Ogilvie, *Modern Language Notes*, 46 (1931), pp. 44-5 and W. F. Bolton, *Alcuin and Beowulf. An Eighth-Century View* (London, 1979), pp. 57-63. Aldhelm's use of alliteration is considered in similar terms by M. Lapidge, 'Aldhelm's Latin Poetry and Old English Verse', *Comp. Lit.* 31. 3 (1979), pp. 218-22.

[3] Cordier (op. cit., p. 19) records $72\frac{1}{2}$ per cent of verses in the *Aeneid* with at least one alliteration and 72 per cent in the *Georgics*.

Alliteration in Alcuin can be as heavily repetitive as it is in Aldhelm:

contemplativos cupiens et carpere flores;
ipse Deo soli solus servire sategit,
ne mundanus honor mentem mutaret alacrem. (660-2)

Tempering its concentration in passages such as this is its distribution in roughly one of every three lines. The skilful, regular, and controlled occurrence of alliteration in Alcuin's poem is one of the signs of his command of the Latin hexameter.

(c) Repetitions, Clichés, Formulae

Alcuin's verse is built around a series of internal echoes. What for other Latin poets was a hallmark of inelegance was for Alcuin a cardinal principle of composition. Just as he draws extensively upon a limited body of sources, reworking them again and again, so repetitions of single words or entire phrases continuously occur within close proximity of one another.

In their simplest form, these repetitions consist of one or two words in a similar metrical position and form: 'in pace' at v. 571 and v. 574 or 'lumina' at v. 582 and 'lumine' at v. 584, for example. These are combined with repeated or similar phrases: 'angelicam . . . agens . . . vitam' at v. 647, 'angelicam . . . vitam . . . agendo' at v. 1392, 'caelestibus inclyta signis' at vv. 392 and 683 are four instances among many. Larger phrases find echoes at different points of the work: 'reflexo est calle reductus' at v. 797, for example, is reworked at v. 1314 as 'directo est calle secutus' and at v. 1628 as 'converso calle reduxit'. Entire lines are repeated with little or no variation:

vox quoque cantantum resonat dulcissima ibidem
(v. 979)
de quo cantantum suavissima vox resonabat (v. 1001)

transit in aetheream laetus feliciter aulam
(v. 875 ~ v. 1568).

The numerous internal echoes of this kind are noted in app. iii. Their frequency precludes any straightforward attempt to identify interpolation on the grounds of sheer repetitiveness (comm. to vv. 576 and 871-2). Written formulae, which are so marked a feature of every page of Alcuin's text, are also to be found in Aldhelm's poetry.[1] They reflect a method of learning versification and Latin style which Alcuin describes in his Lives of St. Willibrord.[2] Memorized, refashioned, and repeated, these formulae are one of Alcuin's principal tools of composition.[3]

(iv) *Metre and Prosody*[4]

1. *Dactylic Rhythm* is favoured in the first four feet, DDSS being the most common pattern (e.g. v. 3). Monotony is avoided by the use, common among dactylic poets, of DSSS, the second most frequent pattern, and by the rarer SDSS (e.g. v. 5). Lines which are predominantly spondaic (e.g. v. 12) or predominantly dactylic (v. 33) occur infrequently. The variation of dactyls and spondees throughout all six feet distinguishes Alcuin's verse from the repetitive spondaic lines of Aldhelm[5] and links it to Bede's lighter dactylic rhythm.

2. *Caesura*: the common pattern of strong caesura of the third and fourth feet is prevalent in Alcuin (e.g. v. 1). Third strong caesura alone (e.g. v. 3) is also frequent, although less monotonous than it is in Aldhelm. Caesura between the third trochaic and fourth strong (e.g. v. 57) is uncommon; hephthemimeral caesura is rare. Caesura is virtually absent from vv. 376, 705, 1146, 1372.

3. *Elision*[6] of one long syllable by another is most common

---

[1] Discussion in Lapidge, *Comp. Lit.* 31. 3 (1979), pp. 223 ff.
[2] See p. lxxxvi above.   [3] Cf. *SM* (3ᵃ Ser.) 20. 2 (1979), pp. 560 ff.
[4] Selective examples of each feature are provided. The following study is introductory, pending the Cambridge University Ph.D. dissertation of N. Wright, 'The Anglo-Latin Hexameter *c.*675-800: Theory and Practice'. Remarks on Alcuin's prosody are to be found in Burghardt, 'Philologische Untersuchungen . . .' (p. xxv, n. 1), *passim*, and Traube, *Karolingische Dichtungen*, pp. 47 ff. Several of the features isolated here are discussed brilliantly by F. Munari, *M. Valerio, Bucoliche*[2] (Florence, 1970), pp. lxiv-lxxviii. On the prosodic and metrical practice of early Anglo-Latin poets, see Ehwald, *Aldhelmi Opera*, pp. 754-5; Jaager, *Bedas metrische Vita S. Cuthberti*, pp. 17-21; Campbell, *Æthelwulf, de Abbatibus*, pp. xli-xliv; M. Lapidge, *ASE* 1 (1972), pp. 86-9 (with bibliographical notes); id., *Comp. Lit.* 31. 3 (1979), pp. 209-31; M. Henshaw, 'The Latinity of the Poems of Hrabanus Maurus' (diss. cit., p. xciv, n. 1), pp. 40-9. See further Klopsch, *Einführung*, pp. 61 ff.
[5] Cf. Lapidge, *Comp. Lit.* 31. 3 (1979), pp. 214 ff.
[6] Occurs 223 times in this text.

(e.g. v. 151), closely followed by elision of short syllables by long. Elision of final long syllables and of a final vowel + *m* by a short syllable is avoided.[1] Ten monosyllables are elided (vv. 293, 296, 399, 435, 467, 541, 709, 800, 812, 1343). Aphaeresis of *est*, which occurs thirty-eight times in different positions throughout the line, most frequently in the thesis of the sixth foot (e.g. v. 770), counts as a distinctive feature of Alcuin's metrical practice. Elision, chiefly concentrated at the thesis of the first foot (e.g. v. 452), the arsis of the second foot (e.g. v. 231), and the thesis of the fourth foot (e.g. v. 26), is avoided in the thesis of the third foot. The line's main caesura is often obscured (e.g. v. 209). Elision in the fifth thesis is as common as it is inelegant (vv. 66, 95, 361, 695, 1181, 1492, 1643).

4. *'Bucolic Diaeresis'*: 54, 468, 917, 1628.

5. *Fifth and Sixth Feet*

(*a*) Fifth-foot spondees, eschewed by Bede and Aldhelm and proscribed in their works on metre,[2] never occur in Alcuin's poem.[3]

(*b*) There are few final monosyllables. E.g.: vv. 515, 996 (where it is part of a deliberate enjambment with v. 997).

(*c*) Quadrisyllabic hexameter endings at 60, 71, 310, 595, 829, 833, 835, 1456.

(*d*) Quinquesyllabic hexameter endings at 483, 914, 1421, 1556, 1557.

(*e*) Failure to observe 'Hermann's bridge', a hazard of the dactylic fourth foot, is common, e.g. v. 77 *coepit habere potentes*.
The result is a flat, if regular, homodyne line ending.

6. *End-stopping and Internal Stops.* Approximately one-third of Alcuin's lines are end-stopped. Internal stops are used, almost exclusively, to introduce direct speech (e.g. v. 339) or for breaks at the third strong caesura.

7. *Licences of Prosody*:[4] *affatim* (75); *anachoreta* (1389);

---

[1] The final long syllable in *circumspexi* is elided at v. 952.

[2] Aldhelm, *De Metris* (Ehwald, p. 83); Bede *De Arte Metr.* i. 10. 7-8; 14. 53-76; 15. 55-60 (Kendall, pp. 109, 124-5, 129).

[3] In the only possible instance of a *spondeiazōn* (508), *Osui* is to be scanned as a dactyl.

[4] See Bede *De Arte Metr.* i. 14, 15 (Kendall, pp. 122-9).

anteă (603); *Bāsilius* (1545); *Britōnum* (41); *cāthŏlĭcūs* (139); *centiĕs* (1354); *collĕga* (482); *concīnnere* (1271); *daemoniāca* (704); *dĕdicaverat* (1503); *deīnde* (335); *donēc* (165); *ecclĕsiae* (80); *ferĕbantur* (916, 1060; but cf. 305, 569, 881); *lavācro* (393); *lĭquerat* (1015); *lŭgubris* (1569); *nēc* (1069); *orŏma* (93); *orphānis* (1402); *Panā* (747); *pārălȳsīs* (325); *pāriĕtĭbūs* (278), *posteă* (1033); *praefinĭta* (1464); *pŭtidum* (947); *quadragintă* (1140); *rēpertus* (1190); *rĕspondit* (172); *rŏditque* (256); *sacerdŏtii* (1425); *Saxōnum* (123); *scōlasticus* (462); *sciŏ* (477); *sĭcut* (603); *stātim*[1] (111); *stātu* (1609); *stīpem* (295); *sŭēto* (179); *theōricam* (1025); *trigintă* (1348); *trucīdant* (1056); *vidĕretur* (962).

8. Final syllables preceding initial *h*[2] or double consonants beginning in -*s* are *communes*.[3]

(*a*) Before *h*: *ignotūs habitu* (97); *vibrāt hastilia* (184); *ingreditūr, heres* (266); *veniebāt hospes* (400); *tetigīt haec* (422); *postquām hinc* (751); *prō huius* (1165).[4]

(*b*) Vowels are both left short before *s impura*—e.g. *undiquĕ sceptris* (38); *defenderĕ scutis* (44), and improperly lengthened—e.g. *a regē stipem* (295); *orē spumare* (317).[5]

9. *vēnă cŭī* (1124).[6]

10. *fidĕi* in mid verse (133, 163, 214), *fidēi* at end of hexameter (1045, 1052, 1332), *fidē* (433, 1086, 1208, 1313).

11. *Common shortening of the final* -e *of adverbs*—e.g. *maximĕ* (1624),[7] *valdĕ* (927).

12. *Unusual lengthening of syllables with ictus*: *nĕc audet* (387), *ampullā* (1505).

13. *Treatment of* -o

(*a*) Common shortenings of final -*o*:[8] *adhibendŏ* (21);

---

[1] Cf. Munari, ed. cit., p. lxviii.   [2] Norberg, *Introduction*, pp. 7–8.
[3] Bede, *De Arte Metr.* i. 3. 22–34 (Kendall, p. 89); Norberg, *Introduction*, p. 8.
[4] Ibid. i. 3. 13–20.   [5] Ehwald, p. 755, col. 2.
[6] For this scansion and the one listed at 11 below, see Bede, *De Arte Metr.* i. 14 (Kendall, pp. 122–7). Cf. Alc. *Carm.* xc. 21. 3, Paul. Nol. xxi. 349, Prud. *Cath.* xii. 67, *Contra Symm.* ii. 114.
[7] Norberg, *Introduction*, p. 9.
[8] A feature also of Aldhelm's versification and of late Latin.

aestimŏ (787); *agnoscŏ* (942); *ambŏ* (762); *caligŏ* (174); *carŏ* (309); *cernŏ* (933); *credŏ* (818); *ergŏ* (781); *estŏ* (171); *idcircŏ* (1347); but *idcircō* (1031); *Leŏ* (1544); *leŏ* (255); *Marŏ* (1554); *mirandŏ* (420); *praecŏ* (1401); *precandŏ* (698); *quaesŏ* (1004); *rogŏ* (896); *sermŏ* (1632); *signandŏ* (1108); *virgŏ* (410).

(b) Common shortenings of long -o: *quandŏque* (669); *quŏmodo* (690); *quŏusque* (837).

(c) Common lengthenings of short -o: *dōmusque* (724); *duō* (1044); *prōfatur* (484).

14. *Synizesis: pāriĕtĭbūs* (278; cf. Section 7, above); *semīanimisque* (1196); *Cēŏlfridus* (1295); *Ēanbaldus* (1516, 1523); *Hīeronymus* (1541).

15. *Syncope: vinclis* (405 *et passim*); *periclis* (1134); *dextra* (178, 703); *imposta* (329); *prendere* (949).

In licences of prosody, varied dactylic rhythm, use of elision, regularity of final homodynes, and the end-stopped character, tempered by enjambment, of its verses, Alcuin's poem on York corresponds to the metre and prosody advocated in Bede's *De Arte Metrica* and observed in his metrical Life of St. Cuthbert.

Conclusion

The conservative character of Alcuin's Latinity marks a natural stage in the development of a written language. Grammar, syntax, metre, and prosody display no radical departure from the cultivated practice of earlier Medieval Latin poets. In aspects of his diction, in his use of symmetry within the verse and of alliteration throughout, Alcuin shows a nice discrimination. His marked reliance upon a limited number of memorized sources, and the repetitious, formulaic, character of his versification point to a laborious attempt at composition in an acquired language. The leading scholar of the Carolingian *renovatio* was a competent, if undistinguished, writer of Latin verse.

x. Orthography

We have no comprehensive guide to Alcuin's orthography. No identified autograph of any of his works survives.[1] Neither the sole extant medieval manuscript of the poem on York (Reims, Bibliothèque municipale 426), which is of the early twelfth century,[2] nor a seventeenth-century copy of another medieval codex now lost[3] are reliable witnesses to Alcuin's spelling.

The best evidence of Alcuin's orthography is provided by his tract *De Orthographia.*[4] Manuscripts written under his influence, at Tours, such as BL Harley 2793,[5] and the orthography of Bede, provide supplementary data. None of these sources is complete or reliable.

Alcuin's *De Orthographia* is not a dictionary but a selective guide to a number of specific problems. We cannot assume uncritically that Alcuin (or any other writer) held fast to his own statement of orthographical principles or that his spelling remained fixed throughout his career. Even a manuscript produced at Tours and containing Scripture—*the* cardinal text in Alcuin's eyes—represents at most the practice of only the last eight years of his life (796-804). Manuscripts such as BL Harley 2793 therefore provide useful, but not primary, evidence for Alcuin's spelling. The orthography of manuscripts of Northumbrian provenance containing Bede's *HE* and other works, together with Bede's own tract *De Orthographia,*[6] permit one in certain cases to make an informed guess as to how Alcuin might have spelled. They do not enable us to solve an orthographical crux. The combination of these three pieces of evidence enables one to indicate, although not firmly to determine, the possible orthography of most of Alcuin's poem on York.

[1] Alcuin's autograph marginalia are discussed by B. Bischoff, 'Aus Alkuins Erdentagen', *Medievalia et Humanistica* 14 (1962) [= *Mittelalterliche Studien*, ii (Stuttgart, 1967), pp. 12-18], and see now id., *Paläographie des römischen Altertums und des abendländischen Mittelalters* (Berlin, 1979), p. 64 and n. 56. Useful remarks on orthography in J. Huemer's review of Dümmler's edition, *Deutsche Literaturzeitung*, 1881 (22), col. 890 and ibid. 1887 (7), col. 242.

[2] See pp. cxx ff. below.   [3] See pp. cxv ff. below.

[4] The best edition is still that of H. Keil, *Grammatici Latini*, vii (Leipzig, 1880), pp. 295-312. See also A. Marsili, *Alcuini Orthographia* (Pisa, 1952). Supplementary evidence is preserved in the *De Grammatica* (*PL* ci, cols. 850 ff.) and in *Ep.* 162, *MGH Epp.* iv, pp. 260 ff.

[5] See B. Fischer, *Die Bibel von Moutier-Grandval . . .* , p. 63.

[6] Ed. C. W. Jones, *Bedae Venerabilis Opera* i, *Opera didascalica*, *CCSL* cxxiii. A (Turnhout, 1975), pp. 1-57.

The chief exception to this generalization is the vexed problem posed by the Anglo-Latin orthography of Anglo-Saxon proper names and of place-names. Their irregular spelling, unfamiliar and difficult to a later and/or continental copyist, made them particularly liable to corruption. For Alcuin's possible orthography of these names the closest near-contemporary evidence is provided by Bede's *HE* and the early material in the Durham *Liber Vitae*.[1] An example will illustrate some of the difficulties posed by the spelling of these words.

Euboricensis, the adjectival form of the place-name, is transmitted in the manuscript tradition of the poem on York. It has often been altered to the classical *Eboracensis/ Eburacensis* found in Bede.[2] However, the form *Eubora(i)ca*, attested in Alcuin's letters, is once preserved by a tradition that is both early and good.[3] This Latin spelling is perhaps connected with the OE pronunciation of *Eoforwic*, the vernacular name for York.

The popular etymology which produced *Eoforwic*[4] implies that the first element of the OE name for York was pronounced like the word for 'boar'. In the second half of the eighth century, when back-mutation had affected *efur* (> *eufur*),[5] Alcuin would have pronounced the OE name with an *eu/eo* diphthong. Moreover, intervocalic *b* does not exist in OE of this period, and the voiced allophone of *f* would be an obvious sound-substitute for it. Alcuin's vernacular pronunciation of this name, transferred to his Latin pronunciation, may thus be reflected in the orthography of the manuscripts; and the existence

[1] See R. Müller, *Untersuchungen über die Namen des nordhumbrischen Liber Vitae, Palaestra* ix (Berlin, 1901) and T. J. M. van Els, *The Kassel Manuscript of Bede's 'Historia Ecclesiastica Gentis Anglorum' and its Old English Material* (Nijmegen, 1972).

[2] Listed in full in P. F. Jones, *A Concordance to the Historia Ecclesiastica of Bede* (Cambridge, Mass., 1929), s.v. p. 169.

[3] *Ep.* 121, *MGH Epp.* iv, p. 177. 9; cf. *Ep.* 43 ibid., p. 43. 1.

[4] Cf. *Parker Chronicle* (*c.*891) *s.a.* 644 in C. Plummer, *Two Anglo-Saxon Chronicles Parallel*, i (repr. Oxford, 1972), p. 26.

[5] I follow the chronology of K. Luick, *Historische Grammatik der englischen Sprache*, i. 1 (repr. Stuttgart, 1964), pp. 209, 228, n. 5, and A. Campbell, *Old English Grammar* (Oxford, 1959), pp. 88, 210. See further A. H. Smith, *Three Northumbrian Poems*[2] (London, 1968), p. 31, and H. Ström, *Old English Personal Names in Bede's History* (Lund, 1939), p. 117.

of this possibility should give editors reason to pause before emending to the form *Eboracensis.*

In the tenuous state of our evidence, much of Alcuin's orthography, especially in the case of proper names and place-names, remains necessarily speculative. Where it is consistent, the manuscript transmission of these names is preserved, except when it departs significantly from the criteria outlined above.[1] Spellings explicitly prescribed in Alcuin's *De Orthographia* are adopted in the text.[2]

xi. *History of the Text*

An account of the textual transmission of Alcuin's poem on York in the Middle Ages is inseparable from an analysis of its editorial history. Although there survives only one medieval manuscript containing this work, lost codices can be distinguished by examining the papers of its seventeenth century editors, Thomas Gale and Jean Mabillon.[3]

The first edition of any part of Alcuin's poem was printed by Mabillon in 1672.[4] Under the title *Fragmentum Historiae de Pontificibus et Sanctis Ecclesiae Eboracensis Scriptae a Poeta Anonymo . . .* Mabillon published vv. 1-98 (omitting v. 66) and vv. 1205-1658. He chose not to print the work in its entirety, but only what its author had added to Bede's *Ecclesiastical History*, which Mabillon recognized as the principal source of the poem on York.[5] Mabillon's text was founded on a manuscript from the monastery of Saint-Thierry near Reims discovered by the

---

[1] e.g. v. 358 A*edilredi,* *Osthryda* (cf. Bede, *HE.* iii. 2); vv. 575-6 *Ecgfrido*; v. 753 *Aedilthryda*; v. 843 *Aldfrido*; v. 1274 E*adberctus* (where his reading is little more than an expansion of *R*); v. 1388 *Echha.*

[2] e.g. *affatim,* not *adfatim* (Marsili, p. 108, 38); *exsilium,* not *exilium* (Marsili, p. 111. 11) and, by analogy, *exsul*; *gnatus,* not *natus* (Marsili, p. 112. 28); *pene,* not *paene* (Marsili, p. 115. 42); *solemnia,* not *sollemnia* (Marsili, pp. 118. 46, 119. 1), etc.

[3] Preliminary studies of this problem are published in my 'Mabillon, Ruinart, Gale et l'*Eboracum* d'Alcuin', *Revue Mabillon,* lix (1978), pp. 254-60 and 'The Textual Tradition of Alcuin's Poem on York', *Mlat. Jb.* 15 (1980), pp. 35-50. See further F. Dolbeau, ibid. 17 (1982, forthcoming).

[4] *AASSOSB* iii. 2, pp. 556-69.

[5] '. . . tantum ea quae adiecit historiae Venerabilis Bedae, a quo cetera mutuatus est' (p. 556).

Benedictine Christophe Daubin.[1] In that codex, according to Mabillon, the title given to the poem was *Historia anglica carmine heroico a quodam sapiente facta* (p. 557). Without identifying the poet, Mabillon recognized that this text was the work of a pupil of Ælberht, archbishop of York, and that vv. 1529-30 imply that its author's name had been affixed to the autograph.[2] His edition contains two conjectures and brief marginal notes indicating the subject of each section.[3]

The *editio princeps* of the entire poem was published by Thomas Gale in 1691.[4] Gale was the first to attribute the work to Alcuin, and this ascription has been correctly and almost universally accepted ever since.[5] Gale stated that his text was based on manuscripts from Saint-Thierry and Saint-Remi, generally supposed to be two in number and now presumed to be lost. He reproduces Mabillon's marginal notes beside those parts of the text that Mabillon had edited in 1672, to which Gale added v. 66. How his edition was constructed and on which manuscript sources it was based are problems that have never been resolved.

Gale declares in his preface that he owed his text of Alcuin's poem on York to Mabillon.[6] Later editors have linked this acknowledgement to their assumption that Mabillon received from Daubin a transcription of a Saint-Thierry manuscript containing the work. They have inferred either that the transcription attributed to Daubin, supplemented by readings from a Saint-Remi codex, was passed on to Gale by Mabillon; or that Gale

[1] '. . . poematium istud haud inelegans e ms. codice Monasterii S. Theodorici prope Remos *eruit* noster Christophorus Daubin', ibid. (my italics: on this verb, see below, p. cxv).

[2] See comm. ad loc. and on the title pp. cxvii, cxxiv, pp. 2-3^a.

[3] *certatim* for *sepulchri* at v. 36 and *carmen* for *canna* at v. 1271. He indicated a lacuna of one word (*terra*) at the beginning of v. 1381 and tacitly omitted *ibi* at v. 1298, *est* at v. 1461, together with v. 66.

[4] *Historiae Britannicae, Saxonicae, Anglo-Danicae Scriptores XV* (Oxford, 1691), pp. 703-32.

[5] The earliest debate on the attribution of the poem is recounted in *Mlat. Jb.* 15 (1980), pp. 39-40 (especially n. 5). On the ill-founded doubts expressed by Casimir Oudin in 1722 see ibid., p. 34, n. 4.

[6] '. . . hoc poëma beneficio . . . *J. Mabillonii* accepi', Gale, *Historiae* . . . *scriptores XV*, preface (unpaginated).

himself collated the Saint-Thierry and Saint-Remi manu-
scripts.[1] The second of these inferences is untenable
because Gale never travelled out of Britain.[2] The first
is belied by Gale's copy-text, the Trinity College, Cam-
bridge manuscript 1130 (0.2.26),[3] in which the script of
Daubin never appears. Nor is there other evidence that
Daubin did more than discover ('eruit')[4] a manuscript of
the poem at Saint-Thierry. The hand which produced most
of Gale's copy-text was that of Thierry Ruinart, and can
be identified from his surviving letters.[5] Ruinart was the
scholar whose investigation of manuscripts extant at
Reims in the mid 1680s contributed most to the publica-
tion of Alcuin's complete poem, yet until recently his
name has not figured in its editorial history.[6]

Ruinart was responsible for writing into Gale's copy-
text the part of Alcuin's poem on York which had not
been published by Mabillon in 1672: vv. 99–1205 (omit-
ting v. 578 of my edition).[7] The remainder of the poem—
vv. 1–98 (omitting v. 66) and vv. 1205–1658—as it
appears in that copy-text, is in the script of two French
amanuenses. These palaeographical facts establish
Ruinart's involvement in the early stages of Gale's publica-
tion. They are supported and clarified by a number of
letters and drafts for letters between Gale, Ruinart, and

[1] Wattenbach, p. 81 (followed by Dümmler, *MGH PLAC* i, p. 162) and Raine, p. lxv.

[2] On Gale's life and work, see now E. Jeauneau, 'La traduction érigénienne des *Ambigua* de Maxime le Confesseur. Thomas Gale (1636–1702) et le *Codex Remensis*', in *Jean Scot Érigène et l'Histoire de la Philosophie*, Colloques Inter-nationaux du CNRS, no. 561 (Paris, 1977), pp. 135–44.

[3] See M. R. James, *The Western Manuscripts in the Library of Trinity College, Cambridge* iii (Cambridge, 1920), p. 120 (no. 1130, 0.2.26 [= m.g. No. 417]).

[4] See p. cxiv, n. 1.   [5] *Mlat. Jb.* 15 (1980), pp. 39 ff.

[6] On Ruinart see H. Leclercq, *Dictionnaire d'archéologie chrétienne et de liturgie*, xv. 1 (Paris, 1950), cols. 163–82, and H. Jadart, *Dom Thierry Ruinart* (Paris, 1886), and id., 'L'Origine de D. Mabillon à Saint-Pierremont et sa liaison avec D. Thierry Ruinart', *Mélanges et documents publiés à l'occasion du 2e centenaire de la mort de Mabillon* (Paris, 1908), pp. 30 ff. For a recent account, with extensive bibliography, of the circle of Ruinart and Mabillon see B. Neveu, 'Mabillon et l'historiographie gallicane vers 1700. Erudition ecclesiastique et recherche historique au XVIIIe siècle', *Historische Forschung im 18. Jahrhundert. Organisation. Zielsetzung. Ergebnisse*, ed. K. Hammer and J. Voss, Pariser Histor-ische Studien 13 (Bonn, 1976), pp. 27–81.

[7] Preserved only in Reims 426, a manuscript discussed below. See comm. ad loc.

Mabillon that survive in the Bibliothèque Nationale, Paris and the British Library, London and enable us to reconstruct what have seemed lost stages in the text's transmission and edition.[1]

As early as 1679 Thomas Gale had been interested in the poem on York, and had recognized that it was the work of Alcuin.[2] In March 1685 Gale requested from Mabillon a transcription of the Saint-Thierry manuscript upon which his *Acta* edition had been based. Between April 1685 and July 1686 Mabillon made the *iter italicum* of which he wrote a famous account.[3] During that period he entrusted the task of examining relevant manuscripts to his colleague and assistant at Saint-Germain-des-Prés, dom Thierry Ruinart, as a letter of Ruinart's makes clear.[4]

Ruinart was unable personally to collate the Saint-Thierry manuscript used for Mabillon's edition. He had seen it at Saint-Thierry in 1684 and could remember a year later that it ·preserved no indication of the poem's authorship. Ruinart wrote a number of times for the codex to Saint-Thierry. By 22 October 1685 he had received a reply that it was not to be found, and he sent a letter to Gale apologizing for the consequent delay. For Ruinart, the only means of access to Mabillon's Saint-Thierry manuscript was therefore Mabillon's *Acta* edition of vv. 1-98 (omitting v. 66) and vv. 1205-1658. That is why he had two amanuenses reproduce this part of the poem in Trinity 1130 (0.2.26), the transcription that was to become Gale's copy-text.

In the same letter Ruinart announced his discovery of an older manuscript from Saint-Remi at Reims containing the poem on York together with Bede's *HE* and *De Die Iudicii*. He recorded that it was some 700 years old, thus implicitly assigning it to the tenth century, and carried it

---

[1] In the following pages I refer to the edition of these letters in *Mlat. Jb.* 15, with redatings established in *Mlat. Jb.* 17 (art. cit., above, p. cxiii, n. 3).

[2] *Mlat. Jb.* 15 (1980), pp. 46-7.

[3] *Iter Italicum Litterarium* in *Museum Italicum* . . . , i (Paris, 1687), pp. 2-244.

[4] *Mlat. Jb.* 15 (1980), pp. 48-9, no. 3 [= the draft]. The letter has been identified by P. Petitmengin as BL Additional MS. 4277, ff. 147-8 (*The British Library, Catalogue of Additions to the Manuscripts, 1756-1782* (London, 1977), pp. 83-4, 622). Its date is XI cal. nov. 1685 (= 22 October).

off with him to Paris, whence he promised to send a tran-
scription to Gale.

In a draft of a letter written in early or mid November
1685[1] Ruinart went on to describe his Saint-Remi manu-
script. He suggested that Mabillon's Saint-Thierry codex
had been copied from this *Remigianus*, noting the fre-
quency of such a pattern of transmission; and conjectured
that the manuscript had belonged to the poet and historian
Flodoard (893/4–966).[2]

Ruinart distinguished two hands in his Saint-Remi manu-
script. The first of them had produced the body of the
text; while the second, of roughly the same date, which
Ruinart identifies with that of Flodoard himself, was re-
sponsible for a number of marginal notes. Ruinart observed
that the first scribe did not know who had written the poem
because he recorded next to the incipit that it was composed
'a quodam sapiente'. A list of variants and marginal annota-
tions accompanied the letter which Ruinart sent to Gale.
His statement of the date and provenance of the Saint-Remi
manuscript, repeating the fact that it was distinct from
Mabillon's Saint-Thierry codex, is confirmed in a note of
26 November 1685.[3]

The main body of Gale's copy-text, as it survives in the
Trinity manuscript, therefore represents two stages of
research on this poem: a transcription of vv. 1–98 (ex-
cluding v. 66) and vv. 1205–1658 from Mabillon's 1672
edition, together with its marginal notes; and a transcrip-
tion, in the hand of Ruinart, of vv. 99–1204 from his
Saint-Remi manuscript, sent to Gale on 26 November
1685. The first readings of Gale's copy-text in vv. 1–98
(excluding v. 66) and vv. 1205–1658 may be eliminated
because they derive from Mabillon's edition, which there-
fore emerges, at this stage of the text's history, as the

---

[1] *Mlat. Jb.* 15 (1980), pp. 47–8. Classified 4 Nov. 1685. An allusion to
Mabillon's return to Rome after his journey to Naples does not prove that this
letter was written on a date after 16 Nov. (H. Leclercq, *Mabillon*, i (Paris, 1953),
pp. 376–7), for Ruinart may be recounting Mabillon's travel plans rather than his
actual journeys.

[2] On Flodoard's reading see P. C. Jacobsen, *Flodoard von Reims. Sein Leben
und seine Dichtung 'De Triumphis Christi'*, Mittellateinische Studien und Texte
10 (Leiden and Cologne, 1978), especially pp. 88–199.

[3] *Mlat. Jb.* 15 (1980), p. 49.

primary witness to the readings of Mabillon's Saint-Thierry manuscript. Whether the 1672 edition can retain this status is a problem which will be examined below. For the readings of Gale's copy-text of vv. 99–1204, our nearest extant witness to Ruinart's Saint-Remi manuscript, the siglum T is adopted.

The marginal and interlinear variants of Gale's copy-text may be divided into three classes, the first of which is indicated by the siglum T^1.

T^1 represents those variants which can be proved to have derived from Ruinart's *codex Remigianus*. They occur only in vv. 1–98. Between p. 5 and p. 6 of the Trinity manuscript is an unnumbered page, in the same format as the rest of Gale's copy-text, on which Ruinart himself lists seven variants (including v. 66), specifying that they derive from his *codex Remigianus*.[1] Six of these variants are recorded in the text or in the margin of pp. 1–5 of the Trinity manuscript: five of them by Gale,[2] and one by an amanuensis.[3] These variants are all that can be certainly identified with a number of *variae lectiones* from the Saint-Remi manuscript sent to Gale by Ruinart in his letter of early to mid November 1685.[4] Their special authority is therefore marked by a distinct siglum.

The second class of marginal or interlinear variants in Gale's copy-text is represented by the siglum T^2. Five of them occur in vv. 1–98. Two of these indicate, by means of numbers, a word-order different from that of Mabillon's edition.[5] The other three are in the hand of Gale.[6] It is unlikely that Gale made no use of further variants communicated to him by Ruinart from the Saint-Remi

---

[1] The variants Ruinart specifies are: v. 36 *spe lucri*; v. 54 *illa*; v. 59 *movebat (del.)*; v. 64 *per*; v. 61 *tibi*; v. 66 entire; v. 95 *adivit*. Below these variants Ruinart copies vv. 99–109.

[2] All variants listed in the preceding note, with the exception of v. 66, are recorded by Gale with notes indicating that their source was the *Remigianus*.

[3] v. 66 is inserted without indication of its source. The variant to v. 59 deleted by Ruinart is not recorded in the Trinity manuscript, pp. 1–5. It is eliminated from the following account.

[4] See p. cxvii and n. 1.

[5] v. 48 *duritiam*^{2} *dicti* ^{1}*propter*; v. 49 *hanc placuit ducibus* ^{5}*donis conducere* ^{4}*regni*.

[6] v. 18 *gratis*; v. 28 *oceano, vela*.

manuscript, but the absence of any internal evidence of their source in the Trinity manuscript makes it as impossible to determine as it is tempting to speculate whether these four variants are independent conjectures or readings derived from Ruinart's Saint-Remi manuscript. The same is true of the variants in vv. 1205-1658 of Gale's copy-text, which are also represented by the siglum T^2.

The third class of variants occurs only in T, vv. 99-1204. They are all in the autographs of Ruinart and Gale. Since Gale, in this part of the poem, had only Ruinart's transcription of vv. 99-1204 of the *Remigianus* before him, variants in his autograph represent his own conjectures and are therefore ascribed to him by name.[1] Variants in the hand of Ruinart pose a greater problem. They could represent his own conjectures or his corrections of an earlier transcription of the *Remigianus* from the manuscript itself. Although variants in Ruinart's hand are assigned to him by name in my edition, one may not exclude the possibility that they reflect a second and more accurate collation by him of the *Remigianus*. The ambiguous status of these variants will affect our argument at a later stage.[2]

The Trinity manuscript 1130 (0.2.26), together with Mabillon's edition of 1672 and the correspondence of Ruinart, thus enables us to distinguish with some exactitude the state of the text of Alcuin's poem on York when Gale handed it to his printer. Mabillon's edition, reproduced in Gale's copy-text, was the chief witness to the readings in vv. 1-98 (excluding v. 66) and vv. 1205-1658 of an inaccessible manuscript from Saint-Thierry. That part of the poem, supplemented by six variants from Ruinart's Saint-Remi manuscript (T^1) and by other variants of uncertain origin (T^2), was combined with the text of vv. 99-1204 copied by Ruinart from his *Remigianus* (T) and annotated by Ruinart's own corrections or conjectures and by those of Gale. This state of affairs was to remain essentially unchanged until the twentieth century.

---

[1] Gale's corrections and clarifications, chiefly of an orthographical nature, to Ruinart's transcription are not recorded in the apparatus criticus.

[2] pp. cxxvi-cxxvii.

Gale's edition of 1691 has no authority independent of Mabillon's text, T, T^1, T^2 and the corrections and conjectures of Ruinart and Gale as recorded in T. It may be eliminated from any future apparatus criticus. Its elimination marks a discontinuity in the editorial history of the poem. Alcuin's eighteenth- and nineteenth-century editors[1] simply added to Gale's printed text historical commentary and conjectural criticism, in which none of them, save Wattenbach, made any notable advance.[2] No separate edition of the poem on York has ever been published. Not until the MS. Reims, Bibliothèque municipale 426 became accessible[3] have editors been in a position substantially to improve on the state in which Gale left this text in 1691.

Reims 426 is a Saint-Thierry manuscript which contains Isidore's *Etymologiae*, Alcuin's poem on York, and a compendium of Bede's *HE*. Ff. 1–117 are of the early ninth century; the remainder (ff. 118–216) dates from the early twelfth century.[4] The twelfth-century *ex-libris* occurs *passim* and establishes the Saint-Thierry provenance of the codex as a whole; on folio 2^r appears the signature of the fifteenth-century abbé Arnoult d'Anglade.[5] The manuscript, cited in Montfaucon's catalogue of 1739,[6] measures 315 × 210 mm.

---

[1] Discussed and evaluated in *Mlat. Jb.* 15 (1980), p. 34.

[2] Wattenbach anticipates a number of readings contained in R: e.g. v. 86 *fluctus*; v. 105 *suo*; v. 176 *si sit*; v. 299 *comprendit*, v. 384 *percipit*; v. 520 *bello*; v. 596 *qua*; v. 1273 *item*; v. 1490 *ubi.*

[3] Recorded by H. Loriquet, *Catalogue général des manuscrits des bibliothèques publiques de France*, xxxviii (Paris, 1902), pp. 568–9. Signalled by K. Strecker *MGH PLAC* iv. 3, p. 1128 (where the manuscript as a whole is assigned to the ninth century) and W. Levison, *Antiquity*, 14 (1940), p. 290, n. 18 and id., *England and the Continent*, p. 197, n. 2. I have collated this manuscript.

[4] F. M. Carey, 'The Scriptorium of Reims during the Archbishopric of Hincmar (845–882)', in *Classical and Medieval Studies in Honour of Edward Kennard Rand* (New York, 1938), p. 57, dates ff. 1–117 to 800–25, and (p. 59) ff. 118–210 to 1000–1100. See further M. de Lemps and R. Laslier, *Trésors de la Bibliothèque municipale de Reims* (Reims, 1978), no. 4 (unpaginated) and M.-P. Lafitte, 'Esquisse d'une bibliothèque mediévale. Le fonds de manuscrits de l'Abbaye de Saint-Thierry', in *Saint Thierry, une abbaye du VIe au XXe siècle*, Actes du Colloque international d'Histoire monastique, Reims–Saint-Thierry, 11–14 octobre 1976 (Saint-Thierry, 1979), p. 94, no. 70.

[5] Laffitte, art. cit., p. 84, n. 58, p. 94.

[6] *Bibliotheca bibliothecarum manuscriptorum nova* (Paris, 1739), ii, p. 1235, no. 70. Michael Reeve points out that this part of the work had probably been drawn up by 1720 (i, praef. p. i).

Its written surface area is 255 × 160 mm. There are 32 lines per folio.

Alcuin's poem on York is contained on ff. 210^r-214^v, and 215^r,[1] of Reims 426. This part of the manuscript was produced by two scribes, the first of whom wrote most of ff. 210^r-211^v and the second of whom wrote most of the rest, with the first scribe taking over from time to time in shortish passages of between 10 and 20 lines. Ff. 210-11 have three columns per folio, while f. 212 has four columns in cramped script. Ff. 213-15 return to the earlier three-column format.

The reason for the interest of these two scribes in Alcuin's poem on York is suggested by the contents of the manuscript itself. The poem appears immediately after a text of Isidore's *Etymologiae*. The only part of Alcuin's text to be glossed is vv. 1434-49, which describe the teaching of the seven liberal arts at York under Egbert. Not merely are individual words provided with glosses, but couplets are given their own 'subheadings'. Before vv. 1435-6, for example, the first scribe wrote *de grammatica et rhetorica* in the main body of the text. Before vv. 1436 ff. he wrote *de dialectica et musica.*[2] The interest in Alcuin's poem of the first scribe, whose hand is to be found in marginal notes and glosses throughout the text of Isidore's *Etymologiae* on folios 1^r-210^r, clearly lay in what it had to say about the seven liberal arts. The second scribe, immediately after the apparent end of the poem on f. 214^v, made in conjunction with the first a compendium of the earlier parts of Bede's *HE*, together with a list of Bede's other writings. His interest in early English history and in Bede suggests his motive for producing a text of Alcuin's poem, which draws extensively on Bede, supplementing the account of eighth-century Northumbria provided in the *HE*. This dual interest in English intellectual tradition and history may explain the motives behind the production of Reims 426.

There are a few marginal notes in the codex and these are confined to ff. 210^{r-v}.[3] Word-division within the line is not systematic. The often cramped format of Reims 426 results

[1] See pp. cxxii.
[2] Recorded in full in the comm. to vv. 1434-49.
[3] See pp. cxxiv, n. 1 below.

in words being split at the end of the line and completed at the end of the preceding or following verse where there is greater space.[1] The two scribes often correct one another (*dator* at v. 1341, for example, is emended to *datur* by the second hand) or add variants (*hisdem* for *isdem* at v. 876 is an instance). There are signs of erasure at several points where correction is made: the crux at vv. 871–2 arrived in its present form in Reims 426 after words had been rubbed out. The state of the codex, with its numerous variants and corrections and omissions later filled, suggests corruption in its exemplar. I propose the siglum *R* to designate the main body of the text in Reims 426 and the siglum *r* to represent any variant or correction either by the first or by the second scribe.

Reims 426 was collated from photographs by M. L. Hargrove for her unpublished Cornell dissertation of 1937.[2] She noted a mark of omission in the first column of f. 211[r] immediately after v. 285, which is then followed by v. 338, and therefore assumed a loss or omission from *R* of 51 lines. However, the omission mark immediately after v. 285 on f. 211[r], column 1 of Reims 426, is repeated on f. 215[r], column 3, where vv. 286–337 are copied after what is chiefly a compendium of Bede's *HE*. Reims 426 preserves, therefore, a complete twelfth-century witness to the text.

The text established by Hargrove in her 1937 dissertation relies heavily on Reims 426. To that extent it marks an improvement over Dümmler's edition of 1881. Hargrove recorded a conjecture of H. Caplan's which is patently correct,[3] and made seven proposals of her own, none of which has been received into the present text.[4] She collated Trinity 1130 from rotographs, and drew attention to a number of places where errors committed by Gale and perpetuated by other editors might have been eliminated by consulting this manuscript.[5]

The scholarly papers of Ruinart and Gale, which elucidate the different stages of the text embodied in Trinity 1130,

---

[1] See p. cxxv (*adiuit*).

[2] 'Alcuin's "Poem on York". The Latin Text, with an Introduction, an English Translation and Notes' (Ithaca, N.Y., 1937).

[3] v. 58 *ducti*.   [4] See app. i to vv. 435, 592 (*ter*), 698, 872, 1464.

[5] Her collation is far more systematic than that of Jaffé or Raine (pp. 7–8).

were inaccessible to Hargrove. Her attempt to investigate the affiliations of Reims 426 and Gale's copy-text, through no fault of her own, thus begins from false premises. Hargrove's dissertation contains an English translation, at times substantially independent of its Latin original, and a number of brief and sometimes pertinent textual notes. Her apparatus criticus represents the first attempt to supply anything worthy of that name to Alcuin's poem on York.

The chief problem now posed by the history of this text is the relationship of the Saint-Thierry and Saint-Remi manuscripts presumed to be lost with Reims 426. Is Reims 426 the *Theodoricanus* used by Mabillon? Was Ruinart's *Remigianus* the exemplar of Reims 426?[1]

We know from the signature of Arnoult d'Anglade on f. 2^r of Reims 426 that the manuscript was at Saint-Thierry at the end of the fifteenth century. That it remained there until the eighteenth century is attested both by the seventeenth-century *ex-libris* and by the appearance of the manuscript in the catalogue of Montfaucon.[2] On external grounds it is therefore possible that Reims 426 was accessible to Mabillon. Four criteria enable one to test this hypothesis. I begin with the internal evidence which supports it.

1. *Agreements in Error of Mabillon's edition with Reims 426 where T^1 or T^2 have the truth*

36	sepulcri	1346	iuvenis
54	illi	1371	lenius
1298	ibi *omitted*	1398	bonus
1310	qui	1469	annis
		1626	complexibus

Mabillon's *Theodoricanus* and Reims 426 are therefore related, nor is the apparent evidence against their proximity provided by our second and third criteria sufficient to shake this hypothesis.

---

[1] This question is implied by Ruinart's observation on Mabillon's Saint-Thierry manuscript: 'fallor nisi ex codice Remigiano isdem sicut plerique alii Theodoricani excriptus sit' (*Mlat. Jb.* 15 (1980), p. 48).

[2] See above, p. cxx and n. 6.

2. *The marginalia of Mabillon's edition and Reims 426.* The marginalia to vv. 1205-1658 published by Mabillon do, not occur in Reims 426.[1] There is, however, no indication that they derive from Mabillon's *Theodoricanus*, and their summary style of reference to events, figures, and places in the text indicates that they, like the marginalia in the text of Flodoard following (pp. 569-608), are of Mabillon's own invention.

Mabillon records (p. 557) that 'Istius Poëmatis inscriptio sic se habet in cod. ms: *HISTORIA ANGLICA CARMINE HEROICO A QUODAM SAPIENTE FACTA.*' Reims 426 has no such inscription. In the margin to vv. 1 ff., *r* reads: 'A quodam sapiente facta dei sanctorumque eius invocacio in adiutorium sequentis sui operis hoc ponitur in prohemio.'

Mabillon used a transcription of his *Theodoricanus* supplied by a copyist who was less than reliable.[2] The discrepancy between the inscription recorded at p. 557 of Mabillon's edition and the reading of *r* to vv. 1 ff. can be explained if the copyist supplied Mabillon with a paraphrase of the subject of Alcuin's poem, perhaps incorporating the first three words of *r*'s marginalia, and provided no further account of it, thus leaving Mabillon to infer that this was what his Saint-Thierry exemplar had as an inscription.[3]

3. *True readings in Mabillon's edition not contained in Reims 426*[4]

    52 collaudat *Mabillon*: colladat *R*
  1220 summi *Mabillon*: summis *R*
  1240 quo *Mabillon*: quos *R*
  1242 reliquit *Mabillon*: leliquit *R*
  1322 caerula *Mabillon*: cerulam *R*
  1403 bonis *Mabillon*: bonus *R*

---

[1] *R* is paraphrased by *r* in the margin to vv. 1 ff.; 18-27, 46-50, 68-76, 79-83, 90-4.   [2] See below 3, 4.

[3] Cf. the descriptive entry in Montfaucon (p. cxx, n. 6 above): 'In hoc cod. continentur *historia* Ecclesiastica Anglorum *a quodam sapiente poëtice*, soluta oratione a Beda' (my italics).

[4] The readings of both *R* and *r* are taken into account. When *r* anticipates Mabillon's reading the variant in *R* cannot be used to demonstrate this point. e.g. v. 13 vos *r Mabillon*: quos *R*; 1219 fretus *r Mabillon*: fletus *R*; v. 1385 penitus *r Mabillon*: petimus *R*; v. 1524 decus *r Mabillon*: ductus *R*; v. 1561 scribi *r Mabillon*: scripsi *R*; v. 1575 magistri *r Mabillon*: patroni *R*; v. 1640 et *r Mabillon*: ad *R*; v. 1653 verenter *r Mabillon*: reverenter *R*.

1448 maxima *Mabillon*: maxime *R*
1495 supra *Mabillon*: super *R*
1504 ut *Mabillon*: *om. R*
1530 prodent *Mabillon*: prodant *R*
1562 postulat *Mabillon*: postulet *R*
1619 manibus *Mabillon*: remanibus *R*
1623 ubi *Mabillon*: ut *R*
1652 quae *Mabillon*: quem *R*

This evidence is insufficient to prove the independence of Mabillon's edition from Reims 426. In every case the reading of *R* is so patently corrupt and the remedy is so simple that one need only postulate a modest capacity for obvious correction on the part of Mabillon's copyist or, more probably, of Mabillon himself. We come to our fourth and final criterion.

4. A number of disagreements between *R* and Mabillon's edition can be explained by assuming that misunderstanding of *R* arose through its irregular word-division and cramped format,[1] through the carelessness and the inability of Mabillon's copyist correctly to interpret abbreviations, or by simple error.

Disagreements of Reims 426 with Mabillon's edition due to mistakes and mis-readings

29 iam *R*: ut *Mabillon* ($\overline{\text{ia}}$ confused with $\overline{\text{tc}}$)
48 duritiam propter dicti *R*: duritiam dicti propter *Mabillon*
56 ubi digna *R*: indigna *Mabillon*
64 (cf. 1348) per *R*: post *Mabillon*
66 *om. Mabillon*
86 fluctus *R*: fluctu *Mabillon*
93 oroma *R*: orama *Mabillon*
95 adivit *R*: deinde *Mabillon* ($\partial\partial$ in *R*, with *-ivit* at end of 93, interpreted by the copyist as *deinde*)
97 vir *R*: vix *Mabillon*
1207 haec *R*: hic *Mabillon*
1211 vivens *R*: iuveni *Mabillon*

---

[1] See pp. cxxi–cxxii above.

1215 proprius *R*: propius *Mabillon*
1273 item *R*: idem *Mabillon*
1274 ãberctus *R*: Adbertus *Mabillon*
1313 actu *R*: acta *Mabillon*
1348 per *R*: post *Mabillon*
1380 nisu pelagi *R*: pelagi nisu *Mabillon*
1381 terra *R*: *om. Mabillon*
1434 gnaviter *R*: graviter *Mabillon*
1442 zonas *R*: conas *Mabillon*
1445 volucrum atque *R*: volucrumque *Mabillon*
1461 est *R*: *om. Mabillon*
1475 vasti *R*: vasta *Mabillon*
1479 non *R*: nec *Mabillon* (n̄)
1490 ubi *R*: ut *Mabillon*
1537 per *R*: pro *Mabillon*
1543 acutus *R*: avitus *Mabillon*
1545 coruscant *R*: coruscans *Mabillon*
1565 quaternos *R*: quot annos *Mabillon*
1594 gramina *R*: germina *Mabillon*
1597 hic *R*: sic *Mabillon*
1604 rexit *R*: vexit *Mabillon*

On internal grounds a case cannot be established against the affiliation of Reims 426 and Mabillon's *Theodoricanus*. It is highly probable, on both internal and external evidence, that his edition derives, through an imperfect copy, from Reims 426. From this it follows that Mabillon's edition may be excluded from the apparatus criticus except where its aberrant readings account for a variant being recorded in Trinity 1130. Reims 426 is thus an independent witness. Whether Ruinart's lost Saint-Remi manuscript served as its exemplar[1] is therefore a historical and not an editorial problem.

The *Remigianus* was presumably destroyed, as Loriquet first supposed,[2] in the fire of 15 January 1774 which ravaged the library of Saint-Remi. Its loss throws us back on *T*[1] and *T*. *T* contains variants in Ruinart's hand which may represent

---

[1] The lost manuscript is not identical with, nor does it descend from, Reims 426, as is shown by the dates of Ruinart's *Remigianus* (*s.* x, according to Ruinart, p. cxv) and of Reims 426 (*s.* xii *in.*, p. cxx nn. 3, 4), together with the evidence on p. cxxvii. [2] *Catalogue*, p. 569.

either his own conjectures or his corrections, after a second reading, of a first collation of the *Remigianus*, or both. The indeterminable origin of these variants requires them to be excluded from an analysis of the internal evidence for and against the possiblity that Ruinart's Saint-Remi manuscript was the exemplar of Reims 426, and yet their exclusion may lead to unavoidable distortions of *T*'s exemplar. As Reims 426 and Trinity 1130 are independent of each other, it is natural that each contains both truths and corruptions not found in the other,[1] even though they sometimes agree in error.[2] However, no analysis of these variants could show the exact relationship of Reims 426 and the *Remigianus* from which *T* descends.

Only slight external evidence as to the possible affiliations of the *Remigianus* and Reims 426 is provided by the extant manuscript's appearance and by the correspondence of Ruinart. In his letter of early to mid November 1685[3] Ruinart notes that the words *a quodam sapiente* occur in the margin to v. 1 of his *Remigianus*. The same marginalia are recorded by *r* at the same place in Reims 426, and may have been copied from its exemplar. The numerous signs that the two scribes of Reims 426 found difficulty in reading their exemplar (pp. cxxi–cxxii) seem to arise from its corruption, a hypothesis borne out by the high incidence of error in *T* and perhaps supported by the fact that the copyist of Ruinart's *Remigianus* did not know who had written the poem. These points, however, are in themselves insufficient to demonstrate the dependence of Reims 426 on Ruinart's lost manuscript.

Given the ambiguous status of the readings T^2 and of the variants recorded by Gale and Ruinart in Trinity 1130 (see above, pp. cxviii–cxix), the inconclusive nature of the internal evidence, and the absence of firm external evidence, the hypothesis that Ruinart's *Remigianus* was the exemplar of

---

[1] References are to the apparatus criticus here and in the next note; only selected examples are provided:
  (i) corruptions in *T* absent from *R*: 105, 186, 238, 314, 778, 840, 1111, etc.;
  (ii) Corruptions in *R* absent from T^1 and *T*: 36, 54, 353, 669, 914, 1155, etc.
[2] *T* and *R* agree in error against a variant in the hand of Ruinart at (e.g.) vv. 545, 695, 951, 1034; and against editorial conjectures at (e.g.) 282, 357, 920.
[3] *Mlat. Jb.* 15 (1980), p. 47.

Reims 426 can be neither confirmed nor denied. The following stemma is therefore tentative:

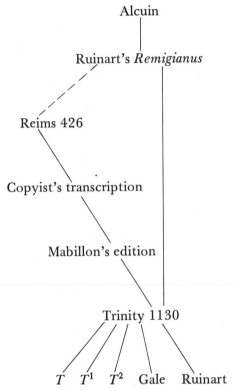

Alcuin

Ruinart's *Remigianus*

Reims 426

Copyist's transcription

Mabillon's edition

Trinity 1130

T T^1 T^2 Gale   Ruinart

In tabular form the manuscripts to be used in the present edition appear thus:

vv. 1–98	R, T^1, T^2.
vv. 99–1204	R, T (with marginal or interlinear variants by Gale and Ruinart)
vv. 1205–1658	R, T^2.

The exclusively continental tradition of Alcuin's poem on York corresponds to the pattern of transmission of several other works of Anglo-Saxon authorship from the eighth and ninth centuries, the survival of which also depends on manuscripts produced on the Continent.[1] Due weight must be

---

[1] See Brown, *Spoleto . . . Settimane*, 22 (1974), pp. 280–1.

given to the disruptions caused both by natural loss and by the Viking invasions of the ninth century. It would be rash to assume that Alcuin's earliest extant compositions were his first. We know so little about the Latin poetry which he may have written in his youth or early manhood at York[1] as a result of the yawning gaps in its textual transmission. Similarly, it is certain that his poem on York had a limited diffusion in England,[2] but its availability there cannot be assessed in terms of surviving manuscripts.

On the Continent, Reims emerges as the area which preserved Alcuin's poem on York since at least the tenth century. The palaeographical interest of this area is not confined to the crucial role it played in the transmission of Alcuin's verse; it is also enhanced by the general importance of Reims in the textual history of early Medieval Latin poetry. In the ninth century Reims produces such remarkable collections of late Antique and early Carolingian poetry as Bibliothèque Nationale lat. 9347[3] and Vatican, Reginensis lat. 2078.[4] In the time of Flodoard, and in the early twelfth century, the reconstructible textual history of Alcuin's *Versus de . . . Sanctis Euboricensis Ecclesiae* centres wholly upon the area of Reims. A full palaeographical study of the part played by Reims in the transmission of early Medieval Latin poetry would therefore seem a real desideratum.

xii. *Construction of this Edition*

1. Alcuin's extensive borrowings from Bede are indicated by references in the left-hand margin of the Latin text. Italics in the body of the text indicate those passages which are verbally closest to Bede's *HE* and Lives of St. Cuthbert.

---

[1] See pp. xxxvi, xxxix above.   [2] pp. xliv–xlv above.

[3] See p. lxxi above. Further bibliography in F. Leo, *MGH AA* iv. 1, pp. v ff.; W. Meyer, 'Über die Handschriften der Gedichte Fortunats', *Nachrichten von der königlichen Gesellschaften der Wissenschaften* (Göttingen), *phil.-hist. Klasse* (1908), pp. 82–114; R. Koebner, *Venantius Fortunatus. Seine Persönlichkeit und seine Stellung in der geistigen Kultur des Merowinger Reiches*, Beiträge zur Kulturgeschichte des Mittelalters und der Renaissance 22 (Leipzig and Berlin, 1915), pp. 125–43; and K. Langosch, *Geschichte der Textüberlieferung . . .* , ii, *Überlieferungsgeschichte der mittelalterlichen Literatur*, edd. H. Hunger and O. Stegmüller (Zürich, 1964), p. 40 and n. 89.

[4] On this manuscript see Bischoff, *Karl der Grosse*, ii, p. 238 and n. 38.

2. Below the Latin text are three apparatus, the purposes of which are as follows.

Apparatus i. The apparatus criticus records the evidence needed to determine what Alcuin wrote and to illustrate the affiliation of the manuscripts. It is not intended to provide a comprehensive history of scribal or editorial practice.[1]

Apparatus ii lists the principal sources and nearest analogues of the text.[2]

Apparatus iii contains evidence of Alcuin's use of repeated phrases, formulas, and clichés, traces the continuity of his poetic diction in his other works, notes the use of similar sources by poets contemporary with and later than Alcuin and records the influence of his poem on York.

The passages directly germane to these purposes are cited *verbatim*; in other cases a reference without quotation is provided. Square brackets indicate doubtful parallels, which are generally discussed in the Introduction and/or commentary, e.g.: *app.* ii and *app.* iii to vv. 1325[-6] with commentary ad loc.

3. Facing the Latin text is a Translation.

4. The commentary follows apparatus iii.

---

[1] Examples of readings excluded: v. 36 certatim *Mabillon*; v. 246 substernite *Froben*; v. 1272 vicibus *Froben*; etc.

[2] Dr M. T. Van Poll-van de Lisdonk's dissertation on the sources of vv. 1–604 (*Alcuins Versus de Sanctis Euboricensis Ecclesiae, vers 1–604. De Brunnen van een Carolingisch Epos* (Nijmegen, 1981) appeared after this book had gone to press. I will review it in *Medium Ævum*.)

SIGLA AND
EDITORIAL ABBREVIATIONS

R	Reims, Bibliothèque municipale 426 (*saec.* xii *in.*).
r	any variant or correction by the first or second scribe in *R*.
T	the readings of Ruinart's lost Saint-Remi manuscript as represented by the transcription of vv. 99–1205 (excluding v. 578) preserved in Trinity 1130 (0.2.26) (*saec.* xvii *ex.*).
T^1	variants in vv. 1–98 from Ruinart's lost Saint-Remi manuscript recorded in Trinity 1130.
T^2	variants of unspecified origin in vv. 1–98, 1205–1658 of Trinity 1130.
Gale	Gale's marginal or interlinear variants in Trinity 1130.
Ruinart	Ruinart's marginal or interlinear variants in Trinity 1130.

EDITIONS

Mabillon	J. Mabillon, 'Fragmentum Historiae De Pontificibus et Sanctis Ecclesiae Eboracensis, Scriptae à Poeta anonymo, Ælberti Episcopi discipulo, circiter annum DCCLXXXV', *AASSOSB Saeculum* III, Pars II (Paris, 1672), pp. 558-69.
Froben	F. Froben, 'Poema de Pontificibus et Sanctis Ecclesiae Eboracensis', *Beati Flacci Albini seu Alcuini abbatis, Caroli magni regis ac imperatoris, magistri Opera. Post primam editionem, a viro clarissimo D. A. QUERCE-TANO curatam, de novo collecta, multis locis emendata, et opusculis primum repertis plurimum aucta, variisque modis illustrata cura ac studio FROBENII, S.R.I. principis*

et abbatis ad S. Emmeramum Ratisbonae, ii. 1 (Regensburg, 1777), pp. 242-58 [= *PL* ci, cols. 812-48].

Wattenbach   W. Wattenbach, 'Alcuini de Pontificibus et Sanctis Ecclesiae Eboracensis Carmen', *Monumenta Alcuiniana*, edd. P. Jaffé, W. Wattenbach and E. Dümmler, *Bibliotheca Rerum Germanicarum*, vi (Berlin, 1873), pp. 80-131.

Raine   J. Raine, 'De Pontificibus et Sanctis Ecclesiae Eboracensis Carmen [Auctore Alcuino]', *The Historians of the Church of York and its Archbishops*, i (London, 1879), pp. 349-98.

Dümmler   E. Dümmler, '[Versus de Patribus Regibus et Sanctis Euboricensis Ecclesiae]', *MGH PLAC* i (Berlin, 1881), pp. 169-206.

Hargrove   M. L. Hargrove, 'Alcuin's Poem on York' (Ph.D. dissertation, Cornell University, 1937).

Godman   P. Godman, 'Alcuin's Poem on York and the Literature of his Times' (2 vols.) ii (Ph.D. dissertation, University of Cambridge, 1980).

SUPPLEMENTARY TEXTUAL CRITICISM

Dümmler, Add.   *MGH PLAC* i, *Addenda* p. 632.

Traube   L. Traube, *Karolingische Dichtungen*, Schriften zur Germanischen Philologie i (Berlin, 1888), p. 47.

VERSUS DE PATRIBUS REGIBUS ET SANCTIS EUBORICENSIS ECCLESIAE

VERSUS DE PATRIBUS REGIBUS ET SANCTIS EUBORICENSIS ECCLESIAE[a]

CHRISTE deus, summi virtus sapientia patris,
vita, salus, hominum factor, renovator, amator,
unica lingua Dei, donorum tu dator alme,
munera da mentis, fragili da verba poetae
irrorans stolidum vivaci flumine pectus,   5
ut mea lingua queat de te tua dicere dona;
te sine nulla valet dignum quid dicere lingua.
Vos quoque suppliciter cives contestor Olympi,
o sancti, populus fortis, gens diva Tonantis,
victrices aquilas caeli qui fertis in arcem   10
aethereo regi regalia dona ferentes,
qui vestri causa sacratum sponte cruorem

1 ff. A quodam sapiente facta dei sanctorumque eius invocacio in adiutorium sequentis sui operis hoc ponitur in prohemio *r in marg*: a quodam sapiente *Ruinart*

---

1 1 Cor. 1: 24 Christum Dei virtutem et Dei sapientiam; Sedul; *Carm. pasch.* i. 312; Paul. Nol. xxii. 135; Publ. Optat. Porf. xxiv. 18; *Syll. Epig. Cantab.* 23.1 1–2 Prosper *Carm. de Ingrat.* 979 vita salus virtus sapientia gratia Christi; Drac. *Laud. Dei* ii. 2   3 Paul. Nol. xvi. 213   4 Arat. *de Act. Apostol.* i. 227 munera da linguae, qui das in munere linguas; [id. *Ep. ad Parth.* 85]; Bede *Vit. S. Cuthb. metr.* 38 munera da verbi linguae tua dona canenti; Aldh. *de Virg. metr.* 37 auxilium fragili . . . dedere servo   5 id. *Ænigm. pref.* 15 inspirans stolidae pia gratis munera menti; Ven. Fort. *Vit. S. Mart.* i. 131 fontibus ingenii sitientia pectora rorans   6–7 Paul. Nol. xv. 45–6 tua non queo fari / te sine; id. ii. 3 quid dignum   7 Virg. *Georg.* iii. 42 te sine nil altum mens incohat; Bede *Vit. S. Cuthb. metr.* 36 Te sine nam digne fari tua gratia nescit 8–9 1 Petr. 2: 9 vos . . . gens sancta, populus; Paul. Nol. xxvii. 213 vos etiam, sancti, subplex deposco   10 Prud. *Psych.* 645 victrices aquilas; Aldh. *de Virg. metr.* 2287   11 Virg. *Aen.* ii. 49 dona ferentis

---

1 Alc. c. i. 1 Christe deus; id. xx. 8 patris virtus, sapientia Christus   2 *cf.* vv. 267, 1399; Paul. Diac. iv. 1. 28; Joseph Scott. v. 1   4 Hrab. Maur. xviii. 3 da munera linguae   5–6 Æthelw. *de Abbat.* 15–16   6 Paul. Diac. xxxiv. 1–3 Christe . . . / annue . . . ut tua . . . dona queamus / dicere   8 *cf.* v. 562; Alc. c. i. 6 vos quoque . . . rogo   10 *cf.* v. 569; Alc. cix. 17. 4

---

[a] Alcuin's poem descends to us without a title. The above title, by which it is generally known, is of editorial confection and adapted from vv. 1654–5. The copyist of his Saint-Remi manuscript, according to Ruinart (Introduction, p. cxvii), did not know who had written the poem. If Ruinart was correct in assigning this manuscript to the tenth century, then medieval knowledge of Alcuin's authorship

POEM ON THE BISHOPS, KINGS, AND SAINTS OF THE CHURCH OF YORK[a]

CHRIST divine, strength and wisdom of the Father Almighty,
life, salvation, creator, redeemer, and lover of mankind,
sole voice of God, kindly bestower of gifts,
grant inspiration, grant words to this feeble poet,
bedewing my dull heart with the waters of life
that by you my tongue may proclaim your gifts;
without you no tongue can speak worthily about you.
Citizens of Olympus, you too I humbly beseech,
o saints, valiant host, divine race of the Thunderer,
who bear the standards of victory to the heights of Heaven,
carrying royal gifts to the heavenly king,
who, for your sake, chose to shed his hallowed blood

had perished early in the poem's textual tradition. It is a reasonable assumption
(shared by both Ruinart and Gale) that vv. 1529-30 imply that Alcuin's name had
been affixed to the autograph. On the inscriptions and marginalia to the poem see
Introduction, pp. cxiv, cxvii-cxix, cxxi, cxxiv.

1 ff. The tripartite proemium—1. invocation of Christ (vv. 1-7); 2. appeal to
the saints (vv. 8-16); and 3. statement of theme (vv. 16-18)—introduces Alcuin's
account of Roman York. Parts 1 and 2 of Alcuin's proemium are modelled chiefly
on the late antique Biblical epic (see Introduction, pp. lxix-lxx, lxxx-lxxxii,
lxxxviii-lxxxix, with bibliography). New to Medieval Latin narrative poetry is
Part 3: the statement of Alcuin's historical and regional theme (comm. to vv.
16-18). On conventions of the proemium in Latin narrative poetry earlier than
and contemporary with Alcuin, see D. Schaller, *Fm. St.* 10 (1976) pp. 140 ff.
(with bibliography) and Klopsch, *Einführung* pp. 7 ff. On the stylistic features of
this proemium see Introduction, p. ciii (iii) (*a*) 2.

1. **deus**: one of Alcuin's less common adjectival uses of the substantive (Intro-
duction p. xciv (i) (*a*)). For the vocative, see Löfstedt, *Syntactica*, i², pp. 92 ff.
On its use in invocations cf Schaller-Könsgen, pp. 165 ff.

2. **renovator**: see Introduction, p. cii 3. Cf. 2 Cor. 5: 17 and the liturgical
terms for redemption listed by Blaise, *Vocabulaire latin*, pp. 375-6.

3. Christ is invoked as divine *Logos*.

6. **de[te]**: causal-instrumental (and antithetical to *te sine* at v. 7). For the
replacement of the causal and instrumental ablative by *de* cf. Leumann-Hofmann-
Szantyr, ii, p. 261; Löfstedt, *Kommentar*, p. 104. On Alcuin's use of this preposi-
tion, see Introduction, pp. xcvi-xcvii (*e*).

8-9. **Olympi . . . Tonantis**: the application of these Classical allusions to a
Christian subject, frequent in late and early Medieval Latin verse, is an integral
feature of Alcuin's poem (Introduction, pp. ciii (iii) (*a*) 2 *ad fin.*) and serves to
heighten his style. Only once (vv. 747 ff., with comm. ad loc.) are the pagan and
Christian deities opposed.

fuderat in terris, ut vos salvaret ab umbris
inque Dei patris secum deduceret aulam!
Mecum ferte pedes, vestris componite carmen   15
hoc precibus, patriae quoniam mens dicere laudes
et veteres cunas properat proferre parumper
Euboricae raris praeclarae versibus urbis!
Hanc Romana manus muris et turribus altam
fundavit primo, comites sociosque laborum   20
indigenas tantum gentes adhibendo Britannas—
nam tunc Romanos fecunda Britannia reges
sustinuit, merito mundi qui sceptra regebant—
HE ii. 3   *ut foret emporium terrae commune marisque*
et fieret ducibus secura potentia regni   25
et decus imperii terrorque hostilibus armis;
esset ab extremo venientibus hospita portu

13 vos *r*: quos *R*   15 pedes *R*: preces *Froben*   componite *R*: com-
mendite *Traube*   18 raris *R*: gratis *T*^{2} 23 sustinuit merito, *Dümmler*
27 portu *R*: portus *Froben*

---

13 Juvenc. *Evang.* iii. 1 fuderat in terras   15 Virg. *Georg.* i. 11 ferte simul . . .
pedem   16 id. *Ecl.* vi. 6 dicere laudes   17 id. *Aen.* iii. 105
18 ibid. iv. 655   19 1 Mcc. 4: 60; *cf. Laud. Mediol. civ.* i–iv (1–12); *Laud.
Veron. civ.* ii (4–6)   20 Stat. *Silv.* v. 2. 35 comitem belli sociumque laborum
22 Aldh. *de Virg. metr.* 878 fecunda Britannia cives; [Ven. Fort. viii. 3. 155 (=
Bede, *HE* i. 7)]   23 Aldh. *de Virg. metr.* 1095 mundi qui sceptra regebat; Gild.
de Excid. v. 1 reges Romanorum cum orbis imperium obtinuissent   25 Ps.
144: 11   26 Lucan *Bell. civ.* ix. 747; Virg. *Aen.* xi. 83 hostilibus armis
27–8 id. *Georg.* iii. 362 puppibus . . . hospita

---

13 *cf.* v. 580   15 *cf.* vv. 1408–9 versifico . . . pergere gressu / . . . mecum
18 Moduin, *Egloga* ii. 36 carmina rara   19 *cf.* vv. 38, 196   22 Alc.
Vit. S. Willibr. metr. i. 5 fecunda Britannia [ibid. xxxiii. 3]   26 Alc. lxxxii. 2

15. Traube's conjecture *commendite* is attractive and consistent with Alcuin's
poetic style (cf. xx. 25; li. 5.5 *et passim*). *Componite*, however, completes the in-
vocation. Alcuin calls first on Christ and then on the saints to inspire his poem:
by a well-attested *topos* the poet is represented as the instrument of divine or
saintly will (cf. Klopsch, *Einführung*, pp. 24–5).

16–18. This is the earliest instance in extant Medieval Latin of a major narra-
tive poem which begins with praise of a country and a city. See Curtius, pp.
157–8; Introduction, pp. xlvii–xlviii (on this poem and the urban encomium) and
pp. xlviii–xlix, li, lv, lx (on Alcuin's sense of *patria*); comm. to v. 30.

mens . . . properat: Among the sources known to Alcuin I have found no true
parallel for this expression. As at v. 7 so here Alcuin may have adapted Virg.
Georg. iii. 42 (*mens incohat*). For *mens* in the sense of 'will' or 'intention' see
T.L.L. VIII, 725, II A, 26, 44 ff. and with verbs ibid. 731 II A, 4. 62–78. (Note-
worthy CL examples of the idiom include Horace, *Ep.* i, 14, 8 and Ovid, *Met.* i, 1).
For the convention see Curtius, *Z.f.r.Ph.* 59 (1939) p. 137.

on earth to save you from the shades and
lead you away with him into the mansion of God the Father.
Keep pace with me, compose this my poem with your prayers,
for my mind is eager to speak in praise of my homeland
and swiftly to proclaim the ancient foundation
of York's famed city in rare verse!
York, with its high walls and lofty towers, was first built
by Roman hands, that summoned only the native Britons
as comrades and partners in the labour—
for at that time the Romans, rightly supreme
throughout the world, held fertile Britain in their sway—
to be a general seat of commerce by land and sea alike,
both a powerful dominion, secure for its masters, and an
ornament to the empire, a dread bastion against enemy attack;
as a haven for ocean-going ships from the farthest ports,

18. raris: The sense ('scant' or 'meagre' rather than 'excellent' and antitheti-
cal to *praeclaris*) represents only a slight extension of this word's numerical con-
notations at v. 535. Cf. vv. 431, 437, 741-6, 783, and 1649-56, where Alcuin
emphasizes, in a self-deprecatory manner, that his treatment of his theme should
be brief, twice (vv. 437, 742) using verbs of rapid movement like *properat* at
v. 17. There is no exact parallel to this usage in CL, the nearest being Stat. *Theb.*
ii 377. In early Carolingian poetry Moduin of Autun (*app.* iii ad loc) is closest.

19 ff. Alcuin's account of the foundation of York owes nothing to any extant
literary source. Archaeological evidence shows, however, that some of the build-
ings of Roman York were still extant in Alcuin's lifetime. The *principia* of the
legionary fortress continued to be used and repaired into the late Saxon period.
A stone tower on the fortress wall between the western angle and the north-west
gate was built, possibly c.650, to strengthen and supplement the Roman defences.
Of these, only the north-west and north-east sides remained in use. Evidence is
summarized by M. Biddle in *Archaeology*, p. 117, with p. 145, nn. 131-6. For a
survey of the monuments of Roman York see *Ebvracvm.* Recent accounts of the
Roman foundation of York in *Soldier and Civilian*, pp. 45-54, and of its early
defences ibid., pp. 97-106; Salway, pp. 325-8. On the growth and development
of the city, see *Bibliography*, C (v) pp. xxx-xxxi.

22-3. This is Alcuin's only reference to Roman rule over Britain. Elsewhere
he refers chiefly to Romanist tradition in the Church (*MGH Epp.* iv, p. 627, cols.
2-3 and Introduction, pp. xlix, li-lii). On the political usage of *Britannia*, see
E. John, *Orbis Britanniae* (Leicester, 1966), pp. 5 ff. and comm. to v. 88.

24. emporium: Alcuin adapts Bede's description of London (*HE* ii. 3 'mult-
orum emporium populorum terra marique venientium'). See further vv. 36-7
with comm.

25-6. York was a centre of land communications for the Roman legions. On
its strategic importance see *Ebvracvm*, pp. xxix ff., 1-48; *Soldier and Civilian*,
pp. 55 ff.; Salway, pp. 136-7, 221-2, 384, 528, 564.

27-9. Sea-going ships of this period could navigate the Ouse. Supplies were
also conveyed by the water transport which linked York with the Fenland
(*Ebvracvm*, p. xxxi). On the commercial significance of Roman York see
Ebvracvm, pp. 49-144 and *Soldier and Civilian*, pp. 127-42.

navibus oceani, longo sua prora remulco
navita qua properans iam sistat ab aequore fessus.
Hanc piscosa suis undis interluit Usa 30
florigeros ripis praetendens undique campos;
collibus et silvis tellus hinc inde decora:
nobilibusque locis habitatio pulchra, salubris
fertilitate sui multos habitura colonos.
Quo variis populis et regnis undique lecti 35
spe lucri veniunt quaerentes divite terra
divitias, sedem sibimet, lucrumque laremque.
Hinc Romana manus turbatis undique sceptris
postquam secessit cupiens depellere saevos
hostes Hesperiae regnum sedemque tueri, 40
urbis tunc tenuit sceptrum gens pigra Britonum.
HE i. 12-13 Quae fere continuis Pictorum pressa duellis
servitii pondus tandem vastata subivit,
nec valuit propriis patriam defendere scutis
vel libertatem gladiis revocare paternam. 45
Est antiqua, potens bellis et corpore praestans
Germaniae populos gens inter et extera regna,

28 occeani *R*: oceano T^2 prora *R*: vela T^2 36 spe lucri T^1: sepulcri *R*

28-9 Isid. *Etym.* xix. 4. 8 Hic mea me longo succedens prora remulco / laetantem gratis sistit in hospitiis   29 Virg. *Aen.* v. 715   30 ibid. iii. 418-19   34 Arat. *de Act. Apostol.* i. 99 fertilitate sui; Lucan *Bell. civ.* iv. 807 civisque habitura beatos   35 Virg. *Aen.* viii. 723; Arat. *de Act. Apostol.* i. 553   37 Virg. *Georg.* iii. 344 tectumque laremque   38 ff. Gild. *de Excid.* xviii   40 Virg. *Aen.* iv. 355 regno Hesperiae   41 ff. Gild. *de Excid.* xix-xxi   42 Bede *Vit. S. Cuthb. metr.* 610 Pictorum . . . premeret dum regna duello   43 Juvenc. *Evang.* iii. 480 servitiique premit . . . pondere   44 Virg. *Aen.* ii. 447   44-5 Lucan *Bell. civ.* ii. 282   46 Virg. *Aen.* i. 531 antiqua, potens armis; ibid. i. 71   47 ibid. iv. 350 extera regna

28 Alc. iv. 4 praelongo . . . prora remulco   30-2 Alc. xxiii. 3-5, 7-8 Undique te cingit ramis resonantibus arbos, / silvula florigeris semper onusta comis. / Prata salutiferis florebunt omnia et herbis / . . . flumina te cingunt florentibus undique ripis, / retia piscator qua sua tendit ovans   31 *cf.* v. 968   33 Alc. xxiii. 1   35 Poet. Saxo i. 299   35 ff. *'Karolus Magnus'* 495-6   40 ff. Poet. Saxo ii. 211 ff.   41-5 Alc. *Ep.* 17 (p. 47, 17 ff.) Legitur vero in libro Gildi . . . quod . . . ipsi Brettones propter . . . pigritiam . . . et malos mores populi patriam perdiderunt   42 Poet. Saxo i. 324 continui premerentur pondere belli   44-5 *cf.* v. 60   45 Poet. Saxo i. 348 libertate . . . prisca patriaque carerent   46 Alc. *Vit. S. Willibr. metr.* xxi. 1 Est antiqua, potens muris et turribus ampla   46-8 id. *Ep.* 17 (p. 47, 12 ff.) Patres itaque nostri, Deo dispensante, licet pagani, hanc patriam bellica virtute . . . possederunt

where the eager sailor, weary from the sea, could
at last moor his ship with its long tow-rope.
Through York flows the Ouse, its waters teeming with fish,
along its banks stretch fields laden with flowers,
all about the countryside is lovely with hills and woods,
and this beautiful, healthy place of noble setting
was destined to attract many settlers by its richness.
To York from divers peoples and kingdoms all over the world,
they come in hope of gain, seeking wealth from the rich land,
a home, a fortune, and a hearth-stone for themselves.
After the Roman troops, their empire in turmoil,
had withdrawn, intending to rout their savage foe
and to defend Italy, their native realm,
the slothful race of Britons then held sway over York.
Overwhelmed by almost unending struggle against the Picts,
finally vanquished, they yielded to burdensome slavery,
unable to shield their fatherland or with the sword to regain
the liberty enjoyed by their forefathers.
Between the peoples of Germany and the outlying realms
there is an ancient race, powerful in war, of splendid physique,

28. **sua prora**: Here neut. acc. pl; but see Introduction p. xciv (i) (*a*).

30 ff. A standard feature of the ancient and early medieval urban encomium (Curtius, pp. 157 ff., pp. 195 ff., C. J. Classen, *Die Stadt im Spiegel der descriptiones und laudes urbium* (Hildesheim and N.Y., 1980) pp. 37 ff.), this description of the site of York as an ideal landscape was adapted by Alcuin later in the 790s in his *Carm*. xxiii, an elegy on his second intellectual and spiritual home at Aachen (cf. app. iii ad loc. and Godman, *SM* (3ª Ser.) 20.2 (1979), pp. 555-83).

33. **habitatio** occurs only twice in eighth-century poetry: here and at Alcuin *Carm*. xxiii. 1. On this usage see *TLL* vi. 3. 2469-70. 2B. II 2. 64 ff.

35-6. In the eighth century there was a colony of Frisian merchants at York (Altger, *Vita Liutgeri*, i. 12 (*MGH SS* ii, p. 408) [= Whitelock, pp. 788-9]).

36-7. Evidence for commercial activity at York between the Roman occupation and Alcuin's times is slight. Three York 'thrymsas' of the seventh century (described in C. H. V. Sutherland, *Anglo-Saxon Gold Coinage* . . . (London, 1948), p. 94, no. 75 a-c, discussed by P. Grierson, *British Numismatic Journal*, 31 (1962), pp. 8 ff.) suggest the maintenance there, as in the south-east, of a gold standard (M. Dolley, *Archaeology*, p. 351). See further D. M. Metcalf in *Coins and the Archaeologist*, edd. J. Casey and R. Reece, British Archaeological Reports 4 (Oxford, 1974), pp. 206 ff., especially p. 211, and I. Stewart in *Scripta Nummaria Romana*, edd. R. Carson and C. Kraay (London, 1978), p. 155 (on the Wigmund *solidus*).

38 ff. See H. G. Ramm, *Soldier and Civilian*, pp. 179-200, and P. Hunter Blair, 'The Origins of Northumbria', *Archaeologia Aeliana* (Ser. 4) 25 (1947), pp. 1-51.

41-5. The disdain for the Britons, implicit at vv. 21-2, is now made plain. See further comm. to vv. 71-9.

duritiam propter dicti cognomine saxi.
HE i. 14 Hanc placuit ducibus donis conducere missis,
ut foret auxilio patriae pavor hostibus atque.   50
Ore favet vulgus clamoso mobile statim
et bona collaudat patrum consulta suorum.
Atria gazarum rumpunt regalia, genti
mittere dona parant ignotae, quo magis illa
annuat, ut placitae feriant sibi foedera pacis.   55
Ast ubi digna vident tantis exenia votis,
legatos exire iubent, vada salsa carinis
iam sulcare citis. Ducti formidine vota
ingeminant lacrimis, quoniam sic ipse monebat
libertatis amor, patriae spes ac redimendae.   60
HE i. 15 Quid tibi plura canam? Properans exercitus ecce
venerat undosi vectus trans aequora ponti
subsidium sociis referens, hostemque nefandum
expulit et vicit multis per bella triumphis
donec Pictus atrox timido simul agmine fugit,   65
contentus propriis sese defendere in oris.

48 duritiam propter dicti *R*: duritiam[2] dicti propter $\overset{1}{\text{propter}}$ T^2 saxi *Traube*: Saxi
edd.   49 donis conducere missis *r*: donis conducere regnis *R*: donis condu-
cere regni *Mabillon*: dŏnis conducere [4] regni T^2 52 collaudat *Mabillon*: col-
ladat *R*   54 illa T^1: illi *R*   56 ubi digna *R*: indigna *Mabillon*
58 ducti *H. Caplan (Hargrove, pp. 50, 251-2)*: dulci *R*   59 monebat *R*:
movebat T^1 (*del.*)   61 tibi T^1 *R*: iam *Mabillon*   64 per T^1 *R*: post
Mabillon   65 Pictus atrox *Munari*: Picto ferox *Mabillon*: Pocto ferox *R*
66 *sic* T^1 *R edd.*: *om. Mabillon*

48 Isid. *Etym*. ix. 2. 100 Saxonum gens . . . appellata quod sit durum et validis-
simum genus hominum; Ven. Fort. iii. 9. 103; Virg. *Aen*. i. 530 cognomine dicunt
49 Gild. *de Excid*. xxii   50 Ven. Fort. ix. 1. 25   55 Lucan *Bell*.
civ. iv. 365 placuerunt foedera pacis; Aldh. *de Virg. metr*. 779   57 Virg. *Aen*.
v. 158 sulcant vada salsa carina [Arat. *de Act. Apostolorum* i. 989]   58-9 Virg.
Aen. iii. 261 votis precibusque iubent exposcere pacem; Bede *Vit. S. Cuthb. metr*.
340-1 precamina . . . / vocibus ingeminat   59 Virg. *Aen*. vii. 110
sic . . . ipse monebat   60 ibid. vi. 821, 3 pro libertate . . . / . . . amor patriae
62 Virg. *Georg*. i. 469   62 ff. Gild. *de Excid*. xxiii   64 Ven. Fort.
Vit. S. Mart. i. 264   65 Paul. Nol. xxvi. 192

48 *cf*. vv. 657, 1013, 1289; Alc. *Vit. S. Willibr. metr*. xxxiii. 13 dictus cogno-
mine; Poet. Saxo i. 32; [Widukind *Res gest. Sax*. 6, 7]   55 Alc. lx. 9
58-9 Ermold. *In hon. Hlud*. iv. 523 ingeminantque preces precibus   60 *cf*.
v. 118; Poet. Saxo i. 105 libertatis iam spes viteque tenende   61 *cf*. vv.

called by the name of 'rock' because of its toughness. This
people the Britons' leaders tried to enlist by sending bribes
to protect their fatherland and ward off their foe.
With loud applause the fickle commoners at once
praised and approved their elders' decrees.
Bursting open the royal treasure-troves, they prepared gifts
to send to the unknown people and gain its assent
to striking an acceptable treaty of peace.
When they felt that their gifts matched their high hopes
they sent emissaries swiftly to sail across the briny ocean.
Driven by fear, with tears in their eyes, they redoubled
promise upon promise, spurred on by love of liberty
and the hope of regaining their fatherland.
Let my poem be brief. In haste an army came,
borne over the billowing ocean-waves,
bringing aid to its allies, driving out the dread foe,
victorious and triumphant in many a battle,
until, in faltering rank, the barbarous Picts fled,
glad to defend themselves on their own shores.

1409, 1654; Alc. xliv. 49 quid tibi plura canam   65–6 *'Karolus Magnus'* 536
propriisque repulsus ab oris

48. For the reading of *R*, cf. anastrophe with *propter* at vv. 473, 817, 1353,
1480.

saxi / Saxi: Editorial capitalization implies a proper name. Alcuin never uses
the noun *Saxus* for Saxon: he always uses *Saxones* (vv. 123, 482, 1050) or
Saxonia (583). His poetic usage is in keeping with his prose usage, and with that
of Bede. For the construction *dictus cognomine*, cf. vv. 657, 1013–14, 1289.
With the word-play *saxum / Saxo*, cf. v. 1545 *Basilius . . . Fulgentius . . . coruscant*.
On Alcuin's attitude to the pagan Anglo-Saxon forefathers see app. iii to vv. 46–8
and Introduction, p. xlviii.

49 ff. Archaeological evidence for the presence of Saxon *foederati* at York is
summarized by Cramp, *Anglian and Viking York*, p. 2 with nn. 5–6.

50. End-stopped *atque* is eschewed in CL verse. *Atque* in final position is
found in classical poets but is not attested as the final word in the sentence. See
the useful survey in O. Schumann, *Lateinisches Hexameter-Lexikon*, i, A–C,
(Munich, 1979), pp. 155 ff.

60. **patriae spes**: Alcuin's poem on Northumbrian history, partly for metrical
reasons, contains no specific term for Northumbria. *Patria*, employed (as here)
in a broad sense, can point a contrast between man's earthly and heavenly home-
lands (e.g. v. 1015) and refer not only to Northumbria (e.g. v. 239) but also
to foreign parts (v. 463). Cf. comm. to v. 88. On Alcuin's departure here from
Gildas and Bede see Introduction, pp. xlviii–xlix.

61. The specific audience of the poem, as vv. 1409 ff. make clear, is the
studious youth trained at York by Ælberht and his successors. For the reading
tibi cf. app. iii ad loc; but see also Alc. ix 111.

Haec inter maiora dari stipendia poscit
externus sibimet miles: haec causa duelli
in sociam fuerat gentem convertere ferrum
et segnem populum patrio depellere regno.　　　　70
Hoc pietate Dei visum, quod gens scelerata
ob sua de terris patrum peccata periret
intraretque suas populus felicior urbes,
qui servaturus Domini praecepta fuisset.
Quod fuit affatim factum, donante Tonante　　　75
iam nova dum crebris viguerunt sceptra triumphis
et reges ex se iam coepit habere potentes
gens ventura Dei. Rexit tunc temporis almus
HE i. 23, ii. 1　Gregorius praesul, toto venerabilis orbi,
ecclesiae sedem Romanae maximus, atque　　　80
agrorum Christi cultor devotus ubique
plurima perpetuae dispersit semina vitae.
Vomere nec solum Latios confregerat agros,
sed bonus atque pius peregrini cultor agelli
oceani tumidos ultra sulcavit aratro　　　85
[596]　pectora divini fluctus gentilia Verbi
arida mellifluis perfundens arva fluentis,
de quibus aequorei potus hausere Britanni
iam sibi perpetuae, Christo donante, salutis.
HE ii. 12　Eduin interea veterum de germine regum,　　　90

69 Virg. *Aen.* ix. 427　　　70 ibid. i. 620 finibus expulsum patriis
72 Lev. 26: 38-9 peribitis inter gentes . . . et propter peccata patrum suorum et sua
adfligentur; Virg. *Aen.* ix. 137 ferro sceleratam exscindere gentem　　　74 Joh.
15: 10　　　79 Ven. Fort. viii. 16. 3 toto venerabilis orbe　　　82 Sedul.
Carm. pasch. i. 55 semina vitae　　　84 Aldh. *de Virg. metr.* 2750 cultor agelli
85-6 Ven. Fort. *Vit. S. Mart.* iii. 161 alloquiis fera pectora cultor arare　87 Aldh.
Carm. eccl. iv. 10. 14 arida divinis irrorans corda scatebris; Is. 44: 3 effundam
aquam super sitientem et fluenta super aridam　　　88 Prosper *Epigr.* (*PL* li. cols.
151, 194) aequorei . . . Britanni [= *HE* i. 10]　　　89 Aldh. *de Virg. metr.* 1089
Christo donante, salute　　　90 Ven. Fort. iv. 8. 11

74 *cf.* v. 1231　　　75. Alc. xxviii. 25 donante Tonante　　　79 Alc. ix.
49. id. cx. 17. 1 praesul, toto venerabilis orbe　　　82 *cf.* vv. 206, 1012
87 *cf.* v. 1432; Alc. lxxxix. 5. 4 imbribus aethereis arida rura rigans　　　89 *cf.*
vv. 581, 609; Alc. *Vit. S. Willibr. metr.* viii. 5 perpetuae, Christo pandente,
salutis

71-9. Like Gildas, Alcuin employs the language of Scripture to censure the
Britons; but he goes beyond both Gildas and Bede in this panegyric of the Saxons
as God's people. By v. 78 the *externus miles* of v. 68 has become the new Israel.

In the meantime the foreign soldiers demanded higher pay:
this was the cause of the conflict which turned the sword
against an ally and drove a slothful people
from its ancestral kingdom. In His goodness
God determined that the wicked race
should lose its fathers' kingdoms for its wrongdoing
and that a more fortunate people should enter its cities,
a people destined to follow the Lord's commands.
God's will was abundantly fulfilled: for, by His grace, through
repeated victories a new power came into the ascendant
and God's destined race began to produce
from its own ranks powerful kings.
At that time the blessed Gregory, universally revered,
ruled as supreme pontiff the see of Rome.
A thoroughly ardent tiller of the fields of Christ,
he scattered abroad manifold seeds of everlasting life.
Not only did he plough the fields of Latium,
but, a kindly and pious tiller of foreign fields, far beyond the
reaches of the swelling ocean, with the plough of God's word
he furrowed too the hearts of pagans,
on those dry fields pouring honey-sweet waters, from
which the Britons, dwellers by the sea, quenched their thirst
in draughts of everlasting salvation granted by Christ.
 Meanwhile Edwin, the descendant of ancient kings,

On the terms *gens* and *populus* see H. Vollrath-Reichelt, *Königsgedanke und Königtum bei den Angelsachsen*, Kölner Historische Abhandlungen (Cologne and Vienna, 1971), pp. 43 ff.

 79 ff. The cult of Gregory the Great (*c.*540–604), celebrated at length by his anonymous Whitby biographer and by Bede, was commemorated by a *porticus* or chapel in the cathedral church of St. Peter's at York (as at Canterbury and Whitby), in which the head of King Edwin was buried. Bede counselled Egbert, archbishop of York, to study Gregory's *Cura Pastoralis* (Plummer, i, p. 406), and Alcuin gave the same advice to archbishop Eanbald II (*Ep.* 113, *MGH Epp.* iv, p. 166. 9–13). The metrical Calendar of York, contemporary with Alcuin, records Gregory's feast-day at v. 14. Vv. 79 ff. of this poem are the first full expression of the saint's cult in Anglo-Latin poetry. See further Introduction, p. xlix.

 86-7. For the metaphor, see D. Schaller, *Mlat. Jb.* 1 (1964), pp. 59–64.

 88. aequorei . . . Britanni: the expression occurs only once in the *HE* where it is borrowed from Prosper of Aquitaine (Plummer ii, p. 22). Alcuin uses it elsewhere in his poem (vv. 140, 461, 567) to describe the territory or people of Britain. The term *Britannus*, in his usage, can refer both to the native Britons (v. 123) and to the Anglo-Saxons (vv. 455, 723), just as *Britannia* is applied indifferently to Roman Britain (v. 22) and Anglo-Saxon England (vv. 233, 433, 501).

Euborica genitus, dominus per cuncta futurus,
pulsus in exsilium fugit puer invida regna
oroma gentilis qua viderat ipse supernum
nocte soporata, solus dum tempore quodam
anxia corda gerens curis loca congrua adivit   95
et tacitus sedit sublustri lumine lunae.
Vir stetit ignotus habitu vultuque repente
ante oculos iuvenis, verbisque affatur amicis:
'Quae te dura coquit, iuvenum fortissime, cura?
Rex Deus aeternus caeli qui sidera fecit,   100
quae tu pulchra vides, solatia dat tibi certa.
Ecce tuam vitam quaerenti servat ab hoste;
insuper imperium latum tibi terminat undis:
rex Deus ille tibi totum sit semper in aevum!'
Imponensque suo capiti pro foedere dextram: 105
'Haec tibi', dixit, 'erunt nostri signacula pacti.'
Nuntius his dictis subito discessit ab illo.
Cui vigor affatim venas discurrit in omnes,
pulsa procul fugiens et desperatio fibras
liquerat. Eventus venientis dicta probavit   110
hospitis: occubuit statim rex ense nefando
invidus imperii vitae simul illius atque.
Tunc iuvenis rediens intravit amabilis urbes
iam patrias, populi procerumque favore receptus.

93 oroma R: orama Mabillon   95 adivit T¹ R: deinde Mabillon   gerens
curis, Dümmler   104 sit semper T: semper sit r: semper R   105 suo
R: tuo T   107 his T: iis R   108 discurrit R: decurrit T   113 tunc
T: tun R   114 iam T: in R

92 Virg. Aen. x. 852 pulsus ob invidiam solio sceptrisque paternis   93 Aldh.
de Virg. metr. 1276 oroma per noctem cernebat rite supernum   94 Bede
Vit. S. Cuthb. metr. 775 soporata . . . nocte   95 Paul. Nol. xvi. 45 anxia corda
regens; Aldh. de Virg. metr. 2048   96 Paul. Nol. xviii. 372 sublustri lumine
noctis   97 id. vi. 41 vultuque habituque   98 Bede, Vit. S. Cuthb.
metr. 500 dictisque illam . . . affatur amicis; [Virg. Aen. x. 466]   99 Virg.
Aen. vii. 345 curaeque . . . coquebant; id. Georg. iv. 445   100 Prud. Apoth.
153 qui lucida sidera fecit   102 Jr. 19:9   103 Virg. Aen.
i. 287 imperium oceano . . . terminat   104 id., Ecl. i. 7 erit ille mihi semper
deus   106 ibid. v. 74 haec tibi . . . erunt   110 Gen. 41: 13 postea
. . . rei probavit eventus   112 Ecclus. 18: 33   113-14 Virg. Aen. xi.
793

93 Alc. Vit. S. Willibr. pr. ii intempesta noctis quiete caeleste in somnis vidit
oroma   93-4 Paulin. Aquil. v. 7. 1-2 in nocte soporatus . . . / vidit
somnia   95 Alc. Vit. S. Willibr. metr. xxxiv. 42 loca . . . congrua corde suo

a native of York and the future lord of all the land,
was driven into exile as a boy and fled the realms of his foes.
There, while still a pagan, he witnessed in the depths of night
a vision sent from on high. Once, lonely and careworn,
he came to a spot which suited his mood, and sat in silence
by the glimmering light of the moon. Suddenly before
the young man's eyes appeared a man, strangely dressed and of
unfamiliar appearance, who addressed him in friendly words:
'What care torments you so, brave young man?
God the everlasting king, who made the stars in Heaven,
that you see in their beauty, grants you certainty and support.
Lo, he will save you from the enemy who seeks to take your life,
and limit your wide empire only by the waves:
let him be your God and king for all time!'
Placing his right hand on Edwin's head in token of a promise:
'Let this', said he, 'be a sign of our bond.'
With these words the messenger suddenly left him.
Strength coursed through his veins
and despair, put to rout, fled his being.
The outcome proved the stranger's words: for
the king, who coveted Edwin's kingdom and menaced his life,
soon perished by the murderous sword.
Then the young man returned once more to his ancestral cities,
popular and acclaimed by the people and nobles alike.

100 *cf.* v. 104   104 *cf.* v. 155   105 *cf.* v. 1199

---

91. Euborica genitus: Bede never says that Edwin was born at York. Alcuin's statement may reflect an authentic tradition, or it may be part of his general attempt to focus the events of Edwin's reign on that city.

92-3 ff. exsilium . . . qua: Edwin fled from his enemy, Æthelfrith of Northumbria, first to Mercia and then to the court of Raedwald, king of the East Angles. His exile is incisively set in historical context by J. Campbell, *Bede's 'Reges' and 'Principes'* (Jarrow Lecture, 1979), pp. 9-10.

In what follows Alcuin departs from Bede's narrative in two chief respects: he omits Æthelfrith's attempt to have Edwin assassinated (*HE* ii. 12) and he places the account of Edwin's *imperium*, marriage, and reception of Paulinus (*HE* ii. 9 [= vv. 131 ff.]) after the vision described at *HE* ii. 12 [= vv. 90-119]. The entire events of Edwin's reign are made to proceed from this prophetic vision.

101. solatia = 'support', 'help'; see Löfstedt, *Late Latin*, pp. 148-9.

110. The victory of Edwin's protector Raedwald over Æthelfrith at the battle of the river Idle in 616 led to Edwin's acceptance as king in both Bernicia and Deira.

114. iam: Alcuin uses *intrare* twelve times in the poem, eleven of them transitively, without the preposition *in*; cf. vv. 73, 344, etc. (the exception is v. 982 with *quo*). *In* therefore runs counter to his poetic usage. For *iam* cf. v. 29.

[616] Qui mox accipiens sceptri regalis honorem 115
quaesivit propriae genti bona, largus in omnes,
nec per sceptra ferox, sed de pietate benignus,
factus amor populi, patriae pater, et decus aulae,
assiduis superans hostilia castra triumphis,
HE ii. 5, 9 imperioque suo gentes superaddidit omnes, 120
finibus atque plagis qua tenditur insula longa.
Iamque iugum regis prona cervice subibant
Saxonum populus, Pictus Scotusque, Britannus.
HE ii. 16 Interea placida regni dum pace tribunal
rexerat armipotens, sopitis undique bellis, 125
iustitiae validis populos frenabat habenis.
Nec rapit arma furor, legum sub pondere pressus
ultrices timuit capiti quia quisque secures,
provida ni toto servaret pectore scita,
quae posuit populis rector servanda subactis. 130
HE ii. 9 Accipit uxorem australi de parte fidelem,
moribus egregiam patrumque ab origine claram
[625] omnibus ac sanctae Fidei virtutibus almam.
Cui datur antistes vitae servator honestae,
nomine Paulinus, civis clarissimus urbis 135
Romanae, magno meritorum fretus honore,
qui fuit ore simul verax et pectore prudens,

115 sceptri *T*: regni *R* 116 propriae genti *T*: propria egenti *R*
121 longa *T R*: longe *Froben* 128 capiti *R*: capitis *T* 134 datur
T r: dator *R* 135 civis *r*: cives *T R* 137 pectore *R Gale*: pectora *T*

---

115 Aldh. *Carm. eccl.* iv. 12. 4 regni sceptra regebat 116 1 Macc. 14:4
quaesivit bona genti suae 117 Paul. Nol. xxi. 43 pietate benignus 118 Ven.
Fort. vii. 16. 37 amor populi; id. viii. 21. 6 pater patriae 119 Aldh. *de
Virg. metr.* 2020 assiduis . . . triumphis 122 Jr. 27: 11 gens quae subiecerit
cervicem suam sub iugo regis; Bede *Vit. S. Cuthb. metr.* 403 124–5 Virg.
Aen. viii. 325 placida populos in pace regebat 126 Aldh. *Carm. eccl.* i. 4
populi . . . frena gubernant 127 Virg. *Aen.* i. 150 furor arma ministrat;
Aldh. *de Virg. metr.* 2401 pondere pressus; Ven. Fort. vi. 2. 86 pondera . . . legum
128 Virg. *Aen.* ii. 130 quae sibi quisque timebat 132 id., *Georg.* iv. 286
134 Lucan *Bell. civ.* ii. 389 servator honesti 137 Aldh. *de Virg. metr.*
1130 prudens pectore

---

115 *cf.* vv. 576, 1274 118 Alc. xlv. 3 amor populi; id. vii. 15 pater o
patriae, decus; 'Karolus Magnus' 92 amor populique decusque 119 *cf.* vv.
254, 1330; Alc. *Vit. S. Willibr. metr.* ix. 2 gentes superando triumphis 127 Alc.
ix. 189 132 *cf.* vv. 268, 649 134 Paul. Diac. iv. 1. 19 136 *cf.*
v. 1219

Readily accepting the royal office of king, he sought
the best interests of his people; generous to all, not harsh
in the exercise of power, but gentle and kindly, he became the
nation's idol, father of his country, the paragon of the court.
Ever victorious over the camps of the foe,
he annexed to his own empire all the peoples
that this long island holds within its far-flung bounds.
And now in total submission there came under his kingly yoke
the Saxon peoples, the Picts, Irish, and Britons.
In the calm of peace throughout his realm,
this warrior-king ruled as a judge, with war at a lull,
holding his peoples in check with firm reins of justice.
Under the weight of law, men's anger turned not to violence,
since everyone feared the axe of vengeance on his own head,
if he failed wholeheartedly to observe the wise decrees
which the leader had determined his subjects should uphold.
Edwin took a wife from the South country,
a faithful woman of excellent character and illustrious descent,
endowed with all the virtues of the holy Faith.
Accompanying her was a priest staunch in the upright life
called Paulinus, a Roman citizen of high renown
and great distinction assured by his own achievements.
His words were truthful and his heart was wise,

120. imperium: on this much-discussed term see now Vollrath-Reichelt (op. cit.) pp. 79 ff. (with bibliography).

123. Alcuin, as noted by Dümmler, *MGH PLAC* i, p. 172, n. 3, adds the Picts and the Irish to Bede's account of the extent of Edwin's overlordship. On his dealings with the peoples listed here, see Stenton, pp. 80-1.

124-30. On the kingly virtues embodied in the peace of Edwin's reign see Wallace-Hadrill, *Early Germanic Kingship*, pp. 81, 87 (Bede and Alcuin); *Early Medieval History*, pp. 106-7.

131-3. Æthelburh, daughter of king Æthelberht of Kent, one of the first warrior-converts to Christianity (*HE* ii. 5). Pope Boniface V's letter to her is recorded by Bede at *HE* ii. 11. Her life and role in Edwin's conversion are set in context by J. Nicholson, *Medieval Women, SCH Subsid.* 1, ed. D. Baker (Oxford, 1978), p. 24 and by R. Hill in *Saints, Scholars, and Heroes. Studies . . . in Honour of Charles W. Jones* i, edd. M. H. King and W. M. Stevens (Ann Arbor, 1979), p. 68.

134-44. Paulinus probably went North with Æthelburh not in 625, as recorded by Bede (*HE* ii. 9), but in 619. The implications of this date are discussed by D. P. Kirby, 'Bede and Northumbrian Chronology', *EHR* 78 (1963), p. 522. Alcuin mentions Paulinus's mission at *Ep.* 16 (*MGH Epp.* iv, p. 43, 1-3). See further Introduction, p. xlix and P. Hunter Blair in *England Before the Conquest. Studies . . . presented to Dorothy Whitelock*, edd. P. Clemoes and K. Hughes (Cambridge, 1971), pp. 5-13.

iustitiae cultor, verus pietatis amator,
catholicus doctor, caelestia dona ministrans
gentibus aequoreis. Solis ceu Lucifer ortum   140
praecurrens tetras tenebrarum discutit umbras
atque diem monstrat mundo venisse serenum,
sic pater ille pius divino lumine Verbi
HE ii. 12 expulit humanis tetricas de cordibus umbras.
Quique die quadam constanti pectore regem   145
aggressus retulit signum, quod diximus olim
nocte sub obscura iuvenem vidisse paternis
finibus expulsum, posuitque in vertice dextram.
HE ii. 13 Territus agnoscens praedictae signa salutis
rex solio supplex statim descendit ab alto   150
et ruit ante pedes venerandi antistitis, atque
'Omnia nunc faciam', dixit, 'quaecumque spospondi,
atque Deum caeli credens venerabor ubique,
qui mihi concessit vitam regnique coronam;
namque erit ille mihi solus Deus omne per aevum!   155
Sed modo dic nobis, sit qualiter ille colendus.'
Cui prompto gaudens respondit episcopus ore:
'Foeda procul fugiat primum cultura deorum,
nec pecorum sanguis falsis plus fumet in aris,
nec calidis omen fibris perquirat aruspex,   160
nec cantus volucrum servet vanissimus augur:
omnia sternantur fundo simulacra deorum!'
Hinc pius antistes Fidei mysteria coepit

138 Ven. Fort. vi. 1^a. 21 iustitiae cultor pietatis amore coruscans; [Lucan *Bell. civ.* ii. 389]   139 Bede *Vit. S. Cuthb. metr.* 565 caelestia dona ministrans 140-1 Bede *Hymn.* viii. 16. 3-4 praecurrat . . . / solem rubens ut lucifer; Ven. Fort. vii. 8. 45-8   141 Virg. *Georg.* iii. 357 discutit umbras   143 id. *Aen.* x. 875 sic pater ille   144 Bede *Vit. S. Cuthb. metr.* 1-3 Multa suis dominus fulgescere lumina saeclis / donavit, tetricas humanae noctis et umbras / lustraret divina poli de culmine flamma   147 Juvenc. *Evang.* ii. 177 nocte sub obscura; [Virg. *Georg.* i. 478]   147-8 id. *Aen.* i. 620 finibus expulsum patriis 149 Aldh. *de Virg. metr.* 852 signa salutis   150 Virg. *Aen.* viii. 541 solio se tollit ab alto   151 Ven. Fort. i. 13. 3 venerandi antistitis; id. *Vit. S. Mart.* iii. 350 conruit ante pedes   155 ~ Virg. *Ecl.* i. 7   158 Prud. *Psych.* 29; Aldh. *de Virg. metr.* 1518   159 ff. Arat. *de Act. Apost.* ii. 183-4 162 Aldh. *de Virg. metr.* 1331 sternuntur fundo simulacra

138 *cf.* v. 1401; Alc. xcix. 22. 3   140 *cf.* v. 856   140-4 Alc. *Vit. S. Willibr. pr.* ii ceu solem praecedens lucifer . . . luce veritatis caliginosos tenebrarum errores discutit [Willibrordus]. (*Cf.* id. *Vit. S. Richar.* vi)   143 *cf.* v. 1341   144 *cf.* vv. 455-7, 580   149 Alc. lxxxix. 2. 4

a pillar of justice, a true lover of piety,
a doctor of the Church, he bestowed the gifts of Heaven
upon the peoples dwelling by the sea. Like the morning star,
hastening before sunrise, dispelling the foul shades of gloom,
and announcing to the world the coming of bright day,
that holy father, by the light of God's word,
drove the ugly darkness from men's hearts.
One day, without wavering, he approached the king,
recalling the sign that, as I have just mentioned, Edwin
had witnessed in the depths of night, while a young man
exiled from his homeland. On his head Paulinus placed his hand.
Terrified, but recognizing the sign that foretold his salvation,
the king immediately descended from his high throne,
and fell in entreaty at the revered priest's feet, saying:
'Now I shall fulfil all my promises and as a believer
shall worship in every respect the God in Heaven
who granted me life and the crown of this realm.
He will be my only God for ever and ever!
But now tell me how he should be worshipped.'
Joyously and eagerly the bishop replied:
'First banish afar the foul worship of idols,
on their profane altars let the blood of animals smoke no more,
nor the soothsayer look for omens in the warm entrails,
nor the meaningless augur attend to the songs of birds:
let all images of the gods be smashed to the ground!'
Then the pious bishop began calmly to expound

155 *cf.* vv. 300, 758, etc.   158 *cf.* v. 1054   163 *cf.* vv. 873,
1104, 1144, 1228

---

138. On the sources of this verse see Wallach, *Alcuin and Charlemagne*, pp. 194-7.

144. For the liturgical connotations of the language, cf. Blaise, *Vocabulaire latin*, p. 558.

145. quique = *qui* ('fossilized *-que*'). Cf. vv. 677, 1604, *et passim*. On this idiom see Löfstedt, *Vermischte Studien*, pp. 42-3, Norberg, *Beiträge*, pp. 92-6.

145 ff. The anonymous author of the Whitby *Vita Gregorii Magni* xvi (Colgrave, p. 101), unlike Bede, identifies Paulinus with the heavenly messenger of vv. 97-107.

146. olim: on this usage in Medieval Latin, see H. Hoffmann, *Deutsches Archiv* 28 (1972), pp. 45-57.

149 ff. In omitting Bede's account of Edwin's hesitation before his conversion and of the council that preceded it, Alcuin's poem excludes perhaps the most poetic simile in Bede: the likeness of human life to a sparrow's flight through a mead-hall (*HE* ii. 13).

testificare palam constanter in ordine cunctis,
donec ipse Fidem concepit pectore toto   165
rex pius et populo persuasit credere Christum.
Ecce sacerdotum Coefi tunc temporis auctor
errorumque caput fuerat. Cui rex ait: 'Eia,
arripe tela tibi prius inconsueta, sacerdos,
et iaculo celsum primus tu pollue fanum!   170
Qui fueras scelerum doctor, nunc esto salutis!'
Annuit his dictis senior, paucisque respondit:
'Hactenus incerto mea stamine vita pependit,
obruit et dubiis animum caligo tenebris;
exhinc certa sequar cupiens agnoscere verum   175
aeternumque Deum, vel si sit vita futura,
an tormenta malis, maneant an praemia iustis.'
His rapuit dextra dictis hastile minaci
atque marem conscendit equum non more sueto,
cui per colla iubae volitant, tumet ardua cervix,   180
pectore sublato velox fodit ungula terram,
impatiensque morae quatiebat morsibus aurum.
Terribilis qualis curvo fit Parthus in arcu,
vel si longa levis vibrat hastilia Maurus,
talis et ipse petit iaculo fastigia fani.   185
O nimium tanti felix audacia facti!
Polluit ante alios quas ipse sacraverat aras.
Plena fides patuit, nec adhuc in fonte lavatus

---

167 tunc *T*: fuerat tunc *R*   170 fanum *T*: templum *R*   172 his *T*:
iis *R*   176 vel si sit *R*: vel sistit *T*   184 levis . . . Maurus *Godman*
(*cf.* Lucan *Bell. civ.* i. 210): brevis . . . Maurus *R*: levis . . . in auris *T*: leves . . . in
auras *Gale*   186 tanti *R Gale*: tanta *T*

---

164 Bede *Vit. S. Cuthb. metr.* 536   165 Lucan *Bell. civ.* v. 163
167 Virg. *Aen.* ii. 318 ff.   167-8 ibid. xi. 361 caput . . . et causa malorum
172 Bede *Vit. S. Cuthb. metr.* 923   173 ibid. 700-1 in dubio pendit . . . /
stamine; Paul. Nol. xxvii. 289 mea vita pependit   174 Act. 13: 11
177 Paul. Nol. vi. 281 malis poenas et praemia iustis   180 Virg. *Aen.* xi.
497 iubae per colla; id. *Georg.* iii. 79 ardua cervix   181 Job 39: 21 terram
ungula fodit   182 Lucan *Bell. civ.* vi. 424 impatiensque morae   183 ibid.
ix. 267   184 ibid. i. 210 levis si lancea Mauri   186 Virg. *Aen.* iv.
657; [Ovid *Ep.* xviii. 195 felix audacia]   187 Virg. *Aen.* ii. 501-2 per aras
/ . . . quos ipse sacraverat ignis   188 Virg. *Ecl.* iii. 97

---

164 Alc. *Vit. S. Willibr. metr.* xxii. 22   166 Poet. Saxo i. 307   173 Alc.
cxvi. 1   185 *cf.* v. 364

the mysteries of the Faith openly and systematically to all,
until the pious king wholeheartedly embraced the creed
and persuaded his people to believe in Christ.
At that time Coifi was the chief priest
and fountain-head of error. To him the king said: 'Go,
priest, seize weapons that you have not handled before,
and be the first to defile the lofty shrine with a spear!
Once you were a teacher of sin: now be a guide to salvation!'
The old man assented to these words, and briefly replied:
'My life to this moment has hung by a thread of uncertainty,
my spirit has been darkened by the shadows of doubt;
henceforth I shall follow the truth, longing to know
the real and eternal God, whether there is a life to come,
punishments for the evil and rewards for the just.'
With these words, brandishing a spear in a gesture of threat,
he flouted custom by mounting a stallion
whose mane flowed over a neck arched high in pride.
The steed reared up, its eager hoof pawed the ground;
impatient with delay, it chafed the bit of gold.
Just as the dread Parthian pulls taut the curved bow
or the nimble Moor lets fly his long spear,
so the priest aimed his dart at the lofty temple.
O great deed! Happy boldness! Before others
he defiled the very altars he had consecrated.
Revealed before baptism in the fullness of his faith,

168 ff. In Bede, Coifi himself suggests desecrating the pagan altars, partly
because his former faith had failed to reveal to him truth, partly through its lack
of material advantage. Alcuin has king Edwin urge Coifi to the act, and emphasizes
the ethical benefit of Christianity through a speech (vv. 173-7) in which the
pagan high priest declares his longing for it.

170. fanum/templum: *fanum* always refers to a heathen temple in Alcuin's
usage (cf. vv. 185, 192); *templum* to a Christian church (vv. 281, 306).

177. an . . . an: see Norberg, *Beiträge*, pp. 100 ff.

178 ff. The first of three passages, modelled partly or chiefly on Virgil, which
lend epic colouring to Alcuin's poem (cf. vv. 255 ff.; 517 ff.). Through this
description of Coifi, filled with conviction and cast in the mould of an epic
hero, Alcuin turns Bede's striking but single exploit into a total triumph for the
faith.

184. levis/brevis . . . Maurus: for the use of *brevis* to describe human stature,
see *TLL* ii. 10. 2182. 42 ff. I find no true parallel for this usage in eighth-century
poetry. Moreover, the contrast pointed by *brevis* between the shortness of the
Moor and the length of his spear borders on the comical. I am inclined to see
in *brevis* a scribal corruption of *levis*, the reading of *T* and an imitation of
Lucan.

explevit virtutis opus pietate fideli.
Turba salutiferum sequitur mox tota magistrum,   190
viribus unanimis sternunt caeduntque sacellum.
Tunc erecta ruit fani structura profani,
funditus in cineres etiam destructa fatescit.

HE ii. 14   Affuit interea tempus paschale per orbem,
quo rex cum populo statuit baptisma subire   195
[627]   Euboricae celsis etiam sub moenibus urbis,
in qua tecta Deo iussit cito parva locari,
sumeret ut sub eis sacram baptismatis undam.
Dum festiva dies inluxit temporis almi,
cum gnatis ducibusque simul, cum plebe sequenti,   200
undecimo regni Christo sacratus in anno est
fonte salutifero praefatae in moenibus urbis,
cuius abhinc culmen sublimius extulit ille,
metropolimque sui statuit consistere regni.

HE i. 29   Sic quoque Gregorius praesul decreverat olim,   205
semina dum vitae Romana misit ab arce
gentibus Anglorum: confestim praecipit urbem
hanc caput ecclesiis et culmen honoris haberi,
pallia pontificesque in ea vestire sacratos.

193 destructa *R*: distructa *T*   fatescit *R T*: fatiscit *edd.*   198 sacram
T: sacri *R*   203 abhinc *R*: ab hinc *T*   209 pontificesque *T*:
pontificisque *R*

---

189 Virg. *Aen.* x. 469 virtutis opus; Paul. Nol. xvi. 266 pietate fideli; Rustic.
Helpid. 66   190 Paul. Nol. xvi. 233 salutiferum . . . magistrum   191 Lucan
Bell. civ. iv. 558 sternuntque caeduntque   192 Ven. Fort. *Vit. S. Mart.* i. 319
fana eruit; Aldh. *Carm. eccl.* iv. 3. 11 fana profana   193 ['Lactant'. *De Ave*
phoen. 98 solvitur in cinerem]   194 Ven. Fort. *Vit. S. Mart.* iv. 284 dies
aderant paschalia festa gerentes; Juvenc. *Evang.* ii. 153   195–6 Bede *Vit. S.*
Cuthb. metr. 398 celsis statuit sub moenibus   198 Aldh. *de Virg. metr.*
1136   199 Ven. Fort. iii. 8. 1 inluxit festiva dies   205 ff. Aldh. *de*
Virg. metr. 875 Gregorius praesul . . . descripserat olim; *cf.* Bede *Ep. ad Ecgbert.*
ix. sanctus papa Gregorius . . . duodecim . . . episcopos . . . ordinandos esse decre-
vit; in quibus Eboracensis antistes, accepto a sede apostolica pallio, metropolitanus
esse deberet

---

190   Poet. Saxo i. 350   magna   salutiferum   suscepit   turba   lavacrum
191 Æthelw. *de Abbat.* 145   192 Alc. *Vit. S. Willibr. metr.* ii. 7 ruunt . . .
fana profana; Poet. Saxo i. 74 fani subversio . . . profani   193 *cf.* v. 1053
196 *cf.* v. 202   198 *cf.* 597, 1490   208 *cf.* vv. 674, 1406, 1484

---

197 ff. 'Edwin of Deira's baptism in the church that Easter may suggest
that there was already a royal residence in the city and that, as in Winchester, the

with unwavering piety he performed the virtuous deed.
Soon the entire crowd followed his guide to salvation;
in strength united, they levelled and destroyed the shrine.
Then that building erected as a heathen temple
crashed to the ground, collapsed, scattered in ashes.
At the coming of Easter throughout the world,
the king decided to be baptized together with his people
under the lofty walls of the city of York; there,
in the little church which he had swiftly built in honour of God,
to receive the waters of holy baptism.
When the festive day of that hallowed season dawned,
with his children and nobles and a train of the people,
in the eleventh year of his reign, Edwin was dedicated to Christ
at the font of salvation, beneath the walls of that city,
whose heights he then raised to greater eminence,
by choosing to make it the chief city of his realm.
This was in keeping with what pope Gregory had decreed,
when he sent the seeds of life from the lofty city of Rome
to the English people. His immediate command was
that this city be a capital and prime see of the Church,
and that archbishops be enrobed and consecrated there.

church was established in the first instance to serve the residence' (Biddle, *Archaeology*, p. 47). See further comm. to vv. 220-2.

202 ff. Alcuin envisages York as the political and ecclesiastical capital of Northumbria, in accordance with the plans of Edwin and of Gregory the Great. The city had been a metropolitan see of Roman Britain (J. C. Mann, *Antiquity*, 35 (1961), pp. 316-20; S. Frere, *Britannia* (London, 1967), p. 332), and its special status in the early Northumbrian church may reflect the preservation of a sub-Roman British tradition (E. John, *Agricultural History Review*, 18 Suppl. (1970), p. 48; cf. J. Campbell, *SCH* 16 (1979), pp. 119-21) or simply Pope Gregory's desire to revive antique sees (Cramp, *Anglian and Viking York*, p. 4).

203. abhinc: see Norberg, *Beiträge*, p. 76.

204. metropolim: this word, meaning 'capital', is used by Bede twice of Canterbury and once of London (J. Campbell in *Names, Words, Graves: Early Medieval Settlement*, ed. P. H. Sawyer (Leeds, 1979), pp. 38-9, 43). Alcuin applies this term to York in the same manner at v. 204, with which cf. *Ep.* 16 'Euborica civitate . . . que caput est totius regni' (*MGH Epp.* iv, p. 43. 17-18).

209. The *pallium*, or archbishop's scarf of lamb's wool (see Plummer ii, pp. 49-52), sent to Paulinus in 634, reached him only after his flight from Northumbria. Egbert was thus the first archbishop of York *de iure et de facto* (Plummer ii, p. 117 and v. 1280, with comm.). Alcuin stresses the importance of the *pallium* at *Ep.* 125: 'de patria mea venerunt et civitate mea more canonico atque apostolico beati Gregorii praedicatoris nostri sacri pallei depraecari dignitatem . . . valde illis in partibus sacri pallei auctoritas necessaria est ad opprimendam improborum perversitatem et sanctae ecclesiae auctoritatem conservandam' (*MGH Epp.* iv, p. 184. 27 ff.).

HE ii. 17 Sic pius antistes primum Paulinus habebat   210

  .   .   .   .

qui Domini legem meditans in nocte dieque,
sedulus in populos sparsit praecepta salutis;
plurima quapropter convertit milia Christo
et Fidei flammis virtutis et igne coruscans
frigora bis ternis borealia depulit annis   215
HE ii. 20 rex, quibus egregius regnaverat Eduinus idem,
disposuitque suas iusto moderamine leges,
inlicitans servare Fidem donisque minisque,
ecclesiasque suis fundavit in urbibus amplas.
Ex quibus Euboricae, solidis suffulta columnis,   220
nobilis illa manet celso speciosa decore,
qua statione sacra fuit ille lavatus in unda,
quamque diu vixit Christi praecepta tenebat.
Illi quapropter clemens meliora parabat
tradere regna Deus, luci sociata perenni;   225
nam sibi praescriptae mortis dum venerat hora,
belliger occubuit subito socialibus armis.
O res caeca nimis terreno fidere regno,
quod praeceps Fortuna rotat, fatisque malignis
vertitur et variis semper mutatur in horis!   230
Ecce decem et septem postquam regnaverit annis,
Eduinus occubuit regum clarissimus ille,

210-11 *a lacuna lies between these verses*   216 Eduinus *T*: eduin *R*
217 disposuitque *T r*: deposuitque *R*   222 lavatus *T*: levatus *R*   230 mutatur
R: motatur *T*   231 regnaverit *T R*: regnaverat *Gale*

---

211 Ps. 1: 2 in legè Domini ... meditabitur die ac nocte   213-14 Aldh. *de Virg. metr.* 2111-12 plures nam Christo convertit ... / ... coruscans   217 Juvenc. *Evang.* ii. 575 iusto moderamine legis   218 Stat. *Theb.* vi. 319   220 Paul. Nol. xxvii. 393   223 Juvenc. *Evang.* i. 7 legis praecepta tenebant   224 Ven. Fort. iv. 4. 3 meliora paravit   225 id. viii. 3. 41 luci sociata perenni   226 Juvenc. *Evang.* iii. 556 ubi tertia venerat hora   227 Aldh. *de Virg. metr.* 2850; Ven. Fort. *Vit. S. Mart.* i. 112

---

211 Alc. *Vit. S. Willibr. metr.* xiii. 10 legibus in sacris meditans noctesque diesque   212 Alc. lxvi. 1. 3   213 *cf.* vv. 608, 852, 1306   217 *cf.* v. 884; Theodulf xxviii. 63 legum et moderamine iustus   220 *cf.* v. 1509 228-30 Alc. xi. 10-11 adversis variant prospera cuncta cito / omnia tristifico mutantur gaudia luctu; *cf.* id. ix. 5-12; xxiii. 24

210-11. habebat lacks the necessary accusative. I posit a lacuna of one verse, lying between v. 210 and v. 211, referring to Paulinus's metropolitan authority.
220-2. Edwin's cathedral, encompassing the wooden oratory in which he was

And so York's first archbishop was the devout Paulinus

. . . .

who meditated on God's law both day and night;
zealously spreading the word of salvation among the people,
he converted many thousands to Christ. For six years,
shining with the flames of Faith and the fire of virtue
he fought off the chill disbelief of the North.
During these years reigned Edwin, the excellent king,
whose laws were ordered with justice and fairness.
By gifts and by threats he incited men to cherish the Faith,
and founded spacious churches in the cities of his realm.
Among them the church of York, supported by strong columns,
survives to this day, lofty, splendid and graceful.
In that place Edwin was baptized with holy water,
who upheld Christ's teaching as long as he lived.
And so God in His mercy prepared for that king
finer dominions, realms joined to eternal light;
for when the appointed hour of his death arrived,
the warrior-king was suddenly murdered by his allies.
What blindness it is to put much trust in worldly power,
which giddy fortune wheels about, with cruel strokes of fate
changing, ever mutable with each passing hour!
Edwin, the finest of kings, was slain
after a reign of seventeen years,

baptized, is described by Bede at *HE* ii. 14: 'curavit . . . maiorem ipso in loco et
augustiorem de lapide fabricare basilicam, in cuius medio ipsum, quod prius
fecerat, oratorium includeretur. Praeparatis ergo fundamentis in gyro prioris
oratorii per quadrum coepit aedificare basilicam.' This church, begun by Edwin
soon after 627 and dedicated to St. Peter, was completed by king Oswald. Used
from the first as a royal mausoleum, it was still standing *c.*1080 (Harrison,
Y. Arch. Jnl. 40 (1959-62), pp. 233-4, 240-1). Its actual site remains unknown.
Recent archaeological evidence indicates that the Roman basilica at York survived
into Edwin's time and beyond. It is possible that St. Peter's was built in the open
ground of the Roman basilica's southern courtyard (B. Hope-Taylor, *Under York
Minster. Archaeological Discoveries 1966-1971* (York 1971), pp. 38-9. Conjec-
tural plan in Taylor, p. 701; recent discussion (1977) by R. Hill, *History of York
Minster*, pp. 5-6. Bibliography and *testimonia* (up to 1970) in K. H. Krüger,
*Königsgrabkirchen der Franken, Angelsachsen und Langobarden zur Mitte des 8.
Jahrhunderts* (Munich, 1971), pp. 290 ff. See Introduction, pp. lx-lxi.

227. Edwin was killed at the battle of Hatfield, 12 Oct. 633, by the forces of
Cadwallon, king of Gwynedd, and of Penda of Mercia.

228 ff. On the language and theme of mutability, recurrent in Alcuin's poetry,
see Godman, *SM* (3ª Ser.) 20. 2 (1979), pp. 577-82.

231. **regnaverit**: on the interchangeability of the perfect, future perfect, and
pluperfect tenses see Introduction, p. xcix (*h*) (2).

post quem non habuit praeclara Britannia talem.
HE iii. 1-2 Hoc tamen Omnipotens fieri non passus inultum est,
sed dedit Osuualdum regis regnare nepotem.   235
[635] Qui subito veniens externis exsul ab oris,
firmiter invictae Fidei confisus in armis,
agmina parva rapit properans et pergit in hostem
vastantem patriam ferro flammisque crementem
milibus innumeris, spoliis nimiumque superbum.   240
Sed pius Osuualdus numero non territus ullo
alloquitur propriam constanti pectore turmam:
'O quibus est semper bellorum vivida virtus,
nunc, precor, invictas animis adsumite vires,
auxiliumque Dei cunctis praestantius armis   245
poscite corde pio; precibus prosternite vestros
vultus ante crucem, quam vertice montis in isto
erexi, rutilat Christi quae clara trophaeo,
quae quoque nunc nobis praestabit ab hoste triumphum.'
Tunc clamor populi fertur super astra precantis   250
et cruce sic coram Dominumque Deumque potentem
poplitibus flexis exercitus omnis adorat.
His etiam gestis, promptus processit in hostem
caedibus inrumpens hostilia castra cruentis.
Ut leo cum catulis crudelis ovilia vastat   255
et pecus omne ferus mactat manditque roditque,
haud secus Osuualdus rex stravit ubique phalanges
barbaricas. Victor gradiens per tela, per hostes,
caedit et inculcat, fugientesque atterit alas.

---

238 parva *R Ruinart*: prava *T*   rapit *R*: trahit *Gale: om. T*   239 creman-
tem *R Gale*: vorantem *T*   241 osuualdus *R*: Oswaldus *T*   256 roditque
T R: trahitque *Gale*   257 haud *T*: haut *R*   Osuualdus *R*: Osvaldus *T*

---

236 Ven. Fort. iv. 1. 17 exul ab oris   237 Bede *Vit. S. Cuthb.*
metr. 803 confisus in armis   239 Lucan *Bell. civ.* vii. 261 patriam ferro flam-
misque   240 Virg. *Aen.* viii. 202 spoliisque superbus   241-2 Aldh.
de Virg. metr. 1585 pius alloquitur . . . catervas   243 Lucan *Bell. civ.* ix.
379 o quibus; Virg. *Aen.* v. 754 bello vivida virtus   244 ibid. vi. 261 nunc
animis opus   247 ibid. xi. 526   248 Bede *Vit. S. Cuthb. metr.* 383
crucis rutilo fugat arma tropheo   250 Aldh. *de Virg. metr.* 582 vulgi clamor
ferit aethera; id. *Carm. eccl.* i. 8 populorum vota precantum   251 Ven. Fort.
Vit. S. Mart. iii. 200 dominumque deumque; Virg. *Aen.* vi. 621 dominumque
potentem; Juvenc. *Evang.* iv. 49   252 Aldh. *Carm. eccl.* iv. 7. 10 poplitibus
flexis; Bede *Vit. S. Cuthb. metr.* 281 et genibus dominum positis veneratus adorat
255-6 Virg. *Aen.* ix. 339-41 impastus ceu plena leo per ovilia turbans / . . .

and fair Britain has not had such a ruler again.
Omnipotent God did not allow this to go unavenged,
but granted the kingdom to Oswald, nephew of Edwin.
Returning immediately from exile in foreign lands,
with firm trust in the weapons of invincible Faith, Oswald
assembled in haste a small army and advanced on the foe
as they ravaged and razed the fatherland, by sword and by fire,
their number countless in thousands, their pride overweening
in their spoils. Undaunted by numbers, the devout Oswald
addressed his warband with unwavering heart:
'O staunch and courageous champions in battle,
resolve now, I pray, to be valiant and invincible;
with pious heart implore God's aid, that is
more mighty than any weapon. Prostrate yourselves in prayer
before the cross I have set up on that mountain-top,
where it shines brightly as a sign of Christ's triumph,
and even now will ensure our victory over the foe.'
The din of the host's prayers was carried beyond the stars,
and so, before the cross, the entire army
worshipped its Lord God on bended knee.
This done, they marched directly on the enemy,
bursting in bloody slaughter upon his camp.
Just as the cruel lion and its cubs ravage the sheepfolds,
killing in its fury, devouring and tearing at the flock,
so king Oswald laid low the barbarian hosts on every side.
Advancing in triumph through the armed battalions of the foe,
cutting and trampling, he crushed their fleeing ranks.

manditque trahitque / molle pecus   258 Virg. *Aen.* ii. 358 per tela per hostis
259 id. *Georg.* iv. 203-4 alas / attrivere

---

237 *cf.* vv. 522, 790   238 *cf.* v. 253   250 *cf.* vv. 680, 692,
1063, 1362, 1648; Alc. lxxxviii. 3. 9 populi clamantis ad astra   252 '*Karolus*
Magnus' 455-6 [= 501-2] exercitus omnis . . . fusus adorat   258 Alc. ix. 253

---

235 ff. Alcuin omits any mention of the collapse of the Northumbrian king-
dom at Edwin's defeat or of its split into the two component parts of Deira and
Bernicia (*HE* iii. 1). Oswald succeeded Edwin after Osric, the dead king's cousin
and ruler of Deira, had been defeated and killed by Cadwallon in 633 and Ean-
frith, son of Æthelfrith, and pretender to the Bernician throne, had sued for
peace. Cadwallon's ravages in Northumbria, described at vv. 238-40, were
checked by Oswald at the end of 633. After Cadwallon's defeat and death,
Oswald was accepted as king in both Deira and Bernicia. The succession thus
reverted to the line of Æthelfrith.

Opprimit Osuualdi sternendo exercitus hostes,   260
sanguineos campis rivos post terga relinquens,
donec ipse luens cecidit Caduuala nefandus
perfidiae poenas, moriens in strage suorum,
claraque magnifico cessit victoria regi.
Hostibus occisis regnum sanctissimus Osuuald   265
ingreditur, heres veterum condignus avorum:
vir virtute potens, patriae tutator, amator,
moribus egregius, Christi mandata secutus,
pauperibus largus, parcus sibi, dives in omnes,
iudiciis verax, animi pietate benignus,   270
excelsus meritis, summissus mente sed ipsa,
hostibus horribilis, cunctis iocundus amicis:
ut bello indomitus, sic pacta in pace fidelis.

HE iii. 3 Invaluit postquam sceptris et culmine regni,
exstruit ecclesias donisque exornat opimis,   275
vasa ministeriis praestans pretiosa sacratis.
Argento, gemmis aras vestivit et auro,
serica parietibus tendens velamina sacris
auri brateolis pulchre distincta †coronis†

260 opprimit *R*: premit *T*: praevenit *Gale*   263 perfidiae *T*: perfidia *R*
265 Osuald *T*: Osuualdi *R*   266 heres *R*: heros *T*   268 secutus *T r*:
securus *R*   271 sed *R*: sub *T*   279 brateolis *R*: blateolis *T*   coro-
nis *T r*: coloris *R*: coronas *Wattenbach*: coruscis *Reeve*: coronans; *Godman*

263 Lucan *Bell. civ.* iv. 797 ceciditque in strage suorum   267 Arat. *de Act.*
Apost. ii. 78   269 Bede *Vit. S. Cuthb. metr.* 559 pauperibus qui dives,
inops sibi   270 Paul. Nol. xxi. 43   273 Lucan *Bell. civ.* viii. 364
indomitus bellis   276 Ven. Fort. *Vit. S. Mart.* iv. 171   278 Aldh. *de*
Virg. metr. 1146 serica . . . praebens velamina; id. *Carm. eccl.* iii. 71   279 id.
Ænigm. xcvi. 11

260 Alc. xlv. 51 opprimit et miseros quorundam saeva potestas   261 Theo-
dulf xxviii. 123   262-3 Poet. Saxo i. 298   264 *cf.* v. 430
267 Alc. *Vit. S. Willibr. metr.* i. 2   269 *cf.* v. 1019   273 *cf.* v. 571
275 *cf.* v. 1229   276 *cf.* v. 1224; Alc. lxxxix. 1. 11-12 officiis domini fecit
quoque vasa sacrata / argento, necnon aurea tota quidem   277 *cf.* vv.
389, 1267, 1492; Theodulf l. 9 argento, gemmisque exornat et auro   278 *cf.*
v. 1268

263. **perfidiae:** in Alcuin's political vocabulary this term and its cognates are
highly charged. Describing to Offa the anger of Charlemagne at king Æthelred's
(790-6) murder by the Northumbrians, he writes (*Ep.* 101): 'in tantum iratus est
contra gentem ut ait: "illam perfidam et perversam et homicidam dominorum
suorum", peiorem eam paganis aestimans' (*MGH Epp.* iv, p. 147, 13-15). *Perfidia*,
for Alcuin, is the worst attribute of pagan enemies, treacherous allies, and faith-

So Oswald's army overpowered and annihilated its enemy,
leaving the battlefield behind it in rivers of blood
until the wicked Cadwallon himself fell, paying the price
for his treachery, dying amid the massacre of his men,
and yielding a brilliant victory to that splendid king.
His enemies slain, the holy Oswald entered his realm,
a worthy heir of its ancient line:
a man of mighty virtue, guardian and lover of the fatherland,
following Christ's commands with outstanding character;
generous to the poor, self-denying, but unstinting to all,
true in his judgments, kindly and pious of spirit,
of signal distinction but humbly tempered, terrible
to his enemies but genial to each of his friends, as invincible
in war as he was scrupulous to maintain peace treaties.
His position secured on the throne and throughout the realm,
he built churches and endowed them with fine gifts,
providing precious vessels for the office of worship.
He arrayed the altars with silver, gold, and jewels,
hanging on the hallowed walls silken tapestries
beautifully picked out with gold leaf; †chandeliers†

less subjects: it is an offence against the ideal of *fidelitas* which he regarded as the root of political stability (cf. Wallace-Hadrill, *Early Medieval History*, pp. 164–5).

265–73. Again, the language of Alcuin's panegyric on Oswald's regal virtues is of a piece with the advice he gave in letters to the kings of his own times. Cf. *Ep.* 18 (to Æthelred of Northumbria, in 793): 'Regis est omnes iniquitates pietatis suae potentia obprimere; iustum esse in iudiciis, pronum in misericordia . . . sobrium in moribus, veridicum in verbis, largum in donis, providum in consiliis' (*MGH Epp.* iv, p. 51. 19–22).

275–83. Oswald's benefactions to the Church are stressed by Alcuin but scarcely noted by Bede (cf. Plummer ii, p. 140). Less than thirty years after Oswald's death, Wilfrid I, at his accession in 669, found St. Peter's in a state of grave disrepair (Eddius, *Vita Wilfridi*, xvi [Colgrave, p. 35]). In the period of war and internal dissension that followed Oswald's death, and during the years of the Celtic Church's ascendancy in Northumbria, York Minster appears to have been neglected. It is significant that Alcuin, in his panegyric on Oswiu (vv. 565–76), never mentions any gifts to the church. See further Hill, *History of York Minster*, pp. 6–8.

279. If Wattenbach's proposal is adopted, a semi-colon must be placed before *coronas*. Difficulty lies in the (exceptional) interruption of sense and subject that requires *coronas* to be taken with the following line. Reeve's proposal removes this difficulty and provides an adjective in keeping with Alcuinian style (cf. vv. 505, 678, 1232, 1644). An alternative is to read *coronans*, and to place a semi-colon at the end of the verse. The present participle would thus stand parallel to *tendens* in v. 278 and the construction would be *velamina* / . . . *auri brateolis* . . . *coronans*: 'encircling the tapestries . . . with gilding of gold'. Cf. Bede, *Hist. Abbat.* ix: 'picturas, quibus totam . . . ecclesiam in gyro coronaret', and Latham, *Dictionary*, ii, C, p. 495, col. 3. 4a.

sanctaque suspendit varias per tecta lucernas,   280
esset ut in templis caeli stellantis imago;
christicolasque greges duxit devotus in illa,
ut fierent Domino laudes sine fine canentum.
O pietas, o celsa fides! Nam quidquid habebat
prodigus in Domini gazarum sparsit honorem.   285
Quapropter titulis virtutum claruit atque
signorum celebri fama est vulgatus ubique,
quae modo per mundum chartis inscripta leguntur,
quorum pauca libet lyrico nunc tangere plectro,
et partes cantus calamo currente referre.   290
HE iii. 6 Tempore nam quodam praesul sanctissimus Aedan
cum rege et populo paschalia festa peregit;
eius rex monitis nam omni servivit in actu.
Plurima per plateas inopum tunc turba iacebat
a rege stipem rogitans clamore frequenti.   295
Ingrediens recubat iam et rex simul atque sacerdos,
argentique pius pensantem plurima discum
pondera cum dapibus statim direxit egenis.
Vidit ut hoc praesul, dextram comprendit et infit:
'Incorrupta, precor, maneat manus ista per aevum!'   300
Quod fuit et factum; *sancto nam rege perempto,*
HE iii. 12 *gentili gladio praecisam a corpore dextram*
stipite suspendunt. Veniens rex illius heres,
Osuui germanus germani et sanguinis ultor,

282 illa *Godman*: illas *T R*   285 domini *Gale*: dominum *R*: deum *T*
286-337 *om. R, f. 211ʳ; recorded f. 215ʳ*   289 libet *T*: liber *R*   293 omni
T r: omnis *R*   servivit *T*: sevivit *R*   294 tunc *T*: *om. R*   297 pius
R: prius *T*   299 comprendit *R Ruinart*: comprehendit *T*   304 Osuui
R: Oswi *Ruinart*: Osulus *T*

281 Stat. *Theb.* vi. 579 caeli stellantis imago   282 Arat. *de Act. Apostol.*
ii. 928 christicolas . . . greges   283 Bonif. *Carm.* iv. 5 dominum semper
laudant sine fine dicantes   284 Ven. Fort. *Vit. S. Mart.* ii. 217 O pietas et
celsa fides!   284-5 *Syll. Epig. Cantab.* 41. 9-10 quicquid habebat / in tua
distribuit munera   286 Bede *Vit. S. Cuthb. metr.* 562   287 Virg.
Aen. i. 457   288 Aldh. *de Virg. metr.* 544 quae modo per mundum chartis
inserta leguntur   289 Bede *Vit. S. Cuthb. metr.* 563 quae lyrico liceat
cursim contingere plectro   291 Aldh. *de Virg. metr.* 838   295-8 ibid.
682   303 Aldh. *Carm. eccl.* iii. 18

280 Alc. lxxxix. 1. 9   283 Alc. xcix. 7. 8   284 *cf.* vv.
1576, 1589   284-5 Alc. lxxxviii. 14. 3-4 nam quidquid habebat /
sparserat   286 *cf.* v. 578; Hrab. Maur. xlvii. 6   287 *cf.* v. 613

and lanterns he placed throughout the holy buildings,
there to represent the starry heaven,
and led the faithful in their droves into the temples
to hymn the Lord in unending songs of praise.
O piety, o noble faith! Prodigal of his treasure,
he distributed freely all his possessions in honour of the Lord.
And so his outstanding virtue won him fame,
and he swiftly became a universal byword through his miracles,
which are now on written record throughout the world.
I will now touch on a few of them with lyric strain,
and record some of this theme with my swift pen.
On one occasion the holy bishop Aidan
celebrated Easter with the king and his people;
on every issue Oswald would follow his advice.
At that time a great throng of beggars lay in the streets,
clamouring again and again to the king for alms.
King and bishop went indoors, but as they sat down
pious Oswald commanded that a silver dish of great weight
with the food upon it should immediately be given to the poor.
When the bishop saw this, he took the king's right hand and
said: 'May this hand, I pray, remain incorruptible for ever!'
And so it came about: for after that holy king was slain,
they hung his right hand, severed by a pagan's sword,
upon a stake. King Oswiu his heir,
his brother, and the avenger of his blood came,

289 *cf.* vv. 746, 1439; Alc. iv. 59 lyrico . . . tangere plectro   289–90 Compare v. 378; Alc. *Vit. S. Willibr. metr. praef.* 4; ibid. xxxiv. 57 currenti tangere plectro   292 Poet. Saxo ii. 432   298 *cf.* v. 1254   299 *cf.* vv. 625, 974

289–90. pauca . . . / . . . calamo currente: Alcuin repeatedly emphasizes the modesty and brevity of his verse account (cf. vv. 378, 431, 437-8, 741-6, 783, 1649-56), and at v. 1206 he formulates an explicit *ius brevitatis* to which at vv. 1561-2 he refers again. (See Introduction, pp. lxxxvii-lxxxviii.)

lyrico . . . plectro carries no specific overtones of genre but is used as a general expression for poetry cf. vv. 746, 1439, and the description of Alcuin in Theodulf of Orléans's *Carm.* xxv. 132: 'qui potis est lyrico multa boare pede' (*MGH PLAC* i, p. 486).

296. sacerdos: 'bishop'. See Blaise, *Vocabulaire latin*, pp. 500 ff.

301 ff. Oswald was defeated and killed by Penda on 5 August 641. His body was dismembered, and his relics were venerated in different places (summarized in Farmer, *Dictionary*, pp. 304-5, with bibliography; Plummer ii, pp. 157-60). Generally Alcuin follows Bede's account, both in detail and in emphasis upon Oswald's posthumous deeds (Introduction, p. l).

303-4. See comm. to vv. 506 ff.

arripuit dextram Bebbamque ferebat in urbem,   305
argenti condens loculo sub culmine templi,
quod prius ipse Deo statuit sub nomine Petri.
Hactenus integram fore signo est ungula crescens,
flexilis et nervus, viridis caro, forma venusta.

HE iii. 9   *Cuius quanta fides fuerat vel vis meritorum,*   310
[642]   *post mortem nituit magis ac magis undique signis.*
Namque ubi pro patria pugnans a gente peremptus
pagana cecidit, fiunt de pulvere multa
signa salutifero. Quidam tunc forte viator
egit iter iuxta, fuerat qua scamma duelli,   315
cuius equus subito totis lassescere membris
coeperat et frendens ore spumare cruento
atque ruens campo volvi moriturus in illo,
inque locum versans venit, quo rex pius Osuuald
occubuit quondam, tunc statim corpore sano   320
exsurgens avide carpebat amoena virecta.
Intellexit eques quicquam praestantius illo
esse loco; titulum ponens equitabat abinde,
hospitium veniens quo tenderat. Ecce puella
tabida paralysis gelido languore iacebat,   325
ultima congeminans miserae suspiria vitae.
Cumque domus neptim patris turbata gemebat,
suggerit hospes eam duci, quo forte caballus
sanatus fuerat; carroque imposta puella
ducitur, ut iussit monstrans loca sancta viator,   330
et sita corpus humi paulum dormivit ibidem,
evigilansque suam persensit adesse salutem.
Inde petivit aquam, faciem sibi lavit et ipsos
composuit crines, caput et velamine texit

---

310 quanta *T*: cuncta *R*   314 tunc *R*: om. *T*: dum *Gale*: nam *Wattenbach*
317 et frendens *T r*: extendens *R*   323 abinde *R*: ab inde *T*   324 quo
R Gale: quod *T*   325 gelido *T*: gelida *R*   328 suggerit *R Ruinart*:
suggerat *T*   caballus *T*: caballas *R*

---

306 Ven. Fort. x. 6. 13 culmina templi   309 id. iv. 7. 11 forma venusta
310 id. x. 6. 128 quanta fides cuius   311 Lucan *Bell. civ.* i. 395 undique
signis   316 Paul. Nol. xviii. 350 totis . . . membris   317 Virg. *Aen.*
ix. 341 fremit ore cruento   321 ibid. vi. 638 amoena virecta   325 Ven.
Fort. *Vit. S. Mart.* i. 368 tabida paralysis gelido languore puella   326 Aldh.
Carm. eccl. iv. 3. 15 ultima mortalis clausit spiracula vitae   334 Stat. *Achill.*
i. 348

seized that hand, and carried it off into the city of Bamburgh,
where he placed it in a silver casket within the lofty temple,
which he had dedicated to God in the name of St Peter.
As a sign of incorruptibility, its nails grow still,
its sinews are supple, its flesh has life, its shape is handsome.
The greatness of Oswald's faith and the power of his merits
gained added lustre after his death through his miracles
for many wonders were performed by that miraculous dust
from the spot where he had fallen in battle for his fatherland,
slain by a pagan people. A traveller then happened to pass by
the place where the battle had taken place;
his horse suddenly grew weak in every limb,
began to gnash its teeth, to foam with blood at the mouth, and,
falling to the ground, it writhed in that field, about to die.
In its convulsions it came to the spot where once had fallen
pious king Oswald. Then, of a sudden, it recovered,
rose up, and avidly cropped the sweet turf.
Its rider understood that there was something extraordinary
about that place, and, marking it, he rode away,
arriving at the inn which had been his destination.
There lay a girl, wasting away in a chill coma, unable to move,
ending her careworn life in groans and sighs. In an uproar
her father's household was lamenting his niece,
when the guest suggested that she be taken to the spot where
the horse had happened to be cured. The girl was put on a cart
and carried along, as the traveller commanded, while he led the
way to the holy place where her body was placed on the ground.
She slept for a little and, on waking, realized that she had
been cured. Then she found some water, washed her face,
arranged her hair, covered her head with a scarf

306 *cf.* v. 1535   307 *cf.* v. 1493   314 *cf.* v. 721   317 *cf.*
v. 403   318 *cf.* vv. 381, 1190   325 ff. Alc. *Vit. S. Willibr. metr.*
xxx. 1-4 mulier totis paralitica membris ... / ... languit ... / tabida ... / ultima
vix moriens suspiria corde trahebat   327 [ibid. xxii. 1]

308-9. On the body's incorruptibility after death as a sign of sanctity see
Colgrave-Mynors, pp. 240-1, n. 2.
311 ff. Alcuin's attitude to miracles and the miraculous is discussed at Intro-
duction, pp. liv-lv.
327. On the transitive use of *gemere* in poetry see Leumann-Hofmann-
Szantyr ii. p. 32.

ductoresque suos alacris deinde secuta est.   335
HE iii. 10 *Alter iter faciens praefatae per loca pugnae,*
ecce loci spatium campo iocundius omni
unius inspexit, viridique venustius herba.
Haec reputat secum: 'Cecidit vir sanctior istic,
arbitror, idcirco prodest haec terra saluti.'   340
Atque ligans panno tulerat de pulvere secum,
venit et ad quandam lassescens vespere villam.
Plebs epulare casam villae tunc venit in unam,
quam quoque susceptus veniens intraverat hospes,
pulveris ac pannum posta suspendit in alta.   345
Contigit ut subito flammis volitantibus altum
ignis edax culmen raperet nec viribus ullis
exstingui valuit, donec incendia totam
consumpsere domum; nimium res mira sed acta est:
pulvere sacratam postam timet igneus ardor   350
tangere, sed penitus flammis intacta remansit.
Qua virtute quidem visa, stupor omnibus ingens
incubuit statim. Tunc cognovere quod ille
pulvis erat sacro regis cum sanguine mixtus
Osuualdi, multis fuerat qui causa salutis.   355
HE iii. 11 Claruit his signis postquam locus iste peractis,
ecclesiis Christi iocunda et reddita pax est,
regis Aedilredi regina Osthryda fidelis,
quae fuit Osuualdi sancti iam filia fratris,
curavit sancti sacris inducere tectis   360
reliquias patrui dignoque recondere honore.
Ossibus allatis stupuit miracula late

335 deinde *T*: exinde *R*   344 quam *R*: qua *T*   345 posta *R*:
porta *T r*   350 postam *R*: portam *T r*   353 quod ille *T*: quod almus
r: *om. R*   355 Osuualdi *R*: Osvaldi *T*   357 pax est *Wattenbach*:
pace *T R*   358 Edilredi *T*: Hedilredi *R*: Edelredi *Gale*   Osthfrida *T*:
hostrida *R*   359 Osuualdi *R*: Osvaldi *T*

345 Virg. *Aen.* v. 489 malo suspendit ab alto   346 ibid. xi. 751
347 ibid. ii. 758–59 ignis edax summa ad fastigia . . . / volvitur   354 ibid.
ix. 349   362 Aldh. *de Virg. metr.* 665 stupuit miracula

335 *cf.* vv. 688, 1339   341 *cf.* v. 398   347 Alc. ix. 84
355 *cf.* vv. 420, 779   356 *cf.* vv. 678, 1031   361 *cf.* v. 1071

and swiftly followed those who had brought her there.
Journeying by the site of that battle, another man
saw a plot of ground that was more attractive and pleasant
and had greener grass than anywhere in the field.
He mused to himself: 'In that place, I should think,
died a holy man, and so this earth can perform acts of healing.'
He wrapped up some of the dust in a cloth and took it with him.
Wearily, in the evening, he came to a village,
where the folk had gathered together in a cottage for a feast.
He arrived, was received and taken in as a guest,
and hung the cloth with the dust high on a beam.
A consuming fire suddenly sprang up, its flames soaring
to the roof on high. No effort could put it out,
and the inferno finally consumed the entire house.
But then a miracle occurred. The burning heat
flinched from touching the post hallowed by the dust,
and there it stood, completely untouched by the flames.
When this sign of God's power was seen, everyone was
thunderstruck. They then understood
that the dust was mixed with king Oswald's holy blood,
which had brought salvation to many souls. After
the performance of these miracles made that spot famous,
and sweet peace was restored to the churches of Christ,
Osthryth, king Æthelred's faithful queen,
the daughter of sainted king Oswald's brother,
saw to it that the remains of her holy uncle were brought into
that hallowed building and laid to rest again with due honour.
On the translation of the bones of the saint

337-8. loci spatium . . . / unius: the periphrasis is of Biblical origin. Cf. Jos. 10: 13.

341. On partitive *de* see Löfstedt, *Syntactica*, i², pp. 145 ff.

342. villam: as v. 343 makes plain, Alcuin is using this word as a synonym for Bede's *vicum* (cf. *HE* iv. 27(25): *circumpositas . . . villas*). Bede also employs *villa* to mean 'estate' (*HE* ii. 16: *civitates seu villas aut provincias*), 'hall' (*HE* ii. 9 *villa regalis*), and simply 'dwelling' (*HE* v. 4).

358. Osthryth, wife of Æthelred, king of Mercia (*ob.* 697).

362-3. Hargrove took the adverb to show the extent of the onlookers' surprise and compared the ME idiom 'highly amused'. I find no evidence for this usage in early Medieval Latin or in Scripture. The adverb cannot be taken with *accola* (despite Virg. *Aen.* i. 21 *populum late regem*), because *accola* is not adjectival but the main subject, and the line division precludes its close attachment to *late*. The adverb is therefore to be construed in its literal sense with *stupuit* (cf. vv. 936, 1459).

accola Lindissae cernens super illa columnam
ossa viri sancti summi ad fastigia caeli
luminis aetherei tota fulgescere nocte,   365
maior reliquias qua tunc aulea tegebat.
Nam priscis odiis adsumere primitus ossa
inque monasterium saevi deferre negantes
nocte manere foras illa fecere coloni.
Sed dum divini viderunt luminis ignem,   370
quae prius abnuerant secum retinere rogabant,
maneque sarcofago condentes lota parato
ecclesiae tulerant magno sub culmen honore,
divitias terris curantes condere vivas.
In quo multa loco fiunt nunc usque patroni   375
ob meritum tanti in languentes dona salutis,
sanctae si Fidei virtus comitatur eosdem.
E quibus hoc unum properanti tangere plectro
sufficit, ut credas devotus cetera, lector.

HE iii. 12 *Febre puer quidam iacuit per tempora longa,*   380
coenobio languens citius moriturus in illo.
Ecce die quadam miser ad loca sancta sepulcri
ducitur, Osuualdi meritis ne tangeret illum
febris acerba—fides nam percipit omne quod orat.
Credidit ut languens, citus ad sua tecta cucurrit,   385
corpore sanato properans et pectore laeto,
morbida nec audet plus illum tangere febris.
Postea rex felix ornaverat Offa sepulcrum
argento, gemmis, auro, multoque decore,
ut decus et specimen tumbae per saecla maneret,   390
praemia pro modico sumpturus magna labore.
Nec non terra micat caelestibus inclyta signis

366 qua *R*: quas *T*   383 Osuualdi *R*: Osvaldi *T*   384 percipit *R*: praeci-
pit *T*   omne *T*: unde unde *R*   387 nec *T R*: non *Gale*

364 Virg. *Aen.* ii. 758 summa ad fastigia   365 Arat. *de Act. Apostol.* ii.
624 aethereis fulgebat . . . signis; Bede *Soliloq.* 29 nocte refulget   376 Aldh.
de Virg. metr. 411   378 Bede *Vit. S. Cuthb. metr.* 144 tangere sed breviter
exemplis sufficit unum   384 Matt. 7: 7   392 Bede *Vit. S. Cuthb.*
metr. 842 caelestibus inclita signis

365 *cf.* v. 1065   367 ff. Æthelw. *de Abbat.* 229 ff.   376 *cf.* vv. 441, 609
377 Heiric *Vit. S. German.* iv. 335 salus comitatur euntem   378 Alc. *Vit. S.*
Willibr. metr. xiii. 3 quaedam properanti tangere plectro; [ibid. xxxiv. 57]
380 *cf.* v. 489   382 *cf.* vv. 396, 1459   389 *cf.* v. 277   392 *cf.* v. 683

the people who lived in Lindsey were amazed far and wide
to see above the bones of that holy man a miraculous column
of ethereal light shining up to the heights of Heaven all night
in the place where a great pall was covering them.
For the savage country people, because of a long-standing feud,
had at first refused to carry the bones into the monastery,
and had made them stay outdoors that night.
But when they saw the fiery light sent by God,
they then begged to keep what they had earlier refused to have,
and, the next morning, before burying the bones in the tomb
they washed and carried them with pomp into the
lofty church, laying their living wealth to rest in the earth.
There, to this day, through the greatness of that patron saint
many acts of healing are performed on the sick,
if they possess the virtue of holy faith.
It is enough for me, reader, to touch with my swift lyre
on one of them for you devoutly to believe the rest.
For a long time a boy lay ill with fever in that monastery,
growing weaker and weaker, on the point of death.
Then, one day, the poor boy was taken to that holy spot,
where Oswald was buried, to save him from the raging fever
by the saint's virtues—for faith receives its every request.
As soon as the sick boy had faith, he ran swiftly home,
eager, healed in body and happy at heart,
and the deadly fever dared not touch him again.
Later blessed king Offa adorned the tomb
with silver, gold, gems, and much finery,
making of it a splendid and enduring monument,
and winning great rewards for such small effort.
Resplendent with miracles sent from Heaven is the very earth

366. qua: grammatically ambiguous. Although translated as 'in the place where' it may be taken as co-ordinate with *nocte* (= 'in the night *in which*').

367-9. The story Alcuin tells differs subtly from Bede's. Half a century after Oswald's death the monks of Bardney in Lindsey refused to accept his relics 'quia de alia provincia ortus fuerat et super eos regnum acceperat, veteranis eum odiis etiam mortuum insequebantur' (*HE* iii. 11; discussed by Stenton, p. 83). Alcuin makes no mention of the monks. Instead it is the *saevi coloni* who refuse to bear Oswald's bones into the monastery. At every point in Alcuin's narrative the Church is made to appear in a favourable light.

369. foras = *foris*: B. Axelson, *Unpoetische Wörter* (Lund, 1945), p. 96.

388-91. This is our only eighth-century source for Offa's benefactions to the tomb of Oswald. See Introduction, pp. xlv–xlvi.

corporis, ut dixi, quae sancti lota lavacro est,
sumpsit et effectum vincendi tela maligni
daemonis et sanos vexatis reddere sensus.   395

HE iii. 11   *Abbatissa quidem quaedam loca sancta videre*
advenit, sese et meritis committere sancti,
iamque domum rediens tulerat de pulvere terrae,
ablutis sacram quae ex ossibus hauserat undam.
Tempore transacto veniebat hospes ad illam,   400
daemone qui fuerat nocturnis saepius horis
vexari solitus. Clamoribus ecce repente
coeperat horrendis frendens loca lata replere,
morsibus et furiens semet lacerare nefandis.
Et cum nullus eum potuit constringere vinclis   405
vel miseri saevos flagris compescere motus,
haec abbatissae quidam narrare cucurrit.
Illa videns miseros motus vocesque furentis
iusserat adferri sacro cum pulvere capsam.
Et cum virgo ferens veniebat, ut atria tecti   410
intraret, subito tacuit furiosus et omnes
composuit motus, somno quasi membra dedisset.
Quisque rei adstantes spectabant exitus esset.
Post horae spatium vexatus et ipse resedit,
suspirans graviter: 'Sanus sum, sensibus', inquit,   415
'redditus, et vacuas fugit vagus hostis in auras.'
Mirantur cuncti stupidis hinc inde loquelis,
incolumem subito cernentes corpore toto,
ossibus et nervis nec non et mente vigentem.
Inquirunt subitae causam mirando salutis.   420
Qui respondit ovans: 'Ut venit virgo locellum
portans et pedibus tetigit haec atria, statim
discessere procul qui me torquere solebant
daemones, ut fugiunt venienti luce tenebrae.'

---

404 furiens *T R*: furens *edd.*   410 ut *R*: et *T*   424 venienti *T r*:
venientes *R*: veniente *Froben*

---

398 Gen. 13: 16   400 Aldh. *de Virg. metr.* 1251 tempore transacto
402-3 id. *Ænigm.* lxviii. 2   403 Virg. *Aen.* ii. 495 late loca . . . com-
plent   416 Aldh. *Carm. eccl.* iv. 2. 13 in vacuasque procul fugiens . . . auras
419 id. *Ænigm.* xiv. 2 ossibus ac nervis

401-2 Alc. *Vit. S. Willibr. metr.* xxii. 2 saepius incursu vexatur daemonis atri
416 Milo *Vit. S. Amand.* ii. 165 vagus in vacuas fugiens evanuit auras   419 Alc.

washed by water in which, as I said, the saint's body was bathed.
And so it became capable of routing the Devil's attacks
and of restoring sanity to those possessed.
An abbess came to see the place,
with full trust in the saint's virtues and, on returning home,
she took with her some dust from the earth which had
absorbed the holy water that had washed Oswald's bones.
Time passed, and there came to that abbess
a man who was often tormented at night-time by a demon.
All of a sudden he began to groan,
filling the land all about with his terrible cries,
biting and tearing horribly at himself.
When nobody could bind him with chains
or contain with blows the wretch's flailings,
someone ran to tell the abbess about it.
Hearing his tormented cries and seeing him writhing in misery,
she ordered a box containing that holy dust to be fetched.
And when a girl came carrying the relic and entered the house,
the frenzied man suddenly fell silent, ceased to move, and
grew still, as if his limbs were settling to sleep,
and the bystanders looked to see what would happen.
After an hour the possessed man sat up again,
sighing gravely and saying: 'I am healed, restored to my senses,
and the unquiet demon has fled into the empty air.'
All around the onlookers fell silent and marvelled
at seeing his sudden and complete recovery,
that he was healed in bones, nerves, and mind.
Bewildered, they asked how he had recovered so suddenly.
He replied joyously: 'As soon as the maiden carrying that
little box touched this threshold with her step, the demons
which used to torment me retreated afar,
as the shadows flee at the coming of dawn.'

Vit. S. Willibr. metr. xxx. 11 ossibus et nervis

394-5. tela maligni: on the Biblical and liturgical origins of these terms, see Blaise, *Vocabulaire latin*, p. 466.

396. Æthelhild, sister of Æthelwine, bishop of Lindsey, and of Ealdwine, abbot of Partney (Colgrave-Mynors, p. 247, n. 4).

405-6. On the treatment of *vexati a diabolo* cf. Theodore's Penitential (Haddan and Stubbs iii, p. 197).

419. nec non et: on the development of this pleonasm see Löfstedt, *Kommentar*, pp. 95 ff. and, in general, *Syntactica*, ii, pp. 209 ff.

Cui portanda data est secum pars pulveris almi   425
ac post talis ei fuerat vexatio numquam.

HE iii. 2   Te quoque sancta, potens, virtutibus inclyta multis,
crux veneranda, canam, nequeam si promere dignos
laude tua versus. Reparasti perdita pridem;
nunc iterum per te cedit victoria regi   430
Osuualdo, ut quondam paucae cecinere camoenae.
Exin mirificis fulsit tua gloria signis;
ad te tota fide famosa Britannia currit
quaerere pro variis sibimet medicamina morbis,
et spes ad te etiam venientem fallere nescit;   435
namque salutis opes redeuntes saepe reportant.
Nec ego ruricola possum percurrere plectro
omnia, multoties quae per te signa geruntur:

.   .   .   .

et pecora atque homines, etiam iuvenesque senesque.
Denique praecisae de te ducuntur ubique   440
particulae, per quas fiunt pia dona salutis.
Sufficit e cunctis hoc solum dicere signum.
Frater erat quidam casu confractus acerbo,
infractique dolens penitus gemit ossa lacerti,
cumque dolor nimius succreverat et tumor ardens,   445
pectoris ingeminat lacrimans suspiria fessi.
De cruce cui quidam veteres iam vespere muscos

431 Osuualdo *R*: Osualdo *T*   435 spes *Reeve*: spe *T R*: spem *Dümmler*:
ipsa *Hargrove*   te etiam *T R*: temet iam *Traube*: tete etiam *Dümmler*   venien-
tem *T R*: venientum *Dümmler, Add.*   nescit *T R*: nescis *Gale*   437 nec
T R: non *Gale* ·   ruricola *Gale*: ruricula *T*: ruriculo *R*   438-9 *a
lacuna lies between these verses*   439 et *T R*: in *Godman*
444 infractique *T*: infractoque *R*   gemit ossa *T*: gemitos se *R*

427 Virg. *Georg.* iii. 1   427 ff. Arat. *de Act. Apostol.* i. 801–2 Te quoque,
laude potens, caelestibus incluta signis / . . . canimus; Paul. Nol. xix. 716 Nunc ad te,
veneranda Dei crux, verto loquellas   429 Arat. *de Act. Apostol.* ii. 106
435 Virg. *Georg.* ii. 467; id. *Aen.* viii. 218   436 ibid. vii. 285
437 Aldh. *de Virg. metr.* 23 non rogo ruricolas; Bede *Soliloq.* 14 percurrere plectro
437–8 Virg. *Aen.* vi. 625, 627 non . . . / omnia . . . percurrere nomina possum
439 Ven. Fort. iii. 6. 3 iuvenesque senesque   443 Virg. *Aen.* v. 700 casu
concussus acerbo   444 ibid. v. 422 ossa lacertosque

427 Milo *Vit. S. Amand.* iii. 180 Te quoque, sancte   433 *cf.* v. 501
435 Walahfr. ix. 2. 5   436 Alc. lxix. 32   437 id. *Vit. S. Willibr.*
metr. praef. 4 percurrens titulis inclyta gesta citis; ibid. xiii. 2–3   437–8 Er-
mold. *In hon. Hlud.* i. 9, 15 cum sim rusticulus . . . / non ego gestorum per
singula quaeque precurram; Heiric *Vit. S. German.* i. 188 plectro percurrere

He was given a portion of that blessed dust to take with him
and never afterwards suffered from such torment.
Of you, too, shall I sing, holy, powerful, venerable cross,
famed for many miracles, even though my verse is unworthy
to praise you. You bestowed what was lost in the past;
now, once again, by you victory was granted to king Oswald,
as my poor verse has told. From that moment,
your glory shone forth in wondrous miracles,
and all Britain, acclaimed for her faith, thronged to you,
seeking a cure for her various ills,
and hope does not deceive those who come to you,
for they often return taking with them the riches of salvation.
I, a country bumpkin, cannot run in verse through
all the miracles which you have repeatedly performed

.   .   .   .

[on] both beasts and men, young and old.
And so small pieces are cut from your every side,
and holy deeds of healing are performed by them.
From them all it is enough to recount this single miracle.
There was a monk who had suffered a fracture in a bad accident
and was groaning, deeply in pain from his broken arm;
as the suffering grew and the swelling burned,
he wept, heaving sigh upon sigh from his weary heart.
Then, in the evening, someone brought him hoary moss

textum   439 cf. vv. 528, 1587   443 cf. 1191

---

427 ff. Alcuin interrupts his narrative with a hymn on the Cross, to which he
also devoted an acrostic poem (*Carm.* vi; for bibliography see Schaller–Könsgen,
p. 137, no. 01, and, in general, Bischoff, *Mittelalterliche Studien* ii, pp. 284-
303). A survey of this genre is provided by J. Szövérffy, *Hymns of the Holy Cross*
(Brookline and Leyden, 1976). On the cult of the cross in early Northumbria,
reflected in sculpture and in vernacular poetry, see M. Swanton, *The Dream of the
Rood* (Manchester and New York, 1970), pp. 45 ff., and U. Schwab in *Gedenk-
schrift für Richard Kienast* edd. U. Schwab and E. Stutz (Heidelberg, 1978),
pp. 157 ff. The sculpture is discussed by R. Cramp, *Early Northumbrian Sculp-
ture* (Jarrow Lecture, 1965), pp. 8 ff., W. G. Collingwood, *Northumbrian Crosses
of the pre-Norman Age* (London, 1927), pp. 19 ff. and T. D. Kendrick, *Anglo-
Saxon Art to A.D. 900* (London, 1938), pp. 126-42.

435. **spes** justifies *nescit*, removes an impossible hiatus after *spe*, and makes
sense.

438-9. Syntax and sense are disrupted if one reads *et* with the manuscripts at
v. 439. I posit the loss of at least one verse, perhaps referring to the place where
Oswald's host prayed at the battle of Denisesburn and these miracles were per-
formed (as at Bede, *HE* iii. 2). An alternative is to emend *et* to *in* at v. 439.

443. Bothelm, a monk of Hexham, still alive in Bede's lifetime (*HE* iii. 2).

attulit, in gremium sibimet quos proicit aeger;
cumque iret cubitum oblitus deponere muscum,
nescius in gremio somno praeventus habebat.   450
Evigilans medio morbosus tempore noctis,
ecce aliquid gelidi lateri sibi sensit adesse,
admotaque manu sanum se forte fuisse
reperit atque nihil fractura sensit ab illa.

HE iii. 13   Inclyta fama viri non solum iure Britannos   455
inlustrat populos, trans insuper aequora ponti
aspersit radios, quibus et Germania fulsit,
e quibus et quaedam populosa Hibernia sensit.
Sed nobis signum vero inter multa relatu
hoc narrare placet: dirae nam tempore pestis,   460
aequoreos populos lata quae clade peremit,
Scotorum genere scolasticus, acer in arte,
hoc fuerat morbo patria percussus in illa,
librorum studio doctus, sed nulla futurae
cura fuit misero vitae. Sibi cumque videret   465
mortis adesse diem, magno trepidare timore
coeperat ob merita scelerum, ne ad Tartara dira
mortuus Inferni raperetur. Voce gementi
alloquitur socium: 'Frater, mihi mortis amarae
articulus properat, citiusque ad Tartara ducar   470
perpetuae mortis, quoniam non tempore parvo
criminibus tantum penitus servire solebam.
Proh dolor! haec propter novi feralia flammis
Tartara parta mihi. Totis mihi sensibus est hinc,
si velit Omnipotens misero concedere vitam,   475
viribus annisis mores mutare malignos.
Nec tamen esse mei meriti scio vivere tantum,

---

453 manu *T*: manum *R*   455 non *T*: nec *R*   471 quoniam *R*:
quam *T*: quia iam *Gale*: quianam *Raine*

455-7 Bede *Vit. St. Cuthb. metr.* 25 f. Nec iam orbis contenta sinu trans aequora
lampas / spargitur effulgens   465 Paul. Nol. xi. 8   466 Sedul.
Carm. pasch. v. 120 trepidare timore   469-70 Bede *de Die Iud.* 30

---

461 Poet. Saxo ii. 78   469-70 Alc. *Vit. S. Willibr. metr.* xxxii. 10 mortis
in articulo   472 *cf.* v. 712   475 *cf.* v. 627

---

462. scolasticus: Alcuin generally uses the term to refer to a pupil or student

from the cross, which the sick man tossed in his lap.
When he went to bed he forgot to remove it.
Unawares, he left it in his lap, prevented from sleeping.
Lying awake in his illness in the middle of the night,
he felt something cold near his side,
and, touching the fracture, he found
that he was cured and that it gave him no pain.

This saint's splendid fame not only cast proper lustre
upon the peoples of Britain but also spread its rays
over the ocean, enlightening even the peoples of Germany
and touching also upon populous Ireland.
I think it best truly to relate only this one
of many miracles: at the time when a severe plague
was ravaging far and wide the peoples dwelling by the sea,
a scholar of the Irish race, of subtle learning,
was struck down by illness in his fatherland.
Although a scholar, learned and well-read, the unhappy man
had been unconcerned about the life to come. When he saw the
day of his death approach, he began to tremble in great dread
for the due punishment of his sins, afraid of being dragged
after death into the terrible realms of Hell.
With groans in his voice he said to a fellow-monk: 'Brother,
the bitter end is upon me and I shall go down direct
to Hell and perpetual death, for I have long served
in absolute bondage Sin, my only master.
Alas! I know that for these misdeeds the flames of dire Hell
are reserved for me. I am resolved with all my being that,
if Omnipotent God will deign to grant me life in my misery,
I shall from this moment strive to change my wicked habits.
I know that I shall not exist so long through my own merits:

(*Carm.* xxxii. 23; *Ep.* 273: 'per fideles nostros discipulos, Eboracensis aecclesiae scolasticos' (*MGH Epp.* iv, p. 431. 35-6)). Here, following Bede, he describes a mature scholar.

468-9. Alcuin's view of Hell is given vivid expression in *Ep.* 18: 'O quam miser erit, qui semper arsurus erit in igne, qui tenebris circumdatur horrendis, qui nil audiet nisi voces flentium et stridentium dentibus horrorem, qui nil sentit nisi flammas edaces et frigora ingentia et vermium venenatos dentes' (*MGH Epp.* iv, p. 51. 4-6).

477. mei meriti: repeated in this passage (vv. 479, 488) and recurrent throughout the poem; the different senses of this important term are discussed by Blaise, *Vocabulaire latin* (p. 435). For this construction see Löfstedt, *Kommentar*, pp. 278-9.

ni mihi concedat vitae modo munus amatae
sanctorum meritis miserantis gratia Christi.
Audivi quondam celebri rumore referri   480
Osuualdi regis laudes virtutibus amplas.
Tu quia de genere es Saxonum collega natus,
forsan habes eius quicquam modo reliquiarum?'
Cui socius statim fidam profatur in aurem:
'Pars inventa sacri est mecum de stipite ligni,   485
infixum fuerat caput occisi illius in quo;
et si firma tenes Fidei tu pectora credens,
per tanti pietas meritum divina patroni
huius adhuc vitae donat tibi tempora longa;
insuper aeternum praestabit gaudia forsan.'   490
Nec mora quin toto dixit se credere corde.
Tum benedixit aquam socius, partemque sacrati
roboris immittens aegro dedit atque bibendum.
Qui mox convaluit, mortique ereptus ab illa est.
Exhinc incolumis multo iam tempore vixit,   495
ad Dominumque suam vitam converterat omnem,
magnificasque Deo laudes referebat ubique
et Domini famulum magno celebrabat honore.

HE iii. 9 Sanctus ter ternis Osuuald feliciter annis
imperio postquam regnorum rexit habenas—   500
in se quod retinet famosa Britannia gentes

HE iii. 6 *divisas linguis, populis per nomina patrum—*
atque annos postquam ter denos vixit et octo,

[642] Augustas sacra Nonas iam morte dicavit,

---

481 Osualdi *R*: Osvaldi *T*   490 aeternum *R*: aeternae *T*   491 corde
T r: velle *R*   493 bibendum *T R*: bibendam *edd.*   496 suam *T r*:
suum *R*   499 ter ternis *T*: terrenis *R*   Osualt *R*: Osvald *T*   501 in
se *R*: ipse *T*   quod *R*: quas *T r*   502 divisas *T R*: divisis *Gale*

---

479 Paul. Nol. xvi. 283 gratia Christi; id. xix. 164 Christi miserantis   484 Bede
Vit. S. Cuthb. metr. 962 fidam cui fatus in aurem; [Virg. *Aen.* v. 547]   488 Paul.
Nol. xviii. 5   490 Matt. 25: 23   491 Juvenc. *Evang.* ii. 412 se credere
corde fatentur   494 Virg. *Aen.* xii. 157   496 Aldh. *de Virg. metr.*
1864 ad dominum tota conversus mente   497 Juvenc. *Evang.* i. 96 magni-
ficas laudes . . . rependit   498 Virg. *Aen.* v. 58   500 Bede *Vit. S.*
Cuthb. metr. 516 qui regat imperii . . . habenas; Ven. Fort. iv. 4. 19   502 Gen.
10: 31-2

---

479 Alc. *Vit. S. Willibr. metr.* xxxi. 11 miserantis gratia Christi; Paul. Diac.
xxxiii. 14 Christi per miserantis opem   488 Alc. lxxxix. 2. 3   491 Paulin.

the grace of Christ in His mercy, by the intercession of the
saints, must grant me the gift of life which I now love dearly.
I have once heard swift rumour speak in resounding praise
of king Oswald for his virtuous deeds.
Since you too are by birth a fellow-member
of the Saxon race, have you by chance any relic of him?'
His companion immediately declared to his trusting ear:
'I have with me a piece of holy wood found from the stake
on which Oswald's head was nailed after his murder,
and if you believe staunchly at heart in the Faith
God's goodness, through the merit of this great saint,
will grant you a long span in this life,
and perhaps assure you joys for evermore.'
Without hesitation the man declared his wholehearted faith.
Then his companion blessed some water, put in it a piece
of the hallowed wood, and gave it to the sick man to drink.
He soon recovered, saved by it from death.
He then lived a long and healthy life,
completely devoted to the Lord,
offering up splendid praise to Him at every point
and extolling with high honour His servant [Oswald].
Saint Oswald ruled prosperously for nine years
and after holding in his sway the empire—for famed
Britain holds within her bounds peoples divided by language
and separated by race according to their ancestors' names—
after a lifetime of thirty-eight years, he made
the fifth of August a calendar-day by his holy death, ascending

Aquil. i. 9   492-3 Alc. *Vit. S. Willibr. pros.* xxi aquam benedixit . . . ac
aegrotantibus potandum transmisit   494 *cf.* v. 1633   497 Æthelw.
de Abbat. 173   499-500 *Walthar.* 1450 ter denis populum rexit feliciter
annis   500 *cf.* v. 566; Alc. *Vit. S. Willibr. metr.* ix. 1 regales rexit habenas
502 'Karolus Magnus' 495-6 quam varias . . . linguis . . . / miratur gentes; *Walthar.*
2 moribus ac linguis varias et nomine gentes

482. **collĕga** = *socius* (v. 484). See Latham, *Dictionary*, ii, C, *s.v.* p. 380,
col. 2. 1. For the prosody cf. 'David' viii, 21 (*MGH PLAC* i, p. 112): 'O mihi non
prolis tantum, set collĕga fidus.'
493. **bibendum**: cf. Bede *HE* iii. 13 'benedixi aqu*am* et astulam roboris prae-
fati inmittens obtuli egro potand*um*' and cf. app. iii to vv. 492-3.
501. **quod** [= *quia*]. The clause vv. 501-2 is parenthetical, and describes the
imperium of v. 500. On Oswald's supremacy see Stenton, pp. 81-2. On his sanc-
tity and kingship, see E. Hoffmann, *Die heiligen Könige bei den Angelsachsen* . . .
(Neumünster, 1975), pp. 26 ff.; Introduction, p. l.

ascendit meritis caelestia regna coruscis, 505
Osui germano terrestria sceptra relinquens.
HE iii. 13 Interea tenuit multo iam sceptra labore
principio propriae rector novus Osui gentis:
impugnatus enim fuerat hinc inde vicissim
saepius externis praedantibus undique fines. 510
Insuper a propriis perpessus bella propinquis,
qui crudele manu lacerabant viscera regni
cognato implentes sceleratas sanguine dextras,
nec metuunt patrias gentilia castra per urbes
invidia cogente fera deducere, vel sic 515
viribus externis conantes sternere regem.
HE iii. 24 Cui fuit ante alios primis infestus ab annis
hostes rex Pendan fortis virtute doloque,
occisor fratris, regni et vastator acerbus.
Qui ter dena sibi conduxit milia bello, 520
[655] ter denosque duces totidem deducere turmas
disposuit, quorum certus fuit usus in armis.
Hac vastare manu veniensque evertere regnum,
moenia destruxit, homines mucrone peremit.
Imbribus exundans torrens ceu montibus altis 525
sternit agros segetesque rapit silvasque recidit,
sic dux ipse ferox devastans omnia pressit,
dans simul in pessum pueros iuvenesque senesque.
  Nullus eum sexus vel nulla retraxerat aetas
ad pietatis opus, nullo qui iure pepercit. 530

506 Osui *R*: Osuvi *T*   507 tenuit *R*: obtinuit *T*   508 Osui *R*:
Osvi *T*   515 vel sic *T r*: vel sic sic *R*   518 hostes *T R*: hostis *Ruinart* for-
tis *T*: forti *R*   519 et *T*: *om. R*   520 bello *R Ruinart*: bella *T*
523 veniensque *T*: veniens *R*   529 vel *T r*: per *R*   530 qui *T*:
quia *R*

505 Ps. 138: 8; 2 Tim. 4: 18   512 Virg. *Aen.* vi. 833 patriae . . . in
viscera vertite viris; ibid. xii. 98 manu . . . lacerare   513 Lucan *Bell. civ.* iv.
554 cognato implerunt sanguine   514 Virg. *Aen.* xi. 793 patrias . . . urbes
518 ibid. ii. 390 dolus an virtus, quis in hoste requirat?   525 ibid. xii. 523
de montibus altis   525 ff. ibid., ii. 305-7 . . . rapidus montano flumine
torrens / sternit agros . . . / praecipitisque trahit silvas

506 *cf.* v. 576   518 Alc. *Ep.* 149 (p. 242, 21 ff.) tria videntur in hoste
consideranda: virtus, dolus, pax; Poet. Saxo i. 251   521 id. iii. 7
528 Paul. Diac. xxxiii. 21

through his brilliant virtues into the realms of Heaven,
leaving his earthly kingdom to his brother Oswiu.
Oswiu, the new leader of his people,
had to struggle at first to hold the throne,
for time and again he was attacked on all sides
by foreigners pillaging every part of his realm.
He suffered too from feuds with his own relatives,
who cruelly rent the heart of his kingdom,
covering their criminal hands with kinsmen's blood,
not hesitating to bring pagan troops into the cities
of their homeland, spurred by pitiless envy, and so
attempted to overthrow the king by foreign force.
From his earliest years on the throne Oswiu's deadliest enemy
was Penda, a king mighty in strength and in guile, the
murderer of Oswiu's brother and cruel ravager of his kingdom.
Penda raised thirty thousand troops for battle,
appointing thirty captains for as many divisions,
whose experience in arms was tested and proven.
With this force he came to ravage and overturn the kingdom,
smashing down walls, putting men to the sword.
As a torrent, brimming over with rain from the high mountains,
covers the fields, destroys the crops, lays low the woods,
so that barbarian chieftain ravaged and crushed all beneath him,
slaying children, youths, and the old alike.
Neither age nor sex held him to observe
the obligation of mercy; he spared no law.

506 ff. On Oswald's death in 641 Oswiu succeeded in Bernicia. Oswine, son of Osric, became king in Deira (Bede *HE* iii. 14, with Colgrave-Mynors, p. 256, n. 2). In 651 Oswiu invaded Deira, expelling Oswine and having him murdered. These local and factional rivalries are largely eliminated by Alcuin, who consistently treats Northumbria in this period as a unified kingdom (see Introduction, pp. lii–liii). Oswine was succeeded by Æthelwald, a son of Oswald, who placed himself under the protection of Penda of Mercia. Penda in turn attacked Oswiu in 654.

507. tenuit, which accords better with *interea* than *obtinuit*, is confirmed by *HE* iii. 14: 'Et per annos XXXVIII laboriosissime tenuit.'

512. crudele: ablative in *-e, metri causa.*

518. On Penda's position and strategy in 654 see Stenton, pp. 83–4.

520–1. Bede states that Penda had thirty *legiones* with as many *duces* at the battle of Winwaed (on which see Plummer ii, p. 183, and J. O. Prestwich, 'King Aethelhere and the Battle of the Winwaed', *EHR* 83 (1968), pp. 89–95).

530. nullo . . . iure: dative of the pronominal adjective in *-o* (Introduction, p. xcv (i) (*b*) (iv)), probably in agreement with *iure* (dative in *-e, metri causa*). If *iure* is construed as an ablative the object remains *nullo* but the sense is obscure.

Sed rector, cui cura fuit defendere gentem,
seque suosque simul Christi tutarier armis,
legit et ipse viros fortes, atque agmina tanta
venerat haud trepido contra rex pectore promptus
milite cum raro, primo sed numen Olympi   535
fletibus et votis constanti corde poposcit.
His actis etiam hostiles ut vidit ubique
innumeras acies latis discurrere campis,
[Nov. 15] has contra opposuit parvum licet impiger agmen,
milia trina ciens tantum, sed prompta duello.   540
Nec mora quin mediis se immiserat hostibus audax,
proturbans acies Christi testudine fretus.
Mox timor impactas populorum dispulit alas,
qui pugnae immemores, armis telisque relictis,
tuta fugae petiere loca et sua signa revellunt.   545
Palantum cuneos victor rex cedit ubique,
horrisona increpitans fugientes voce phalanges.
Arma cruore natant, mutantur sanguine fontes;
fugit et ipse simul, tanta vix clade coactus,
dux Pendan cernens caedes stragesque suorum.   550
Nec tamen evaluit fugiens evadere mortem,
sed gladio cecidit victrici occisus et ille.
Curritur ad praedam passim et laus digna Tonanti
redditur aeterno, semper qui liberat omnes
in se sperantes clemens et salvat ubique.   555
Hoc erat, hoc etiam multis satis utile bellum;
namque suam gentem rex hostibus eruit acris,

---

534 promptus *R Ruinart*: promptum *T*   536 fletibus *R Ruinart*: preci-
bus *T*   537 etiam hostiles *T r*: hostes etiam hostiles *R*   545 revellunt
Ruinart: repellunt *T R*   547 phalanges *T R*: phalangas *Ruinart*

---

532 Bede *Vit. S. Cuthb. metr.* 147 seque suosque rogans precibus tutarier almi
535 Prud. *Psych.* 197   536 Virg. *Aen.* i. 666 supplex tua numina posco
538 Ven. Fort. *Vit. S. Mart.* i. 77 innumerasque acies; Lucan *Bell. civ.* iv. 733 late
discurrere campis   542 Aldh. *de Virg. metr.* 1024 Christi testudine fretus
545 Lucan *Bell. civ.* vii. 77 signa revellent   548 ibid. vii. 537 mutentur san-
guine fontes   549 ibid. vii. 648 tota vix clade coactus   552 Bede
Vit. S. Cuthb. metr. 365   556 Virg. *Aen.* xii. 259 hoc erat, hoc . . .

---

556 Alc. *Vit. S. Willibr. metr.* xii. 1 Hoc opus, hoc fuerat . . .

---

531 ff. Alcuin omits Oswiu's pledge that, if he won the battle, he would
dedicate twelve estates to religious uses and his infant daughter to God's service.

But king [Oswiu], anxious to defend his people,
to protect himself and his followers with the weapons of Christ,
chose stalwart men and advanced
against those mighty forces with an unflinching spirit
but with a small company invoking first
God in Heaven with tears, vows, and trusting heart.
The prayer ended, he saw their ranks racing back and forth
on every side, spread, countless in number, over the broad field.
Against them he valiantly pitted his small force—calling
up only three thousand men, but they were ready to fight.
Into the enemy's midst he charged with speed and bravado,
relying on Christ's protection, throwing them into turmoil.
Fear soon scattered the thronged battalions of that host
which, forgetting the battle, abandoned all its weapons,
uprooted its standards, and sought safety in flight.
The king cut down on all sides the stragglers' ranks,
taunting their retreating battle-lines in dread tones.
Weapons ran with gore, streams were turned to blood, and
Penda their leader, unwilling, but forced to yield
before his defeat, took flight on seeing the massacre of his men.
Nor did he contrive to avoid death by fleeing,
but perished at the victor's sword. All over the battlefield
men ran after booty, and due praise was given
to eternal God, who at all times and places mercifully
delivers and preserves those who have hope in Him.
This was a war from which many men gained,
for the king saved his people from the cruel enemy

538. **discurrere:** the verse is modelled on Lucan, and the use of the variant *discurrere* here (v.l. *decurrere* in Lucan) may indicate that Alcuin's exemplar of the *Bell. civ.* was related to the family *PGU* isolated by Housman (ed. cit., pp. xiv and 115). On the importance of such variants see J. E. Cross, *PBA* 58 (1972), p. 5 and n. 3.

556. **utile bellum:** cf. Bede, *HE* iii. 24: 'Hoc autem bellum rex Osuiu ... cum magna utriusque populi utilitate confecit.' Gregory the Great had recommended the use of warfare as a means of propagating the Faith: 'bella vos frequenter appetere . . . dilatandae causa rei publicae . . . quatenus Christi nomen per subditas gentes . . . discurrat' (*MGH Epp.* i, p. 93. 16)—discussed by D. H. Green, *The Carolingian Lord* (Cambridge, 1965), p. 296. See further Wallace-Hadrill, *Early Medieval History*, p. 27 and, in general, P. H. Russell, *The Just War in the Middle Ages* (Cambridge, 1975), pp. 21 ff.

557. **acris:** abl. pl. 'Acer facit pluraliter acri, acris pluraliter facit acres' (Alcuin, *De Orthographia*, ed. Marsili, p. 107. 18; cf. Bede, *De Orthographia*, ed. Jones, p. 11. 108).

Merciorum Fidei sceptris et subdidit almis,
sacrato faciens baptismatis amne lavari.
Perque illum donante Deo ditatur uterque   560
magnifico populus caelestis munere doni:
ille heres patriae factus, hic civis Olympi.
Ambo gentiles gemino micuere triumpho,
daemonis ille iugo, terreno hic hoste solutus.
Plurima continuis domuit post regna triumphis   565
Osuui, nobiliter patrias et rexit habenas,
aequoreasque sibi gentes hinc inde subegit,
has terrore premens, illas mucrone coercens:
victrices aquilas per regna ferebat ubique.
Legibus ille etiam fuerat iustissimus aequis,   570
invictus bellis nec non in pace fidelis,
donorum largus miseris, pius, omnibus aequus.
HE iv. 5 Imperium retinens septenos nam quater annos,
[670]   compositis rebus felix in pace quievit,
Ecgfrido tradens proprio diademata gnato,   575
Ecgfrido moriens regalia sceptra relinquens.
HE iv. 13 Tempore nam micuit Uuilfridus episcopus illo
virtutum meritis longe lateque per orbem,
quem Deus omnipotens infudit luce superna,
errorum tetricas terris ut pelleret umbras: 580

558 Merciorum *T r*: Mercunum *R*   566 Osuui *R*: Osvi *T*   570–4 *re-duplicated but deleted in T*   575, 576 Egfredo *T R*   576 *doublet or interpolation?*   577 Uilfridus *R*: Vilfridus *T*   578 *sic R*: *om. T*

563–4 Ven. Fort. *Vit. S. Mart.* i. 445, 447 Iste hostis laqueis, erroribus ille solu-tus / . . . uterque . . . gemino micuere triumpho   570 Bonif. *Carm.* i. 41
572 Ven. Fort. ix. 15. 15   574 Virg. *Aen.* i. 249 placida compostus pace quievit   576 Bede *Vit. S. Cuthb. metr.* 512   577–8 Paul. Nol. xix. 11–12 longe lateque per orbem / . . . emicuit   578 Aldh. *de Virg. metr.* 896 virtutum meritis   580 Bede *Vit. S. Cuthb. metr.* 22 discutit errorum vera iam luce tenebras

565 ff. Poet. Saxo iv. 330–1 innumeras postquam gentes hostesque triumphis subdiderat   572 Alc. *Ep.* 119 (p. 174, 13) esto largus in miseris, pius . . . *cf.* v. 1235; Æthelw. *de Abbat.* 411   574 *cf.* v. 1043   576 *cf.* v. 1274; Ermold. *in laud. Pipp. reg.* ii. 39   578 Alc. vii. 25 virtutum meritis; Heiric *Vit. S. Germ.* i. 177 signorum titulis longe lateque celebris   578–9 Æthelw. *de Abbat.* 93–4   580 *cf.* vv. 144, 656

565 ff. By his victory at the battle of Winwaed Oswiu earned the overlordship of all the southern kingdoms, until in 657 his rule was undermined by a revolt of

and brought the Mercians under the gentle sway of the Faith
causing them to be bathed in the hallowed river of baptism.
Through him, by God's grace, both peoples were enriched
by a splendid gift from on high: the one regained
its homeland, the other won entry into Heaven.
In the light of this double triumph both peoples were bathed,
one freed from the Devil's yoke, one from an earthly foe.
With unbroken victories Oswiu conquered many a realm,
reigning nobly over his fathers' kingdom and subduing
to his command all the peoples dwelling by the sea,
crushing some by terror, compelling others by the sword,
bearing his standards of victory throughout the realm.
He was a paragon of justice with equitable laws,
invincible in battle and trustworthy in peace,
open-handed to the needy, kindly and fair to all.
After a reign of eight and twenty years,
amid peace and order, he died in happiness,
bestowing the crown on Ecgfrith his son,
leaving to Ecgfrith the royal sceptre.

At that time bishop Wilfrid's fame shone far and wide
throughout the world by virtue of his achievements.
Omnipotent God filled him with light from Heaven
that he might drive from the land foul shades of ignorance.

the Mercian nobles that restored Penda's son Wulfhere (Stenton, pp. 84-5).

570 ff. Cf. the panegyrics of Edwin (vv. 115 ff.) and Oswald (vv. 265 ff.).
Oswiu completes Alcuin's favoured group of seventh-century Northumbrian
kings (Introduction, pp. l-li, liv).

576. Here, as at v. 872 (see comm. ad loc.), there may be reason to suspect
interpolation. Against this must be set the tendency to repetitious stylistic varia-
tion which is so pronounced a feature of Alcuin's writing (Introduction, pp.
cvi-cvii (iii) (c)) and the (speculative) possibility that these lines are authorial
alternatives preserved from an earlier draft.

577 ff. On Alcuin's highly selective treatment of Wilfrid, see Introduction,
pp. li-lii. It is noteworthy that Alcuin never mentions the repairs to St. Peter's
at York commissioned by Wilfrid and recorded only by Eddius Stephanus, *Vita
Wilfridi* xvi (Colgrave, p. 35; comm. to vv. 275-83). The omission of this signifi-
cant fact about the Minster's history, the absence of any reference in the poem to
Eddius' work, together with Alcuin's consistent reliance upon Bede, make it
improbable that he used (or knew) the Life of Wilfrid while writing his own
account of Wilfrid's life.

578. Of the authenticity of this verse, preserved only in *R*, there can be little
doubt. It provides an opening to the passage consistent with its tone of warm
praise. And it embodies the characteristically Alcuinian expression *virtutum
meritis.* With the example cited ad loc. in app. iii cf. Alc. *Carm.* x. 10; xcix. 11. 2;
xxviii. 7; lxii. 2, 4. For *longe lateque per orbem*, cf. id. *Carm.* lxxxvii. 15. 11.

per loca perpetuae quapropter multa salutis
gentibus et populis doctrinae lumina sparsit.
Illius australis studio Saxonia Christum
credidit et claro perfusa est lumine vitae.
Nec solum populos animae de morte maligna   585
illos antistes doctrinis eruit almis,
sed nece de praesente simul salvavit eosdem.
Tempore continuis illo nam sub tribus annis
non ros, non imber sitientes inrigat agros,
arida flammigeris tabescit terra sub astris   590
et victum pariter hominique feraeque negabat,
atque famem sequitur morientum cladis acervus,
praecipitesque ruunt multi de rupibus altis;
ast alii rapidis se demersere sub undis,
ut sibi praeriperet longum cita mors cruciatum.   595
Ipsa namque die, qua gens susceperat illa
doctrinis imbuta sacris baptismatis undam,
descendit pluvia telluribus aura serena,.
et terris rediit specimen viridantibus arvis:
florigero campi montesque ornantur amictu.   600
Frugifer agricolis laetantibus inditur annus,
inque Deum carnes cunctorum cordaque vivum
exultaverunt, cecinit sicut antea David,
certius aeternis inhiantes pectore donis,
quo sumpsere prius sibimet terrena per Illum.   605

HE v. 19   Hic quoque compulsus Romam properabat adire,
[677]   sed prius est ventis Fresonum vectus in oras

---

584 lumine *R*: lampade *T*   588 continuis *Godman*: contiguis *T R*   592 at-
que *T*: neque *R*: unde *Hargrove*   cladis *T*: cladᵭ *R*: clades *Hargrove*   acervus
Gale: acerbae *R*: acervae *T*: acerba *Hargrove*   593 praecipitesque *T*: per-
cipitesque *R*   594 se dimersere *R*: ṣese mersere *T* (demergere *HE* v. 14;
i. 33)   595 longum *T*: dirum *R*   596 qua *R*: quo *T*
598 pluvia telluribus *T R*: pluvia et telluribus *Gale*   599 terris *R*: terrae *T*
600 campi *T r*: campo *R*   602 vivum *Ruinart*: virum *T*: virorum *R*   cor-
daque *T*: corda *R*   606 hic *T R*: hinc *Godman*

---

589 2 Sam. 1: 21 nec ros nec pluviae veniant super vos; Ps.-Prosper *de Prov. Dei*
682; Aldh. *de Virg. metr.* 260 ff. aridus ut nullis roraret nubibus aether / atque
negarentur latices   591 Virg. *Aen.* iii. 142 victum seges aegra negabat; ibid.
x. 245 caedis acervus   593 ibid. xi. 673 praecipites pariterque ruunt, Bede
Vit. S. Cuthb. metr. 471-2 me . . . celsa de rupe . . . / praecipitem mittunt; [Virg.
Georg. iii. 273]   598 [Matt. 7: 25]   599 Ven. Fort. i. 20. 7 viridantibus
arvis   601 Bede *Vit. S. Cuthb. metr.* 785 laetantibus indidit   602 Ps. 83:

Thus he spread the light and teaching of eternal salvation
through many places, nations, and peoples.
By his efforts the South Saxons came to believe in Christ
and were suffused in the shining light of life.
Not only did that bishop by his holy teaching save those
people from the hideous death of the soul,
but he preserved them too from doom on this earth.
At that time, for three years without respite,
neither dew nor rain watered the parched fields
and the earth wasted in dryness beneath the flaming stars,
denying food to man and beast alike.
Mass suicides followed the famine,
many people raced headlong from the high cliffs,
while others cast themselves beneath the swirling waves,
to deliver themselves from long torment by a swift death.
The very day on which that people, imbued
with holy teaching, received the waters of baptism,
a breeze settled with a calm shower on the earth,
the fields grew green, and beauty returned to the land: the
plains and the mountains were arrayed in a flowering mantle.
To the farmers' delight the harvest was fruitful,
in flesh and at heart, all men rejoiced in the living God,
even as David has sung in times past,
yearning more firmly at heart for eternal gifts,
since they had taken earth's bounty from Him before.
    Driven by compulsion, he hastened to Rome,
but first he was carried by the winds to the Frisian coast,

---

3 cor meum et caro mea exultaverunt in Deum vivum   603 Aldh. *de Virg.*
metr. 1912 ut cecinit dudum; id. *Ænigm. praef.* 34 cecinit quod carmine David

---

582 Alc. lxxxix. 19. 3; *Walthar.* 1384   588 *cf.* vv.
565, 860; Alc. *Vit. S. Willibr. metr.* xxx. 2 continuis . . . septenis . . . annis
607 *cf.* v. 1466

---

588. continuis: the required sense is not one of proximity but of duration.
In Alcuin's poetry this is expressed by *continuus*, of which the reading of *T* and
R is a facile corruption. Cf. the passages cited in app. iii ad loc.
598. The subject is *aura. Pluvia serena* is an ablative of accompaniment; the
expression is taken from *HE* iv. 13.
599. terris: poetic plural, parallel to *telluribus*; cf. vv. 13, 1594.
606. hic/hinc: for the conjecture cf. vv. 38, 958: *Hinc compulsus* ('driven
from here')—a further stage in Wilfrid's travels.

atque ibi mox populi convertit milia Christo
plurima perpetuae demonstrans dona salutis.
Et quocumque pedem movit, pia semina sevit,   610
pectora perfundens arentia rore superno,
inclyta caelesti complevit et horrea fructu,
et celebri fama lato laudatur in orbe.

[704] Dum pius illud iter gestit complere sacerdos,
ecce repente fuit morbo perculsus acerbo,   615
perque dies multos valido crescente dolore
venit ad extremum confecto corpore finem.
Bis binosque dies sensu sine corporis omni
exanimis iacuit pene et spiraminis exsors,
voce carens, membrisque stupens, in pectore tantum   620
frigida vix tenui duxit suspiria flatu.
Discipuli socii stabant hinc inde gementes
lugentesque sui funus lacrimabile patris.
Ecce die quinta subito pater ipse resedit
atque levans oculos socios conspexit et infit: 625
'Quid iuvat atroci tantum indulgere dolori?
Cui vult, omnipotens poterit mitescere iudex,
extremamque novum vitam convertere in ortum.
Namque suum clemens legatum misit ab astris,
qui steterat niveo nimium praeclarus amictu   630
et mihi flammigero praedixit talia vultu:
"Me pius altithronus Michaelem misit Olympo
dicere, quod morbo nunc confortaberis isto
pro meritis sanctae matris precibusque Mariae,
quae gemitus, lacrimas, sociorum et vota tuorum   635
auribus e solio caelesti audivit apertis
deposcens tibimet vitam simul atque salutem.

---

613 lato *T R*: laeto *Froben*   619 exsors *T*: exors *R*   622 socii
T r: socios *R*   623 lugentesque *T*: lugentes *R*   628 extremamque
R Gale: extra namque *T*   629 clemens *R Ruinart*: demens *T*

---

613 Aldh. *de Virg. metr.* 800 crebro mundus rumore celebrat   615 Bede
Vit. S. Cuthb. metr. 235 perculsus . . . pavore; ibid. 575 morbo . . . acerbo
620 Aldh. *Ænigm.* xxxi. 3 voce carens   621 Paul. Nol. xv. 273 tenui cernit
. . . suspiria flatu   626 Virg. *Aen.* ii. 776 quid tantum insano iuvat indulgere
dolori?   629 Arat. *de Act. Apostol.* i. 234 misit ab astris   630 Sedul.
Carm. pasch. v. 328 niveo praeclarus amictu   632 Aldh. *Carm. eccl.*
ii. 17 cum pater altithronus Gabrihel misisset ab astris; [id. *de Virg. metr.* 1695]

there soon to make thousands of converts to Christ,
revealing to them the manifold gifts of eternal salvation.
And wherever he set foot, he sowed seeds of piety,
watering their parched hearts with dew from Heaven,
filling their noble granaries with food from on high,
and his fame was celebrated throughout the wide world.
While that devout bishop was longing to reach his journey's
end, an acute illness suddenly struck him,
and for many days the pain grew stronger,
until his weakened body reached the limit of its endurance.
For four days he lay insensible,
half-dead and almost devoid of breath,
mute, his limbs benumbed, heaving only
chill sighs and feeble gasps.
About him stood his pupils and comrades, groaning
and lamenting the tearful death of their father.
Then, on the fifth day, he suddenly sat up,
raised his eyes, and, gazing at his companions, said:
'What point is there in giving way to such wild grief?
The omnipotent judge can take pity upon whom He chooses
and can transform death into rebirth.
Mercifully He sent His messenger from the stars
who stood before me, resplendent in snow-white garb,
with fiery countenance, and made this prophecy to me:
"God enthroned on high sent me, Michael, from Heaven
to say that you will be restored from this illness
through the good offices and prayers of our holy mother Mary,
who to your comrades' groans, tears, and petitions
has listened attentively from her heavenly throne,
interceding for your life and salvation.

635 Bede *Vit. S. Cuthb. metr.* 119 vota suorum   636 Bede *de Die Iud.* 35
auribus . . . nunc exaudit apertis

608 *cf.* v. 1038   611 *cf.* vv. 87, 1463; Alc. *Vit. S. Willibr. metr.*
i. 12-13 sitientia rura rigare . . . rore superno   613 Alc. xliii. 17; id. xlv. 73
615 *cf.* v. 927   616 = v. 886   618 *cf.* v. 1194   621 *cf.* v.
1159; Theodulf xvii. 29-30 . . . suspiria pectus anhela, / et tenui sonitu vox geme-
bunda sonat   637 Alc. lxxv. 3. 1 pacis simul atque salutis; *Walthar.* 955

629 ff. Cf. the vision related at vv. 1607 ff.

Esto tamen quarto veniente paratus in anno;
ipse ego tunc iterum veniam te visere, nam tu
tempore tranquillo patriae morieris in oris." '   640
Angelicos sequitur monitus mox vita salusque,
nec non expletos post quatuor exitus annos
praesulis egregii praedicto est fine secutus.
Sic et in ecclesia, quam Petri erexit honore,
[709] Hripensi est positus, felix in pace sepultus.   645
HE iv. 27(25) Vir quoque temporibus sanctus fulgebat in illis,
angelicam Cuthberctus agens in corpore vitam,
qui fuit a puero signis insignis apertis:
moribus et meritis statim succrevit honestis,
atque manens monachus primaevo tempore clarus   650
doctor apostolicus fuit hinc et presbyter almus,
et loca fructiferis implens inculta virectis
fontibus aeternis sitientia prata rigabat;
divina et cunctos firmans virtute sequaces
dogmatis aetherei radios spargebat ubique   655
discutiens tenebras errorum luce serena.
HE iv. 28(26) Est locus oceano dictus cognomine Farne,
insula fontis inops et frugis et arboris expers.
Hanc petit intrepidus Christi bellator opimus
contemplativos cupiens et carpere flores;   660
ipse Deo soli solus servire sategit,
ne mundanus honor mentem mutaret alacrem.
Hic heremita sacer non parvo tempore vixit;

638 veniente *Froben*: venienti *T R*   paratus *Gale*: partus *T R*   639 ve-
niam te *R Gale*: veni ante *T*   640 oris *T r*: annis *R*   641 monitus
R Gale: monitis *T*   645 Hripensi *T*: Hypensi *R*   647 Cuthberctus
R: Cuthbertus *T*   652 implens *R*: replens *T*   654 firmans *R*: for-
mans *T*

640 Ven. Fort. vi. 8. 5 patris . . . ab oris   647 Bede *Vit. S. Cuthb. metr.*
28 Cuthbertus agens per sidera vitam   656 Aldh. *Carm. eccl.* iii. 66 luce
serena; Bede *Vit. S. Cuthb. metr.* 22 discutit errorum vera iam luce tenebras
657 Virg. *Aen.* iii. 163 Est locus, Hesperiam Grai cognomine dicunt   657-9 Bede
Vit. S. Cuthb. metr. 390 Farne petit   658 ibid. 406 fontis inops; Ven. Fort.
Vit. S. Mart. i. 150 insula frugis inops   660-1 Aldh. *de Virg. metr.* 944-5
contemplativos carpens . . . maniplos / dum solus soli Christo famularier optat

638 *cf.* vv. 729, 1583   641 *cf.* v. 688   647 *cf.* v. 1392
648 *cf.* vv. 765, 1090   653 *cf.* v. 1089; Alc. *Vit. S. Willibr. metr.* i. 12
sitientia rura rigare   654 ibid. i. 14 auxiliisque Dei famulum firmavit honestis
659 ff. ibid. xxxiv. 40 ff   660 *cf.* v. 1094; Alc. *Vit. S. Willibr. metr.* xxxiv.

None the less be prepared four years from now:
I shall come to visit you again, for you will die
in peace on the shores of your native land." '
Life and health soon followed the angel's prophecy,
and, after four years had run their course,
that excellent bishop died, as had been predicted.
He was buried in the church that he had built in honour of
St. Peter at Ripon, and was laid to rest in happiness and peace.
Another holy man was a shining light at that time:
Cuthbert, who led the life of an angel while still on this earth.
From boyhood he was set apart by manifest signs:
his virtue increased, his character became ever nobler.
He was from the beginning an outstanding monk,
then became a teacher of the Gospel and a holy priest,
filling the wastelands with flowering greenness,
watering the dry meadows with eternal fountains
and strengthening all his followers in virtue;
he spread everywhere the rays of heavenly teaching,
dispelling the shades of error with serene light.
There is a place in the ocean called Farne,
an island with little water, barren of crops and trees.
Fearlessly, Christ's excellent champion sought out this place,
and wishing to gather the flowers of contemplation,
he strove to serve the one true God in isolation
that worldly honour might not sway his intent mind.
There, for a long time, he lived in sanctity as a hermit.

43 aetherios possit decerpere flores; id. lxxxviii. 10. 14

644-5. Wilfrid is named in the metrical Calendar of York (vv. 22-3). Recent summaries of his life and work by Farmer, *Dictionary*, pp. 402-3, and id., *Saint Wilfrid at Hexham*, ed. D. P. Kirby (Newcastle upon Tyne (1974) pp. 35-59). If Wilfrid campaigned for York's metropolitan status (M. Gibbs, *Speculum* 48 (1973), pp. 213-46), it is surprising that his efforts are never mentioned by York's principal apologist in this poem.

646 ff. The place of St. Cuthbert (*c.* 634-87) in Alcuin's work is discussed on pp. lii-liii. The saint's links with York were close. According to the (later) *Historia de Sancto Cuthberto*, at his consecration at York in 645, Cuthbert was granted by king Ecgfrith 'all the land that lies from the wall of St Peter's church to the great west gate, and from the wall of St Peter's church to the city wall towards the south' (Harrison, *Y. Arch. Jnl.* 40 (1959-62), pp. 234, 241). His name is recorded at v. 15 of the metrical Calendar of York. Notice in Farmer, *Dictionary*, pp. 94-6.

650. manens: 'being' (~ the non-existent present participle of *esse*).

651. apostolicus: on the application of this term to bishops see Blaise, *Vocabulaire latin*, p. 520.

saepius angelicis felix affatibus usus
toxica mortiferi vincebat tela draconis.   665
Attamen abstractus multis rogitantibus inde
tandem consensit secretam linquere sedem,
pontificisque gradum, populis et rege coactus,
quandoque suscepit cunctis orantibus illum;
nobiliter binis digne quem rexit in annis,   670
plurima conquirens animarum lucra Tonanti,
et bene commissum sibimet servavit ovile,
ne lupus insidians Christi deroderet agnos.
Sed mox mundani culmen vitavit honoris
ipse petens iterum soliti secreta cubilis   675
atque ibi praesentis spectaverat ultima vitae;

HE iv. 29(27)   quaeque Dei famuli sacrata est insula morte.
[687]   Nam locus ille nitet signis hucusque coruscis,
ex quo pontificis linquens ergastula carnis
spiritus alta petens scandit super astra polorum.   · 680
Nec non et claris fiunt miracula rebus
facta loco, sacrum pausat quo corpus humatum,
cuius tota fuit caelestibus inclyta signis
usque diem mortis primaevo tempore vita.
Omnia quae dudum praeclarus Beda sacerdos   685
prosaico primum scripsit sermone magister
et post heroico cecinit miracula versu:

---

669 orantibus *T*: hortantibus *R*   670 digne quem *T*: quem digne *R*
677 quaeque *T R*: sicque *Munari*   682 loco *R Ruinart*: locum *T*   sacrum
R Ruinart: sacro *T*   684 primaevo tempore *T R*: primaevo a tempore *Winter-
bottom*   686 prosaico *T R*: prosaice *edd.*

---

664 Arat. *de Act. Apostol.* i. 52 angelicis . . . affatibis usa   672 Sedul.
Carm. pasch. i. 82-3 servat . . . / pastor ovile; *Syll. Epig. Cantab.* 28. 7-8 commis-
sumque . . . servasti / . . . gregem   672-3 Bede *Ep. ad Egbert.* xiv te . . .
deprecor . . . ut commissum tibi gregem sedulus ab irruentium luporum improbi-
tate tuearis   673 *Syll. Epig. Cantab.* 3.8 ne lupus insidians vastet ovile dei;
[Virg. *Georg.* iii. 537; Joh. 10: 12]   678 Bede *Vit. S. Cuthb. metr.* 381
nitens per signa coruscus   679 Aldh. *de Virg. metr.* 1403 linquens ergastula
680 Virg. *Aen.* v. 508   682 Aldh. *Carm. eccl.* iv. 5. 17 pausat in . . . corpore
684 Bede *Vit. S. Cuthb. metr.* 729 primaevo a flore

---

665 Alc. cxiv. 2. 7 tela draconis   671 *cf.* v. 852; Alc. *Vit. S. Willibr.
metr.* xii. 2 plurima . . . animarum lucra tonanti   672-3 Alc. ix. 229-30
ut pius egregium conservet pastor ovile, / ne . . . rapidis capiat hoc lupus insidiis

Often communicating with angels, he succeeded
in thwarting the poisoned weapons of the deadly serpent.
At many people's request he was induced to return
and eventually agreed to leave his retreat;
at the urging of the people and the king he eventually assumed
the office of bishop, as everyone begged him to do,
discharging it nobly for two years,
winning great riches in souls for God,
he guarded well the fold committed to his care,
stopping the prowling wolf from devouring the lambs of Christ.
Soon he escaped from this high worldly honour
in search of the privacy of his former cell,
and there ended his life on this earth.
That island is hallowed by the death of God's servant,
for, to this day, it has been resplendent with brilliant miracles,
since the time when, escaping the confines of the flesh,
the bishop's spirit mounted up beyond the stars in Heaven.
Miracles and wondrous deeds are performed in the spot
where his holy body was buried and now rests.
Cuthbert's entire life, from the day of his birth to the hour
of his death, was marked out by signs from Heaven.
Bede, that famous priest and teacher, wrote all about
these miracles, first in prose
and then in hexameter verse:

673 *cf.* v. 1472; Alc. *Ep.* 130 (p. 193, 24-5) ne . . . lupus insidians aliquos ex grege Christi devorare valeat   674 *cf.* vv. 1406, 1484   676 *cf.* vv. 874, 1290   679 Alc. *Vit. S. Willibr. metr.* xxviii. 3 linquens ergastula carnis   680 *cf.* v. 1648   682 *cf.* v. 1161   684 *cf.* v. 1021; Alc. *Vit. S. Willibr. metr.* xviii. 14 usque diem mortis   685-7 Alc. ix. 175-6 Dum prius heroicis praeclarus Beda magister / versibus explicuit inclita gesta patris

679. On the metaphor see Blaise, *Vocabulaire latin*, p. 540.

685-7. Alcuin confuses the order of composition of the two parts of Bede's work. Bede wrote first the metrical then the prose *Vita.* In the preface to his metrical Life Bede says 'spero me in alio opere nonnulla ex his, quae praetermiseram, memoriae redditurum' (Jaager, p. 57) and in the epistle to Eadfrith, prefatory to the prose Life, he writes: 'vitam . . . , quam vobis prosa editam dedi . . . heroicis dudum versibus edidi. . . . In cuius operis praefatione promisi me alias de vita et miraculis eius latius esse scripturum. Quam videlicet promissionem in praesenti opusculo . . . adimplere satago' (Colgrave, p. 146). This error does not prove in itself that Alcuin's exemplar of Bede lacked the prefaces to the Lives of St. Cuthbert.

687. heroico . . . versu = 'hexameters'. Cf. *HE* v. 24 'vitam . . . Cudbercti, et prius heroico metro et postmodum plano sermone descripsi.'

Vit. S. Cuthb.
rubr.

pr. ii: *m.* ii   qualiter angelicos monitus medicina secuta est,
                 dum tumor in tenero succrevit corpore fervens;
pr. iii: *m.* iii aut quomodo ipse puer ventis per caerula puppes   690
                 iactatas precibus revocabat ab aequore quinas;
pr. iv: *m.* iv   qualiter aut animam ferri super astra videbat
                 praesulis Aedani, teneros dum pasceret agnos;
pr. vii: *m.* vii caelicolam quomodo terreno pane fovere
                 dum cuperet, meruit caelestes sumere ab illo;   695
pr. x: *m.* viii ut beluae gelidum villo flatuque fovebant,
                 cernentem fratrem morbo culpaque relaxat;
pr. xi: *m.* ix   utque precando famem proiectus ab aequore nautis
                 expulit et certum praedixit adesse serenum;
pr. xii: *m.* x   aut quomodo ex aquila delato pisce cibandum   700
                 se sociumque suum praedixit, et est ita factum;
pr. xiv: *m.* xii aut quomodo ardentes avertit ab aedibus ignes
                 incumbens precibus, iuvenum quos dextra nequibat;
pr. xv: *m.* xiii daemoniaca quidem vel qualiter uxor ab illo
                 sit sanata, prius quam tecta rogantis inisset;   705
pr. xvii: *m.* xv daemones aut quomodo sanctus de Farne malignos
                 expulerit, iuxta faciens sibi tecta manendi;

690-1 puppes . . . quinas *T*: quinas . . . puppes *R*   695 caelestes
Ruinart: caelestis *T R*: caelestem *Godman*   696 ut beluae *R Gale*: urbe
lue *T*   698 proiectus *T*: praeiectus *R*: praeclusus *Hargrove*   nautis *Ruinart*:
nauta *T R*   699 expulit *R*: extulit *T*: abstulit *Ruinart*   praedixit *R*
Ruinart: perdix *T*   703 quos *Froben*: quas *T R*   707 expulerit *R*
Ruinart: expuleret *T*   iuxta *Ruinart*: iussu *T R*   sibi *Ruinart*: ibi *R*: ubi *T*
manendi *T R*: manenti *Munari*

---

688 Bede *Vit. S. Cuthb. metr.* 91 monitus medicina secuta est   688-9 [*see
commentary*] quomodo genu dolente claudus effectus sit et angelo medicante
sanatus   690 Bede *Vit. S. Cuthb. metr.* 104 per caerula puppis
690-1 quomodo ventis oratione mutatis rates oceano delapsas revocaverit ad litus
691 Virg. *Aen* i. 29 iactato aequore   692-3 quomodo cum pastoribus positus
animam sancti Aidani episcopi ad coelum ab angelis ferri aspexerit   693 Bede
Vit. S. Cuthb. metr. 120f teneros . . . dum . . . agnos pasceret   694-5 quo-
modo angelum hospitio suscipiens dum panem querit ministrare terrenum, coelesti
ab eodem remunerari meruerit   696 Bede *Vit. S. Cuthb. metr.* 229 gelidas
villo flatuque foventia plantas   696-7 quomodo animalia maris, in quo per-
nox oraverat, illi egresso praebuerint obsequium, et frater qui haec videbat prae
timore languescens eius sit oratione recreatus   697 Bede *Vit. S. Cuthb. metr.*
247 culpamque relaxat   698-9 Quomodo nautis tempestate praeclusis sere-
num mare ad certum diem praedixerit et orando cibos impetraverit   700-1 quo-
modo iter faciens aquila ministra viaticum et percepturum se esse praedixerit et
perceperit   702-3 quomodo flammas domus cuiusdam [*pr.* vero igne] ardentis
orando restrinxerit   703 Bede *Vit. S. Cuthb. metr.* 336 iuvenum quae dextra

how he was cured by following an angel's command
when a swelling turned to fever in his weakened body;
how, when a boy, by his prayers he called back from the sea
five rafts tossed by wind on the ocean waves;
or how he saw bishop Aidan's soul borne above the stars
as he tended young lambs which were grazing;
how, by being willing to feed an angel with earthly bread,
he rightly gained heavenly manna from him;
how with their fur and breath the wild beasts warmed him, or
how he saved from illness and sin a monk who watched this;
how, thrown up by the sea, he averted the sailors' hunger
by his prayers, and certainly foretold calm weather; or
how Cuthbert prophesied that he and a companion would eat
a fish brought by an eagle, and so it was done;
or how, by the ardour of his prayers, he turned a raging fire
from some houses, which strong young men could not do; or
how a married woman possessed by a demon was cured by him
before he entered her house, as invited by her husband;
how that saint drove evil demons away from Farne,
making a place nearby to live in himself;

nequibat 704-5 qualiter daemonium ab uxore [*pr.* praefecti, *m.* cuiusdam]
necdum adveniens eiecerit 706-7 [*pr.*] qualiter sibi in insula Farne pulsis
daemonibus habitationem fecerit

---

688 *cf.* v. 1147 690 *cf.* v. 1322 692 *cf.* v. 725
699 Paul. Diac. xxxiii. 18

688-740. These lines are based on the rubrics to Bede's prose and metrical
Vitae S. Cuthberti, supplemented by a number of other quotations, chiefly from
the metrical Life. The entries in the margin of the text indicate the chapters of
the prose and verse accounts which Alcuin summarizes. App. ii records the rubrics
to these chapters (without repeating the references). When the rubrics to both
versions are (near-)identical a single entry is given. When they differ substantially
variants are recorded within square brackets. Alcuin's source for vv. 735-6 and
739-40 is the metrical Life of St Cuthbert alone. At vv. 702-3, 708-9, 719-22,
731-2 his summary is nearest to Bede's verse, while at vv. 706-7, 733-4, 737-8
it follows the prose. See further Introduction, pp. lii-liii, lxxxviii.
695. **caelestes/caelestem:** acc. sing. with *panem* understood from v. 694.
But cf. Bede, *Vit. S. Cuthb. metr.* 202: 'Tres inibi e nitido fulgentes polline
panes.'
707. iuxta: cf. vv. 315, 1161.
sibi: this reading is supported by the rubric to the prose *Life*.
tecta manendi: genitive of the gerund with a concrete noun, a usage generally
avoided in CL. The sense is final-causal. See Löfstedt, *Syntactica*, i², pp. 169 ff.
Cf. *HE* v. 2 *manendi locum* and see further Druhan, *Syntax*, p. 131.

Vit. S. Cuthb.
rubr.

pr. xviii: ex sicco ut liquidam produxit caespite lympham,
m. xvi   quae ad votum patris praestabat in ore saporem;
pr. xix: qualiter ipse sibi messem sevisset in agro   710
m. xvii   et volucres verbo tantum pepulisset ab illa;
pr. xxi: *m.*xix ut mare cum beluis sancto servire solebat;
pr. xxiv: plurima veridico praedixit et ore futura
m. xxi   de se deque aliis, quae praescius ante videbat;
pr. xxix: qualiter uxori comitis, cui miserat undam   715
m. xxiii   sacram, restituit depulsa peste salutem;
pr. xxx: chrismate sic quandam sanaverat ipse pedunctam
m. xxiv   a morbo lateris capitisque dolore puellam;
pr. xxxi: ut benedictus item delatus panis ab illo
m. xxv   immissis lymphis quendam sanaverat aegrum;   720
pr. xxxii: aut quomodo iuvenem moriturum forte viator
m. xxvi   repperit, orando cui reddidit ipse salutem;
pr. xxxiii: ut pius atque pater, morbo vastante Britannos,
m. xxvii   praedixit matri gnati domusque salutem;
pr. xxxiv: qualiter aut animam pastoris ab arbore lapsi   725
m. xxxi   angelicos caelo coetus inferre videret;
pr. xxxviii: atque suum aegrotans curaverat ipse ministrum,
m. xxxv   profluvii ventris fuerat qui tabe gravatus;
pr. xlii: qualiter undecimo post mortem corpus in anno
m. xxxviii integrum fuerat tota cum veste repertum;   730
pr. xli: *m.* xl   daemoniacus humo, supra quam funditur unda,

715 uxori *Ruinart*: uxorem *T R*   721 aut quomodo *R*: qualiter aut *T*
731 humo *T R*: homo *Froben*   quam *T R*: quem *Gale*

708-9 [*m.*] qualiter precibus aquam de arida produxerit, qui etiam bibendo
quondam aquas in vinum convertit   709 Virg. *Georg.* iv. 277   710-11 quali-
ter a messe, quam sua manu seruerat, verbo volucres abegerit   712 qualiter
[*pr.* eius necessitatibus etiam, *m.* eidem] mare servierit   713 Bede *Vit. S.
Cuthb. metr.* 491 praedixerat ore futurum   713-14 [*m.* prophetia eiusdem,
pr. quod sciscitanti eidem Elfedge] de vita Ecgfridi regis et episcopatu suo [*pr.*
praedixerat]   715-16 [*pr.* quomodo] uxorem comitis per presbyterum suum
aqua benedicta sanavit   717-18 [*pr.* quomodo] puellam crismate perunctam
a dolore capitis laterisque curavit   718 Bede *Vit. S. Cuthb. metr.* 571-2
laterali tacta dolore / virgo premebatur capitisque gravedine   719-20 [*m.*]
pane a viro dei benedicto sanatur infirmus   721-2 [*m.*] oblatum in
itinere iuvenem moriturum oratione revocarit ad vitam   723 Bede *Vit. S.
Cuthb. metr.* 589 pestis vastabat dira Britannos   723-4 [*pr.* quo-
modo] tempore mortalitatis morientem puerum matri sanum restituerit
724 Bede *Vit. S. Cuthb. metr.* 596 cuius dicta salus puerique domusque secuta est

how he brought flowing water from the arid turf,
which, in answer to his prayer, provided that father with drink;
how he sowed for himself a crop in a field,
and by only a word kept the birds from it;
how the sea as well as wild beasts used to obey the saint;
how in words of truth he prophesied many future events
which he had foreseen, concerning himself and others;
how the wife of a *gesith* on whom he sprinkled holy water
was restored to health and the plague driven from her;
how, by anointing a girl with holy oil,
he cured her from a pain in the side and an aching in the head;
how, likewise, bread that had been blessed and offered up by
him cured a sick man when it was mixed with water;
or how on a journey he happened to find a young man
on the point of death and restored him to health by praying;
how, when Britain was swept by an epidemic, that father
prophesied to a mother safety for her son and household
or how he saw a company of angels bearing up to heaven
the soul of a shepherd who had fallen from a tree;
and how, although sick himself, Cuthbert cured
one of his attendants who was gravely ill with diarrhoea;
or how, ten years after his death,
his body was found intact with all its robes;
how a boy vexed by evil spirits was cured by the earth

725-6 [*pr.*] [quomodo] animam cuiusdam, qui de arbore cadendo mortuus est, ad coelum ferri conspexerit   727-8 [*pr.* quomodo] ministrum suum a profluvio ventris [*pr.* ipse aegrotus] sanaverit [*m.* aegrotus]   728 Bede *Vit. S. Cuthb. metr.* 764   729-30 quomodo corpus ipsius post undecim [*m.* sit] annos sine corruptione [*pr.* sit] repertum   731-2 [*pr.*] quomodo puer daemoniacus sit humo cui lavacrum corporis infusum est in aquam missa sanatur

713 *cf.* v. 1393   715 *cf.* v. 1144   728 *cf.* v. 1578   730 *cf.* v. 767

715. **comitis:** *gesith.* On this term and the words for *thegn* see H. Loyn, 'Gesiths and Thegns in Anglo-Saxon England from the Seventh to the Tenth Century', *EHR* 70 (1955), pp. 529–49.
731. **humo . . . quam:** cf. Bede *Vit. S. Cuthb. pr.* xli: 'venit clanculo ad locum ubi noverat effusam fuisse aquam, qua corpus eius defunctum fuerat lotum, tollensque inde modicam humi particulam, immisit in aquam. Quam deferens ad patientem infudit in ore eius. . . . Qui . . . mane de somno simul et vesania consurgens, liberatum se a demonio quo premebatur beati Cuthberti meritis et intercessione cognovit.' The true reading had already been recognized by Jaager, in his note on the rubric to *Vit. S. Cuthb. metr.* xl (ed. cit., pp. 123-4).

Vit. S. Cuthb.
rubr.   sanatur, sacros patris quae laverat artus;

pr. xliv: aegra trahens quidam suspiria qualiter orans
m. xli   illius ad tumulum morbo est sanatus ab illo;

m. xlii   languidus utque oculis tangens oraria vatis,   735
             illius ex visu dolor et caligo recessit.

pr. xlv: Calciamenta patris resoluto corpore quidam
m. xliii   induit et sanis perrexit gressibus inde.

m. xliv   Qualiter infirmi curentur tegmine, sub quo
             spiritus astra petit sancti terrena relinquens: 740
                haec breviter tetigi, ne tota tacere viderer
             inclyta rurali perstringens carmine gesta,
             haec quoniam cecinit plenis cum versibus olim
             praeclarus nitido Beda sermone magister.
             Ni praevenisset nostras pius ille camoenas,   745
             inciperem lyricas omnes extendere fibras,
             non Pana rogitans Phoebi nec numen inane,
             sed tua cum toto suffragia corde precarer,
             ut mihi rorifluam donares, Christe, loquelam
             ad narranda pii digne praeconia patris.   750

E iv. 19(17) Belliger Ecgfridus postquam hinc inde triumphos
             gesserat et gentes domuit sub marte feroces,

734 morbo est sanatus . . . *R*: morbo sanatus est . . . *T*: morbo sanatus ab illo
est *Gale*   735 utque *T R*: ut quae *Gale*   tangens *R Gale*: frangens *T*   vatis
T R: vasis *edd.*   745 ille *T R*: ipse *Froben*   747 Pana *T R*: Panem
J. Huemer (*Dümmler, Add.*)   751 Egfridus *T R*

732 Bede *Vit. S. Cuthb. metr.* 187 artus abluitur sacros [ibid. 855]   733 Bede
Vit. S. Cuthb. metr. 585 aegre suspiria saeva trahentis   733-4 [*pr.*] qualiter
aegrotus ad tumbam eius orando sit curatus   735 Bede *Vit. S. Cuthb. metr.*
873 oraria vatis   736 ibid. 872 dolor et caligo   735-6 [*m.*] oculos
quidam languentes orario illius adtactos sanavit   737-8 [*pr.* quomodo] para-
liticus sit per eius calciamenta sanatus   739-40 Quod tegmine parietis eius
infirmi curentur   740 Bede *Vit. S. Cuthb. metr.* 892; *Syll. Epig. Cantab.*
32. 3 spiritus astra petit   742 Sedul. *Carm. pasch.* i. 96 perstringere pauca
relatu   746 Paul. Nol. xxvii. 100 lyricas . . . chordas; id. xv. 26 totis inten-
dere fibris   747-50 *cf.* id. xv. 30 ff.; Aldh. *de Virg. metr.* 23 ff.; Bede *HE*
iv. 20(18). 2-8

732 *cf.* v. 775   734 *cf.* v. 1318   737 Milo *de Sobr.* i. 532
740 Alc. *Vit. S. Willibr. metr.* xxviii. 4 spiritus astra petit   742 *cf.* v. 1655; Alc.
vii. 2 rurali carmine laudes; id. *Vit. S. Willibr. metr. praef.* 4 percurrens titulis in-
clyta gesta citis   744 *cf.* vv. 1207, 1547   747 Ermold. *In hon. Hlud.*

on which had been poured the water that had washed
Cuthbert's holy limbs; how a man sighing in illness
was cured by prayers at Cuthbert's tomb;
how a man with an eye complaint touched the prophet's robe,
and the darkness and pain in his sight were relieved.
A man stricken with paralysis put on that priest's sandals
and walked away, his body healed and his step firm.
The sick are cured by the covering beneath which that holy
man's spirit left this earth and set forth for the heavens.
    Not to seem wholly silent I have touched briefly
on these things, passing swiftly over his wondrous deeds
in my rude verse; for Bede, the peerless master, once wrote
a full-scale poem on this subject in splendid style.
Had not pious Bede written his poem before mine,
I should expand on this theme in lyric strain,
not invoking Pan nor Apollo, that hollow deity,
but praying with all my heart to Christ for aid
to grant me power of expression flowing like dew
to proclaim as I should the praises of that devout father.
    After Ecgfrith had won victories on all sides,
and subdued fierce peoples in battle,

praef. 13 ff. nec rogo Pierides, nec Phoebi tramite limen . . . ; Walahfr. *Vit. Mamm.*
praef. 6-7   750 Heiric *Vit. S. German.* i. 197 nostri . . . praeconia . . . patris

---

741-6. Cf. vv. 685 ff., 781-5, 1207-9, where Alcuin defers to Bede. For
parallel passages stressing the brevity of this account, see comm. to vv. 18, 289-90.
    747-50. A *topos* of rejection of the pagan deities of profane verse (see
Curtius, pp. 234 ff.; Klopsch, *Einführung*, pp. 26 ff.). Curtius, p. 237 and *Z. f. r.
Ph.* 59 (1939) pp. 147-8, uses this passage to illustrate his contention that Alcuin
distinguished between secular poetry, in which the Muses were allowed a role, and
spiritual verse, from which they were banned. In the sacred sphere, according to
Curtius, Alcuin decreed that the Muses could have no place. That is true of vv.
747 ff. The Muses have no place in this context. They are not even mentioned.
For Alcuin, as for Aldhelm (cf. app. ii ad loc.), Pan and Apollo were symbolic
of a style which he attacked; the Muses, on the other hand, were innocuous. In
this text alone there are seven allusions to the Muses: vv. 1077-8 and 1393-5
refer to its personified subject; vv. 431, 745, 882, 1091 describe its verse by
metonymy; and at vv. 1597-8 Thalia is invoked as the presiding spirit of the
poem. Curtius's distinction between secular and spiritual poetry cannot be
upheld. Naturally assimilated into Alcuin's style, the Muses did not need to be
banned.
    751 ff. The chronology of Ecgfrith's reign (670-85) is analysed by K. Harrison,
Y. Arch. Jnl. 43 (1971), pp. 79-84.

accepit sponsam Aedilthrydam nomine dictam,
nobilium genitam regali stirpe parentum,
nobilior longe casta quae mente manebat.   755 ·
Nam licet illa foret thalamo coniuncta superbo,
regia bis senos pariter iam sponsa per annos,
intemerata tamen permansit virgo per aevum,
inter iura thori vincens incendia carnis.

HE v. 7   *Virginis alma fides, regis patientia mira!*   760
[*Epitaph.*   Vincitur hic precibus, sed amore Tonantis et illa;
Caedw. 15] ambo sacris Fidei ferventes ignibus intus,
permansere simul coniunx cum coniuge casti.
Quamque integra foret vivens in corpore virgo,
post mortem Dominus signis patefecit apertis: 765
nam caro sex denos etiam tumulata per annos
incorrupta quidem tota cum veste reperta est.
Corpus erat vegetum nervis et flexile totum
et facies rutilo fulgebat sancta decore;
et quod iure magis multum mirabile dictu est: 770
ante dies mortis binos in corpore vulnus,
quod medicus fecit, nimio cogente timore,
apparet sanum, tenuissima visa cicatrix
ulceris obtendens veteris vestigia tantum.
Vestis item, sacros quae texit virginis artus,   775
expulit atrocem de obsessis saepe chelydrum.
Nec non tumba prior, tenuit quae virginis almae
sacrosancta sinu sub terris membra receptans,

---

753 Adiltruda *T R*   768 flexile *R Ruinart*: flexibile *T*   778 recep-
tans *R*: receptas *T*: recepta *edd.*

---

754 Ven. Fort. viii. 5. 1 regali de stirpe   757 Juvenc. *Evang.* i. 281
bissenos . . . annos   758 Virg. *Aen.* xi. 583–4 virginitatis amorem / intemerata
colit; Aldh. *de Virg. metr.* 707 permansit virgo perennis   759 ibid. 804
763 Ven. Fort. iv. 26. 69   765 Bede *Vit. S. Cuthb. metr.* 711 certis . . .
patescere signis   768 ibid. 830 flexile iam tota corpus conpage videtur
774 Virg. *Aen.* iv. 23 veteris vestigia   775 Aldh. *de Virg. metr.* 2327 artus
virgineos; Bede *Vit. S. Cuthb. metr.* 832 sanctos quae texerat artus   777 Aldh.
de Virg. metr. 1789–90 tumbam, qua clausum virginis almae / . . . corpus

---

753 *cf.* v. 1397   754–5 *cf.* vv. 1252–3   757 *cf.* vv. 766, 1135
760 *cf.* v. 997   763 Theodulf xliii. 27 coniunx . . . cum coniuge casto
764 *cf.* v. 1346   769 *cf.* v. 1223   772 *cf.* v. 1338
773 *cf.* v. 978   775 Flor. Lugd. xix. 13 sacrati corporis artus

he took a wife called Æthelthryth
of royal descent and noble parentage,
who became far nobler by remaining chaste of spirit.
Although in marriage she made a proud alliance,
although wedded to the king for twelve years,
she remained an immaculate virgin throughout her life,
vanquishing the fires of the flesh in the sacrament of marriage.
How pure was her faith, how wondrous his patience!
He was won over by her prayers, and she by love of God!
Afire, both of them, with inward flames of the holy Faith,
in chastity they remained together as husband and wife.
The truth of Æthelthryth's purity during her life on earth
the Lord revealed after her death by undeniable signs.
Sixty years after her burial her flesh was found
uncorrupted, with all her clothes undecayed.
The sinews in her body had life, nor was her corpse stiff;
her holy countenance was aglow with high colour and grace,
and—what is indeed far more wondrous to tell—
an incision which a doctor had made
with great concern two days before her death
was seen to be healed, leaving only a very fine scar
just covering the traces of the tumour which she had suffered.
Similarly, the clothes covering that maiden's hallowed limbs
would often drive the hideous demon from those possessed.
Just so, the original tomb, which had held in its underground
embrace the sacrosanct limbs of that sweet virgin,

778 *'Karolus Magnus'* 116 (receptans)

---

753 ff. St. Æthelthryth, daughter of Anna, king of East Anglia and founder of the double monastery at Ely, married Ecgfrith in 660. Recent notices in Farmer, *Dictionary*, pp. 138-9, and J. Nicholson, *Medieval Women, SCH Subsid.* i, ed. D. Baker (Oxford, 1978), p. 21.

754-5. **nobilium . . . stirpe parentum / nobilior . . . mente:** on this hagiographical *topos*, common in Bede, see Plummer ii, pp. 90-1. Its occurrence in the *Vita Alcuini* ('vir Domini Albinus nobili gentis Anglorum exortus prosapia, nobilior Christi Iesu regeneratus undis extitit vitalibus', Arndt i, p. 24 = *Monumenta Alcuiniana*, i, p. 6) has led modern critics to doubt the literal truth of Alcuin's noble descent. See D. A. Bullough, *Spoleto . . . Settimane*, 20 (1971) pp. 580-1.

760-3. Alcuin omits Bede's account of Ecgfrith's impatience at Æthelthryth's refusal to consummate their marriage, together with Bede's insistence that the royal saint's virginity was not to be doubted (*HE* iv. 19).

exstiterat multis optatae causa salutis
atque aegris oculis praestaverat ipsa medelam.   780
HE iv. 20(18) Istius ergo sacrae praedictus Beda puellae
in laudem fecit praeclaris versibus hymnum;
quapropter tetigi parcis haec pauca libellis,
utpote commemorans veteris proverbia dicti:
'Tu ne forte feras in silvam ligna, viator.'   785
HE iv. 22(20) Tunc quoque forte fuit quiddam memorabile gestum,
aestimo quod multis prodesse legentibus ista
(si tamen haec quisquam reputabit digna legendo).
[679] *Exstinctus regis frater fuit Ælfuine bello,*
in quo miles item quidam prostratus in armis   790
nobilis occubuit, crudeli strage peremptus,
exanimisque diem duxit cum nocte sequenti.
Qui tamen, exstinctos anima redeunte per artus,
redditus est vitae, et sumpta virtute valescens
atque ligans sibimet refluentia vulnera fesso   795
coepit abire gradu, sed captus ab hostibus atque
ad comitem quendam reflexo est calle reductus.
Cui comes instituit de se narrare quis esset.
Ille tamen metuit clara se stirpe fateri
progenitum, dicens: 'Pauper sum et rusticus unus   800
atque maritali vivebam iure ligatus.'
Quem comes accipiens primo curare sategit;
ne tamen aufugeret vinciri iussit. At ille
vinciri numquam potuit, nam cuncta resolvi
vincula sponte sua mirando more solebant.   805
Haec dum cernebant stupefactis mentibus hostes,

783 libellis *T*: labellis *R*   785 tu ne *R Gale*: tunc *T*   789 Aelfuine
T R: Aelfwine *Gale*   792 sequenti *T*: sequente *R*   795 fesso *T R*:
festo *edd.*

779 Aldh. *de Virg. metr.* 2433   785 [Hor. *Serm.* i. 10. 34]   793 Aldh.
de Virg. metr. 1411 anima redeunte; Sedul. *Carm. pasch.* iii. 293 virtus regressa
per artus   796 Paul. Nol. xix. 549 gradu coepisset abire   797 Aldh. *de
Virg. metr.* 1074 reflexo tramite

785 Alc. *Ep.* 126 (p. 187, 18) Ego vero veteris immemor proverbii: 'Non feres
ligna in silvam'; [*Ep.* 28 (p. 70, 27; p. 71, 1)]   792 *cf.* v. 1113   797 *cf.*
vv. 1314, 1628

became well known to many as a source of healing,
and provided a cure for diseases of the eye.
Bede, of whom I have spoken, wrote in splendid verse
a hymn in honour of that holy maid,
and so I have only touched on this subject in sparing style,
remembering the words of the old proverb:
'Don't carry wood into the forest.'
Another memorable event occurred,
which I think will be of value to many readers
(should anyone think these lines worth reading).
In the battle at which Ælfwine the king's brother perished,
a *thegn* was also laid low,
slain in action amid that terrible massacre.
For a day and the following night he lay lifeless.
The soul however returned to his lifeless body
and he was restored to life, regaining his vigour and strength,
and, staunching his bleeding wounds, he set off
with weary step, but was captured by the enemy
and led back along a winding path to a *gesith*.
The *gesith* instructed him to say who he was.
Afraid to admit that he was of distinguished birth,
he said: 'I am a poor man, a peasant,
and I lived within marriage's bonds.'
The *gesith* took him in, ensured that he was cared for,
and ordered him to be tied up to prevent him from fleeing.
But the prisoner could never be shackled, for of their own
accord, wondrously, his chains would become unfastened.
While the enemy gazed on this in utter amazement,

781-2. For Bede's alphabetical and epanaleptic hymn on Æthelthryth see Plummer ii, p. 241.

783. **libellis:** on the poetic usage of this term, see TLL vii. 2: 1269. ii, B 9 ff.

785. This quotation had long been proverbial (cf. A. Otto, *Die Sprichwörter der Römer* (repr. Hildesheim and N.Y., 1971) p. 323), and is used as such by Alcuin in the letter quoted in app. iii. It proves nothing about his direct knowledge of Horace (cf. Schaller, *Verfasserlexikon* i, col. 246; P. v. Winterfeld, *Rheinisches Museum*, 60 (1905) pp. 31 ff.).

789. Ælfwine died in 678 at the battle of Trent (Stenton, p. 85). His body was carried to York (Eddius, *Vita Wilfridi*, xxiv (Colgrave, p. 50)).

790. Called Imma in Bede. His brother's name was Tunna (v. 813). This incident is discussed by Wallace-Hadrill, *Early Medieval History*, pp. 84 ff.

798. **instituit:** used generally by Alcuin of education (cf. vv. 1018, 1438), the verb is here employed in the sense of 'command'.

artibus ex magicis seu scriptis esse putantes,
saepius addebant priscis nova vincula vinclis.
Haec comes ammirans secrete convocat illum
et cur non posset vinciri inquirit ab illo,   810
an prius aut magicas didicisset forsitan artes.
Nosse nihil studiis se ex talibus ille fatetur:
'Est mihi sed frater devoti pectoris,' inquit,
'quem scio quod Christo pro me solemnia cantat
missarum, quoniam meme putat esse peremptum.   815
Et si forte animam nunc altera vita teneret,
illius illa preces propter missasque frequentes
libera, credo, foret poenasque evaderet omnes.'
Tunc cognovit eum responsis ille receptis
dux fore praeclara genitum de stirpe parentum;   820
et quamvis sibimet visus sit iure necandus
eripit hunc morti, cuidam sed vendidit illum,
qui quoque temptat eum duris vincire catenis.
Nec potuit: quoniam, praedicto more solutus,
liber ab impositis remanebat corpore vinclis.   825
Saepius haec equidem sed praestitit hora diei
tertia, qua frater missarum dona solebat
corde offere pio. Dominus dum talia cernit
mira, facultatem dat ei sese redimendi.
Liber et ille redit pretii sub iure redemptus   830
atque domum repetens narraverat omnia fratri,
sed referente illo cognovit tempora frater
illa, quibus vinclis resolutum se referebat,
haec eadem fieri, quibus et solemnia semper
missarum celebrasse Deo sese recolebat.   835

[684]   *Praefuit Ecgfridus regno feliciter annis*
HE iv. 26(24) *ter quinis faciens victricia bella, quousque*

809 haec *R*: hoc *T*   811 prius *T*: *om. R*   815 meme *R*: me *T*
816–20 *in marg. R*   823 duris *R*: diris *T*   826 equidem *R Gale*:
quidem *T*   833 illa *R*: illo *T*   836 Egfridus *T R*

818 Virg. *Georg.* iv. 485 casus evaserat omnes   822 id. *Aen.* ii. 134
836 Sedul. *Carm. pasch.* ii. 12   837 Aldh. *de Virg. metr.* 852

807 Walahfr. *Vit. Mamm.* xvi. 22   826 *cf.* v. 1195   835 *cf.* v. 1265
836 Alc. xlv. 11 regnet multis feliciter annis   836 ff. Æthelw. *de Abbat.*
35 ff.; 'Hib. Exul' xix. 7–8

thinking that it happened by magic arts and written charms,
they added fresh chains upon chains to the old ones.
Astonished by what was happening, the *gesith* summoned him
privately, and asked him why he could not be fettered,
and whether he had perhaps learnt magic.
The captive declared that he knew nothing of such arts, and
explained: 'I have a brother whose heart is devout and
I know that he offers up High Mass to Christ on my behalf,
for he thinks that I have perished.
And if by chance my soul were to be held in the other life,
because of the prayers and masses that he says so often, it
would now be free, I believe, and would escape all punishment.'
The *gesith* then realized from his prisoner's replies
that his captive was of distinguished birth,
and, although he knew he should have been slain,
he saved him from death, and sold him to another man,
who also tried to bind him with hard chains. This could not
be done, for he was unbound in the way I have mentioned, and
his body remained free of the shackles which were put on it.
This happened most often at the third hour of the day,
when it was his brother's habit to say mass with pious heart.
When his master noticed these wondrous events,
he gave the captive a chance to ransom himself.
Then, freed and duly ransomed, he returned home
and recounted everything to his brother.
As he told his tale, his brother realized that those times
when he told of being released from the chains
were invariably one and the same as those at which
he remembered celebrating High Mass to God.
    For fifteen years Ecgfrith reigned with success,
waging victorious wars, until, with savage intent,

---

807. artibus ex magicis seu scriptis: *seu* in Alcuin, as in Bede (Druhan,
Syntax, p. 150), is virtually equivalent to *et* (Introduction, p. xcix (i) (*h*) 5).
Scriptis is therefore a past participle in agreement with *artibus* and parallel to
magicis: 'by magic arts and written charms' (Alcuin's version of Bede's *litteras
solutorias*). Alcuin envisaged both spells pronounced before battle to secure the
man from captivity, and magical charms employing written techniques. He
probably refers to an amulet of parchment, bone, or wood, with letters written or
inscribed on it and a text either providing a magical formula or using magical
symbols, such as those cited by G. Storms, *Anglo-Saxon Magic* (The Hague,
1948), p. 311, no. 86, and R. I. Page, 'Anglo-Saxon Runes and Magic', *Journal of
the British Archaeological Association* (Ser. 3) 27 (1964), pp. 21–2.

agminibus missis animo trans aequora saevo,
praecipiens gentes Scotorum caede cruenta
vastare innocuas, Anglis et semper amicas,   840
mox adversus eum Pictis bellantibus ipse
occubuit victus misera cum clade suorum

[685] imperii linquens Aldfrido regmina fratri,
qui sacris fuerat studiis imbutus ab annis
aetatis primae, valido sermone sophista,   845
acer et ingenio: idem rex simul atque magister.

HE iv. 12 Praefuit ecclesiae venerandus Bosa sacerdos,
condignis gradui meritis tunc temporis alto,
vir, monachus, praesul, doctor moderatus, honestus,
quem divina sacris virtutum gratia sertis   850
compserat et multis fecit fulgescere donis.
Plurima quapropter congessit lucra Tonanti:
retia mundanas immittens sacra per undas
aequoreas Christo praedas ad litora traxit.
Vir sine fraude bonus, dives pietate superna   855
inque domo Domini fulsit ceu Lucifer ardens.
Hic pater ecclesiae cultum decoravit et illam
moribus a plebis penitus secernit et uni
deservire Deo statuit simul omnibus horis:
ut lyra continuo resonaret mystica plectro,   860
aethereas Domini decantans laudibus odas
vox humana quidem superum pulsaret Olympum,

---

840 Anglis *R Ruinart*: angelis *T*   843 Altfrido *T*: Agfrido *R*
852 lucra *T r*: dona *R*   856 domo *R*: domum *T*

---

839 Aldh. *de Virg. metr.* 1046   847 ibid. 693; Ven. Fort. iii. 3. 3
849 Ven. Fort. *Vit. S. Mart.* i. 221 vir monachus   852 *Syll. Epig. Cantab.*
32. 14 domino . . . plurima lucra   853–4 Matt. 4: 18–19; Aldh. *de Virg.*
metr. 537 retibus angelicis raptos ex aequore mundi   855 Juvenc.
Evang. ii. 112 virtutem puram servant sine fraude maligna. Ven Fort. v. 5. 11
ditans virtute superna   860 Bede, *Vit. S. Cuthb.* 820 resonat
lyra mistica cantu   862 Aldh. *de Virg. metr.* 1537 celsum pulsabat Olym-
pum; [Virg. *Aen.* x. 216 medium pulsabat Olympum]

845–6 Theodulf xvii. 55 sophista potens . . . rex inclytus; '*Karolus Magnus*' 70
summus apex regum, summus quoque in orbe sophista; *Walthar.* 104   857 Alc.
lxxxix. 8. 2   858 ff. Æthelw. *de Abbat.* 219 ff.   862 '*Karolus Magnus*'
518 vox ardua pulsat Olympum

840-2. Ecgfrith's expedition of 684 against the Irish was followed the next

he sent troops across the sea, ordering them
to slaughter and ravage the innocent Irish race,
which had always been friendly to the English.
The Picts soon made war against him and he fell,
vanquished, amid a terrible massacre of his followers,
leaving the throne to his brother Aldfrith,
a man from the earliest years of his life imbued with love
of sacred learning, a scholar with great power of eloquence,
of piercing intellect: a king and a teacher at the same time.
At the head of the church was the revered bishop Bosa,
a man whose merits were equal to his high rank,
a monk, a bishop, a staunch and upright teacher,
whom divine grace had adorned with garlands
of holy virtue, and made resplendent by many a gift.
And so he amassed great treasures for the Lord,
casting his holy nets through the oceans of the world,
and netting from that sea prizes for Christ.
A good and guileless man, rich in piety towards Heaven he
shone in the house of the Lord like the blazing morning star.
This father of the church endowed its fabric
and made its clergy live a life apart from the common people,
decreeing that they should serve the one God at every hour:
that the mystical lyre should sound in unbroken strain,
that human voices, forever singing heavenly praises
to the Lord, should beat upon the heights of Heaven;

year by a raid upon the Picts. On 20 May 685 he and his army were destroyed at
the battle of Nechtanesmere.

843-6. Alcuin's rapid summary of the reign of Aldfrith (685-704), son of
Oswiu, hardly indicates the importance of the security that king provided for the
Northumbrian church in the age of Bede. Aldfrith was educated for the priest-
hood (v. 844), perhaps at a school in Wessex, as may be deduced from a letter
of Aldhelm to him (*MGH AA* xv, pp. 61-2); later he studied in Ireland and
Iona. Aldhelm dedicated his treatise on metre to Aldfrith; Adamnan's *De Locis
Sanctis* was copied at the king's behest for use in Northumbria. Aldfrith's learning
is praised both by Bede and by Eddius (concise appraisal in Stenton, pp. 88-9).

847 ff. Bosa (678-86 and 691-705), the first of three monks of Whitby who
became bishops of York (Introduction, p. liv). This passage of Alcuin's poem,
apart from scattered references in Bede, is our largest primary source for Bosa's
career and the only one to mention his endowments of the church at York. Bosa
is recorded in the metrical Calendar of York (vv. 61-2).

854. aequoreas . . . praedas: the metaphor is of scriptural origin (see app. ii
to vv. 853-4), and the adjective *aequoreas*, used of the Anglo-Saxons throughout
the poem (see comm. to v. 88), fits neatly into Alcuin's description of Bosa as the
fisher of men's souls. (Other examples of word-play are noted at comm. to v. 48.)

omnia dispensans alternis tempora causis:
lectio nunc fieret, sed nunc oratio sacra.
Quisque Dei laudes praeferret corporis usu,   865
iusserat hunc raptim complere negotia carnis:
omnibus ut fieret parvus sopor, esca sub ictu,
non terras victusque, domus, nummismata, vestes,

HE i. 27   *nec quicquam proprium sibimet iam vindicet ullus,*
omnia sed cunctis fierent communia semper.   870
†Qui terrena sibi celorum possidet heres
gaudia qui cunctis speret communia regnit†

.   .   .   .

Hic pius antistes magnis virtutibus huius
implevit postquam praesentis tempora vitae,
transit in aetheream laetus feliciter aulam.   875

HE v. 12   Visio temporibus memorabilis acta sub isdem,

---

863 dispensans *T*: dispensas *R*   865-6 Quisque . . . usu. / Iusserat . . .
Dümmler   866 hunc *T R*: hinc *Wattenbach*   867 parvus *Ruinart*:
parvo *T R*   sopor *T*: sapor *R*   sub ictu *Godman* (*cf.* Ven. Fort. *Vit. S. Mart.*
ii. 412): sub actu *Gale*: subiectu *T*: sub estu *R*   871 possidet *R*: vel possit
T: vel petit *Gale*   871-2 *in ras. R*   872 qui *T R*: hic *Hargrove*   speret
R: fieret *T*   876 isdem *T R*: hisdem *r*

863-4 [I Cor. 14: 40]; Ven. Fort. *Vit. S. Mart.* ii. 414-15 tempus utrumque
dicans causis repetendo duabus: / lectio nunc resonans sibi, nunc oratio cur-
rens   865 Sedul. *Carm. pasch.* iii. 91 corporis usu   866 ff. Ven. Fort.
Vit. S. Mart. ii. 408-9, 411-12 otia nulla terens et nulla negotia carnis, / quidquid
agendum esset totum velociter implens / . . . / non cibus et somnus nisi quod natura
necessat: / tardus edax, velox vigilans sopor, esca sub ictu   868 ff. Act.
2: 44-7 omnes etiam, qui credebant, erant pariter et habebant omnia communia.
Possessiones et substantias vendebant et dividebant illa omnibus prout cuique opus
erat . . . conlaudantes Deum; [Act. 4: 32-4; *Reg. S. Ben.* xxxiii. 6]   874 Aldh.
Carm. eccl. iv. 6. 20 praesentis tempore vitae   875 id. *de Virg. metr.* 708
aetheream . . . migraret in aulam

869-70 Alc. *Ep.* 168 (p. 276, 14 ff.) Hanc [vitam] primitiva per apostolos in
Iudaea initiavit aecclesia, quibus omnia communia esse leguntur, et nemo aliquid
suum esse dicebant   874 id. *Vit. S. Willibr. metr.* 8. 8-9 tempora vitae /
praesentis complens   875 ~ v. 1568   876 ff. *cf.* v. 1070; Æthelw.
de Abbat. 321 ff.

863-4. Cf. *Ep.* 114 (to Eanbald II, archbishop of York, 796): 'Omnia vestra
honeste cum ordine fiant. Tempus statuatur lectioni, et oratio suas habeat horas'
(*MGH Epp.* iv, p. 168, 1-2).
865. **praeferret:** Hargrove translates this as 'prefer', taking *usu* as a rare dative

regulating every hour with alternate duties:
now a reading, now a holy prayer. Whoever wished to proclaim
the Lord's praise by his treatment of the flesh
he commanded swiftly to satisfy his physical needs:
that all should sleep but little and take what food was to hand,
that no one should claim lands, food, houses, money, clothes,
or anything as his private property,
that everything should always be shared.

† . . . .

. . . . †

. . . .

After that pious bishop had completed his span in this life,
amid great and virtuous achievements, he passed
with blissful happiness into the realms of Heaven.
At that time occurred a memorable vision

in -*u*. Thus the line, in her view, means: 'he determined . . . each one to prefer the praises of God to physical enjoyment.' *Praeferre* in Alcuin means 'to carry forth' or 'to proclaim'; cf. vv. 1012, 1431. *Usu* is ablative.

865-6. The sense is obscured by Dümmler's punctuation; Wattenbach's conjecture *hinc* is unnecessary. A comma should be read after v. 865 because the line is a relative clause defining *hunc* in v. 866, not an independent clause, as Dümmler's punctuation implies. The construction is *quisque . . . hunc*: 'whoever'; *quisque* being used as the equivalent of *quisquis* (Introduction, p. xcvi, *d*).

867. **sub ictu**: 'within range', i.e. 'to hand' (cf. *TLL* viii. 1. iii c, 171. 53 ff.). For its corruption into *subiectu* in *T*, and thence to *sub actu / estu*, cf. the variants to Ven. Fort. *Vit. S. Mart.* ii. 412 (Leo, *MGH AA* iv. 1, p. 327 ad loc.).

871-2 are neither sense nor Latin. Since Gale's edition of 1691 they have been consistently obelized. Vv. 865-72 contrast what each man should not desire with what he should, the general object being their common good. Vv. 871-2 in the original presumably formed a transition from the community of earthly goods achieved by Bosa's ecclesiastical reforms to the common joys of heaven to which vv. 873-5 consign the bishop. Without radical emendation neither v. 871 nor v. 872 can stand. V. 871 embodies an expression that is characteristically Alcuinian; cf. v. 562, 'ille heres patriae factus, hic civis Olympi', and v. 1215, 'est patriae proprius caelesti redditus heres'. V. 872, however, repeats in almost identical language v. 870. The suspicion that v. 872 was confected from v. 870 to make good a lacuna cannot be proven because of the formulaic and repetitive quality of Alcuin's style (Introduction, pp. cvi-cvii (iii) (*c*); comm. to v. 576).

876 ff. The vision of Dryhthelm is recorded in *The Anglo-Saxon Chronicle* D and E as taking place in 693. On the vagueness of Bede's dating, see Plummer ii, p. 294. The criterion of moral usefulness in relating this vision is copied directly by Alcuin from Bede. Visions of the other world occur frequently in early Anglo-Latin literature. A recent survey of the visionary literature of Alcuin's age is provided by H. J. Kamphausen, *Traum und Vision in der lateinischen Poesie der Karolingerzeit* (Bern and Frankfurt, 1975), expecially pp. 123 ff. (with bibliography), and see discussion by P. Dinzelbacher, *Vision und Visionsliteratur im Mittelalter* (Stuttgart, 1981), pp. 202 ff.

ut reor, in nostro fuerit si carmine scripta,
proderit aeterna multis de morte vocandis.
Posset ut ergo animas vitiis sanare peremptas
mortuus ecce diu surrexit corpore quidam   880
multaque, quae vidit, memoratu digna ferebat,
e quibus hic nostris addemus pauca camoenis.
Ergo domum propriam communi in plebe maritus
atque suam rexit iusto moderamine vitam.
Qui post tactus erat morbo iam carnis acerbo,   885
perque dies multos valido crescente dolore
infirmus recubans extrema pericula duxit;
mortuus ac tandem primo sub tempore noctis,
eius in extrema respirans parte revixit
atque resurgendo cunctos simul inde fugavit   890
funeris exsequias peragentes nocte sub ipsa.
Plus sed amore vigens coniunx ibi sola remansit,
quam nimium pavidam rediens a morte maritus
coeperat hortari, reliquis fugientibus illinc:
'Quae mihi fida satis remanes ex omnibus,' inquit,   895
'te rogo, ne metuas nunc me, dulcissima coniunx.
Vivo equidem, vere surrexi a morte remissus,
sed mihi longe aliter nunc altera vita sequenda est,
gaudia vel luxus meme damnare necesse est.'
Nec mora, divitiis mox omnibus ille relictis   900
iura monasterii devoto est corde secutus
atque ibi tam duro domuit sub pondere corpus,
ut facile ex vita possent cognoscere cuncti
quae vel quanta prius ductus de corpore crevit.
Isto namque modo quae vidit ferre solebat: 905
'Splendidus', inquit, 'erat, qui me de corpore duxit
et contra aestivum solis processimus ortum,
quo ad latam vallem devenimus atque profundam,
cuius in oblongum extensa est sine fine vorago,

---

877 fuerit *T R*: sic erit *Gale*   885 acerbo *R Ruinart*: acervo *T*

---

884 Ven. Fort. iv. 11. 15   886 Bede *Vit. S. Cuthb. metr.* 694 inque dies
. . . cum incresceret . . . ardor   891 Ven. Fort. iii. 9. 59   895 id.
vii. 8. 55 omnibus una manens   896 Bede *Vit. S. Cuthb. metr.* 643 me
rogo ne linquas   897 Virg. *Aen.* iii. 315–16 vivo equidem . . . / vera vides
901 Aldh. *Carm. eccl.* iii. 7

which will help, I believe, to save many men
from eternal death if it is recorded in this poem.
To restore souls ruined by vice
a man who had long been dead rose in the flesh
and told of many memorable things he had seen,
a few of which I shall now include in my poem.
He was a commoner who had been married and had ordered
his household and his life with justice and moderation.
Later he fell ill with a painful disease,
his pain growing sharply over many days.
Lying back in his illness, he was approaching the last pangs,
and at last died at the first night-watch
when, at the end of night, he regained life and breath
and rose up again, putting to flight all those
who were conducting his funeral that very evening.
But his wife's love overcame her fear. She alone remained,
and her husband, coming back from death,
set about encouraging her when the others fled:
'Sweet wife,' said he, 'you are the only one among them all
to remain faithful to me, and I beseech you not to fear me.
I am alive; I have truly risen from the dead.
But now I must follow a very different life
and must put an end to all idle pleasures.'
Without delay he abandoned all his riches
and devoutly followed the monastic law,
there subduing his flesh in such great mortification
that from his manner of life everyone could easily see
the impact of what he had beheld when led from the body.
He used to give this account of what he had seen:
'Radiant was the being that led me from my body,' said he,
'we went in the direction of the rising summer sun
and on our way came to a valley both wide and deep,
along which there stretched an endless abyss,

884 'Hib. Exul' xvii. 13 regit propriam iusto moderamine carnem   891 *cf.*
v. 1160

883-4. Dryhthelm lived, according to Bede, in a district of Northumbria
now identified with Cunningham (see Colgrave-Mynors, p. 488, n. 1). He later
became a monk (v. 901) at Melrose.

quae latus horrendum flammis ferventibus unum   910
atque aliud habuit glaciali grandine plenum.
Haec animabus erat hominum hinc inde repleta,
quae, nimis exustae dum flammas ferre nequibant,
frigoris in medium miserae mox prosiliebant.
Cumque ibi nec poterant requiem reperire, vicissim   915
flammivomum flentes iterum ferebantur in ignem.
Haec cernens mecum meditabar, forte quod esset
poena infernalis, quam saepe audire solebam.
Ductor et ille mihi meditanti talia dixit:
"Non, sicut ipse putas, istic Infernus habetur."   920
Cumque haec aspicerem, pavidum me duxit inante.
Tunc subito vidi tenebris loca cuncta repleri,
intrantesque illas densatae noctis imago
nos circa incubuit, nec quicquam cernere praeter
ductoris speciem potui vestesque nitentes.   925
Et sic ingressi sola sub nocte per umbras,
ecce repente globi flammarum valde tetrarum
sicut de puteo surgunt iterumque residunt.
Tunc aberat subito ductor, solusque remansi
in mediis positus trepidus stupidusque tenebris.   930
Cumque globi flammae peterent alta atque vicissim
motibus alternis repetebant ima barathri,
omnia flammarum fastigia cerno repleri
spiritibus hominum miseris, qui more favillae
cum flammis pariter scandebant atque cadebant;   935
sed nimius foetor late loca cuncta replebat.
Longius haec cernens circumstetit undique terror,
utpote quid facerem, possem quo vertere gressum
inscius, aut misero qui finis forte maneret.
Audio tum subito sonitum post terga gementum   940
nec non ceu vulgi capto super hoste cachinnum;

910 unum *R*: urunt *T*   911 atque *T*: at *R*   914 miserae *T*: misere *R*   915 nec *T r*: non *R*   917 quod *T*: quid *R*   920 sicut *Winterbottom* (*cf.* vv. 603, 975): ut *T R*   924 praeter *R Gale*: propter *T* 928 sicut *R*: sicuti *T*   932 motibus *Ruinart*: montibus *T R*

910 ff. Bede *de Die Iud.* 95   916 Virg. *Aen.* ix. 451 flentes in castra ferebant   926 ibid. vi. 268 ibant obscuri sola sub nocte per umbras   927 id. *Georg.* i. 473 flammarumque globos [Juvenc. *Evang.* i. 341]   932 Prud. *Hamart.* 722 motibus alternantem; Sedul. *Carm. pasch.* i. 302 petit ima profundi;

one side of which was filled with terrible, raging flames
and the other with freezing hail.
It was crowded on both sides with the souls of men, who,
when excessively burned and unable to endure the burning,
would leap in their misery into the midst of the cold.
And when they could find no respite even there, they were
carried back again, wailing, into the fire's belching flames.
Seeing this I mused that it was perhaps
Hell's punishment, of which I had often heard.
But even as I considered this my guide said:
"This is not, as you think, the region of Hell."
As I gazed with fear, he led me in ahead. Then,
suddenly, I realized that on all sides gloom was descending,
and a cover of darkest night settled upon us
as we entered the shades. I could see nothing but
the outline of my guide and his shining garments.
And so, as we entered through the shadows in the lonely night,
balls of hideous flame suddenly rose up
as if from a pit, and then sank back again.
My guide went away and I remained there alone
in the midst of the gloom, terrified and in awe.
As the balls of flame soared up on high and then,
reversing their movement, sank back to the bottom of the pit,
I saw that the tip of every flame was filled
with the spirits of wretched men who, like sparks,
mounted up and fell back with the fire,
and a powerful stench filled everywhere, both far and wide.
As I gazed on this for a long time, utter horror surrounded me,
not knowing what I should do, where I should
turn my step, or what end might await me in my misery.
Then, of a sudden, I heard behind me the groaning of wretches,
like the jeer of the common people at a captured enemy,

Bonif. *Carm.* i. 291 baratri repetant lustrantes ima profundi   936 Virg. *Aen.*
ii. 495 late loca . . . complebat

920 *cf.* v. 975   922 *cf.* v. 936   932 *cf.* v. 944; Paulin. Aquil. i. 97
petit ima profundi; Theodulf. viii. 3. 16   936 *cf.* v. 1459

910 ff. On the extremes of heat and cold endured in Hell, see Plummer ii,
p. 296.
921. inante: see Löfstedt, *Late Latin*, p. 165; Campbell, *Æthelwulf, de
Abbatibus*, p. xxxv.

qui prope dum veniunt, hostes agnosco malignos
ad poenas animas ululantes quinque trahentes
cum quibus in medii descendunt ima barathri.
Flammivomo e puteo quidam deinde maligni   945
daemones ascendunt oculis flammantibus atque
me circumsteterant, putidum de naribus ignem
oreque spirantes, ignitis meque minantur
prendere forcipibus, nec me contingere tantum
iam poterant, quamvis multum terrere valerent.   950
Tunc ego conclusus tenebris et ab hoste coactus
circumspexi oculis, aliquid si forte veniret
auxilii, quo iam salvarer ab hoste cruento.
Tunc mihi post tergum fulsit quasi stella per umbras,
quae magis accrescens properansque fugaverat hostes: 955
dux erat ille meus veniens cum luce repente,
cuius in adventu fugerunt daemones atri.
Hinc convertit iter brumalem solis ad ortum,
noctique ereptum nitidas me duxit in auras,
ante ubi nos murus subito comparuit ingens,   960
qui sine fine sui sic visus longus et altus,
nullus ut extenso videretur terminus illi.
Sed prope dum venimus quo quali nescio certe
ordine, nos fuimus stantes in culmine muri.
Ecce! ibi campus erat magnus pulcherrimus atque,   965
cuius tantus erat fragrantis nidor odoris,
a me foetorem mox ut depelleret omnem,
et lux tanta sacrum perfuderat undique campum,
vinceret ut lucem solis simul atque diei.
In his ergo locis laetas habitare videbam   970
sanctorum turmas, sedesque tenere beatas.
Haec ego conspiciens mecum meditabar, an essent

---

943 quinque *T R*: quasque *Dümmler*   947 putidum *Ruinart*: fetidum
T R   951 coactus *Ruinart*: coactis *T R*   966 nidor *Wattenbach*:
nitor *T R*   968 sacrum *R Gale*: sanctum *T*   perfuderat undique cam-
pum *R Ruinart*: undique perfuderat agrum *T*

---

952 Virg. *Aen.* ii. 68 oculis . . . circumspexit   957 Bede *Vit. S. Cuthb.*
metr. 372 eius ad adventum fugiens; [Virg. *Aen.* vi. 798]; Bede *Vit. S. Cuthb. metr.*
349 daemonis atri   958 Virg. *Georg.* iii. 277   971 id. *Aen.* vi. 639

---

942 *cf.* v. 963   947 *cf.* v. 991   951 Walafr. *Vit. Mamm.* xiv. 17

and as they came nearer I recognized the wicked demons
dragging five howling souls to punishment
with whom they went down to the bottom of Hell.
Then the wicked demons rose up again from the pit
that belched fire and surrounded me, their eyes ablaze,
their mouths and nostrils darting
stinking flames, threatening to seize me
with their fiery tongs. They could not even touch me,
although frighten me they certainly did.
Encompassed by darkness and set upon by the fiends,
I gazed about to see if there might be some help
at hand to save me from that grisly foe.
Behind me there gleamed like a star in the darkness,
growing brighter and brighter, swiftly routing the fiends,
my guide, who suddenly appeared in a burst of light,
and at his coming the black demons fled. From here he
directed our journey toward the rising of the winter sun,
rescuing me from night and leading me into the clear air.
There suddenly rose before us a huge wall,
so endlessly long and high,
that its dimensions seemed limitless.
But as we drew nearer to it, I know not how,
there we were, standing on the top of the wall.
Suddenly there came into sight a large and beautiful plain.
So delicious was its fragrance that it soon
drove from my memory that foul stench.
So radiant a light shone all over that sacred plain
that it surpassed the sunlight of an entire day.
I saw that in this region the saints in joyous throngs
live and dwell in blessedness.
Gazing on them I wondered whether these were

957 Ermold. *In hon. Hlud.* iv. 63   958 *cf.* v. 1629   966 Alc. *Vit.*
S. *Willibr. metr.* xxvi. 1 miri fragrantia odoris

---

942. **hostes . . . malignos** (cf. vv. 945-6): see Blaise, *Vocabulaire latin*, pp.
466 ff.

943. **quinque:** the allusion here is to *HE* v. 12: 'Considero turbam malig-
norum spirituum, quae *quinque* animas hominum merentes . . .'

947. Neither reading scans. I retain *pŭtidum* because of Bede, *HE* v. 12:
'. . . de ore ac naribus ignem *putidum* efflantes angebant'; cf. *pŭtidum* v. 991,
where the adjective may have formed its short vowel on analogy with *pŭteus.*

regna superna poli cunctis promissa beatis.
Haec mihi volventi respondit ductor et infit:
"Non, sicut ipse putas, istic sunt regna polorum."   975
Fulget inante novae maior mihi gratia lucis,
quae nimio superat lucem fulgore priorem,
nam tunc illa prior vere tenuissima visa est.
Vox quoque cantantum resonat dulcissima ibidem,
et cum luce fuit miri fragrantia odoris,   980
ut mihi propter eam parvissima prima putata est.
Quo nos dum laetus sperarem intrare, repente
substitit ipse meus ductor gressumque retorquet,
meque via, per quam nos venimus, inde reduxit.
Intrantesque iterum campi loca pulchra prioris,   985
omnia quae vidi si scirem forte requirit.
"Nescio," cui dixi, statimque haec addidit ille:
"Vidisti vallem flammis et frigore plenam,
in qua nunc animae poenis purgantur acerbis
ac redient iterum purgatae ad praemia vitae.   990
At vero puteus, putidum qui eructuat ignem
est os Inferni: ruerit nam quisquis in illum
forte semel, numquam post haec salvabitur inde.
Floriger iste locus, quem possidet alba iuventus,
est requies, in qua spectant caelestia regna   995
qui bona gesserunt, quamvis ex parte minus quam
postulat alma Fides. Nam qui perfectus ubique est,
ut moritur, statim caeli penetrabit in aulam.
Pertinet ad cuius vicinia fulgidus ille
luce locus nimia, miri quoque plenus odoris,   1000
de quo cantantum suavissima vox resonabat.
Tu quia nunc iterum debes adsumere corpus
atque homines inter moritura vivere vita,
corrige, quaeso, tuos mores et verba vel actus,
ut tua in his sancta reputetur mansio turmis."   1005
Haec ubi dicebat, quomodo sed scire nequivi,
indutum proprio statim me corpore vidi.'

977 superat *Gale*: fuerat *T R*   979 vox quoque *Gale*: voxque *T R*
990 ac *Gale*: hae *T R*   redient *T R*: redeunt *Gale*

---

975 Aldh. *de Virg. metr.* 755   976 Juvenc. *Evang.* iv. 150 gratia lucis
990 Sedul. *Carm. pasch.* i. 341   994 Ven. Fort. ii. 7. 49–50   1005 [Joh.

the heavenly kingdoms on high promised to all the blessed.
As I was reflecting on this my guide answered:
"There are not, as you think, the realms of Heaven."
Before me there gleamed a greater and lovelier light,
which so outshone the other with its surpassing brightness
that the first came to seem very dim indeed.
Sweet voices raised in song resounded there
and with the light came a scent so wonderfully fragrant
that the first in comparison seemed very slight.
I waited, joyously expecting us to go in, when suddenly
my guide halted, turned about again,
and led me back along the road which we had taken.
As we entered the fair field that we had once visited, he
happened to ask me whether I understood all that I had seen.
"I do not," I replied and he immediately added:
"You have seen a valley filled with flames and with ice,
in which souls are purged by bitter punishments
and shall return again, cleansed, to life's rewards.
But the pit which belches forth stinking fire
is the mouth of Hell, and he who chances but once
to fall into it can never again be saved. That pleasance,
filled with flowers, the home of young men clad in white,
is a place of rest, where those who have done good,
although rather less than sweet Faith requires, gaze
upon the kingdom of Heaven. Those who are wholly perfect
will enter into the courts of Paradise as soon as they die.
Close by is that place which shines with great brilliance,
full of wondrous fragrance, where lovely voices
were resounding forth, singing their songs.
Since you must once again enter the body
and live among men a life that will end in death,
I entreat you to reform your character, your words, and deeds,
so that your blessed home may be in that company."
When he had finished speaking, I suddenly saw—I know not
how—that I was covered in the mantle of my own body.'

14: 23]   1006 Virg. *Aen.* ii. 790 Haec ubi dicta dedit

---

979 *cf.* v. 1001   980 *cf.* v. 1000   998 Alc. cix. 17. 4 caeli
penetravit in arcem

HE v. 9   Nec gens clarorum genetrix haec nostra virorum,
quos genuit soli sibimet tunc ipsa tenebat,
intra forte sui concludens viscera regni,   1010
sed procul ex illis multos trans aequora misit,
gentibus ut reliquis praeferrent semina vitae.
E quibus ille fuit, dictus cognomine sanctus
Ecgberct antistes, primis aetatis in annis
qui liquerat patriam patriae caelestis amore,   1015
et peregrina petens Scotis iam maxima vitae
tunc exempla dabat, doctrinae lampade fulgens,
actibus instituens, verbis quoscumque docebat.
Pauperibus largus, sibimet sed semper egenus,
sic bonus egregiae duxit moderamina vitae   1020
usque diem mortis clara pietate coruscans.
Cui fuerat socius meritis et moribus aptus
et comes exsilii Uuibert praeclarus in omni
religione satis, sed post divisus ab illo
theoricam solus vitam districtus agebat.   1025
Inde suae gentis monachis construxit ovile
egregium, vitae meritis et moribus illud
exornans, ovibus Christi studiosus alendis,
ipse per angustam quas recto tramite callem
duxit ad aeterni devotus pascua regni.   1030
Claruit idcirco signis et more prophetae
multa futura videns permansit clarus ubique;
postea caelestis penetravit gaudia vitae.

HE v. 10   Ast alii ratibus vecti trans aequor eoum

1023 Uuibert *R*: Wibert *T*   1026 monachis *R*: monachus *T*
1030 aeterni *T R*: aetherei *Froben*   1032 permansit *T R*: mansit
Ruinart   clarus *R*: praeclarus *T*   1034 aequor *Ruinart*: aequora
T R

1008 Bede *Vit. S. Cuthb. metr.* 25 Nec iam orbis contenta sinu trans aequora
1017 Ven. Fort. vi. 1. 101 lampade fulgens   1029 Is. 26: 7; Ven. Fort. ii.
16. 17 per augustam . . . callem; Aldh. *Ænigm.* lix. 3 directo tramite

1013 Alc. *Vit. S. Willibr. metr.* i. 9   1015 *cf.* v. 1455; Alc. *Vit. S. Willibr.*
pros. iv ob caelestis patriae amorem domo patria cognationeque relicta
1016 ibid. *metr.* i. 8 peregrina petens   1025 *cf.* v. 1097; Alc. *Vit. S.*
Willibr. metr. xxxiv. 40 theoricam cupiens solus adire viam   1032 *cf.* v. 1393
1033 Alc. cxxi. 15.4

This race of ours, mother of famous men,
did not keep her children for herself,
nor held them within the confines of her own kingdom,
but sent many of them afar across the seas,
bearing the seeds of life to other peoples.
One of them was a holy bishop
called Egbert who, early in life, had left
his native country for love of his heavenly homeland
and, travelling abroad, set the Irish an example
of how to live; a shining light in his teaching,
he instructed all manner of men by his words and deeds.
Generous to the poor, but stinting himself,
this goodly man led an excellent life
brilliant with outstanding piety until the day of his death.
His fitting companion by character and achievements
and comrade in exile was Wihtberht, a figure of high renown
for his godliness. Later he separated from Egbert
to lead in strict solitude a life of contemplation.
Then he built an excellent shelter for the monks of his race,
and was a credit to it through his upright and moral life.
Zealous to feed the sheep of Christ,
he led them devoutly, by the straight and narrow,
to the pastures of the eternal kingdom.
So he became famous for his miracles and, prophet-like,
saw much of the future, his fame remaining widespread,
and afterwards entered the joys of eternal life.
Others travelled in ships across the eastern seas

1008 ff. Although Alcuin here follows Bede, his own works provide primary evidence for the Anglo-Saxon missions to the Continent (comm. to vv. 1037-43). On these missions see Levison, *England and the Continent*, pp. 45 ff.

1014-21. Egbert (d. 721), a Northumbrian of noble birth and a monk of Lindisfarne, was staying in an Irish monastery when his companions were killed by the plague of 664. He vowed to go into voluntary exile for life if spared. Later he was to inspire the missionary activities of the Anglo-Saxons Wihtberht and Willibrord described by Alcuin below (Levison, pp. 52-3; Farmer, *Dictionary*, p. 127). Egbert is mentioned in the metrical Calendar of York, vv. 20-1.

1022-33. Wihtberht's career is recorded only by Bede (*HE* v. 9) and by Alcuin (here and at *Vit. S. Willibr. pr.* iv (Levison, pp. 118-19)). His two-year mission in Frisia was fruitless.

1025. theoricam . . . vitam: after returning from the Continent, Wihtberht lived for many years as a hermit in Ireland.

1026-33. These verses are our only source for Wihtberht's foundation of a monastery (in Ireland?) and for his prophecies.

paganum petiere solum, qua verba salutis   1035
spargere temptabant in agrestia corda serendo.
Ut fuit egregius Uuilbrordus episcopus ille,
plurima qui populi Fresonum milia Christo
lucratus monitis fuerat caelestibus atque
pontificale decus multis ornavit in annis,   1040
ecclesiasque Deo plures construxit ibidem
presbyteros in eis statuens Verbique ministros;
[738] omnia perficiens felix in pace quievit.
Illius ecce duo fuerunt exempla secuti
presbyteri, nimio accensi fervore Fidei,   1045
nominis unius Heuualdus uterque vocatus.
Par opus ambobus vitae, sed et exitus unus.
Albus hic, ille niger, distantia sola capillis;
ast niger in libris fuerat studiosior albo.
Ergo hi Saxonum paganae compita plebis   1050
intrabant, aliquos si Christo acquirere possent.
Sed dum forte novos mores habitusque Fidei
agnoscunt miseri, metuunt, ne funditus omnis
iam caderet citius veterum cultura deorum.
Hos subito raptos crudeli morte necarunt,   1055
album sed trucidant statim mucrone cruento,
longa sed exquirunt duro tormenta nigello
atque peremptorum Rheni sub fluminis undas
corpora proiciunt. Quae sed mox ordine miro
contra praevalidos ferebantur fluminis ictus   1060
milia et usque suos socios undena natabant.
Ast quocumque loco veniebant corpora nocte,
maximus hinc lucis radius super astra refulsit,

1037 Uuibrordus *R*: Wilbrordus *T*   1044 fuerunt *T R*: fuerant *Froben*
1045 nimio accensi *T*: accensi nimio *R*   1046 Heuualdus *R*: Heruwaldus *T*:
Hewaldus *Gale*   1061 undena *Traube*: undana *T R*: (milia) ad (usque suos)
passus undaque (natabant) *Dümmler, Add.*

1036 Virg. *Aen.* x. 87; Arat. *de Act. Apostol.* ii. 1167 agrestia corda
1039 Bede *Vit. S. Cuthb. metr.* 918   1040 ibid. 812   1055 Aldh. *de Virg.*
metr. 2267 crudeli morte necaret; [id. *Carm. eccl.* iv. 4. 2]   1056 id. *de Virg.*
metr. 1749   1058 Virg. *Aen.* iii. 389   1063 Aldh. *de Virg. metr.* 1403

1035 Alc. c. 7   1037 *cf.* v. 1201   1040 *cf.* v. 1524   1041-7 Alc.
Vit. S. Willibr. pr. xii mox ecclesias in eis aedificare iusserat, statuitque per eas
singulas presbiteros et verbi Dei sibi cooperatores   1044 Alc. xc. 12. 3
1045 id. xcix. 14. 4   1055 Flor. Lugd. i (*In evang. Matt.*) 194

in quest of pagan lands, where they attempted to spread
the word of salvation by sowing it in barbarian hearts.
Thus was the excellent bishop Willibrord,
who had won many thousands of the Frisian people for Christ
through God's instruction and for many years
had brought glory to his episcopal office,
he built there many a church to God
and set in them priests and ministers of the Word.
After completing all this labour, he ended his life in peace.
Two priests followed his example,
burning with intense fervour for the Faith,
and both of them were called by the same name of Hewald.
Their mission in life was the same; identical were their deaths.
One was fair, the other dark, the only difference being the
colour of their hair; but dark Hewald was keener on learning
than the fair Hewald. They entered the land of the pagan
Saxons, attempting to win some of them over to Christ.
But when the wretches saw the new morals and customs of
the Faith, they were afraid that the cult of their ancient gods
might be subverted rapidly and completely. Suddenly they
laid hold of the monks and put them to a cruel death:
fair Hewald was immediately murderously slaughtered
but rugged dark Hewald, poor wretch, they long tortured,
and tossed the corpses of both into the waters of the Rhine.
The bodies were carried off in a wondrous way
against that river's powerful current,
floating eleven miles back to their companions.
Wherever the bodies touched at night-time,
a brilliant ray of light shone more brightly than the stars

1037 ff. On the Frisian mission see Levison, *England and the Continent*,
pp. 52–69.
1037–43. Alcuin deals briefly with the achievements of his kinsman St.
Willibrord (658–739), about whom he wrote a prose and a metrical *Life* (Intro-
duction, pp. xliii–iv, lxxxv–vii). Willibrord's life and work are brilliantly discussed
by Levison in the chapter of *England and the Continent* cited above (previous
note) and in *Aus rheinischer und fränkischer Frühzeit* (Düsseldorf, 1948), pp.
304–46. Notice in Farmer, *Dictionary*, pp. 406–8.
1055. The two Hewalds, missionaries to the Old Saxons, were martyred on
3 October c.695 (Farmer, *Dictionary*, p. 191). They are commemorated in the
metrical Calendar of York, v. 63.
1061. **undena:** perhaps arose through *XL* [*milia passum*] at *HE* v. 10 being
read as *XI*.

lumen et hoc illi, qui sanctos ante necabant,
aspiciunt omni semper fulgescere nocte. 1065
Alter ab his noctu sociorum visus at uni est:
'Corpora', cui dixit, 'statim reperire potestis
nostra, ubi de caelis lucem radiare videtis.'
Visio tunc socios talis nec illa fefellit;
corpora namque locis sic sunt inventa sub isdem 1070
martyribusque piis digno conduntur honore.

HE v. 11   Ast alii atque alii praefata ex gente ministri
sermonis fuerant illis in partibus orbis.
E quibus egregii Suidberct et Uuira sacerdos
temporibus fulsere suis, qui culmine clari 1075
virtutum fuerant, nostro quos carmine cunctos
tangere non libuit. Nunc namque revertere musam
urbis ad Euboricae fas est—procul inde recessit—
pontifices summos seriemque relinquere regum,

HE v. 18 qui post Aldfridum variarunt tempora regni, 1080
imperio functum denis simul atque novenis
orbibus annorum, qui post sub tempore pacis

[705]   appositus patribus suprema sorte quievit.
    Interea Bosa felicia regna petente,

[686]   accipit ecclesiae regimen clarissimus ille 1085
vir pietate, fide, meritis et mente Iohannes,
pontificalis apex, priscorum formula patrum,
flumina doctrinae fundens e pectore puro,
e quibus intente vivacia prata rigavit,
quem virtutis honor signis comitatur apertis, 1090
quorum pauca libet nostris memorare camoenis.

HE v. 2 Dum pater ipse pius ieiunia sancta gerebat,
parvula saepta viris repetit comitatus honestis,

1064 necabant *T R*: necarant *Munari*   1070 isdem *T*: hisdem *R*
1074 Suidberct *r*: Suidbrect *R*: Suidbert *T*   Uuyraque *Gale*: et Uire *R*:
iureque *T*   1078 inde *T R*: unde *Froben*   1090 honor *T*:
honos *R*

1072–3 Lc. 1: 2 ministri . . . sermonis   1073 Virg. *Aen.* xi. 708
1087 Ven. Fort. i. 15. 33 pontificalis apex   1089 Bede *Vit. S. Cuthb. metr.*
682 vivida prata rigat   1090–1 ibid. 30–1 Hunc virtutis honor . . . / . . .
signis comitatur apertis

1087 Alc. *Vit. S. Willibr. metr.* iv. 1   1090 Hrab. Maur. xiii. 41

and the murderers of these holy men saw
it gleaming on throughout the night.
One of them appeared at night to a comrade of his,
and said: 'You can find our bodies without delay,
where you see the light streaming from the heavens.'
Nor did this vision deceive the Hewalds' comrades,
for they found the corpses in that very place
and buried them with the honour that is due to holy martyrs.

More and more servants of the Word from our people
came to that part of the world. Among them were
the excellent Swithberht and the priest Wira,
who enjoyed outstanding fame in their own time,
and were distinguished for the highest virtue. I cannot deal
with all of them in my poem, for now I should return to the
bishops of the city of York—far from there have I wandered—
and leave the succession of kings
reigning at various times after Aldfrith, who,
discharging his royal duties for a span
of nineteen years, passed away in a time of peace
and was at last laid to rest beside his fathers.

When Bosa had departed for the realms of bliss,
famed John reigned over the church,
a man renowned for his piety, faith, merits, and intellect,
a high pontiff, cast in the mould of the ancient fathers,
from his pure heart pouring forth streams of learning,
with which he eagerly watered the meadows of life.
Honour and virtue attended him with undeniably miraculous
signs, a few of which I am pleased to recount in this poem.
While that devout father was piously fasting
with a company of upright men, he sought out a small retreat

1064. **necabant:** such changes of tense are usual in Alcuin. See Introduction, p. xcix (i) (*h*) 2.

1074. Swithberht (d. 713) and Wira, possibly the bishop of Utrecht (d. *c.* 753). See Levison, *England and the Continent*, pp. 82 (with n. 2)-83, Farmer, *Dictionary*, pp. 364-5, 410.

1078-9. Alcuin refers to the personified theme of his poem: *musa*[*m*], the object of *revertere* and the subject of *recessit. Fas est* governs both *relinquere* and *revertere.* If one reads *unde* with Froben a comma must be placed between *est* and *procul* at v. 1078. My translation adopts the first person, in keeping with ME idiom.

1084 ff. John of Beverley (d. 721) was the second monk of Whitby who became bishop of York (notice in Farmer, *Dictionary*, p. 216). The miracle recounted at 1092-1119 occurred while John was bishop of Hexham.

posset ut aethereos animo decerpere flores
et Domino propriae decimas persolvere vitae, 1095
e quis divitias caelo reperiret opimas.
Intrans ergo locum districtis usibus aptum
tunc inopes iussit per proxima compita quaeri,
per se pauperibus victum ut deferret egenis.
Tunc aeger iuvenis mutusque adducitur illi, 1100
promere qui nullis poterat iam verba loquelis,
cui caput horribili fuerat scabrigine tectum
et pro crine cutis maculis vestita remansit.
Huic pius antistes casulam congessit egeno,
in qua susciperet stipem miser ille suetam; 1105
postque dies septem transacti temporis illum
iusserat adduci mutamque ostendere linguam.
Cui crucis impressit sanctae signando figuram
atque diu tacitam iussit proferre loquelam.
Qui dicto citius patris praecepta secutus 1110
ore loquens prompto taciturna silentia rupit
et pleno est penitus mutus sermone locutus
atque die tota pariter cum nocte sequenti
non cessavit ovans varias proferre loquelas
atque suae mentis secretas pandere causas. 1115
Et cum voce cutis pariter iam sana reversa est,
reddunturque novi crispato crine capilli,
pulcherque est iuvenis factus, promptusque loquela,
sicque domum propriam gaudens sanatus adibat.
HE v. 3 Nec meminisse aliud taedet laudabile signum. 1120
Dum lustrat pastor vigili tutamine mandras,
sanctarum venit famularum visere cellam,
de quarum numero recubat virguncula quaedam,

1096 quis *T R*: queis *Gale*   1098 proxima *T*: maxima *R*
1104 congessit *T R*: concessit *Munari*   1111 rupit *R Ruinart*: rumpit *T*
1112 pleno *T*: plano *R*   mutus *R*: muto *T*   1121 mandras *T*: mandres *R*

1095 Lev. 27: 32   1096 Aldh. *de Virg. metr.* 973   1097 Bede *Vit. S. Cuthb. metr.* 454   1098-9 Juvenc. *Evang.* iii. 79 quaerens per compita victum   1111 Ven. Fort. *Vit. S. Mart.* iv. 220 taciturna silentia rumpens; [Virg. *Aen.* x. 63-4]   1121 Bede *Vit. S. Cuthb. metr.* 135 vigili tutamine mandris; ibid. 583 iam commissa vigil dum lustrat ovilia pastor

---

1094 Alc. *Vit. S. Willibr. metr.* xxxiv. 43 aetherios . . . decerpere flores
1109 *cf.* v. 1114   1110 *cf.* v. 1231   1114 *cf.* vv. 1204,
1455; Æthelw. *de Abbat.* 141   1119 Alc. *Vit. S. Willibr. metr.* xxx. 13 atque

to gather in spirit the flowers of Heaven
and pay tithes to the Lord for his life,
through them to store up splendid riches in Heaven.
And so, on coming to a place suited to fasting and abstinence,
he ordered a search to be made high and low for those in want,
in order to offer food to the poor and the needy himself.
There was brought to him a young man who was ill,
a mute, unable to utter any word in speech,
whose head was covered by a horrible scurf,
the skin filled with sores in place of hair.
The bishop had a small hut built for this poor young man,
in which that sad wretch took his daily rations,
and after seven days had passed, he had him brought forth,
and commanded him to show his speechless tongue.
On it he made the sign of the holy cross,
commanding it to break its long silence.
No sooner was this said than the father's command was obeyed:
the total mute broke his silence and spoke fluently,
replying clearly in eloquent words.
For the entire day and the following night
he never ceased to talk joyously of many things,
revealing the hidden thoughts of his mind.
His skin was restored to health along with his voice
and a new head of curly hair grew on his head.
He became a handsome young man, with a ready tongue.
So, rejoicing and cured, he returned home. It is
interesting to recall another miracle which deserves praise.
When that shepherd was visiting the folds in his charge,
he came to see a community of holy nuns,
one of whom, a young maiden, lay ill.

domum propriis gaudens se currere plantis   1121 Alc. ii [*Epit. Ælb.*]. 4 vigili
tutamine mandras; id. *Vit. S. Willibr. metr.* xii. 5

1112. **pleno / plano . . . sermone:** *plano . . . sermone* has a precise technical
sense in Anglo-Latin of this period, and means 'prose'; cf. *HE* v. 24: 'vitam . . .
Cuthbercti et prius metro heroico et postmodum *plano sermone* descripsi.' Alcuin
wishes to stress the new-found eloquence of the erstwhile mute.

1120-35. This is the first of John of Beverley's miracles that took place while
he held the bishopric of York.

1122. **cellam:** at Watton in the East Riding of Yorkshire. In the poetry of
Alcuin this term is used of a spiritual community and never refers to a single
monastic cell (Godman, *SM* (3^a Ser.) 20. 2 (1979), pp. 567 ff.).

1123. Called Cwenburh in Bede.

vena cui nuper medio est incisa lacerto
et manus obstipuit nimio grassante tumore;   1125
ergo videbatur citius moritura puella.
Hanc sed restituit Domini virtute saluti
antistes sanctus, qui tecta a matre rogatus
virginis intrabat recubamque ex more salutat
atque preces fundens manui benedixerat aegrae.   1130
Invaluit statim fugiente dolore puella,
inque modum mirum toto de corpore tota
cum redeunte foras secessit praesule pestis.
Protinus Altithrono magnis erepta periclis
virgo canit laudes multos victura per annos.   1135

HE v. 4   Huic aliud simili successit in ordine signum.
Ecce comes quidam venerandum iure Iohannem
advocat, ecclesiae Domino qui tecta dicaret.
Uxor erat cuius multis infirma diebus,
quadraginta iacens noctes depressa dolore   1140
algida nec valuit sese relevare cubili.
Lurida cui gelidus pallor praetexerat ora,
naribus alternis tenuis vix flatus anhelat.
Huic pius antistes benedictam miserat undam,
qua prius ecclesiam Domino sacraverat illam,   1145
ut potaret eam atque dolentia membra liniret.
Quod dum fecisset, sequitur medicina per artus
atque salutifero morbi periere sub haustu,
venit et optatae virtus concessa salutis,
surgit et e strato statim tunc femina sospes   1150
atque sacerdoti renovatis viribus almo
pocula deportat, cunctisque impigra ministrat,
reddidit atque Deo proprio cum coniuge grates.

1124 vena *T*: vela *R*   1125 grassante *R*: crassante *T*   1129 intra-
bat *T*: intrabant *R*   ex *R*: a *T*   1136 huic *T*: hinc *R*   1143 flatus
anhelat *Gale*: flabat anhelus *T R*   1153 proprio *T*: propria *R*

1129 Bede *Vit. S. Cuthb. metr.* 80   1134 Virg. *Aen.* iii. 711 tantis . . .
erepte periclis   1143 Aldh. *Ænigm.* lxxi. 4 Spiritus alterno . . . flatu;
Stat. *Theb.* vi. 873 flatibus alternis   1148 Bede *Vit. S. Cuthb. metr.* 581
medellifero morbi cessere sub haustu   1149 Sedul. *Carm. pasch.* iii. 100
1150 Aldh. *de Virg. metr.* 1278 protinus e strato festina surgere; Bede *Vit. S.
Cuthb. metr.* 570 femina sospes   1153 Aldh. *de Virg. metr.* 1114; Ven. Fort.
Vit. S. Mart. iii. 389 coniuge cum propria

A vein had recently been cut in the middle of her upper arm;
as the swelling increased apace, her hand grew numb,
and so it seemed that the girl would soon die. But through
the Lord's power the holy bishop restored her to health.
Entering her home at her mother's request,
he greeted her in the usual way as she lay there,
and, uttering prayers, he blessed her sick hand.
The pain immediately fled, the girl grew well,
and, wondrously, the disease left her body
as the bishop left their house and went outdoors again.
Saved from great danger, the girl, who was destined to live
for many years, sang praises to God enthroned on high.
  Another miracle after this occurred in a similar way.
A *gesith* summoned the revered bishop John
to dedicate a church building to the Lord.
His wife had lain ill for many days,
suffering for forty nights from severe pains,
in a chill and unable to rise from the bed.
A cold pallor had spread over her wan face,
from her nostrils came scarcely a faint breath.
The goodly bishop sent blessed water,
with which he had previously consecrated the church,
for her to drink and use to anoint her suffering limbs.
When she had done this, the medicine flowed through her veins
and her illness vanished with the healing draught.
The vigour and health for which she yearned were granted her,
and immediately she rose up from bed, cured,
her strength renewed, and bore the cup of hospitality
to the ministering priest, serving all with care and,
with her husband, giving thanks to God.

  1129 *cf.* v. 1168   1130 *cf.* vv. 1165, 1360   1138 *cf.* v. 1155
1140 Flor. Lugd. i (*In Evang. Math.*). 74   1143 *cf.* v. 1159; Walafr. lxxxiv.
12 dum flatus anelat; Milo *Vit. S. Amand.* iv. 352 tenuem flatum de nare . . .
efflans   1144 Alc. *Vit. S. Willibr. metr.* xxii. 14 benedictam miserat undam
1145 *cf.* v. 1155

  1125. **grassante:** cf. *Vit. S. Willibr. pr.* xxviii *grassante . . . infirmitate.*
  1128. **a matre rogatus:** the girl's mother was Hereburh, the abbess, who
wished her daughter to succeed her.
  1137. Bede records that the name of the *gesith* was Puch.

HE v. 5 Ast comes hunc alius diverso tempore scisci
fecit ad ecclesiam Domino de more dicandam,   1155
cuius forte puer, mortali peste subactus,
mortuus ex omni membrorum parte remansit,
spiritus excepto quod pectora fessa movebat,
frigida vix tenui geminans suspiria flatu.
Funeris exsequias cui tunc comes ipse parabat   1160
et loculus iuxta stabat, quo corpus humandum
mox fuerat, vitae quoniam spes nulla manebat.
Pro quo pontificem lacrimans dux ipse rogabat,
ut dignaretur puero benedicere presso
atque preces Domino pro huius fundere vita.   1165
Nec quod plena Fides rogitabat iure negabat
vir pius et clemens, statim sed visitat aegrum
et benedixit eum, rediens ex more salutat:
'Mox revalesce puer,' dicens, 'viresque resume!'
Post haec cum praesul vel dux prandere sedebant,   1170
postulat infirmus sitiens sibi pocula ferri.
Cui dominus gaudens quod iam potare valeret,
mox calicem vini benedictum a praesule misit.
Ut bibit hunc, statim sanus surrexit et ibat,
intravitque domum quo dux et praesul edebant,   1175
cumque illis bibere et vesci se velle profatur.
Potat editque sedens laetus laetantibus illis,
post haec et multis vivebat sospes in annis.
HE v. 6 Ast quoque praesul iter per quandam cursibus aptam
planiciem campi cum clero gessit equester;   1180
tunc iuvenes ardent cursu contendere equorum,
sed pius antistes vetuit specialiter unum
ex sociis, ludo ne se misceret inani.
Ille tamen contra vetitum petulanter habenas
solvit equo fidens mediumque erumpit in aequor.   1185
Ergo cavum quoddam dum fervidus ille caballus
transilit et valido iuvenis conamine lapsus
in lapidem cecidit, qui forte aequalis harenae

1154 scisci *Gale*: sisti *R*: scissi *T*   1155 ad *T*: et *R*   domino *T R*: domini
edd.   1158 quod *T*: quo *R*   1164 presso *T R*: praesto *edd.*

1159 Virg. *Ecl.* viii. 14 frigida vix   1161 id. *Aen.* vi. 161 quod corpus
humandum   1166 Arat. *de Act. Apostol.* ii. 939   1181 Virg. *Aen.*
v. 291 contendere cursu   1183 Bede *Vit. S. Cuthb. metr.* 63 levi subdis

At another time, a different *gesith* summoned John
to dedicate a church, as custom demanded.
A servant boy of his was struck down by a mortal illness
and lay there, lifeless in all his limbs,
except that his breathing moved his weary breast,
as he heaved sigh upon sigh, chill and faint.
Even then the *gesith* was preparing his funeral
and a coffin stood nearby in which his body
was soon to be laid, since he had no hope of surviving.
In tears on his behalf, the nobleman asked the bishop
to be kind enough to bless the afflicted boy
and offer up prayers to the Lord for his life.
What the fullness of Faith demanded that goodly and kindly
man did not refuse. He immediately visited the sick boy,
blessed him, and, on returning as usual, gave him this greeting:
'Now be restored to health and strength, my boy.'
Later, as the bishop and *gesith* were sitting down to their meal,
the sick boy asked that a goblet of wine be brought to quench
his thirst. Delighted that he was well enough to drink, his
master sent a glass of wine blessed by the bishop. On drinking,
the boy immediately rose up in good health, began to walk,
and entered the house where the *gesith* and bishop were eating,
declaring that he wished to take food and drink with them.
They rejoiced together, and he sat down to eat and drink
and for many years after lived on in health.

That bishop was once making a journey on horseback
with some of his clergy over a level field well-suited to racing.
The young men longed to compete with one another on
horseback, but the kindly bishop expressly forbade one of
them to take part in his companions' idle sport.
Flouting the prohibition, the young man gave his horse free
rein, and galloped confidently into the middle of the plain.
But, as his hot-blooded stallion was leaping over a ditch,
the young man strained hard, slipped, and fell on to a stone,
which happened to lie hidden in the middle of the field,

per inania ludo; Virg. *Georg.* iv. 105   1185 id. *Aen.* x. 181

1154. Called Addi in Bede.
1158. **excepto quod**: cf. Löfstedt, *Kommentar*, pp. 298-9, Norberg, *Syntaktische Forschungen*, p. 234.

in medio campi latuit sub caespite tectus.
(Nec lapis alter erat campo repertus in illo).   1190
Huic caput atque manum casu collisit acerbo,
verticis et solvit iuncturas; atque cerebro
quassato cunctis iacuit iam sensibus expers
et moribundus erat motu sine corporis ullo.
Septima nempe fuit tunc circiter hora diei,   1195
semianimisque domum sociis defertur ab ipsis.
At vigil in precibus perstabat nocte sacerdos,
venit ad infirmum primo sed mane reversus,
inpositaque manu capiti benedixit eundem
atque illum proprio compellans nomine clamat.   1200
Ergo gravi veluti de somno surgeret, ille
recludens oculos patri respondit amato
convaluitque cito recreatis viribus atque
cras equitavit ovans caro cum praesule pergens.
Multa alia, ut referunt, hic fecit signa Iohannes,   1205
quae modo non libuit brevitatis iure referri.
Diximus haec tantum, posuit quae Beda magister,
indubitante fide texens ab origine prima
historico Anglorum gentes et gesta relatu.
Consenuit postquam praefatus episcopus ille,   1210
tunc alio vivens sedem concessit honoris
atque monasterium devoto corde petivit,
condignamque Deo vitam complevit ibidem,
iuraque tunc tandem terrae peregrina relinquens
[721]   est patriae proprius caelesti redditus heres.   1215
Presbyter egregius successit iure Iohanni
Uuilfridus, heres patri dignissimus almo,
qui prius Euboricae fuerat vicedomnus et abbas,

1207 haec *R*: hic *Mabillon*: hac *T²*   1211 alio vivens *R T²*: alio iuveni
Mabillon: alii vivens *Froben*   1217 Uuilfridus *R*: Wilfridus *T*

1205 Aldh. *de Virg. metr.* 1455 plurima hic gessit virtutum signa sacerdos
1208 Arat. *de Act. Apostol.* i. 953 indubitata fides; Aldh. *de Virg. metr.* 510 ab
origine prima   1209 Ven. Fort. *Vit. S. Mart.* iv. 426 gesta . . . relatu
1215 Paul. Nol. xvi. 257 divitiis . . . patriis possederat heres

---

1197 Alc. xci. 2. 3   1205-6 Milo *Vit. S. Amand.* i. 281 plurima praeteriens
studio brevitatis omitto   1208-9 ibid. iv. 310 historiae manifesta fides

---

1205 ff. With one possible exception (vv. 1291-1318) Alcuin from this point
ceases to draw on the *HE*, which closes in the year 731. The remainder of his

level with some sand and covered by turf.
(No other stone was found in that field.)
Falling badly, he struck his head and hand,
splitting the crown of his head and crushing the brain.
There he lay without any sense of movement or feeling,
on the point of death, his body motionless.
It was then about the seventh hour of the day;
he was carried home unconscious by his comrades.
The bishop stayed up all night praying,
and returned to see him early in the morning.
He placed his hand on the sick man's head, gave a blessing,
and called out to him urgently by his own name.
The sick man rose up as if from a heavy sleep
and, opening his eyes, replied to his beloved father.
He quickly regained his health and strength, and the following
day rode away, rejoicing, in the bishop's company.
This John, they say, performed many other wondrous deeds
which the rule of brevity prevents me from setting out now.
I have related only what Bede the master laid down
with unquestionable accuracy in his historical account of
the English peoples and their deeds from their first beginnings.
When that bishop grew old he yielded his place of honour
in his own lifetime to another man,
and entered a monastery with devout heart,
there ending a life well suited to God,
and, taking leave of his exile on this earth,
he returned, as its true heir, to his heavenly homeland.
John was duly succeeded by an excellent priest
called Wilfrid, a most worthy heir to that good father,
who had been bishop's deputy and abbot at York.

poem constitutes a primary source for Northumbrian history from that date to
*c.*780 (Introduction, pp. xxxix, lv–lx). On the *topos* of brevity see Curtius,
pp. 48 ff.

1210–15. John retired to the monastery of Beverley which he had founded in
717, some four years before his death on 7 May 721.

1216–17. Wilfrid II (d. 744), the third monk of Whitby to become bishop of
York. This is the only extant source for his ecclesiastical benefactions and the
longest for his career. Wilfrid is included in the metrical Calendar of York (vv. 24–
5). Notice in Farmer, *Dictionary*, pp. 403–4.

1218. Euboricae vicedomnus et abbas: on *vicedom(i)nus* see Niermeyer,
Lexicon, s.v. 2, pp. 1093–4. The existence of a *monasterium*, in the sense of a
community of clerks, at York is implied by this verse and by v. 1417, where
Alcuin states that Ælberht in boyhood was committed to a *monasterium* (there

postea sed magno meritorum culmine fretus,
pontificis summi condignus sumpsit honorem,　　1220
ornavitque gradum meritis et moribus almis.
Plurima nam titulis sanctae ornamenta venustis
addidit ecclesiae, rutilo qui vasa decore
apta ministeriis argentea iure sacratis
fecit et argenti lamnis altare crucesque　　1225
texerat auratis: nolensque abscondere gazas
prudens praesul eas divino impendit honori.
Haec pius Euborica faciens antistes in urbe,
ecclesias alias donis ornavit opimis,
nec minus ille pio curam de corde gerebat　　1230
multiplicare greges, Domini praecepta secutus,
doctrinae monitis exemplis atque coruscis.
Hos mentis dapibus, illos sed carnis alebat;
hos fovet aethereis, illos carnalibus auget,
ore manuque simul donorum largus utrisque,　　1235
rem pietatis agens duplici moderamine rector
omnibus acceptus, venerandus, honestus, amatus.
[732]　Ast sua facta bonus postquam compleverat ille
pastor in ecclesiis, specialia saepta petivit,
quo servire Deo tota iam mente vacaret,　　1240
contemplativae seseque per omnia vitae
dans, mundi varias curasque reliquit inanes,
et quamvis ipso resideret corpore terris,

1219 fretus *r*: fletus *R*　　　　　　　1220 summi *Mabillon*: summis *R*
1225 lamnis *corr. Traube* (*Dümmler, Add.*): laminis *R*　　　1240 quo *Mabil-*
lon: quos *R*　　　1242 reliquit *Mabillon*: leliquit *R*

1220 Bede *Vit. S. Cuthb. metr.* 525 pontificis summi . . . honore　　1220–
1 *Syll. Epig. Cant.* 28. 6 sumpsisti meritis pontificale decus　　1221 Aldh.
de Virg. metr. 565 mundum propriis ornabat moribus　　1224 Ven. Fort.
ii. 16. 119 apta ministeriis; 1 Chron. 28: 13　　1225–6 2 Chron. 3: 5
1228 Aldh. *de Virg. metr.* 541 praesul in urbe　　1231 Ez. 36: 37; Sedul. *Carm.*
pasch. iii. 78　　　　1239 *Syll. Epig. Cantab.* 3. 5–6 pastor . . . septa . . . /
servans

1220 *cf.* v. 1575　　　1221 *cf.* vv. 1253, 1302, 1426, 1469; Alc. cix. 24. 3
meritis et moribus almus; Ioseph Scott. i. 7 gradum meritis ornas et moribus almis
1222 Alc. lxxxix. 1. 5　　　1223 *cf.* v. 1489

---

is no evidence that the future archbishop was trained anywhere other than at
York). Bede in his Letter to Egbert (Plummer i, p. 405) says 'cum . . . in
monasterio tuo demorarer'. Discussing the possible elevation of the church at

Later, on the basis of his great merits,
he assumed the highest rank of bishop, as he deserved,
gracing that position by his good deeds and sweet character.
He added many ornaments with fine inscriptions
to the holy church; having vessels of shining lustre
and silver made for the holy services,
covering the altar and crosses with layers
of gilded silver: not wishing to hoard up treasure,
the wise bishop placed it in the church to honour God.
While performing these works in the city of York,
he endowed other churches with fine gifts,
nor did he neglect to fulfil with devout heart the charge
of multiplying his flock, following God's commands,
by the urging of his teaching and his shining example. To some
he gave nourishment for the mind, to others food for the flesh,
some he favoured by heavenly, others by earthly, means.
He was generous both in word and in deed,
a leader performing deeds of piety in a twofold way
welcomed, revered, honoured, and beloved by all.
After that good shepherd had completed his work in the
church, he went in search of a place of retreat,
there to serve God with all his mind, and,
giving himself up entirely to the contemplative life,
he left the varied and empty cares of the world.
Although his body remained on earth,

York to metropolitan status in the same work (Plummer i, p. 413) he states:
'Quod si hoc . . . perfeceris . . . Eboracensis ecclesia metropolitanum possit
habere pontificem. Ac si opus esse visum fuerit, ut tali *monasterio*, causa
episcopatus suscipiendi, amplius aliquid locorum ac possessionum augeri debeat,
sunt loca innumera . . .' It is therefore clear that there was a *monasterium* in
York, closely linked to the episcopal see, at the accession of its abbot Wilfrid to
the bishopric in 718, which was still functioning in 734 when Bede wrote to
Egbert. It seems fair to assume that the *monasterium* existed both before and
after those dates. In 741 the 'York Annals' record that a 'monasterium in Eboraca
civitate' was burned (Arnold, p. 38 [= Whitelock, p. 240]); this has been identi-
fied with St. Peter's (Harrison, *Y. Arch. Jnl.* 40 (1959–62), p. 235). Writing to the
'Euboracensis ecclesiae fratribus' in *c.* 795 Alcuin (*Ep.* 42) refers to 'nostrae frater-
nitatis animas' (*MGH Epp.* iv. p. 86. 14) and enjoins 'regularis vitae vos ordinet
disciplina' (ibid. 30; cf. *Ep.* 43, 'estote . . . concordes in omni regularis vitae
disciplina', p. 88. 9–10). Lupus of Ferrières addresses Altsige of York as *abbati*
in 852 (*MGH Epp.* vi. p. 62. 9). On the character of the York school see Intro-
duction, pp. lx–lxv.

1233–4. See Blaise, *Vocabulaire latin*, pp. 535 ff.
1238–48. Wilfrid II died, twelve years after his retirement, at Ripon.

attamen ex omni iam mente manebat Olympo,
pervigil exspectans caelestis praemia vitae.   1245
Tempore quae certo, vita praesente peracta,
sumpserat angelicis caelo transvectus in ulnis.
Hic pastoralis posuit dum pondera curae,
tradidit Ecgbercto venerandae iura cathedrae,
quem sibi pontificem fecit succedere summum.   1250
Hic fuit Ecgberctus regali stirpe creatus,
nobilium coram saeclo radice parentum,
sed Domino coram meritis praeclarior almis:
dives opum terrae, miseris quas spargit egenis,
ditior ut fieret, caelo dum colligit illas.   1255
Qui curas inopum devotus semper agebat
pauperibus tribuens devoto pectore gazas,
quas terris perdens, sibimet condebat Olympo.
Hic erat ecclesiae rector clarissimus atque
egregius doctor, populo venerabilis omni,   1260
moribus electus, iustus, affabilis atque
efferus in pravos, mitis simul atque severus.
Sacris divisit vicibus noctesque diesque,
impiger assidue spatiosis noctibus orans,
missarum celebrans solemnia sancta diebus,   1265
inque Dei domibus multa ornamenta paravit.
Illas argento, gemmis vestivit et auro,
serica suspendens peregrinis vela figuris

1257 devoto *R*: gaudenti *T*²

1245 Sedul. *Carm. pasch.* i. 341 perpetuae . . . praemia vitae   1246 Arat.
de Act. Apostol. ii. 123   1247 Sedul. *Carm. pasch.* ii. 206 angelicis sub-
vectus . . . ulnis; Aldh. *de Virg. metr.* 709 angelicis vectus caeli ad convexa
1251 Virg. *Aen.* x. 543 stirpe creatus   1252-3 Rom. 12: 17   1254 Virg.
Aen. i. 14 dives opum; Paul. Nol. xviii. 255; Avit. *de Diluv.* 196 sparsit egenis
1254-5 Lc. 1: 53   1257 Ven. Fort. iv. 5. 15   1257-8 Job 36: 6;
Luc. 12: 33; Matt. 6: 19-20; Bede *Vit. S. Cuthb. metr.* 348   1258 Ven. Fort.
ii. 8. 17 terris . . . Olympo   1260 Aldh. *de Virg. metr.* 501 egregius doctor
1263 Virg. *Aen.* vi. 556 noctesque diesque

1247 *cf.* v. 1351; *Cal. Ebor. metr.* 23 angelico gaudens vectus trans culmina coetu
1248 *cf.* v. 1480   1248-50 *HE Contin.* s.a. 732 Ecgberct pro Uilfrido
Eboraci episcopus factus   1259 *cf.* v. 1400   1265 *cf.* v. 1506

1249-50. Egbert's accession to the bishopric on the resignation of his pre-
decessor in 732 is recorded in the *Continuations* to the *HE* (app. iii ad loc.). His
consecration took place in 734 and he received the *pallium* in 735. (These dates
are discussed by Plummer ii, p. 378 and Harrison, *The Framework of Anglo-*

his spirit was entirely in Heaven,
awaiting vigilantly the rewards of eternal life.
These he gained at a determined time, at the end of his present
life, when he was carried to Heaven in the arms of angels.
When Wilfrid laid aside the burden of pastoral duties,
he gave up the direction of his venerable see to Egbert,
whom he made his successor as bishop.
This Egbert was the descendant of kings,
eminent by his royal ancestry in the eyes of men,
but more outstanding in God's sight through his goodly merits;
rich in earthly wealth, he distributed it among the poor and
needy, to become all the richer by amassing treasure in Heaven.
Always concerned with the cares of those in want,
he bestowed his treasures upon the poor with devout heart,
storing up in Heaven the riches he had lost on earth.
He was a famous prelate of the Church and
an excellent teacher, beloved of all his people,
of exceptional character, just, affable, and
relentless to the wicked, both gentle and severe.
The days and nights he divided between various holy duties,
praying with unceasing diligence during the long night-watches,
celebrating holy mass in the daytime,
and preparing many ornaments for the houses of God.
He adorned them with silver, gold, and gems,
hanging silken tapestries of foreign pattern,

Saxon History to 900 (Cambridge, 1976), pp. 107, 113).

1251-3. Egbert was the son of Eata, a descendant of Ida, founder, according to tradition, of the Bernician dynasty. On this *topos* see comm. to vv. 754-5.

1254 ff. The virtues embodied by Egbert were those Alcuin urged upon the bishops of his own day: 'Esto miseris consolator, pauperibus pater . . . sint tibi mores humanitate praeclari, humilitate laudabiles, pietate amabiles. . . . Lectio sanctae scripturae saepius tuis reperiatur in manibus. . . . Vigiliae et orationes assiduae sint tibi . . .' (*Ep.* 17, to Æthelhard, archbishop of Canterbury in 793 (*MGH Epp.* iv, p. 46. 8 ff.)).

1259-60. ecclesiae rector . . . egregius doctor: an epitome of ecclesiastical law, in the form of a series of questions and answers between pupil and master, is set out in Egbert's *Dialogus Ecclesiasticae Institutionis* (Introduction, pp. lxiii-lxiv and n. 1). A description of Egbert's teaching at York is given at *Vita Alcuini* v (Arndt, pp. 186-7 [= *Monumenta Alcuiniana*, i, pp. 9-11]).

1268. peregrinis . . . figuris: Egbert had travelled to Rome, where he was ordained deacon (Bede, *Ep. ad Ecgbert*, xv; see further comm. to vv. 1454-9). This passage provides further evidence for continental influences in early English art (cf. P. Meyvaert, 'Bede and the church paintings at Wearmouth-Jarrow', *ASE* 8 (1979), pp. 63-77).

sacravitque probos altaribus ipse ministros,
ordinibus variis celebrent qui festa Tonantis.   1270
Davidisque alios fecit concinnere canna,
qui Domino resonent modulatis vocibus hymnos.
Cuius frater item Tyrio nutritus in ostro
[737] sumpserat Eadberctus gentis regalia sceptra,
qui dilatavit proprii confinia regni   1275
saepius hostiles subigens terrore phalanges.
Tempora tunc huius fuerant felicia gentis,
quam rex et praesul concordi iure regebant:
hic iura ecclesiae, rex ille negotia regni.
[735] Hic ab apostolico humeris fert pallia missa,   1280
ille levat capiti veterum diademata patrum.
Fortis hic, ille pius; hic strenuus, ille benignus,
germanae pacis servantes iura vicissim,
ex alio frater felix adiutus uterque.
Rexit hic ecclesiam triginta et quatuor annis,   1285
ille annis tenuit ter septem sceptra parentum;
ambo felices meritis in pace sepulti.
Temporibus primis praefati praesulis huius,
presbyter eximius meritis, cognomine Beda,
astra petens clausit praesenti lumina vitae.   1290

1271 canna *R*: carmen *Mabillon in marg.*   1274 āberctus *R*: Adbertus
Mabillon   1290 praesenti *Godman*: praesentis *T R*

1270 Ven. Fort. viii. 3. 264 ordinibus variis   1271 id. *Vit. S. Mart.* ii.
262 davitica canna   1272 Paul. Nol. xxvii. 561   1273 Virg. *Georg.*
iii. 17 Tyrio . . . in ostro; [Bede *Vit. S. Cuthb. metr.* 552]   1279 I Macch.
6: 56   1281 Avit. *de Virg.* 546 diadema . . . in vertice sumat

---

1269 Alc. xxvi. 7-8; id. lxxxix. 1. 13   1270 id. xxiii. 24 ordinibus
variis; Moduin, *Egloga* ii. 112 celebrantes gaudia festis   1271 *cf.* v. 1437
1279 Poet. Saxo ii. 21   1280 Theodulf xvii. 17   1281 *cf.* vv. 1313,
1536; Æthelw. *de Abbat.* 67 suo capiti portare coronam; ibid. 182 levant capiti . . .
coronas   1290 *cf.* vv. 1519-20; Alc. xlv. 13 praesentis tempora vitae

---

1273-6. Eadberht, king of Northumbria (737-58), made extensive conquests
beyond Northumbria's northern border, including the capture of Alcluith, the
British capital, in 756. In 758 he retired to live in his brother's Minster, leaving
the Northumbrian kingdom more secure and further expanded than it had been
since the defeat and death of Ecgfrith (Stenton, p. 92). The charisma of Eadberht's

consecrating upright men to serve the altars
and celebrate God's festive days at their various time.
Others he taught to sing with David's pipe
and resound hymns to God in well-trained voices.
Eadberht his brother, likewise born in the purple,
reigned over the Northumbrian people,
extending the bounds of his own kingdom,
subduing the enemy's forces in many a terrible defeat.
These were fortunate times for the people of Northumbria,
ruled over in harmony by king and bishop:
the one ruling the church, the other the business of the realm.
On his shoulders the one wore the *pallium* sent by the pope,
on his head the other bore his ancestors' ancient crown.
The one was powerful and energetic, the other devout and
kindly, both lived in peace together as kinsmen should:
two brothers helping one another gladly.
For thirty-four years the one ruled the church,
the other wore his ancestors' crown for twenty-one years;
both, happy in their achievements, were buried in peace.
Early in the reign of Archbishop Egbert,
a priest of outstanding merits named Bede closed his eyes
on this present life and sought the kingdom of the stars.

royal birth, to which Alcuin refers at v. 1273, was a matter of prime importance.
The failure of kings in England in his own day was partly attributable to their
low birth (Wallace-Hadrill, *Early Medieval History*, p. 168; *Early Germanic King-
ship*, p. 119).

    1277 ff. On the harmony of Egbert's and Eadberht's reigns see Introduction,
p. xlv and n. 3. Some of the earliest Northumbrian *sceattas* bear the name of the
king and the archbishop together. (Illustrated in *ASE* 5 (1976), Plate VIIIe;
discussed by C. C. S. Lyon, *British Numismatic Journal*, 38 (1955-7), p. 228.)

    1280. Alcuin refers to York's elevation to metropolitan status in 735 (see
comm. to vv. 202 ff. and 209, and app. ii to v. 205), which had been planned by
Gregory the Great, and discussed by Bede in 734, in his *Ep. ad Ecgbert.* x (cited
at comm. to v. 1218). See Levison, *England and the Continent*, p. 243.

    ab apostolico: cf. v. 651 with comm. Substantival use of the adjective to mean
'pope' is common in ML of this period. See *Mlat. Wb.* i. 5, s.v. 764, ii. b 42 ff.
and cf. Alc. *Ep.* 216: 'Apostolicum suos superare adversarios referebat' (*MGH
Epp.* iv, p. 360. 14) and '*Karolus Magnus*' 519, 534.

    1286. Eadberht's retreat from the world is set in context by K. H. Krüger,
Fm. St. 7 (1973), pp. 182-3.

    1288 ff. Alcuin dwells on the life and work of Bede, but displays no know-
ledge of Cuthbert's letter on Bede's death. Bede's posthumous reputation is best
discussed by D. Whitelock, *After Bede* (Jarrow Lecture 1960) [= id., *From Bede
to Alfred. Studies in Early Anglo-Saxon Literature and History* (London, 1980),
pp. 3-16].

HE v. 24 Qui mox a puero libris intentus adhaesit
et·toto studiis servivit pectore sacris,
utpote septennem quem fecit cura parentum
arta monasterii Girvensis claustra subire.
Cui iam praeclarus Ceolfridus praefuit abbas,   1295
qui, peregrina petens Christi deductus amore,
Hist. Abbat. mortuus est exsul Linguanae in finibus urbis
21, 23 atque ibi condigno felix tumulatus honore est.
Cuius corpus erat post tempora multa repertum
integrum penitus, patriamque exinde reductum.   1300
Ergo monasterio Beda enutritus in illo
ornavit teneros praeclaris moribus annos.
HE v. 24 *Discere namque sagax iuvenis seu scribere semper*
fervidus instabat, non segni mente laborans;
et sic proficiens est factus iure magister.   1305
Plurima quapropter praeclarus opuscula doctor
edidit, explanans obscura volumina sanctae
Scripturae, nec non metrorum condidit artem.
De quoque temporibus mira ratione volumen,
quod tenet astrorum cursus, loca, tempora, leges   1310
scripsit et historicos claro sermone libellos;
plurima versifico cecinit quoque carmina plectro.
Actu, mente, fide veterum vestigia patrum
semper dum vixit directo est calle secutus.
Huius vita quidem qualis fuit ante, magistri   1315

1294 arta *R*: arcta *T²*   1298 ibi *T²*: *om. R*   1310 quod *T²*:
qui *R*   1313 actu *R T²*: acta *Mabillon*

1293 Juvenc. *Evang.* iii. 492   1304 Virg. *Aen.* ix. 350 fervidus instat
1310 Paul. Nol. xxii. 129 astrorum cursus; Sedul. *Carm. pasch.* i. 67 . . . cursus,
loca, tempora   1312 Aldh. *de Virg. metr.* 1912 cecinit . . . carmine
1313 Stat. *Silv.* v. 3. 177 patrum vestigia

1294 Alc. lxxxvii. 1. 6   1296 id. *Vit. S. Willibr. metr.* i. 8 peregrina petens
Domini deductus amore; [id. cix. 24. 6]   1310 *cf.* v. 1443   1312 Alc.
Vit. S. Willibr. metr. xxxiii. 9 versifico . . . plectro; [id. xiv. 15]   1313 *cf.* v.
1536

1291-1318. There is every reason to believe that Alcuin could have written
these lines without reference to any written source: his own works display an
intimate familiarity with the entire corpus of Bede's writings; Egbert had been a
protégé of Bede and archbishop Ælberht, Alcuin's teacher, had received requests
for Bede's works. However the outline of Alcuin's account corresponds, once
closely (vv. 1303-4), to Bede's description of his own career and writings at *HE*

From early boyhood he had concentrated intensely on books,
and had devoted himself wholeheartedly to sacred studies.
With loving concern his parents had made him enter at the age
of seven the cloistered precincts of the monastery of Jarrow,
where the famous Ceolfrith presided as abbot.
Led by love of Christ, Ceolfrith went on pilgrimage
and died in exile in the city of Langres,
where that happy man was buried with due honour.
After a long time his body was found wholly uncorrupted,
and brought back from there to his native land.
Bede was brought up in that monastery, and his tender years
were a pattern of outstanding behaviour.
Wise even as a youth, he was always keen and eager
to learn or to write, working with unfailing diligence, and such
was his progress that he made a teacher, as he deserved.
This famous scholar wrote many works,
unravelling the mysterious volumes of Holy Scripture,
and composed a handbook on the art of metre.
He also wrote with marvellous clarity a book on time,
containing the courses, places, times, and laws of the stars.
He was the author in lucid prose of books on history,
and the composer of many poems in metrical style. He followed
the footsteps of the ancient fathers in actions, spirit, and faith
walking the straight and narrow path through all his days.
The quality of this teacher's life was clearly revealed

v. 24. One further detail suggests that Alcuin was drawing on another written source (see comm. to vv. 1297-1300).

1297-1300. The death of Ceolfrith in Langres on 25 September 716 is never mentioned by Bede in the *HE*, although it is recorded at *Hist. Abbatum* 21, 23 and in the anonymous *Hist. Abbatum* 32, 36, and it is on these sources that Alcuin probably drew if he made use of written authority. V. 1300 is our earliest evidence for the translation of Ceolfrith's uncorrupted body from Langres to England.

1300. **exinde:** see Löfstedt, *Syntactica*, ii, pp. 150-1, Norberg, *Beiträge*, p. 76.

1303-4. These lines are a paraphrase of Bede's 'semper aut discere aut docere aut scribere dulce habui' (*HE* v. 24).

1306-13. Alcuin selects only Bede's major writings: the Biblical commentaries, *De Arte Metrica, De Temporum Ratione* (the title of which is paraphrased in verse at v. 1309); his historical and poetical works. These, together with the prose and metrical Lives of St. Cuthbert, were among the principal influences on Alcuin's own work.

1315-18. Alcuin is our only source for this posthumous miracle. It resembles, perhaps by a chance similarity of diction, a famous miracle of St. Cuthbert's recounted at vv. 733-4.

claro post obitum signo est patefacta salutis.
Aeger enim quidam, patris dum cingitur almi
reliquiis, penitus peste est sanatus ab illa.
 Te quoque Pierio tangentes, Balthere, plectro,
et tibi, sancte, locum nostris in versibus istum   1320
signantes petimus, placida tu mente teneto
et rege nunc nostram pelagi per caerula cymbam
inter monstra maris, scopulosas inter et undas
ut possit portum portans attingere tutum.
Est locus undoso circumdatus undique ponto,   1325
rupibus horrendis praerupto et margine saeptus,
in quo bellipotens terreno in corpore miles
saepius aerias vincebat Balthere turmas,
quae sibi multimodis variabant bella figuris.
Qui tamen intrepidus hostilia castra relisit,   1330
tela malignorum semper crucis arma beatus
belliger opponens, galeam scutumque Fidei.
Vir pius ille quidem quodam dum tempore solus
incubuit precibus meditans caelestia tantum,
horribilem subito strepitum simul atque fragorem   1335
audivit, veluti vulgi erumpentis in hostes.
Tunc anima ex superis cuiusdam nubibus eius
ante pedes cecidit nimio tremefacta timore,
quam mox turba minax ingenti horrore secuta est
cum variis miseram poenis torquere volentum.   1340
At pater ille pius placidis amplexibus illam
arripuit gremio, statimque inquirit ab illa

  1322 caerula *Mabillon*: cerulam *R*

  1316 Bede *Vit. S. Cuthb. metr.* 711 certis . . . patescere signis   1318 Arat.
de Act. Apostol. i. 777 sanavit ab illa   1321 Virg. *Aen.* iii. 388   1322 Aldh.
de Virg. metr. 1736 caerula ponti; [Sedul. *Carm. pasch.* i. 136]   1325 ['Lac-
tant.' *de Ave Phoen.* 1 Est locus in primo felix oriente remotus; Ven. Fort. i. 18. 1]
1326 Aldh. *Ænigm.* lvi. 1 praeruptis . . . in margine ripis   1330 Ven. Fort.
Vit. S. Mart. ii. 172 hostilia tela relidens   1331 ibid. i. 264 obtulit arma
crucis [ibid. i. 277]   1332 Ephes. 6: 16   1334 Bede *Vit. S. Cuthb.*
metr. 335 incubuit precibus

  1319 Paul. Diac. xxiii. 4   1319 ff. 'Ann. *Ebor.*' s.a. 756 Balthere
anachoreta viam sanctorum patrum est secutus migrando ad eum qui se reformavit
ad imaginem filii sui [= 'Symeon Dunelm.' *Hist. Reg.* xlii]   1322 *cf.* v. 1657
1325-6 [*The Seafarer* 18-19, 23 þaer ic ne gehyrde butan hlimmam sæ, / iscealdne
waeg . . . / Stormas þaer stanclifu beotan . . .]   1326 *cf.* v. 1367   1339 *cf.*

after his death by a miraculous act of healing:
when a sick man was surrounded by relics of that blessed
father he was completely cured from his illness.

Now I shall touch on you in lyric measure, holy Balthere,
and mark a place for you in this my poem;
with your calm spirit, I pray, preserve and guide
my frail craft through the ocean depths,
among the sea-monsters and waves as high as cliffs,
that it may safely reach harbour with its cargo.
There is a place completely encircled by the ocean waves,
hemmed by terrible crags and steep cliffs, where
Balthere, the mighty warrior, during his life on this earth
vanquished time and again the hosts of the air,
that waged war upon him in countless shapes.
This saint fearlessly crushed his enemy's forces and the arms
of wicked demons, always opposing them with the weapons of
the Cross, the helmet and shield of Faith, in successful combat.
That pious man was once alone and praying fervently,
his only thoughts were of Heaven,
when of a sudden he heard a terrible uproar and din
like that of a host charging the enemy.
From the upper clouds there fell at his feet
a soul which quivered in great fear.
Hard on its trail followed a terrifying, menacing throng
bent on torturing the unhappy man with various punishments.
But that pious father clasped it to his bosom in gentle embrace
and immediately asked it what it was, why it was in flight
vv. 1377, 1412, 1626   1341 *cf.* v. 1626

1319 ff. Balthere ('Baldred of the Bass'). See Bullough, pp. 348 ff., pp. 352 ff.
1322-4. On this nautical metaphor, completed at vv. 1385-7, see comm. to
vv. 1649 ff.
1325 ff. The Bass Rock in late medieval Scottish tradition (Bullough, pp.
353-4). Here Alcuin deliberately inverts the traditional rhetorical description of
a *locus amoenus* (Curtius, pp. 195-202), perhaps implicitly contrasting Balthere's
place of tribulation with such idyllic sites as those depicted in the poem *De Ave
phoenice* attributed to Lactantius or in Venantius Fortunatus, *Carm.* i. 18, to
both of whom Alcuin refers at v. 1553. There is also a resemblance, which should
not be exaggerated, to Anglo-Saxon poetry of exile (for all three references see
app. ii and iii ad loc.).
1327 ff. Alcuin's description of Balthere's fights with the 'hosts of the air'
owes much to a tradition of hagiography influenced especially by Evagrius's
translation of Athanasius's *Vita Antonii*. Cf. Felix, *Vita S. Guthlaci*, xxix-xxxvi
(Colgrave, pp. 94-116).

quae esset, cur fugeret, faceret vel quae mala. Cui tunc
respondit: 'Levita fui, sed mente maligna
feminea amplexus manibus sum pectora tantum 1345
et culpam erubui vivens in carne fateri.
Nunc idcirco feri duris incursibus hostes
per triginta dies meme torquere sequuntur.
Nec captata fui, sed nec secura remansi.'
Tunc terrebat eum clamans ex hostibus unus: 1350
'Non hodie effugies, nec si tenearis in ulnis
Petri, sed meritas patieris, pessime, poenas.'
Sanctus at irascens Petri convicia propter
haec ait: 'Ecce minor meritis sum centies illo
principe apostolico; sed de pietate Tonantis 1355
confidens dico tibi, trux et saeve tyranne:
"Non hodie portabis eam sub Tartara tecum!" '
Tunc pius interventor humo prosternitur atque
cum lacrimis Domino pro culpa supplicat illa,
nec prius ille preces desistit fundere sacras 1360
quam propriis animam ferri vidisset ocellis
altius angelicas caeli super astra per ulnas.
Par quoque iam veteri signumque aequabile signo
hoc de patre pio gessit clementia Christi.
Nam velut aequoreas Petrus calcaverat undas, 1365
sic huic evenit; gradiens nam tempore quodam
rupis in excelsae praerupto margine, casu
contigit ut caderet; sed fluctibus ille marinis
suffultus graditur siccis super aequora plantis,
et ceu rura soli premeret, sic ambulat undis 1370
iam, nisi quod levius susceperat unda ruentem,

1346 vivens T^2: iuvenis R 1348 per R T^2: post *Mabillon*
1371 levius T^2: lenius R

1344 Aldh. *de Virg. metr.* 1850 mente malignus 1346 Lev. 13: 14; Paul.
Nol. xxiv. 827 in carne vivens 1351 Virg. *Ecl.* iii. 49 numquam hodie
effugies 1355 Aldh. *de Virg. metr.* 1514 1363 Matt. 14: 29
1364 Arat. *de Act. Apostol.* ii. 520 dat clementia Christi 1365 Sedul. *Carm.*
pasch. iii. 226 superambulat undas 1369 Aldh. *Ænigm.* xxxviii. 6 pedibus
gradior super aequora siccis 1369–70 Prud. *Apoth.* 655–6 ipse super fluidas
plantis nitentibus undas / ambulat ac presso firmat vestigia fluctu 1370 Sedul.
Carm. pasch. iii. 227 premit arva freti; ibid. iii. 226 superambulat undas

---

1345 *cf.* v. 1646 1351 *cf.* v. 1357 1356 Milo *Vit. S. Amand.*

and what wrong it had done. To him the soul replied:
'I was once a deacon, but with evil intent,
I once laid hands on a woman's breasts—no more.
When I lived on earth I was ashamed to admit my sin.
And so the cruel demons have been pursuing me relentlessly
for thirty days in order to torment me. I have
not been captured, but I have never been free from anxiety.'
Then one of the demons terrifying him cried out:
'Today you will not escape, no, not if you were clasped
in the arms of St. Peter. You will suffer the punishment
you deserve, evil one.' The saint grew angry at the insult to
Peter, and said: 'I am a hundred times less worthy than that
prince of the apostles, but with trust in God's goodness
I say to you, tyrant ruthless and cruel, that you shall not
carry this soul off to Hell with you today!'
Then, in kindly mediation, he prostrated himself on the ground
and implored God with tears for the guilt of that soul,
ceaselessly pouring forth holy prayers,
until he saw with his own eyes that it was carried high over
the stars in Heaven in the arms of angels. In His clemency
Christ achieved another miracle through this pious father,
which was the exact equivalent of one performed in ancient
times. For just as Peter trod the waves of the sea,
so did this holy father. Once, while walking
along the steep border of a high cliff,
he chanced to fall. Buoyed up by the ocean waves
he passed over the water with dry feet,
walking on the waves as if stepping in a country field, except
the wave received him more smoothly when he hurtled down

ii. 170 saeve tyranne   1368-9 Flor. Lugd. i (*In Evang. Matt*).
136 per fluctus graditur, maris aequora calcat; Heiric *Vit. S. German.* iv, *praef.*
47-8   1369 Alc. lxix. 67 siccis super aequora plantis   1370 *cf.*
v. 1375

1344. The correct behaviour of the diaconate had a particular significance for
Alcuin, who held that rank all his adult life. The sixth canon of the Northern
synod of 786, which Alcuin attended, decreed 'ut nullus episcoporum pres-
biterum vel diaconum ordinare praesumat, nisi probatae vitae fuerint' (*MGH
Epp.* iv, p. 22. 33-4).
    1363. veteri . . . signo: the allusion is to Christ's command that Peter walk on
the waters (Matt. 14: 29). Alcuin makes no higher claim for any miracle in this
poem: the anchorite Balther of his own day is represented as a match for the
Apostle Peter.

quam si dura virum accepissent arva cadentem.
Dum ruit, unda fluit, casus ne laederet illum:
gressibus arva manent, illum ne mergeret aequor;
ambulat ergo freto solido ceu tramite terrae,   1375
donec ad undivagam pervenerat ipse carinam,
quam mox ascendit securo calle pedester.
Non in veste liquor, non soccis haeserat humor.
Quod natura negat, hoc dat tua dextera, Christe,
unda tuo iussu pelagi fit pervia iustis;   1380
terra sed econtra vindex fit gurges iniquis:
suffert ista humiles, dum devorat illa superbos.
Nunc sed te petimus devoti, Balthere sancte,
ut sicut unda tuum portabat ab aequore corpus
te sanum penitus revehens ad litora nota,   1385
sic precibus nostras animas evadere fluctus
[756] mundanos facias portumque intrare salutis.

    Claruit his etiam venerabilis Echha diebus,
anachoreta sacer, heremi secreta secutus,
terrenos fugiens iam corpore castus honores,   1390
ut cum rege Deo caelestes posset habere.
Angelicam terris vitam devotus agendo,
multa prophetali praedixit mente futura,
de quo plura vetat narrari Musa recurrens
carminis ad finem propriique ad gesta magistri   1395
qui post Ecgberctum venerandae insignia sedis
[767] suscepit sapiens Ælberctus nomine dictus.

1380 iussu T^2: nisu R 1385 penitus r: petimus R 1389 *sic R*:
secreta secutus heremi T^2

1379 Arat. *de Act. Apostol.* i. 528 Quod natura negat; [Sedul. *Carm. pasch.* iv.
8]; Juvenc. *Evang.* i. 737 tum dextera Christi; [Juvenal i. 79]   1385 Virg.
Aen. ii. 256   1389 Ven. Fort. i. 5. 5 heremi secreta   1392 Bede *Vit.
S. Cuthb. metr.* 480   1393 ibid. 162 prophetali praefatur mente futura;
[Ven. Fort. *Vit. S. Mart.* ii. 116]   1396 Paul. Nol. xv. 112

1388 '*Ann. Ebor.*' s.a. 767 Etha anachorita feliciter in Cric obiit, qui locus
distat ab Eboraca civitate x. miliariis [= 'Symeon. Dunelm.', *Hist. Reg.* xlvi]
1393 Alc. *Vit. S. Willibr. metr.* xxiii. 1 praedixerat ante futura; id. *Ep.* 200 (p. 332,
24 ff.) ad gloriosum. . . regem Carolum . . . adveni, sicut mihi quidam sanctissimus
vir prophetiaeque spiritu praeditus Dei esse voluntatem in mea praedixerat patria;
etiam et ut vir venerabilis totusque Deo deditus meus mihi mandatum dederat
magister   1396 '*Ann. Ebor.*' s.a. 766 Ecgberht archiepiscopus Eboracae
civitatis in pace Christi requievit xiii. kal. Decembris, xxxiv. anno episcopatus sui
[= 'Symeon. Dunelm.', *Hist. Reg.* xlv]

than the unyielding earth would have taken a falling man.
When he fell, the wave flowed to prevent it injuring him,
remaining as firm as earth beneath his step lest he drown,
and so he walked on the sea, as if on a solid path of earth,
until he came to a boat adrift on the waves,
into which he climbed—his journey made safely on foot.
There was not a drop of water on his clothes, no dampness
on his boots: what nature denies Christ's power can dispense;
at Christ's command sea-waves become a path for the just;
the earth is turned into a whirlpool to punish the wicked,
the sea bears up the humble while the land engulfs the proud.
But now, holy Balthere, we reverently implore you
that, just as the wave carried your body from the sea,
bearing you back in perfect safety to familiar shores,
so with your prayers you may help our souls escape
the storms of this world and enter the port of salvation.

Famous in those days was a venerable hermit, Echa,
who, far from men, in the wilderness lived
a life of chastity, shunning worldly honours,
that he might enjoy heavenly ones with God the king.
By leading the life of an angel devoutly on earth
he predicted much of the future like a prophet.
My Muse forbids me to tell more of his story, as she hurries
back to the end of the poem and the deeds of my teacher,
the sage Ælberht, who succeeded Egbert
in the honours of that respected see.

1388 ff. On the anchorite Echa see Introduction, pp. lvi–lvii. Alcuin's interest in contemporary anchorites, reflected in his notices of Echa and Balther, is also attested in a letter of 790 to Colcu, an Irishman teaching in northern England, asking him to distribute 'per singulos anachoritas III siclos de puro argento' (*MGH Epp.* iv, no. 7, p. 33. 4-5).

1393. Alcuin mentions Echa's predictions and then describes his teacher Ælberht. In Alcuin's *Ep.* 200 (app. iii) the archbishop's command that he travel to Francia and the Northumbrian prophecy of his future association with Charlemagne are linked in the same sentence. Identification of Echa with the author of this prophecy must remain speculative, but the inclusion of the anchorite in this poem would gain point if his predictions had personal significance for Alcuin.

1396. Egbert died on 19 November 766. His brother Eadberht was buried with him two years later at York in what the A version of the Anglo-Saxon Chronicle records as 'on anum portice' (*s.a.* 738). Their burial in the Minster may reflect a longstanding custom (comm. to vv. 220-2).

1397. The career of archbishop Ælberht (767-78), Alcuin's teacher, receives Alcuin's special attention (Introduction, pp. lvii, lxii–lxiv). Ælberht served as a pattern for the ideal qualities of a prelate as seen by Alcuin, and this lengthy

Vir bonus et iustus, largus, pius atque benignus,
catholicae fidei fautor, praeceptor, amator,
ecclesiae rector, doctor, defensor, alumnus,   1400
iustitiae cultor, legis tuba, praeco salutis,
spes inopum, orphanisque pater, solator egentum,
trux rigidis, blandusque bonis durusque superbis,
fortis in adversis, humilis fuit inque secundis,
mente sagax, non ore loquax, sed strenuus actu.   1405
Cui quantum crevit cumulati culmen honoris,
tantum mens humili sese pietate subegit.

De quo versifico paulo plus pergere gressu
Euboricae mecum libeat tibi, quaeso, iuventus,
hic quia saepe tuos perfudit nectare sensus   1410
mellifluo dulces eructans pectore succos.
Quem mox a primis ratio pulcherrima cunis
corripuit rerum, summamque vehebat in arcem
doctrinae pandens illi secreta sophiae.
Hic fuit ergo satis claris genitoribus ortus: 1415
ex quorum cura studiis mox traditur almis
atque monasterio puerilibus inditur annis,
sensibus ut fragilis sacris adolesceret aetas.
De puero nec cassa fuit spes tanta parentum.
Iam puer egregius crescebat corpore quantum,   1420
ingenio tantum librorum proficiebat.   .
Sic meritis crescens annis et mente sagaci
iam levita sacer condigno est ordine factus.
Hunc bene dum felix adolescens gessit honorem,
iura sacerdotii iuvenis suscepit honestus,   1425
cresceret ut gradibus, meritis qui creverat almis.

1398 pius *T*²: bonus *R*   1403 bonis *Mabillon*: bonus *R*

1401 Ven. Fort. *Vit. S. Mart.* i. 126 tuba legis, praeco   1402 id. iv. 13.9
1405 Arat. *de Act. Apostol.* i. 404; Ven. Fort. ix. I. 92   1406–7 Paul. Nol.
xxv. 146–7   1409 Virg. *Ecl.* ii. 28 libeat . . . tibi   1410 Virg. *Georg.*
iv. 384 perfundit nectare   1412 (Augustin. *Ep.* xxvi) Licent. *carm.* 37 ratio
pulcherrima mundi   1412–13 Virg. *Georg.* ii. 534 rerum pulcherrima
1415 Aldh. *de Virg. metr.* 1266 claris natalibus ortam   1417 Arat. *Ep. ad
Parth.* 49   1418 Virg. *Aen.* xii. 438 matura adoleverit aetas   1422 Bede *Vit.
S. Cuthb. metr.* 248 inque dies meritis crescenti   1425 Ven. Fort. v. 3. 9 iura
sacerdoti   1426 Paul. Nol. xvi. 241 crevit meritis

1400 Alc. xxvi. 6 ecclesiae rector, defensor, amator   1405 Æthelw. *de
Abbat.* 39   1409 Alc. lix. 10 moenibus Euboricae habitans tu sacra

He was a good and just man, generous, devout, and kind,
a pillar, teacher, and lover of the Catholic faith,
the leader and master of his church, its protector and son,
a lover of justice, a clarion of the law, a herald of salvation,
hope of the poor, father to orphans, comforter of the needy,
strong in adversity and humble in good fortune,
stern to the hardened, gentle to the good, harsh to the proud,
of discerning intellect, not wordy in speech, but energetic to
act; the greater and higher his honours grew,
the more he humbled himself with lowly pride.
   I ask you, please, to walk a little further with me,
keeping step with my poem, young men of York,
for he often steeped your senses in nectar,
pouring sweet draughts from his honeyed soul.
From his earliest days reason, the loveliest of things,
had held him in her sway and carried him to the highest
summit of learning, revealing to him wisdom's secrets.
He was of highly distinguished birth and his family soon
devoted him with care to sacred studies,
attaching him to the monastery in his boyhood, that
he might mature in spiritual powers during his tender years.
Nor were his parents' high hopes in vain.
For as that outstanding boy grew up,
his learning made equal progress.
Thus growing in qualities, in years, and wisdom,
he became a holy deacon at the proper time.
In youth he filled this station successfully and well,
and as an upright young man took vows to the priesthood,
advancing in office, as he grew in holy merits.

iuventus   1415 ff. id. *Vit. S. Willibr. pr.* iii tradidit eum pater . . . fratribus
religiosis studiis et sacris litteris erudiendum, ut fragilior aetas validioribus in-
valesceret disciplinis   1426 Heiric *Vit. S. German.* i. 128 crescebat
meritis

---

panegyric, modelled on Venantius Fortunatus's encomia of bishops (cf. *Carm.*
iii. 8. 15 ff.; iv. 3. 9 ff.; iv. 10. 11 ff.), combines many of the virtues singled out
by Alcuin in earlier bishops and kings (cf. vv. 116-18, 136-40, 266-73, 570-2,
1254-62). On this type of panegyric see A. Georgi, *Das lateinische und deutsche
Preisgedicht des Mittelalters* (Berlin, 1969), pp. 47 ff.
   1417. See comm. to v. 1218.
   1423. The minimal canonical age for ordination to the diaconate was 23/24
and to the priesthood 24/25 (v. 1425). Bede's ordination as deacon at age 19 was
unusually early. (See P. Hunter Blair, *The World of Bede* (London, 1970), p. 5.)

Tunc pius et prudens doctor simul atque sacerdos
pontificique comes Ecgberct coniunctus adhaesit,
cui quoque sanguineo fuerat iam iure propinquus;
a quo defensor clero decernitur omni   1430
et simul Euborica praefertur in urbe magister
ille, ubi diversis sitientia corda fluentis
doctrinae et vario studiorum rore rigabat,
his dans grammaticae rationis gnaviter artes,
illis rhetoricae infundens refluamina linguae.   1435
Istos veridica curavit cote polire,
illos Aonio docuit concinnere cantu,
Castalida instituens alios resonare cicuta
et iuga Parnassi lyricis percurrere plantis.
Ast alios fecit praefatus nosse magister   1440
harmoniam caeli, solis lunaeque labores,

1436 veridica *R*: iuridica *T*²

1433 Ven. Fort. *Vit. S. Mart.* i. 131 sitientia pectora rorans   1433 Deut.
32: 2 concrescat ut pluvia doctrina mea; fluat ut ros eloquium meum
1435 Ven. Fort. *Vit. S. Mart.* i. 29 parvula grammaticae lambens refluamina guttae
1436 ibid. i. 31 cote ex iuridica   1439 Virg. *Ecl.* x. 11 Parnasi . . . iuga;
Aldh. *de Virg. metr.* 473   1441 Virg. *Georg.* ii. 478 solis . . . lunaeque
labores; [id. *Aen.* i. 742]

1427 *cf.* v. 1482; Alc. cx. 17. 2   1433 id. *Vit. S. Willibr. metr.* vi. 6
rore rigans; [ibis. i. 12-13]; id. *Vit. S. Richarii* iv arida corda superno perpetuae
salutis rore inrigavit   1437 Moduin, *Egloga* i. 91 Aonias . . . recitare
camenas   1441-8 Alc. *Ep.* 148 (p. 239, 22 ff.) Quid aliud in sole et luna et
sideribus consideramus et miramur nisi sapientiam creatoris et cursus illorum
naturales? . . . Solebat magister meus mihi saepius dicere: 'Sapientissimi hominum
fuerunt, qui has artes in naturis rerum invenerunt . . .' Sed nunc pusillanimitas
multorum non curat scire rationes rerum, quas creator condidit in naturis. Scis, op-
time, quam dulcis est in rationibus arithmetica, quam necessaria ad cognoscendas
scripturas divinas; quam iocunda est cognitio caelestium astrorum et cursus illorum.

1430. defensor (cf. v. 1400): the term, as applied to bishops, had been used
since the late Roman empire to describe their legal role as guardians of the
clergy's interests. See Niermeyer, *Lexicon* s.v. 6, p. 313 and A. H. M. Jones, *The
Later Roman Empire, 284–662*, ii (Oxford, 1964), p. 911.
1432-3. The following idealized picture is our only first-hand source for
Ælberht's teaching of the *trivium* and *quadrivium*, the place of which in the
curricula of Aldhelm, Bede, and Alcuin is discussed by P. Riché, *Éducation et
culture dans l'occident barbare* (Paris, 1962), pp. 419 ff. and by M. Roger,
L'enseignment des lettres classiques d'Ausone à Alcuin (Paris, 1905), pp. 288 ff.
Alcuin himself discusses the seven Liberal Arts in his *Disputatio de vera Philo-
sophia* (*PL* ci. 849-54), and each of the subjects described here is represented in
his own writings.
1434-5. Glossed in *R* as *de grammatica et de rhetorica*, on both of which sub-

Then, as a pious and wise teacher and priest,
he became a boon companion of bishop Egbert,
to whom he was related by blood
and who marked him out to defend the entire clergy,
making him a teacher in the city of York.
There he watered parched hearts with diverse streams
of learning and the varied dew of knowledge:
skilfully training some in the arts and rules of grammar
and pouring upon others a flood of rhetorical eloquence.
Some he polished with the whetstone of true speech,
teaching others to sing in Aonian strain,
training some to blow on the Castalian pipe,
and run with lyric step over the peaks of Parnassus.
To others this master taught the harmony of the spheres,
the labours of the sun and the moon,

jects Alcuin wrote. For the *De Grammatica*, a new edition of which is badly
needed, see *PL* ci. 854-902. The *De Rhetorica et de Virtutibus* is edited by
C. Halm, *Rhetores latini minores* (Leipzig, 1863), pp. 525-50 and by W. S.
Howell (with translation), *The Rhetoric of Alcuin and Charlemagne* (Princeton,
1941). Studies in Mähl, *Quadriga virtutum*, pp. 109-15 and Wallach, *Alcuin and
Charlemagne*, pp. 29-82.

1436-7. Glossed, probably correctly, in *R* as *de dialectica et musica*. It has
been denied that dialectic had any place in the curriculum of Ælberht and alleged
that law was studied instead (Roger, op. cit., p. 315). This interpretation rests on
the reading *iuridica* at v. 1436, which itself may be a copyist's conjecture, on the
basis of Ven. Fort. *Vit. S. Mart.* i. 31. *Veridica* supplies the third element of the
trivium, defined by Cassiodorus at *Instit.* ii, *pref.* 4 as 'disputationibus subtilis-
simis ac brevibus vera sequestrat a falsis' (cited by Isidore, *Etym.* i. 2 and by
Alcuin's pupil Hrabanus Maurus, *De Clericorum Instit.* iii. 20), of which definition
veridica is an apt rendering. Alcuin, described by Einhard (*Vita Karoli Magni*,
xxv) as Charlemagne's teacher of *dialectica*, is the author of a tract on that subject
(*PL* ci. 950-76), the importance of which he also stresses in his *De Trinitate*
(see further comm. to v. 1550). The full *trivium*, including dialectic, had its place
in Ælberht's curriculum.

1437. Aonio . . . concinnere cantu: glossed *sonare musico* in *R*. Cf. vv. 1271-
2, where the allusion is to hymnody. Teaching in this subject was doubtless avail-
able at York from at least the reign of Egbert to that of Ælberht. Alcuin is said
(*Vit. Alcuini* xxi (Arndt, p. 194) [= *Monumenta Alcuiniana*, xii, p. 28]) to have
written a work *De Musica*, now lost. See Bischoff, *Spoleto . . . Settimane*, 19
(1971), p. 405. On the association of 'Aonian Song' with poetry in early Carolin-
gian verse see Schaller, *Fm. St.* 10 (1976), pp. 165-7.

1438-9. While v. 1438 may refer not only to versification but also to musical
performance (as it is interpreted by *r*, who glosses 'Castalida . . . cicuta' as *musica
fistula*), v. 1439 certainly describes the composition of poetry. In these meta-
phorical terms Alcuin outlines his own training as a poet at the school of Ælberht.
See further comm. to vv. 1551-4.

1441-5. Glossed as *astrologia* in *R*, this section describes astronomy, to which
Charlemagne, according to Einhard (*Vita* xxv), 'plurimum et temporis et laboris

quinque poli zonas, errantia sidera septem,
astrorum leges, ortus simul atque recessus,
aerios motus, pelagi terraeque tremorem,
naturas hominum, pecudum, volucrum atque ferarum,   1445
diversas numeri species variasque figuras,
paschalique dedit solemnia certa recursu,
maxima Scripturae pandens mysteria sacrae;
nam rudis et veteris legis patefecit abyssum.
Indolis egregiae iuvenes quoscumque videbat,   1450
hos sibi coniunxit, docuit, nutrivit, amavit,
quapropter plures per sacra volumina doctor
discipulos habuit diversis artibus aptos.
Non semel externas peregrino tramite terras
iam peragravit ovans, sophiae deductus amore,   1455
si quid forte novi librorum seu studiorum,
quod secum ferret terris reperiret in illis.
Hic quoque Romuleam venit devotus ad urbem,
dives amore Dei, late loca sancta peragrans.

1442 zonas *R T²*: conas *Mabillon*   1448 maxima *Mabillon*: maxime *R*
1449 *Suspected, needlessly, by Wattenbach and Dümmler: cf.* Aldh. *de Virg.
metr.* 1625   1453 aptos *R*: auctos *T²*

1442 Virg. *Georg.* i. 233 quinque tenent caelum zonae   1444 ibid. ii. 479
1445 id. *Aen.* vi. 728 hominum pecudumque genus vitaeque volantum   1447
Aldh. *de Virg. metr.* 1577   1449 ibid. 1625 nam rudis et priscae legis patefecit
abyssum; [Sedul. *Carm. pasch.* i. 146]   1450 I Chron. 12: 28   1452 Aldh.
Carm. eccl. iii. 58   1458 Paul. Nol. xix. 483 Romuleam . . . ad urbem
1459 Ven. Fort. viii. 8. 5. dives amore dei

1442 Walahfr. lvi. 23 errantia sydera septem [Theodulf xlvi. 85]   1450 ff. Alc.
ii [*Epitaph. Ælberht.*] 5–10 Imbuit hic teneros liberalibus artibus annos / sollicita
primo mente docendo meos; / quem quocumque quidem, Christo ducente cucurrit
/ promptus mente pede iamque secutus eram, / dum Romam cunctis venerandam
gentibus urbem, / vel tam Francorum florida regna petit   1451 id. cix. 24.
5 docuit . . . nutrivit, amavit; Paul Diac. xxxviii. 6

---

impertivit' under Alcuin's instruction. His more important letters on this subject
include *MGH Epp.* iv, no. 126, pp. 185–7; no. 148, pp. 237–41; no. 155, pp.
249–53; no. 171, pp. 281–3. The tract *De Saltu Lunae ac Bissexto* ascribed at *PL*
ci. 981–1002 to Alcuin was not written by him (C. W. Jones, *Bedae Opera de
Temporibus* (Camb. (Mass.), 1943), pp. 375 ff.). Alcuin's expansive account of
Ælberht's system appears, by v. 1445, to include natural history, which Bede
also links to *computus* (*De Temp. Rat. praef.*). On the links between these parts of
Ælberht's curriculum, as expounded by Alcuin, cf. Ep. *148* (app. iii ad loc.).
    1446. Geometry and arithmetic (glossed *origo matheseos* in *R*). The *Proposi-
tiones ad acuendos iuvenes*, the oldest collection of mathematical problems in

the five zones of heaven, the seven planets,
the regular motions of the stars, their rising and setting,
the movements of the air, the tremors of the earth and sea,
the natures of men and cattle, of birds and wild beasts,
the diverse forms and shapes of numbers.
He regulated the time for Easter's celebration,
revealing the great mysteries of holy Scripture,
for he fathomed the depths of the rough and ancient law.
Whenever he saw young men of excellent character,
he took them to him, to teach, cherish, and love.
And so this teacher had several pupils whom he trained
in various disciplines by means of the holy writings.
More than once he took the pilgrim's route to foreign lands
with joy, led by love of holy wisdom and hope
of finding new books and studies there
to bring back with him.
He travelled devoutly to the city of Rome,
rich in love of God, visiting holy places far and wide.

Latin, have been ascribed to Alcuin and are now available in the excellent edition
of M. Folkerts (Introduction, p. xxxiv, n. 5 (*cont.*)).

1447. *Computus*, on which Alcuin, following Bede, had written is represented
in a number of his letters about astronomy (see comm. to vv. 1441-5); cf. *MGH
Epp.* iv, no. 170, pp. 278-81. Alcuin's most important letters on computistical
and astronomical questions are assembled in the Vatican manuscript Reg. lat. 226.

1448-9. Alcuin regarded the seven liberal arts as *septem Philosophiae gradus*,
a propaedeutic to the *culmina Sanctarum Scripturarum* (see *Disputatio de Vera
Philosophia, PL* ci. 853-4, with the studies of Brunhölzl and Courcelle cited at
p. xxxiii, n. 5, and M. T. d'Alverny, *Mélanges . . . F. Grat* i (Paris, 1946),
pp. 245 ff.). Cf. further *Ep.* 280 (*MGH Epp.* iv, p. 437. 25-38). Alcuin's works on
Scripture include a critical revision of the Bible (see Fischer, p. xxxiv, n. 2) and
exegesis of a number of Scriptural texts (edited in *PL* c), and systematic theology,
particularly two works *De Trinitate* (*PL* ci. 13-58, 59-64) and the *De Animae
Ratione ad Eulaliam* (*MGH Epp.* iv, pp. 473-8).

1449. The Old Testament.

1450-3. The two most famous pupils of Ælberht's school were Eanbald, the
future archbishop of York, and Alcuin himself (cf. vv. 1515-17 and app. iii ad
loc.). Their number probably also included *Sigulfus presbyter, custos Eboricae
civitatis ecclesiae*, who is cited as a source for the *Vita Alcuini* (Arndt, viii, p. 189
[= *Monumenta Alcuiniana*, v. p. 16]).

1454-9. Ælberht's continental journeys, on which he was accompanied by
Alcuin, took place before his consecration in 767 (see D. A. Bullough, *SCH* 14,
ed. D. Baker (Oxford, 1977), p. 31, n. 16). On the established practice of Anglo-
Saxon pilgrimage to Rome, see Levison, *England and the Continent*, pp. 36 ff.;
W. J. Moore, *The Saxon Pilgrims to Rome and the Scola Saxonum* (Freibourg,
1937), pp. 73 ff.; P. Sims-Williams, *ASE* 5 (1976), p. 15. One of Alcuin's Roman
journeys involved a halt in Murbach (see *Ep.* 271, *MGH Epp.* iv, p. 429).

Inde domum rediens, a regibus atque tribunis   1460
doctor honorifice summus susceptus ubique est,
utpote quem magni reges retinere volebant,
qui sua rura fluens divino rore rigaret.
Ad sibi sed properans praefinita facta magister,
dispensante Deo, patriae prodesse redibat.   1465
Nam proprias postquam fuerat delatus in oras,
mox pastoralem compulsus sumere curam,
[767] efficitur summus populo rogitante sacerdos,
officiumque suis meritis decoraverat almis,
ordinis atque bonus pastorque repertus ubique est.   1470
Namque tuebatur divinum cautus ovile,
ulla ex parte lupus Christi ne laederet agnos;
ille quibus sacri praestabat pabula Verbi,
ne sitis atque fames ullo vexaret acerbo.
De gregeque errantes heremi per devia vastae   1475
ad Domini caulas humeris revehebat amicis,
nolentesque sequi placido sermone vocantem
insequitur iuris terroribus atque flagellis.
Non regi aut ducibus iustus parcebat iniquis,
sed neque decrevit, curarum pondera propter,   1480
Scripturas fervens industria prisca legendi,
factus utrumque: sagax doctor pius atque sacerdos,
sensibus hos augens, illos et moribus ornans.
Nec pater adveniens in tantum culmen honoris

   1464 ad sibi sed ... praefinita facta *T R*: ad sua sed ... post finita facta *Raine*:
at sibimet ... praefinita ad facta *Traube*: sed sibimet ... ad facta *Hargrove*
1469 suis *R*: sui *r*   almis *T²*: annis *R*   1475 heremi per *R*: per
eremi *T²*   vastae *T²*: vasti *R*: vasta *Mabillon*

   1466 Bede *Vit. S. Cuthb. metr.* 252   1471 Aldh. *de Virg. metr. praef.* 19
1475 Stat. *Theb.* v. 248 per devia vastae   1477-8 Jdt. 7: 20
1479 Ps.-Prosper *de Prov. Dei.* 822   1480 Ven. Fort. ix. 1. 123 curarum pondera
portans   1484 id. v. 15. 1

   1461-2 '*Karolus Magnus*' 534-5   1467-8 '*Ann. Ebor.*' s.a. 767 Alberht
Eboracae civitatis et Alchmund Hagustaldensis ecclesiae ordinati sunt episcopi viii.
kal. Mai [= '*Symeon Dunelm.*', *Hist. Reg.* xlvi]   1475 Theodulf xxviii. 29
heremi per devia

   1467-8. Ælberht was consecrated on 24 April 767, the *dies depositionis*
of Wilfrid. It is possible that Alcuin attended this ceremony. The choice of the
date of Wilfrid's consecration probably reflects a cult at York, which may have

Then, returning home, the great teacher was everywhere
received with honour by the mighty of the earth.
Powerful kings wished to keep him with them
to water their fields with his stream of divine learning.
But hastening to the business foreordained for him,
by God's grace, this master returned to serve his homeland.
Arriving back on his native shores,
he was soon made to take on a pastoral charge,
and was elected archbishop by popular acclaim.
By his holy achievements he was a credit to his office,
and proved himself a good shepherd in every respect,
for he guarded God's fold with care, preventing
the wolf from harming the lambs of Christ,
offering them the food of the holy Word,
sparing them from the pangs of hunger and thirst.
Wanderers through the desert's boundless waste
he carried back to the Lord's fold on loving shoulders,
and those unwilling to attend to his gentle preaching
he pursued with the terrible punishment of the law.
In his justice that bishop did not spare evil kings or nobles,
and his former eagerness and zeal for reading Scripture
grew no less under the burden of responsibility.
He was both things at once: a wise teacher and a pious priest,
improving the understanding of some, refining others'
character. When that father advanced to his high honour,

influenced Alcuin's favourable portrayal of Wilfrid (see Introduction, pp. li–lii, liii–liv).

1479. Alcuin's letters to kings reflect the importance he attached to the role of bishops. In 793 he wrote (*Ep.* 16) to Æthelred of Northumbria and his *optimates*: 'Oboedite sacerdotibus Dei. Illi enim habent rationem reddere Deo, quomodo vos ammoneant; et vos, quomodo oboediatis illis' (*MGH Epp.* iv, p. 44. 23–24). See J. Chélini, *Le vocabulaire politique et social dans la correspondance d'Alcuin*, Publications de la Faculté des Lettres d'Aix-en-Provence, Travaux et Mémoirs, 12 (Aix-en-Provence, 1959), pp. 27 ff. Ælberht's chastisement of contemporary rulers was a proper function of his office, lent special urgency by Northumbrian politics (Introduction, pp. lix–lx).

1480–1. One of Alcuin's frequent enjoinders to bishops: cf. *Ep.* 17 (to Æthelhard, archbishop of Canterbury, in 793): 'Lectio sanctae scripturae saepius tuis reperiatur in manibus' (*MGH Epp.* iv, p. 46. 16).

1484–7. Cf. *Ep.* 20 (to Hygebald of Lindisfarne, 793): 'Sint vestimenta tuo gradui condigna . . . Inanis ornatus vestimentorum et cultus inutilis tibi est obprobrium ante homines et peccatum ante Deum. Melius est animam in perpetuum permanentem bonis ornare moribus, quam corpus cito in pulvere putrescens exquisitis comere vestibus' (*MGH Epp.* iv, p. 58. 3–7).

vestibus atque cibis veterem mutaverat usum; 1485
deliciosa nimis fugiens, nec vilia valde
sectatus fuerat, medio moderamine gaudens.
Nec minus interea vario ornamenta decore
addidit ecclesiis, Fidei fervore repletus.
Namque ubi bellipotens sumpsit baptismatis undam 1490
Eduuin rex, praesul grandem construxerat aram,
texit et argento, gemmis simul undique et auro,
atque dicavit eam sancti sub nomine Pauli
doctoris mundi, nimium quem doctor amabat.
Hoc altare farum supra suspenderat altum, 1495
qui tenet ordinibus tria grandia vasa novenis,
et sublime crucis vexillum erexit ad aram
et totum texit pretiosis valde metallis.
Omnia magna satis, pulchro molimine structa,
argentique meri compensant pondera multa. 1500
Ast altare aliud fecit, vestivit et illud
argento puro, pretiosis atque lapillis,
martyribusque crucique simul dedicaverat ipsum.
Iussit ut obrizo non parvi ponderis auro
ampulla maior fieret, qua vina sacerdos 1505
funderet in calicem, solemnia sacra celebrans.
Ast nova basilicae mirae structura diebus
praesulis huius erat iam coepta, peracta, sacrata.
Haec nimis alta domus solidis suffulta columnis,
suppositae quae stant curvatis arcubus, intus 1510
emicat egregiis laquearibus atque fenestris.

1495 supra *Mabillon*: super *R*   1504 ut *Mabillon*: om. *R*

1486 Ven. Fort. vi. 12. 49   1487 Aldh. *de Virg. metr.* 831   1488 Virg.
Georg. ii. 429 nec minus interea   1497 Sedul. *Carm. pasch.* i. 337 crucis
vexilla   1498 Aldh. *Ænigm.* xcvi. 11 fulvis pretiosa metallis   1499 id.
Carm. eccl. iii. 1 pulchro molimine structum   1504 id. *de Virg. metr.* 2182
obrizum . . . metallum

1497 Alc. cxiv. 1. 1 vexillum sublime crucis; Æthelw. *de Abbat.* 737
1499 *Carm. Salisb.* ii. 7

1488 ff. Alcuin records three distinct enterprises at York during the episco-
pate of archbishop Ælberht. The first, described at vv. 1490-1506, involved gifts
to the Minster, and included the dedication of an altar to St. Paul. In 796, the
'York Annals' record that king Eardwulf of Northumbria was consecrated at York

he did not change his former habits in food and dress;
though avoiding luxury, he was no fanatic
for the excessively simple, rejoicing instead in a middle course.
He also endowed the churches with ornaments
of varied beauty, filled with zeal for the Faith.
In the spot where Edwin, the warrior king, was baptized
the bishop raised a great altar
and covered it with gold, silver, and jewels,
dedicating it in the name of St. Paul,
the universal teacher, whom he loved with all his heart.
High above this altar he hung a chandelier,
which held three great vessels, each with nine tiers.
At the altar he erected the noble standard of the cross
covering it entirely with most precious metals.
It was all on a grand scale and built on a lovely design,
weighing many pounds in pure silver.
He erected another altar and covered it too
with pure silver and precious stones,
dedicating it both to the martyrs and to the Cross.
He ordered a large cruet to be made in pure gold
and of great weight, from which the priest
celebrating holy mass could pour wine into the chalice.
During his bishopric a new basilica of wondrous design
was begun, completed, and consecrated.
This lofty building, supported by strong columns,
themselves bolstering curving arches, gleams
inside with fine inlaid ceilings and windows.

'in ecclesia Sancti Petri ad altare beati Apostoli Pauli' (Symeon, *Hist. Reg.* lviii,
p. 58 [= Whitelock, p. 274]). This altar, together with the one to the martyrs and
the Cross described at v. 1503, may have been placed in the transepts at the junc-
tion of the nave and chancel. It has been conjectured that all three altars were
part of an elaborate 'west work' covering a baptistery to the west of Edwin's
church (Cramp, *Anglian and Viking York*, pp. 9-10).

1507 ff. Ælberht's second enterprise, the new basilica at York, dedicated
(unusually) to Sancta Sophia (v. 1520) and containing thirty altars (v. 1514),
supplemented St. Peter's and did not replace it (Harrison, *Y. Arch. Jnl.* 39
(1956-8), p. 436). Its site is unknown. For the conjecture that Sancta Sophia
stood to the east of the present Minster, between the West Front and Central
Tower, see Harrison, *Y. Arch. Jnl.* 40 (1959-62), p. 242. In a letter of 801 Alcuin
announces the gifts of 100 lbs. of tin for roofing the belfry and of four screens of
lattice-work (*MGH Epp.* iv, no. 226, p. 370. 12-14; see further Cramp, *Anglian
and Viking York*, p. 10).

Pulchraque porticibus fulget circumdata multis,
plurima diversis retinens solaria tectis,
quae triginta tenet variis ornatibus aras.
Hoc duo discipuli templum, doctore iubente,   1515
aedificaverunt Eanbaldus et Alcuinus, ambo
concordes operi devota mente studentes.
Hoc tamen ipse pater socio cum praesule templum,
ante die decima quam clauderet ultima vitae
lumina praesentis, Sophiae sacraverat almae.   1520
Ergo ministrator clarissimus ordine sacro,
praesul perfectus meritis plenusque dierum,
tradidit Eanbaldo dilecto laetus alumno
pontificale decus, sibimet secreta petivit
saepta, Deo soli quo iam servire vacaret.   1525
Tradidit ast alio caras super omnia gazas
librorum gnato, patri qui semper adhaesit,
doctrinae sitiens haurire fluenta suetus.
(Cuius si curas proprium cognoscere nomen,
fronte sua statim praesentia carmina prodent.)   1530
His divisit opes diversis sortibus: illi
ecclesiae regimen, thesauros, rura, talenta;
huic sophiae specimen, studium sedemque librosque,
undique quos clarus collegerat ante magister
egregias condens uno sub culmine gazas.   1535

   1514 triginta *Mabillon*: x͞er͞ᵗᵃ *R*   1524 decus *r*: ductus *R*   1530 pro-
dent *Mabillon*: prodant *R*

   1512 Paul. Nol. xxviii. 7 porticibus . . . circumdata longis   1514 id.
xxviii. 28 variis ornatibus   1517 Aldh. *de Virg. metr.* 2049   1522 Gen.
25: 8   1535 Bede *Vit. S. Cuthb. metr.* 699 condere gazas

   1515-17 Alc. *Ep.* 112 (p. 162. 23 ff.) [Eanbaldus] mihi et pater et frater et
amicus fidelissimus, etiam et condiscipulus sub magistro meo   1522 id.
lxxxviii. 15. 15 perfectus meritis pastor plenusque dierum; id. *Vit. S. Willibr.*
metr. xxiv. 5   1524 *cf.* v. 1566   1526 *cf.* v. 1535
1533-5 Alc. *Ep.* 114 (p. 167, 8 ff.) thesauris sapientiae, in quibus me magister
meus dilectus Ælberhtus archiepiscopus heredem reliquit; id. *Ep.* 121 (p. 177,
4 ff.) exquisitiores eruditionis scolasticae libelli, quos habui in patria per bonam et
devotissimam magistri mei industriam

   1512. **porticibus:** 'sanctuary (or mortuary) chapel'; cf. comm. to vv. 220-2
and see H. M. Taylor, 'The Position of the Altar in Early Anglo-Saxon Churches',
The Antiquaries Journal, 53 (1973), pp. 52-8.
   1513. **solaria:** 'upper chambers' or 'galleries', possibly made of wood. See Tay-
lor in *The Anglo-Saxons,* ed. P. Clemoes (Cambridge, 1959), pp. 137 ff.; A. W. Clap-

It shines in its beauty, surrounded by many a chapel
with many galleries in its various quarters,
and thirty altars decorated with different finery.
On their teacher's orders this church was built
by Eanbald and Alcuin, the two working together
with intense devotion to the task.
With his associate bishop,
Ælberht dedicated the church to holy Wisdom
nine days before he closed his eyes on this present life.
And so this minister, famous in the ranks of the clergy,
a bishop of outstanding achievements and full of days,
joyfully handed on his episcopal rank to Eanbald,
his beloved pupil, and retired into solitude,
there to dedicate all his time to the service of God alone.
Father-like, he entrusted his books, treasures he valued above
all, to his other son, who was constantly at his side
and whose thirst for learning Ælberht would satisfy.
(If you wish to know this man's name
the beginning of this poem will reveal it immediately.)
He divided his wealth in different ways, granting to the one
government of the church, treasure, lands, and money, and
to the other his choice learning, his study and collection of
books, which that famous teacher had collected everywhere,
storing these priceless treasures under one roof.

ham, *English Romanesque Architecture before the Conquest* (Oxford, 1930), p. 47.

1515-17. Alcuin never mentions elsewhere the part played by himself and Eanbald in the building of Sancta Sophia. The splendour of its construction, and of the endowments described at vv. 1488 ff., reinforces Alcuin's claims about York's wealth and commercial importance (vv. 35-7).

1518. After Ælberht's 'retirement' in 778 Eanbald, his future successor in the archbishopric, became associate bishop of York (vv. 1523-5). At v. 1587 Eanbald is described as *praesul* when attending Ælberht's funeral.

1521. ministrator: see Introduction, p. cii (3).

1529-30. See p. 2, comm. (*a*).

fronte sua: cf. Bede, *Vit. S. Cuthb. pr., praef.*: 'praefationem aliquam *in fronte* iuxta morem' (Colgrave, p. 142). On the convention see P. Klopsch, 'Anonymität und Selbstnennung mittellateinischer Autoren', *Mlat. Jb.* 4 (1967), pp. 9 ff.

1533-5. Ælberht's third and major achievement was the collection of a library at York. His work doubtless began before his accession to the archbishopric. Boniface and Lul, in a number of letters dating between *c.* 747 and 778 (Tangl, *Epp.* 75, 91, 125, 126), request from Egbert and Ælberht copies of Bede's works. In 773 the Frisian Liutger returned home from York 'habens secum copiam librorum' (Altger, *Vita Liutgeri* i. 12, *MGH SS* ii, p. 408 [= Whitelock, p. 789]), and in 796/7 Alcuin wrote to Charlemagne, expressing regret for the books available at York in his youth (app. iii to vv. 1533-5 [= Whitelock, p. 853]).

Illic invenies veterum vestigia patrum:
quicquid habet per se Latio Romanus in orbe,
Graecia vel quicquid transmisit clara Latinis,
Hebraicus vel quod populus bibit imbre superno,
Africa lucifluo vel quicquid lumine sparsit: 1540
quod pater Hieronymus, quod sensit Hilarius atque
Ambrosius praesul, simul Augustinus et ipse
sanctus Athanasius, quod Orosius edit acutus,
quicquid Gregorius summus docet et Leo papa,
Basilius quicquid Fulgentius atque coruscant,   1545
Cassiodorus item, Chrysostomus atque Iohannes;

1537 per *R*: pro *Mabillon*   1543 acutus *R T²*: avitus *Mabillon*
1545 coruscant *R T²*: coruscans *Mabillon*

1536 Sedul. *Carm. pasch. praef.* 11-12 Illic invenies quidquid . . . / quidquid
. . .   1539 Aldh. *de Virg. metr.* 390 imbre superno   1541 ff. Ven. Fort. viii.
1. 54-9 quidquid Gregorius Basiliusque docent, / acer Athanasius, quod lenis
Hilarius edunt, / quos causae socios lux tenet una duos, / quod tonat Ambrosius,
Hieronymus atque coruscat, / sive Augustinus fonte fluente rigat, / Sedulius
dulcis, quod Orosius edit acutus; Ps.-Isid. *Vv. de Biblioth.* iv-viii

1536 *cf.* v. 1558; Alc. *Vit. S. Willibr. metr.* xiii. 6 illic inveniet

1536 ff. veterum vestigia patrum: the expression is a favourite of Bede's
(see P. Meyvaert, *Famulus Christi*, pp. 62-3, n. 7). What follows is not a catalogue
of Ælberht's library but an outline, with explicit omissions (vv. 1558-62), of the
major authors whom Alcuin claims to have been available at York (Introduction,
pp. lxiv-lxv). Few of his prose works are available in modern critical editions; none
of them dates from his years in England. It is therefore impossible to establish
that a given text was studied by Alcuin in York. Brief bibliographical notices of
a number of Alcuin's works relevant to this outline and of the external evidence
that provides a context for it are provided in the Commentary. MSS. in Insular
script which cannot with absolute certainty be considered English are included
in the commentary below.

1537-40. The *tres linguae sacrae* of early medieval exegesis (W. Berschin,
Griechisch-lateinisches Mittelalter (Bern and Munich, 1980), pp. 31 ff.) with the
addition of Africa, presumably as the homeland of the principal exegetes such as
St. Augustine. Alcuin's first-hand acquaintance with Greek was negligible; his
knowledge of Hebrew less. These verses refer to Latin translations and patristic
commentaries.

1541. A number of Alcuin's exegetical works are largely composed of
excerpts from Jerome. Cf. Alcuin's *Explanationes in Epistolas S. Pauli ad Titum,
ad Philemonem et ad Hebraeos* (*PL* c. 1007 ff.). Jerome's Commentary on Isaiah,
a work abbreviated at Alcuin's prompting by his pupil Joseph Scottus (metrical
preface in *MGH PLAC* i, p. 151), survives in the (probably) Northumbrian MS.
Leningrad, Nat. Publ. Libr. F. V. i. 3, ff. 39-108 (*s.* viii²) [= *CLA* xi. 1600, p. 5].
The Kassel, Landesbibliothek Ms. Theol. f. 21 (*s.* viii, ? Northumbrian) [= *CLA*
viii. 1134, p. 33] contains Jerome, *In Ecclesiasten*, a text also used by Alcuin.
Hilary of Poitiers's *De Trinitate* is exploited in Alcuin's exegetical and polemical

There you will find the legacy of the ancient fathers:
all the Roman possessed in the Latin world,
whatever famous Greece has transmitted to the Latins,
draughts of the Hebrew race from Heaven's showers,
and what Africa has spread abroad in streams of light:
the perceptions of father Jerome and of Hilary,
of bishop Ambrose, Augustine, and
of saint Athanasius, the writings of astute Orosius,
the teachings of Gregory the Great and of pope Leo,
the glowing words of Basil and Fulgentius,
of Cassiodorus and John Chrysostom;

writings, particularly the *Contra Haeresim Felicis* (Blumenshine, p. 35). On Jerome and Hilary in Bede see Laistner, *Intellectual Heritage*, pp. 129 ff., 133 ff.

1541 ff. Alcuin's list falls into coherent sections. Vv. 1541-6 comprise *auctores* of the Church; v. 1547 the chief Anglo-Latin authors before Alcuin; v. 1548 theology and/or translation; v. 1549 history (see comm.); v. 1550 philosophy and rhetoric; vv. 1551-4 poets; vv. 1555-7 grammarians.

1542. Both Ambrose and Augustine are employed in Alcuin's exegesis, particularly his *Expositio super Iohannem* (*PL* c. 733 ff.). Augustine's *De Trinitate* is Alcuin's principal source for the three-book *De Fide Sanctae et Individuae Trinitatis* (*PL* ci. 10 ff.); the pseudo-Augustinian *Categoriae decem* influenced Alcuin's ontology (see J. Marenbon, *From the Circle of Alcuin to the School of Auxerre*, pp. 30 ff.). On Alcuin and Augustine's *De Catechizandis Rudibus* see J.-P. Bouhot, *Recherches augustiniennes* 15 (1980), pp. 176-240. Bede's extensive use of both writers is discussed by Laistner, *Intellectual Heritage*, pp. 128 ff., 130 ff.

1543. Athanasius's Life of St. Antony in Evagrius's Latin translation was employed both by Bede and by Felix in his Life of St. Guthlac (Colgrave, pp. 17, 184 ff.). Cf. comm. to vv. 1327 ff. Orosius's *Historiae*, a source for Bede's *HE* and exegetical works, survives in the Düsseldorf Staatsarchiv MS. 2. 4. No. 2 (*s.* viii, ? Northumbrian). Cf. comm. to v. 1549.

1544. The works of Gregory the Great, preserved in a number of early Northumbrian MSS. and exploited by Bede (see P. Meyvaert, *Bede and Gregory the Great* (Jarrow Lecture 1964)), were a major source of Alcuin's exegetical works. Certain letters and homilies of Pope Leo I figure in Alcuin's controversial writings, although their use in earlier Anglo-Latin authors is slight.

1545. St. Basil of Caesarea's *Hexaemeron*, used chiefly in the Latin versions of Eustathius by Bede for his chronological writings, *HE*, and Scriptural commentaries, hardly appears in Alcuin's work, and may provide an example of a writer available to but unused by him at York. Fulgentius of Ruspe's *Ad Trasimundum*, used by Bede (Laistner, *Intellectual Heritage*, p. 133), is cited by Alcuin in his *De Trinitate*.

1546. Cassiodorus's Commentary on Psalms is preserved in a number of early Northumbrian MSS., of which an abbreviation survives in Durham, Dean and Chapter Library B. II. 30 (*s.* viii *med.*) [= *CLA* ii. 152, p. 11]. The context here suggests this work, quoted extensively by Alcuin in his own Commentaries on Psalms (*PL* c. 569-638) and *Adversus Elipandum*. On Alcuin's use of Cassiodorus, especially Book ii of the *Institutiones*, see P. Lehmann, *Erforschung des Mittelalters*, ii, pp. 89 ff. On Bede and Cassiodorus see ibid., pp. 85 ff. and

quicquid et Althelmus docuit, quid Beda magister;
quae Victorinus scripsere Boethius atque
historici veteres: Pompeius, Plinius; ipse
acer Aristoteles, rhetor quoque Tullius ingens;   1550
quid quoque Sedulius vel quid canit ipse Iuvencus,
Alcimus et Clemens, Prosper, Paulinus, Arator,
quid Fortunatus vel quid Lactantius edunt,
quae Maro Virgilius, Statius, Lucanus et auctor;
artis grammaticae vel quid scripsere magistri,   1555

1552 Alcimus *Froben*: Alcuinus *R*

1551-4 Ven. Fort. *Vit. S. Mart.* i. 14-25 primus enim docili distinguens ordine
carmen / maiestatis opus metri canit arte Iuvencus. / hinc quoque conspicui radia-
vit lingua Seduli / paucaque perstrinxit florente Orientius ore, / martyribusque piis
sacra haec donaria mittens / prudens prudenter Prudentius inmolat actus. / stem-
mate corde fide pollens Paulinus et arte / versibus explicuit Martini dogma magis-
tri. / sortis apostolicae quae gesta vocantur et actus / facundo eloquio sulcavit
vates Arator. / quod sacra explicuit serie genealogus olim, / Alcimus egregio
digessit acumine praesul; Ps.-Isid. *Vv. de Biblioth.* x. 1-6 Si Maro, si Flaccus, si
Naso et Persius horret, / Lucanus si te Papiniusque tedet, / pareat eximio dulcis
Prudentius ore, / carminibus variis nobilis ille satis; / perlege facundi studiosum
carmen Aviti; / ecce Iuvencus adest Seduliusque tibi . . .

1551 ff. Theodulf xlv. 13-18 Sedulius rutilus, Paulinus, Arator, Avitus, / et
Fortunatus, tuque Iuvence tonans; / diversoque potens prudenter promere plura /
metro, o Prudenti, noster et ipse parens. / Et modo Pompeium, modo te, Donate,
legebam / et modo Virgilium, te modo, Naso loquax

Laistner, *Intellectual Heritage*, pp. 85 ff. John Chrysostom, the Latin translation
of whose *Homilies on Hebrews* is cited in Alcuin's *Contra Haeresim Felicis* (Blu-
menshine, p. 38), is used by Bede (Laistner, *Intellectual Heritage*, p. 141). Frag-
ments of a Northumbrian MS. of Chrysostom's *De Compunctione Cordis* and *De
Reparatione Lapsi* survive in Düsseldorf, Heinrich-Heine-Institut B 215 + C 118 +
Staatsarchiv Fragm. 20 (*s.* viii med.) [= *CLA* viii. 1187, p. 46]).

1547. Aldhelm and Bede take their place immediately after Alcuin's patristic
auctores. Their prominence in this list is certainly deliberate (cf. Introduction,
pp. lxviii-lxix, lxxv). Complete works of Alcuin, such as *De Orthographia*, derive
from Bede's treatises on the same subject (see now C. Dionisotti, *Revue béné-
dictine* 92 (1981), pp. 129-41); the influence of Aldhelm on Alcuin's prose
writing is much more restricted.

1548. This combination of names suggests Marius Victorinus, whose influence
on Alcuin is analysed by P. Hadot, 'Marius Victorinus et Alcuin', *Archives d'his-
toire doctrinale et littéraire du Moyen Age*, 21 (1954), pp. 5-19. Alcuin may refer
to the theological tracts of Victorinus and Boethius or to their translations of
Aristotle's *Categories* (cf. v. 1550), or to both. The presence in England before
the ninth century of Boethius's *Philosophiae Consolatio*, used extensively by
Alcuin in his *Disputatio de vera Philosophia* (a work written at Charlemagne's
court), has yet to be demonstrated (see recent discussions by P. Hunter Blair,
Famulus Christi, pp. 253-4, and F. Troncarelli, *Tradizione Perdute. La 'Con-
solatio Philosophiae' nell'Alto Medioevo* (Padua, 1980), pp. 107 ff.).

the teaching of Aldhelm and of Bede the master,
the writings of Victorinus and Boethius,
and the ancient historians Pompey and Pliny,
of keen-minded Aristotle and of Cicero the great rhetorician;
all the poetry of Sedulius and Juvencus,
of Alcimus Avitus and Prudentius, Prosper, Paulinus, Arator,
the works of Fortunatus and Lactantius,
the authoritative writings of Virgil, Statius, and Lucan;
and the masters of the grammatical art;

1549. historici veteres: writers of both political and natural history. **Pompeius** = Pompeius (Trogus), in Justin's epitome. It has been proposed that the MS. Weinheim(?), E. Fischer Sammlung S. N. (*s.* viii *med.*) [= *CLA* ix. 1370, p. 38] was written in York and was the exemplar that transmitted this text to the Continent (Brown, *Spoleto . . . Settimane*, 22 (1975), p. 286). Alcuin uses Pliny chiefly in problems of astronomy and *computus*, as does Bede (Laistner, *Intellectual Heritage*, pp. 124-5; C. W. Jones, *Bedae Opera de Temporibus* (Camb. (Mass.), 1943), p. 129). Extracts from Pliny's *Natural History* are preserved in Leyden, Universiteitsbibliotheek Voss. lat. F. 4. ff. 4-33 (*s.* viii², ? Northumbria) [= *CLA* x. 1578, p. 41]. Alcuin's knowledge of ancient history was limited and while Orosius (v. 1543) figures in his reading, this verse does not require one to posit the availability of even a few classical historians at York (*pace* Brown, loc. cit., 22 (1975) pp. 26-7).

1550. Translations or paraphrases of Aristotle's *Categories* or *De Interpretatione* may have been available in York (cf. J. Isaac, *Le Peri Hermeneias en Occident de Boèce à Saint Thomas* (Paris, 1953), pp. 39-40). Cicero's *De Inventione* et *De Oratore* are among the principal sources of Alcuin's *Dialogus de rhetorica et de virtutibus* (cf. S. Mähl, *Quadriga Virtutum*, pp. 83 ff.); Cicero's *Topica* and *De Inventione* are employed in Alcuin's *De Grammatica.* This verse lists authors unused elsewhere in England at this period but read at the court of Charlemagne.

1551-4. On this section, devoted to the poets, see Introduction, pp. lxix-lxxiii.

1552. Alcimus [Avitus]: Froben's emendation has rightly been accepted by subsequent editors. On the confusion *Alcimus/Alcuinus* see A. Streib, 'Wer ist der Verfasser der *Praecepta vivendi?*', *Münchener Museum für Philologie des Mittelalters*, 2 (1914), pp. 360 ff. and M. Boas, *Alcuin and Cato* (Leiden, 1937), p. 15., n. 52.

Clemens = Prudentius.

1554. Statius: on Alcuin's unusual knowledge of this author see Introduction, pp. lxxii-lxxiii. The theory of A. Klotz that a York exemplar of the *Thebaid* and the *Achilleid* lies behind B.N. Par. lat. 8051 (*Philologus* 63 (N.F. 17) (1904), pp. 157-60) merits further investigation.

1555. This list does not include all the authors, such as Caper, used by Alcuin in his *De Orthographia* or *De Grammatica.* The grammatical sources of this second work are discussed by J. Frey, *Jahresbericht über das königliche Gymnasium zu münster*, 66 (Münster, 1886), pp. 1-14; W. Schmitz, *Alcuins Ars Grammatica: die lateinische Schulgrammatik der karolingischen Renaissance*, diss. Greifswald (Ratingen, 1908); and H. W. Fortgens, 'De paedagoog Alcuin in zijn "Ars Grammatica" ', *Tijdschrift voor Geschiedenis*, 60 (1947), pp. 57-65. On grammarians used by Insular authors see now V. Law, *The Insular Latin Grammarians* (Woodbridge, 1982).

quid Probus atque Focas, Donatus Priscianusve,
Servius, Euticius, Pompeius, Cominianus.

Invenies alios perplures, lector, ibidem
egregios studiis, arte et sermone magistros,
plurima qui claro scripsere volumina sensu,   1560
nomina sed quorum praesenti in carmine scribi
longius est visum quam plectri postulat usus.

[780]   His ita dispositis complens sua tempora summus
[Nov. 8] antistes, totus meritis maturus et annis,
post annos binos, menses simul atque quaternos,   1565
ex quo saepta sacer praesul secreta petivit,
discipulis coram pastor, patriarcha, magister,
transit ad aetheream laetus feliciter aulam.

Hanc tamen, hanc citius, lugubris mea fistula, partem,
desere, ne pereas lacrimarum gurgite mersa;   1570
dum properas portum velis hucusque secundis,
quid memorare studes nobis maestissima fata,

1561 scribi *r*: scripsi *R*   1562 postulat *Mabillon*: postulet *R*   1565 quater-
nos *R*: quot annos *Mabillon*

1558 Virg. *Ecl.* ii. 73 invenies alium   1562 Prud. *Psych.* 609 quam postu-
let usus; Paul. Nol. xx. 6   1566 Virg. *Aen.* viii. 463 secreta petebat
1570 Aldh. *de Virg. metr.* 1448   1571 Virg. *Aen.* iii. 683 ventis . . . vela
secundis; id. *Georg.* iv. 116 ff.

1556 Alc. iv. 33-4 patres et profer honestos / Priscianum, Focam   1562
Flor. Lugd. v. 160   1567 Alc. xc. 25. 1

1556. Probus: Alcuin can only have known the excerpts from the geniune
Probus cited in later grammarians. Among the suppositious works attributed to
Probus the *De Nomine* is cited by Insular grammarians (Law, op. cit., pp. 26-7).
Focas: The *Ars de Nomine et Verbo* of this mid-fifth-century grammarian
was used by both Aldhelm and Boniface (Law, p. 22). On its manuscript trans-
mission see C. Jeudy, *Viator* 5 (1974), pp. 61-156. Cf. **Priscianus** below.
Donatus: both the *Ars major* and the *Ars minor* of Aelius Donatus were used
in Alcuin's *De Grammatica*. For the conjectures that Alcuin knew Tiberius
Claudius Donatus's commentary on Virgil at York and that the MS. Florence,
Bibl. Med. Laurenziana pl. XLV, 15 ff. 1-56 (*s.* viii²) [= *CLA* iii. 297a and b, 7]
was copied there, see P. Hunter Blair, *Famulus Christi*, pp. 251-2. The succinct
discussion of L. Holtz, *Donat et l'enseignement de la tradition grammaticale*
(Paris, 1981), pp. 318 ff., especially p. 321, is indispensable.
Priscianus: the *Institutiones Grammaticae* are a principal source for Alcuin's
De Grammatica and *De Orthographia*. On Alcuin's excerpts from Priscian, see
J. R. O'Donnell, 'Alcuin's Priscian' in *Latin Script and Letters, AD 400-900
(Festschrift . . . L. Bieler)*, edd. J. O'Meara and B. Naumann (Leiden, 1976),
pp. 222-35. Some of Priscian and Phocas was probably available at York. *Carm.*
iv, which was written in 780-1 (pp. xxxvi and n. 6, p. xxxix) at York, records
Alcuin's despatch of works by these two grammarians to Beornrad of Sens, abbot
of Echternach (app. iii to this line).

the works of Probus and Focas, Donatus and Priscian,
Servius, Eutyches, Pompeius and Cominianus.
There, reader, you will find many others,
teachers outstanding for their learning, art, and style,
who wrote many volumes with clear meaning.
But to include all their names in this poem
would take longer than poetic usage demands.
After ordering his affairs in this way the archbishop came
to the end of his life, in rich maturity of age and achievements.
Two years and four months after his retirement
into solitude, in the presence of his pupils,
this shepherd, patriarch, and teacher
passed joyously into the courts of Heaven.
Leave swiftly this part of the tale, my mournful poem,
lest you perish, drowned in an ocean of tears,
as you hurry to port, the wind fair behind you until now.
Why do you remind me of events so sad,

1557. Servius: probably *De Finalibus*, though its use in Alcuin is minimal.
Cf. the Spangenberg fragment, with OE glosses, of Servius's Commentary on
Virgil, Spangenberg, Pfarrbibliothek S. N. (*s.* viii[1]) [= *CLA Supp.* 1806, p. 39].
On Insular symptoms in the textual transmission of Servius's commentaries see
C. H. Beeson, *SM* N.S. 5 (1932), pp. 81-100.
Euticius: the *Ars de Verbo* of Eutyches (*s.* vi). On its textual tradition see
C. Jeudy, *Mélanges F. Labande* (Poitiers, 1974), pp. 421-36.
Pompeius: this fifth-century grammarian is quoted by Alcuin in his *De Grammatica*. On the transmission of Pompeius's *Commentum artis Donati* see L. Holtz,
Revue de philologie 45 (1971), pp. 48-53.
Cominianus: as known through the *Ars grammatica* of the fourth-century
scholar Charisius. Rarely cited by Alcuin.
1558-62. Alcuin's reference to his own omissions is plainly true. An outline
of Ælberht's books that fails to mention the Bible and Gildas, *inter alia*, is not
representative of even major texts which were studied at York; nor does Alcuin's
list include all the authors whose works were needed to teach a curriculum on the
scale described at vv. 1432-49. He omits technical literature, such as books on
canon law or ecclesiastical councils, together with anonymous works, such as
some saints' lives. Specific details of this list are not verifiable (comm. to vv.
1536 ff.) but the dominance of patristic *auctores* and grammarians in it suggests
a library at York which in general emphasis was comparable to those which
can be reconstructed from Bede's reading and from the catalogues of early ninth-
century monastic libraries on the Continent (cf. especially the oldest catalogue of
Reichenau, ed. G. Becker, *Catalogi bibliothecarum antiqui* (Bonn, 1885), no. 6,
pp. 4-13). See further Bischoff, *Spoleto . . . Settimane*, 19 (1971), pp. 389-92.
1569 ff. Alcuin's lament for Ælberht, the central figure in his own intellectual
development (Introduction, p. lxii), expands into personal elegy the *Epitaphium*
he composed for the archbishop (app. iii to vv. 1450 ff.).
1569-71. The mixed metaphors, pastoral and nautical, for poetry occur earlier
in the poem (vv. 742, 1322-4). See further vv. 1649 ff. with comm. ad loc.

cum subito ante oculos cunctis mors invida nostros
lumina supremo clausit veneranda sopore
pontificis summi, nostri patris atque magistri?   1575
O nobis, o nigra dies! O clara sed illi!
Nos sine patre dies orphanos ille reliquit
fletibus, exsilio duroque labore gravatos.
Reddidit ast illum patriae patrique superno,
fletibus, exsilio duroque labore solutum   1580
iam cui Christus amor, potus, cibus, omnia Christus,
vita, fides, sensus, spes, lux, via, gloria, virtus.
Qui decimo et quarto summi dormivit in anno
ordinis accepti, octavo sub sole Novembris,
dum gravis illa dies sexta fulgebat in hora.   1585
Eius ad exsequias magnum concurrerat agmen,
cum clero praesul, populus iuvenesque senesque,
patris honorifice curantes condere corpus.
O pater, o pastor, vitae spes maxima nostrae,
te sine nos ferimur turbata per aequora mundi,   1590
te duce deserti variis involvimur undis,
incerti qualem mereamur tangere portum.
Dum sol noxque sibi cedunt, dum quatuor annus
dividitur vicibus, crescunt dum gramina terris,
sidera dum lucent, trudit dum nubila ventus,   1595
semper honos nomenque tuum laudesque manebunt!
    Hic ego dum volui certo te fine, Thalia,
claudere, res nostris occurrit gesta diebus.
Fessa licet paucos quapropter adhuc cane versus

1575 magistri *r*: patroni *R*   1578 gravatos *R*: solutum *T*²

    1576 Virg. *Aen.* vi. 429 atra dies; id. v. 43 clara dies   1581-2 Ven. Fort.
Vit. S. Mart. ii. 440-1 cui Christus amor, Christus honor, omnia Christus, / flos
odor esca sapor fons lux via gloria Christus   1587 Virg. *Aen.* ix. 309
1589 ibid. ii. 281; Sedul. *Carm. pasch.* ii. 97 spes maxima vitae; [Bede *Soliloq.*
31]   1590-1 (Augustin. *Ep.* xxvi) Licent. *carm.* 76-7, 81 sine te nullos promit-
tunt carbasa portus / erramusque procul turbata per aequora vitae / . . . miseri
volvuntur in undis   1591 Sedul. *Carm. pasch.* i. 85 te duce; Virg. *Aen.* v. 629
volvimur undis   1593 ibid. i. 607 ff.   1594 Aldh. *de Virg. metr.*
167 dum promit germina tellus   1596 Virg. *Aen.* i. 609 semper honos
nomenque tuum laudesque manebunt; [id. *Ecl.* v. 78]

    1578 *cf.* v. 1580; Alc. ix. 3   1582-3 '*Ann. Ebor.*' s.a. 780 Eodem anno
Alberht archiepiscopus ex hac luce migravit ad aeternae lucis perennitatem
[= 'Symeon Dunelm.', *Hist. Reg.* 1]; *Vit. Alc.* viii (v) laetus sanctus pater Elcbertus
episcopus migravit ad Deum 6. Idus Novembris, quem pius Albinus ut matrem

when before our gaze Death, our general enemy, suddenly
closed in his last sleep the hallowed eyes
of that archbishop, our father and teacher?
Black was that day for us, but how radiant it was for him!
That day left us fatherless and orphaned,
bowed by tears, exile, and grim suffering,
but him it restored to his homeland and father in Heaven,
winning him freedom from tears, exile, and grim suffering.
Christ was his love, his food and drink, his all; life, faith,
understanding, hope, light, the way, glory, and virtue.
In the fourteenth year of his term as bishop,
on the eighth of November he closed his eyes forever,
while that doleful sun shone in the sixth hour.
A great throng attended his funeral,
the bishop with the clergy, the people, young and old alike,
careful to bury their father's body with honour.
O father and shepherd, greatest hope of our life,
without you we are buffeted on the waters of the world,
bereft of your guidance we are tossed by countless waves,
not knowing which harbour we will reach. While day yields
to night and night to day, while the year divides
into four seasons, so long as the grass grows on the earth,
the stars shine, and the wind sweeps away the clouds,
your honour, fame, and praise will remain forever!
     When I wanted to close my poem here
there came to mind an event that happened in my own time.
Tired though you are, my rustic Muse, sing a few more verses

deplorans lacrimis, nolebat tamen consolationem recipere   1583-5 Alc. *Vit.*
S. Willibr. metr. xxiv. 5-8 Qui postquam vitae meritis perfectus in annis, / bis
octena pius complevit lustra sacerdos, / ter quater et menses, mensis iam iamque
Novembri / Idibus octenis caeli migravit ad aulam   1589 id. xcix. 12. 6 vitae
spes maxima nostrae   1590 Milo *Vit. S. Amand.* ii. 247 se sine non passus
fluctus portarier illos   1590-3 Moduin *Egloga* i. 7-9 Nos egra variis agitati
mente procellis, / fluctibus in mediis ferimur per naufraga ponti. / Litora nulla fuit
mihimet spes certa videnti   1596 Flor. Lugd. xxix. 50   1597 Joh.
Fold. 11 (Thalia); Ermold. *In laud. Pipp. reg.* i. 1 ff.

     1597. **Thalia** is not simply invoked as a Muse of poetry (Manitius, *Geschichte*,
p. 555, n. 3) but expressly as the Muse of Pastoral, the humblest literary genre.
Alcuin lays stress on the rusticity of his poem, on its countrified, unpolished
quality (vv. 437, 742, 1655). By calling on Thalia as the tutelary Muse of his work
Alcuin emphasizes the humility of his subject and the rusticity of his style. On
bucolic terms in Alcuin's verse, see Schaller, in *Medium Ævum Vivum. Festschrift
für W. Bulst*, edd. H. R. Jauss and D. Schaller (Heidelberg, 1960), p. 32.

atque mei pueri causam succinge parumper, 1600
cui quoque praesentem testem me contigit esse.
  Ergo fuit quidam iuvenis nutritus in urbe
Euborica, simplex animo, sed fervidus actu,
quique meae rexit puerilis tempora vitae
consilio. Solus quadam qui nocte suetis 1605
insistit precibus Christi genetricis in aula.
Tunc lux alma domum subito repleverat illam,
et cum luce simul venit vir vestibus albis,
fulgidus aspectu, statu sublimis honesto
et blandis iuvenem nimio terrore cadentem 1610
elevat alloquiis, librumque ostendit apertum.
Perlegit hunc iuvenis, dixit cui codice clauso
candidus ille: 'Sciens iterum maiora videbis.'
His dictis subito nitidus disparuit hospes.
Hinc quoque post aliquos non longo tempore menses 1615
percutitur iuvenis currenti peste per artus,
aegrotusque diu dubia sub morte iacebat,
angustis retrahens perituram naribus auram;
inque meis recubans manibus, tunc spiritus eius
est raptus subito, corpusque remansit inane. 1620
Post spatium rediens iterum sed membra movebat
et mihi narrabat, quidam quod duxerit illum
ad loca pulchra nimis, multos ubi vidit ovantes,
ignotos notosque simul, sed maxime sanctae
illius ecclesiae laetos agnovit alumnos. 1625
Qui mox suscipiunt placidis amplexibus illum

1619 manibus *Mabillon*: remanibus *R*   1623 ubi *Mabillon*: ut *R*
1626 amplexibus *T*²: complexibus *R*

1604 Aldh. *de Virg. metr.* 464   1609 ibid. 2369   1616 Bede
Vit. S. Cuthb. metr. 510 mors . . . diffunditur . . . per artus   1617 Sedul.
Carm. pasch. iii. 301 dubia sub morte   1618 Ven. Fort. *Vit. S. Mart.* i. 374
trahens . . . perituram naribus auram

1600 Paulin. Aquil. i. 134 carmine succincto   1602 ff. Æthelw. *de Abbat.*
692 ff.   1603 Alc. *Vit. S. Willibr. metr.* i. 3 fervidus actu   1604 Æthelw.
de Abbat. 63   1623-5 Alc. *Ep.* 42 (p. 86, 13-15) sicut puer noster Seneca
se vidisse testatur, nostrae fraternitatis animas in eodem laetitiae loco congregan-
das esse credimus   1626 *cf.* v. 1646

1600 ff. See Introduction, p. lxviii. In a letter of 795, addressed to the com-
munity at York (app. iii to vv. 1623-5), Alcuin seems to refer to this vision in
a manner which suggests that it had formed a local tradition. Certain details of the
vision may indicate which text of Bede's *HE* was used by Alcuin. The manuscript

and touch briefly on an experience of my boyhood,
which I happened to witness personally.

There was a young man reared in the city of York,
simple of spirit, but energetic to act,
who deeply influenced my boyhood with his counsel.
One night he was praying fervently, as usual,
alone in the chapel of the mother of Christ.
A gentle light suddenly filled that house
and with the light there appeared a man dressed in white,
of shining countenance and tall, upright bearing.
The young man fell in terror at his feet; he raised him up
with gentle words and showed him an open book.
The youth read it and, when he closed the book,
the resplendent figure said to him: 'Now that you know
you will witness even greater things.' With these words,
the shining messenger disappeared and, a few months
later, the youth was stricken by a disease in his limbs.
For long he lay there, with death impending,
straining to draw breath which was about to fail.
As he rested in my arms, his spirit was suddenly
snatched away, and his body remained there as if dead.
Then, coming to life after a space, he moved his limbs again
and told me how he had been led to a beautiful place,
where he had seen many men rejoicing,
some known to him, others unfamiliar; but he recognized
especially the happy members of that holy church.
They welcomed him with gentle embraces,

transmission of the *HE* divides into two main classes (Colgrave–Mynors, pp. xl ff.). The 'M-type'—so named after the Moore manuscript of this text (Colgrave-Mynors, pp. xliii–xliv)—preserves an additional and authentic chapter (iv. 14) which transmits a posthumous miracle of St. Oswald. Bede's account of this miracle bears a marked resemblance to the vision related here by Alcuin: a boy, lying gravely ill in a monastery, is visited by messengers from Heaven who offer him a vision of the other world which holds out special hope for his own community. Later the boy dies. In specific details Bede's account differs from Alcuin's. Yet it remains possible that Alcuin cast the vision he had witnessed in boyhood on the lines of the one related at *HE* iv. 14, just as he modelled his own account of Northumbrian history on Bede's work. If so, Alcuin read the *HE* in a text of the 'M-type'. As the 'Moore-Bede' (Cambridge University Library MS. Kk. 5. 16) belonged to the palace library of Charlemagne (Bischoff, *Karl der Grosse* ii, p. 56) and was produced in Northumbria during Alcuin's lifetime, it is a tantalizing possibility that the manuscript itself was brought to the Frankish court by Alcuin, and that a copy of his own exemplar of the *HE* thus sired the family of that text most widely diffused on the Continent.

et secum penitus semper retinere volebant,
sed cito ductor eum converso calle reduxit
ad proprium corpus, dicens quod: 'Solis ad ortum
iam melius habiturus eris; de fratribus alter   1630
sed hodie moriturus erit cuiusque paratam
vidisti sedem.' Iuvenem nec sermo fefellit.
Nam cito convaluit, dum sol rutilabat ad ortum;
ante diem medium fuerat sed mortuus alter.
Ille tamen iuvenis parvum post tempus eodem   1635
anno percutitur populantis peste doloris
atque mihi statim morbo praedixit in illo:
'Hac lue iam moriar, cito carnis claustra relinquam.'
Nec secus evenit, quoniam vis magna doloris
crevit et extremam iuvenem deduxit in horam.   1640
Qui tenui moriens animam traducere flatu
dum coepit, fuerat vigilans e fratribus unus,
vir probus et verax, vidit qui culmine ab alto
descendisse virum facie seu veste coruscum
et posuisse suum mox os morientis ad ora.   1645
Blandius amplexus manibus quoque membra cubantis,
regressusque animam solvens de carcere carnis
evexit volitans secum super astra polorum.
    Haec ego, nauta rudis, teneris congesta carinis
per pelagi fluctus et per vada caeca gubernans   1650
Euboricae ad portum commercia iure reduxi,
utpote quae proprium sibi me nutrivit alumnum

1635 tamen *r T²*: stamen *R*   1640 et *r*: ad *R*   1652 quae
Mabillon: quem *R*

1628 Arat. *de Act. Apostol.* i. 54 calle citato   1632 Virg. *Aen.* vi. 691
1645 Paul. Nol. xv. 294 morientis ad ora   1647 Bede *Vit. S. Cuthb. metr.*
535; Paul. Nol. xxxi. 334   1649 ff. Ven. Fort. *Vit. S. Mart. pref.* 1 nauta
rudis; id. viii. 3. 397, 398–400 opto, per hos fluctus, animas tu, Christe, guber-
nes / . . . / ut post emensos mundani gurgitis aestus / in portum vitae nos tua
dextra locet; Paul. Nol. xvii. 173–6 per . . . / vada caeca . . . / donec optatos liceat
salutis / tangere portus   1650 Virg. *Aen.* i. 536   1650–1 Ven. Fort.
Vit. S. Mart. iv. 1 post mare fluctivagum repetens ad litora portum . . .

1632 Alc. *Vit. S. Willibr. metr.* xxx. 8   1635–6 *HE Contin.* s.a. 759 magna
tribulatio mortalitatis venit et duobus ferme annis permansit, populantibus duris
ac diversis egritudinibus, maxime tamen dysenteriae languore   1649–50 Alc.
lxv. 4. 1 nauta rudis pelagi, ut saevis ereptus ab undis   1652–3 Alc. *Ep.* 114
(p. 167, 7) in aecclesia, ubi ego nutritus et eruditus fueram; [*Ep.* 42 (p. 85,

wanting to keep him with them for ever and ever,
but his guide swiftly led him back along the path
to his own body, saying: 'At sunrise
you will recover, but another of the brothers
will die today, and his dwelling you have seen
prepared.'   His words were true.   When the sun
glowed red in the dawn the young man swiftly recovered,
but before midday another brother was dead.
None the less, a short time later in the same year
that young man was struck down by a raging epidemic,
and in that illness at once foretold to me: 'I shall die
of this sickness, soon I shall leave the bounds of the flesh.'
So it happened, for the pain grew mightily,
and brought that young man to his last hour.
As he lay dying and his soul ebbed with fleeting breath,
one of the brothers who was keeping watch,
an upright and truthful man, saw descend from the heavens
above a being of radiant countenance and shining dress,
who kissed the lips of the dying man,
gently embracing the prostrate body;
he freed its soul from the prison of the flesh
and carried it off with him, flying over the stars in Heaven.
Like a rough sailor with these goods loaded on my fragile bark,
sailing through the ocean waves and the hidden shallows,
I have brought them back, as I should, to the port of York,
which reared me as its foster-son,

21 ff.)] ; *Epytaph. Civ. Pap.* i. 1 me sibi praeclarus doctor nutrivit .

1635-6. The *Continuations* to the *HE s.a.* 759 (app. iii ad loc.) record a series
of 'malignant diseases that wasted the people' of Northumbria in the years 760-1.
The continuator uses language similar to that employed here by Alcuin to
describe the epidemic which killed his boyhood friend. There is no evidence for
another calamity on this scale in Northumbria between 730 and 780. If these
two catastrophes are identical and Alcuin's friend died a *iuvenis*, when Alcuin
was a *puer*, then we have a clue to Alcuin's date of birth. *Pueritia*, according to
the definition given by Isidore (*Etym.* iii. 2. 3) and observed by Alcuin, began at
the age of 7 and ended at that of 14. It would follow that Alcuin was born 737/8-
745/6. A date some five to ten years later than the one currently accepted is, on
this hypothesis, no more shaky than c. 735, which coincides, perhaps too conveni-
ently, with Bede's obit (Introduction, p. xxxvi and n. 1).

1649 ff. On the nautical metaphor for literary composition, developed earlier
in the poem, see Curtius, pp. 128-30; D. Schmidtke, *Geistliche Schiffahrt*
(Tübingen, 1969), pp. 357 ff.; E. de Saint-Denis, *Le rôle de la mer dans la poésie
latine* (Lyons, 1936).

imbuit et primis utcunque verenter ab annis.
Haec idcirco tibi propriis de patribus atque
regibus et sanctis ruralia carmina scripsi.   1655
Hos pariter sanctos, tetigi quos versibus istis,
deprecor, ut nostram mundi de gurgite cymbam
ad portum vitae meritis precibusque gubernent.

1653 verenter *r*: reverenter *R*   1654 tibi *R*: cui *T*²

wisely training me from my earliest years.
And so for you have I written this rustic poem
about its bishops, kings, and saints.
I beseech too those saints, upon whom I have touched
in my verse, to guide my light vessel from the sea of the world
by their intercession and prayers to the port of life.

APPENDIX

Bishops and Archbishops of York
and Kings of Northumbria
until Alcuin's Death (804)

(i) BISHOPS AND ARCHBISHOPS OF YORK[1]

	Consecration	Accession	Termination of Office
Paulinus	21 July 625	625	resigned 633 to Rochester
Vacancy 633–64	—	—	—
[Chad	664	664	resigned 669 to Lichfield]
Wilfrid I	664/5	669	deprived 678 (Selsey 680)
Bosa	678	678	deprived 686
Wilfrid I		restored 686	deprived 691 (Leicester 692)
Bosa		restored 691	c. 705
John of Beverley	687	705 (translated from Hexham)	718
Wilfrid II	718	718	resigned 732
Egbert	732	732 archbishop 735	19 November 766
Ælberht	24 April 767	767	8 November 780
Eanbald I	780	780	10 August 796
Eanbald II	14 August 796	796	c. 808

[1] Following F. M. Powicke and E. B. Fryde, *Handbook of British Chronology*[2] (London, 1961), with reference to K. Harrison, *The Framework of Anglo-Saxon History to 900* (Cambridge, 1976). Square brackets indicate a bishop not mentioned by Alcuin (see Introduction, p. li). Bibliography of the dispute which has arisen over some of these dates is omitted from this Appendix.

(ii) KINGS OF NORTHUMBRIA[1]

	Accession	Death
*Edwin	616	633
*Oswald	633	642
*Oswiu	654	670
*Ecgfrith	670	685
*Aldfrith	685	704/5
Eadwulf	704/5	704/5
Osred I	705	716
Coenred	716	718
Osric	718	729
Ceolwulf	729	760/4 deposed and restored 731 resigned 737
*Eadberht	737	768 resigned 758
Oswulf	758	758
Æthelwald 'Moll'	758/759	unknown expelled 765
Alchred	765	unknown exiled 774
Æthelred I	774	796 exiled 778/9 restored 790; killed 796
Ælfwald I	778/9	788
Osred II	788	792 expelled 790
Osbald	796	799 expelled 796
Eardwulf	796	unknown expelled 806/8

[1] Asterisks indicate kings mentioned in the poem.

CONCORDANCE OF EDITIONS

I Concordance of Dümmler's edition with the present edition

The table shows on which pages of the present edition the first word of each page of Dümmler's edition is to be found. References in italics are to line-numbers of the poem.

Dümmler	Godman	Dümmler	Godman	Dümmler	Godman
169, *1*	2	182, *545*	46	195, *1153*	90
170, *10*	4	183, *595*	50	196, *1199*	94
171, *53*	8	184, *641*	54	197, *1242*	96
172, *96*	12	185, *687*	56	198, *1285*	100
173, *140*	16	186, *732*	62	199, *1329*	104
174, *183*	18	187, *779*	66	200, *1377*	108
175, *230*	22	188, *820*	68	201, *1419*	110
176, *276*	26	189, *866*	72	202, *1458*	114
177, *321*	30	190, *912*	76	203, *1502*	118
178, *365*	34	191, *961*	78	204, *1542*	122
179, *410*	36	192, *1012*	82	205, *1586*	128
180, *456*	40	193, *1060*	84	206, *1631*	132
181, *504*	42	194, *1105*	88		

II Concordance of the present edition with Dümmler's edition

The table shows on which page of Dümmler's edition the first word of each page of the present edition is to be found. References in italics are to the line-numbers of the poem.

Godman	Dümmler	Godman	Dümmler	Godman	Dümmler
2, *1*	169	28, *280*	176	54, *638*	183
4, *13*	170	30, *305*	176	56, *664*	184
6, *28*	170	32, *335*	177	58, *688*	185
8, *48*	170	34, *363*	177	60, *708*	185
10, *67*	171	36, *393*	178	62, *732*	186
12, *91*	171	38, *425*	179	64, *753*	186
14, *115*	172	40, *448*	179	66, *779*	187
16, *138*	172	42, *478*	180	68, *807*	187
18, *164*	173	44, *505*	181	70, *838*	188
20, *189*	174	46, *531*	181	72, *863*	188
22, *210*	174	48, *558*	182	74, *877*	189
24, *233*	175	50, *581*	182	76, *910*	189
26, *260*	175	52, *608*	183	78, *942*	190

Godman	Dümmler	Godman	Dümmler	Godman	Dümmler
80, *973*	191	100, *1269*	197	118, *1485*	202
82, *1008*	191	102, *1291*	198	120, *1512*	203
84, *1035*	192	104, *1316*	198	122, *1536*	203
86, *1064*	193	106, *1343*	199	124, *1547*	204
88, *1094*	193	108, *1372*	199	126, *1556*	204
90, *1124*	194	110, *1398*	200	128, *1573*	204
92, *1154*	195	112, *1427*	201	130, *1600*	205
94, *1189*	195	114, *1442*	201	132, *1627*	205
96, *1219*	196	116, *1460*	202	134, *1653*	206
98, *1244*	197				

INDEX OF QUOTATIONS
AND ALLUSIONS[1]

(i) SCRIPTURE

Genesis		Isaiah		
10:31-2	502	26: 7		1029
13:16	398	44: 3		87
25: 8	1522			
41: 13	110	Jeremiah		
		19: 9		102
Leviticus		27: 11		122
13: 14	1346			
26: 38-9	72	Ezekiel		
27: 32	1095	36: 37		1231
Deuteronomy		1 Maccabees		
32: 2	1433	4: 60		19
		6: 56		1279
2 Samuel		14: 4		116
1: 21	589			
		Matthew		
1 Chronicles		4: 18-19		853-4
12: 28	1450	6: 19-20		1257-8
28: 13	1224	7: 7		384
		25		598
2 Chronicles		14: 29		1363
3: 5	1225-6	25: 23		490
Judith		Luke		
7: 20	1477-8	1: 2		1072-3
		53		1254-5
Job		12: 33		1257-8
36: 6	1257-8			
39: 21	181	John		
		10: 12		673
Psalms		14: 23		1005
1: 2	211	15: 10		74
83: 3	602			
138: 8	505	Acts		
144: 11	25	2: 44-7		868 ff.
		4: 32-4		868 ff.
Ecclesiasticus		13: 11		174
18: 33	112			

[1] References on the left of the column are to the work cited; references on the right of the column are to the text of Alcuin's poem.

(ii) CLASSICAL, PATRISTIC, MEDIEVAL

INDEX NOMINUM ET VERBORUM[1]

a (*prep.*) 295, 302, 312, 511, 648, 718, 858, 893, 897, 967, 1128, 1173, 1291, 1412, 1430, 1460
ab 13, 27, 29, 102, 107, 132, 150, 206, 236, 249, 454, 494, 517, 629, 691, 695, 698, 702, 704, 711, 719, 725, 734, 796, 810, 825, 844, 951, 953, 1024, 1066, 1196, 1208, 1280, 1318, 1342, 1384, 1643, 1653
abbas, -atis 1218, 1295
abbatissa, -ae 396, 407
abeo, -ire 796
abhinc 203
abinde 323
abluo, -ere 399
abnuo, -ere 371
abscondo, -ere 1226
abstraho, -ere 666
absum, -esse 929
abyssus, -i 1449
ac 60, 133, 311, 345, 426, 888, 990
accendo, -ere 1045
accipio, -ere 115, 131, 753, 802, 1085, 1237, 1372, 1584
accola, -ae 363
accresco, -ere 955
acer, -ris, -re 462, 557, 846, 1550
acerbum, -i 1474
acerbus, -a, -um 384, 443, 519, 615, 885, 989, 1191
acervus, -i 592
acies, -iei 538, 542
acquiro, -ere 1051
actus, -us 293, 1004, 1018, 1313, 1405, 1603
acutus, -a, -um 1543
ad 342, 364, 382, 385, 400, 433, 435, 467, 470, 496, 530, 553, 617, 709, 734, 750, 797, 854, 908, 943, 958, 990, 999, 1030, 1078,

1155, 1198, 1376, 1385, 1395 (*bis*), 1458, 1464, 1476, 1497, 1568, 1586, 1623, 1629 (*bis*), 1633, 1645, 1651, 1658
addo, -ere 808, 882, 987, 1223, 1489
adduco, -ere 1100, 1107
adeo, -ire 95, 606, 1119
adfero, -ferre 362, 409, 448
adhaero, -ere 1291, 1428, 1527
adhibeo, -ere 21
adhuc 188, 489, 1599
adiuvo, -are 1284
admoveo, -ere 453
adolescens, -centis 1424
adolesco, -ere 1418
adoro, -are 252
adsto, -are 413
adsum, -esse 194, 332, 452, 466, 699
adsumo, -ere 244, 367, 1002
advenio, -ire 397, 1484
adventus, -us 957
adversa, -orum 1404
adversus (*prep.*) 841
advoco, -are 1138
aedes, -ium 702
aedifico, -are 1516
aeger, -ra, -rum 448, 493, 720, 733, 780, 1100, 1130, 1167, 1317
aegroto, -are 727
aegrotus, -a, -um 1617
aequabilis, -e 1363
aequalis, -e 1188
aequor, -oris 29, 62, 456, 691, 698, 838, 1011, 1034, 1185, 1369, 1374, 1384, 1590
aequoreus, -a, -um 88, 140, 461, 567, 854, 1365
aequus, -a, -um 570, 572
aerius, -a, -um 1328, 1444
aestimo, -are 787
aestivus, -a, -um 907

[1] References are to the line-numbers of Alcuin's poem. Place-names and proper names appear in the Latin form which occurs in the text. Words obelized in the text are placed in square brackets in this Index.

anxius, -a, -um 95

Aonius, -a, -um 1437

apertus, -a, -um 636, 648, 765, 1090, 1611

apex, -icis 1087

apostolicus, -a, -um 651, 1355

apostolicus, -i 1280

apparere 773

appono, -ere 1083

aptus, -a, -um 1022, 1097, 1179, 1224, 1453

aqua, -ae 333, 492

aquila, -ae 10, 569, 700

ara, -ae 159, 187, 277, 1491, 1497, 1514

Arator 1552

aratrum, -ri 85

arbitror, -ari 340

arbor, -oris 658, 725

arcus, -us 183, 1510

ardeo, -ere 445, 702, 856, 1181

ardor, -oris 350

arduus, -a, -um 180

areo, -ere 611

argenteus, -a, -um 1224

argentum, -i 277, 297, 306, 389, 1225, 1267, 1492, 1500, 1502

aridus, -a, -um 87, 590

Aristoteles 1550

arma, -orum 26, 127, 227, 237, 245, 522, 532, 544, 548, 790, 1331

armipotens 125

arripio, -ere 169, 305, 1342

ars, -tis 462, 807, 811, 1308, 1434, 1453, 1555, 1559

articulus, -i 470

artus, -a, -um 1294

artus, -us 732, 775, 793, 1147, 1616

aruspex, -spicis 160

arva, -orum 87, 599, 1372, 1374

arx, -cis 10, 206, 1413

ascendo, -ere 505, 946, 1377

aspectus, -us 1609

aspergo, -ere 457

aspicio, -ere 921, 1065

assidue 1264

assiduus, -a, -um 119

ast 56, 594, 1034, 1049, 1062, 1072, 1154, 1179, 1238, 1440, 1501, 1507, 1526, 1579

astra, -orum 250, 590, 629, 680, 692, 740, 1063, 1290, 1310, 1362, 1443, 1648

at 803, 991, 1066, 1197, 1341

ater, -ri, -rum 957

Athanasius 1543

atque 50, 80, 84, 112, 121, 142, 151, 153, 179, 286, 296, 318, 341, 439, 454, 493, 503, 533, 592, 608, 625, 637, 650, 676, 723, 727, 780, 795, 796, 801, 831, 846, 884, 890, 902, 908, 911, 931, 935, 946, 965, 969, 1003, 1039, 1058, 1072, 1081, 1109, 1113, 1115, 1130, 1146, 1148, 1151, 1153, 1165, 1191, 1192, 1200, 1203, 1212, 1232, 1259, 1261, 1262, 1298, 1335, 1341, 1358, 1398, 1417, 1427, 1443, 1445, 1460, 1470, 1474, 1478, 1482, 1485, 1493, 1502, 1511, 1541, 1545, 1546, 1548, 1556, 1565, 1575, 1600, 1637, 1654

atria, -orum 53, 410, 422

atrox 65, 626, 776

attamen 666, 1244

attero, -ere 259

attingo, -ere 1324

auctor, -oris 167, 1554

audacia, -ae 186

audax 541

audeo, -ere 387

audio, -ire 480, 636, 918, 940, 1336

aufugio, -ere 803

augeo, -ere 1234, 1483

augur, -uris 161

Augustinus 1542

augustus, -a, -um 504

aula, -ae 14, 118, 875, 998, 1568, 1606

aulea, -ae 366

aura, -ae 416, 598, 959, 1618

auratus, -a, -um 1226

auris, -is 484, 636

aurum, -i 182, 277, 279, 389, 1267, 1492, 1504

australis, -e 131, 583

aut 690, 692, 700, 702, 706, 721, 725, 811, 939, 1479

auxilium, -ii 50, 245, 953

averto, -ere 702

avide 321

avus, -i 266

Ælberhtus 1397

Ælfuine 789

et (*cont.*)
　1433, 1439, 1449, 1483, 1492 (*bis*),
　1497, 1498, 1501, 1516, 1542,
　1544, 1547, 1552, 1554, 1559,
　1564, 1583, 1608, 1610, 1622,
　1627, 1640, 1643, 1645, 1650,
　1653, 1655
etiam 193, 196, 253, 435, 439, 537,
　556, 570, 766, 1388
Euboricus, -a, -um 18, 91, 196, 220,
　1078, 1218, 1228, 1409, 1432,
　1603, 1651
Euticius 1557
evado, -ere 551, 818, 1386
evaleo, -ere 551
eveho, -ere 1648
evenio, -ire 1366, 1639
eventus, -us 110
everto, -ere 523
evigilo, -are 332, 451
ex 77, 220, 399, 679, 700, 708, 736,
　807, 812, 895, 903, 996, 1011,
　1072, 1157, 1168, 1183, 1244,
　1284, 1337, 1350, 1416, 1472,
　1566
exanimis, -e 619, 792
excelsus, -a, -um 271, 1367
excipio, -ere 1158
exemplum, -i 1017, 1044, 1232
exenium, -ii 56
exeo, -ire 57
exercitus, -us 61, 252, 260
exhinc 175, 495
eximius, -a, -um 1289
exin 432
exinde 1300
exitus, -us 413, 642, 1047
exorno, -are 275, 1028
expello, -ere 64, 144, 148, 699, 707,
　776
expers 658, 1193
explano, -are 1307
expleo, -ere 189, 642
exquiro, -ere 1057
exsequiae, -arum 891, 1160, 1586
exsilium, -ii 92, 1023, 1578, 1580
exsors 619
exspecto, -are 1245
exstinguo, -ere 348, 789, 793
exsto, -are 779
exstruo, -ere 275
exsul, -ulis 236, 1297
exsurgo, -ere 321

extendo, -ere 746, 909, 962
externus, -a, -um 68, 236, 510, 516,
　1454
exterus, -a, -um 47
extremus, -a, -um 27, 617, 628, 887,
　889, 1640
exulto, -are 603
exundo, -are 525
exuror, -uri 913

facies, -iei 333, 769, 1644
facile (*adv.*) 903
facio, -ere 100, 118, 152, 301, 336,
　369, 559, 701, 707, 772, 782,
　837, 851, 938, 1147, 1155, 1205,
　1225, 1228, 1250, 1271, 1293,
　1305, 1343, 1387, 1440, 1482,
　1501
factor, -oris 2
factum, -i 186, 1238, 1464
facultas, -atis 829
fallo, -ere 435, 1069, 1632
falsus, -a, -um 159
fama, -ae 287, 455, 613
fames, -is 592, 698, 1474
famosus, -a, -um 433, 501
famula, -ae 1122
famulus, -i 498, 677
fanum, -i 170, 185, 192
Farne 657, 706
farum, -i 1495
fas 1078
fastigium, -ii 185, 364, 933
fateor, -eri 799, 812, 1346
fatesco, -ere 193
fatum, -i 229, 1572
fautor, -oris 1399
faveo, -ere 51
favilla, -ae 934
favor, -oris 114
febris, -is 380, 384, 387
fecundus, -a, -um 22
feliciter 499, 836, 875, 1568
felix, -icis 186, 388, 574, 645, 664,
　1043, 1084, 1277, 1284, 1287,
　1298, 1424; felicior, -ius 73
femina, -ae 1150
femineus, -a, -um 1345
fenestra, -ae 1511
fera, -ae 591, 1445
feralia, -ium 473
fere 42
ferio, -ire 55

866, 873 (*bis*), 882, 912, 917, 921, 937, 970, 972, 974, 987, 993, 1005, 1006, 1008, 1048, 1050, 1055, 1064, 1066, 1104, 1127, 1136, 1144, 1154, 1165, 1170, 1174, 1178, 1191, 1205, 1207, 1228, 1233, 1234, 1248, 1251, 1259, 1277, 1279, 1280, 1282 (*bis*), 1285, 1288, 1315, 1354, 1364, 1366, 1379, 1388, 1410, 1415, 1424, 1434, 1451, 1458, 1483, 1495, 1508, 1509, 1515, 1518, 1531, 1533, 1563, 1569 (*bis*), 1597, 1612, 1614, 1638, 1649, 1654, 1656

Hieronymus 1541

Hilarius 1541

hinc 32, 38, 163, 417, 474, 509, 567, 622, 651, 751, 912, 958, 1063, 1615

historicus, -i 1549

historicus, -a, -um 1209, 1311

hodie 1351, 1357, 1631

homo, -inis 2, 439, 524, 591, 912, 934, 1003, 1445

honestus, -a, -um 134, 649, 849, 1093, 1237, 1425, 1609

honor, honos, -oris 115, 136, 208, 285, 361, 373, 498, 644, 662, 674, 1071, 1090, 1211, 1220, 1227, 1298, 1390, 1406, 1424, 1484, 1596

honorifice 1461, 1588

hora, -ae 226, 230, 401, 414, 826, 859, 1195, 1585, 1640

horrendus, -a, -um 403, 910, 1326

horreum, -ei 612

horribilis, -e 272, 1102, 1335

horrisonus, -a, -um 547

horror, -oris 1339

hortor, -ari 894

hospes, -itis 111, 328, 344, 400, 1614

hospita, -ae 27

hospitium, -ii 324

hostilis, -e 26, 119, 254, 537, 1276, 1330

hostis, -is 40, 50, 63, 102, 238, 249, 253, 258, 260, 265, 272, 416, 518, 541, 557, 564, 796, 806, 941, 942, 951, 953, 955, 1336, 1347, 1350

Hripensis, -e 645

hucusque 678, 1571

humanus, -a, -um 144, 862

humerus, -i 1280, 1476

humilis, -e 1382, 1404, 1407

humo, -are 682, 1161

humor, -oris 1378

humus, -i 331, 731, 1358

hymnus, -i 782, 1272

iaceo, -ere 294, 325, 380, 619, 1140, 1193, 1617

iacto, -are 691

iaculum, -i 170, 185

iam 29, 58, 76, 77, 89, 114, 122, 296, 359, 398, 447, 495, 504, 507, 757, 869, 885, 950, 953, 1016, 1054, 1101, 1116, 1172, 1193, 1240, 1244, 1295, 1363, 1371, 1390, 1420, 1423, 1429, 1455, 1508, 1525, 1581, 1630, 1638

ibi 608, 676, 892, 902, 915, 965, 1298

ibidem 331, 979, 1041, 1213, 1558

ictus, -us 867, 1060

idcirco 340, 1031, 1347, 1654

idem, eadem, idem 216, 377, 587, 834, 846, 876, 1070, 1199, 1635

ieiunium, -ii 1092

igneus, -a, -um 350

ignis, -is 214, 347, 370, 702, 762, 916, 947, 991

ignitus, -a, -um 948

ignotus, -a, -um 54, 97, 1624

ille, -a, -ud 54, 104, 107, 112, 143, 155, 156, 203, 221, 222, 224, 232, 282, 303, 318, 322, 353, 363, 369, 381, 383, 387, 400, 408, 454, 463, 486, 494, 552, 560, 562, 564, 568, 570, 577, 583, 586, 588, 596, 605, 614, 646, 669, 678, 695, 704, 711, 719, 734 (*bis*), 736, 745, 756, 761, 799, 803, 809, 810, 812, 817 (*bis*), 819, 822, 830, 832, 833, 857, 900, 919, 923, 956, 962, 978, 987, 992, 999, 1011, 1013, 1024, 1027, 1037, 1044, 1048, 1064, 1069, 1073, 1085, 1100, 1105, 1106, 1145, 1176, 1177, 1184, 1186, 1190, 1200, 1201, 1210, 1230, 1233, 1234, 1238, 1255, 1267, 1279, 1281, 1282 (*bis*), 1286, 1301, 1318, 1333, 1341 (*bis*), 1342, 1354, 1359, 1360, 1368, 1373, 1374, 1382, 1414, 1432, 1435, 1437, 1457, 1473, 1483,

nectar, -aris 1410
nefandus, -a, -um 63, 111, 262, 404
nego, -are 368, 591, 1166, 1379
negotium, -ii 866, 1279
nempe 1195
nepos, -otis 235
neptis, -is 327
neque 1480
nequeo 428, 703, 913, 1006
nervus, -i 309, 419, 768
nescio, -ire 435, 963, 987
nescius, -a, -um 450
nex, necis 587
ni 129, 478, 745
nidor, -oris 966
nigellus, -a, -um 1057 .
niger, -ra, -rum 1048, 1049, 1576
nihil 454, 812
nimis 228, 913, 1486, 1509, 1623
nimium (adv.) 186, 240, 349, 630, 893, 1494
nimius, -a, -um 445, 772, 936, 977, 1000, 1045, 1125, 1338, 1610
nisi 1371
niteo, -ere 311, 678, 925
nitidus, -a, -um 744, 959, 1614
niveus, -a, -um 630
nobilis, -e 33, 221, 754, 755, 791, 1252
nobiliter 566, 670
nocte 1062, 1197
noctu 1066
nocturnus, -a, -um 401
nolo, nolle 1226, 1477
nomen, -inis 135, 307, 502, 753, 1046, 1200, 1397, 1493, 1529, 1561, 1596
non 179, 233, 234, 241, 392, 419, 455, 471, 571, 589 (bis), 642, 663, 681, 747, 777, 810, 868, 920, 941, 975, 1077, 1114, 1206, 1304, 1308, 1351, 1357, 1378 (bis), 1405, 1454, 1479, 1504, 1615
Nonae, -arum 504
nos, nostrum 156, 249, 459, 924, 960, 964, 982, 984, 1572, 1576, 1577, 1590
noster, -ra, -rum 106, 745, 877, 882, 1008, 1068, 1076, 1091, 1320, 1322, 1386, 1573, 1575, 1589, 1598, 1657
notus, -a, -um 1385, 1624
Novembris, -is 1584

novenus, -a, -um 1081, 1496
novi, nosse 812, 1440
novus, -a, -um 76, 473, 508, 628, 808, 976, 1052, 1117, 1456, 1507
nox, noctis 94, 147, 211, 365, 369, 451, 792, 888, 891, 923, 926, 959, 1065, 1113, 1140, 1263, 1264, 1593, 1605
nubes, -is 1337
nubila, -orum 1595
nullus, -a, -um 7, 405, 464, 529 (bis), 530, 962 1101, 1162
numen, -inis 535, 747
numerus, -i 241, 1123, 1446
nummisma, -atis 868
numquam 426, 804, 993
nunc 152, 171, 244, 249, 289, 375, 430, 633, 816, 864 (bis), 896, 898, 989, 1002, 1077, 1322, 1347, 1383
nuntius, -ii 107
nuper 1124
nutrio, -ire 1273, 1451, 1602, 1652

o 9, 186, 228, 243, 284 (bis), 1576 (ter), 1589 (bis)
ob 72, 376, 467
obitus, -us 1316
obliviscor, -sci 449
oblongus, -i 909
obrizum, -i 1504
obruo, -ere 174
obscurus, -a, -um 147, 1307
obsessus, -a, -um 776
obstipesco, -ere 1125
obtendo, -ere 774
occido, -ere 265, 486, 552
occisor, -oris 519
occubo, -are 111, 227, 232, 320, 791, 842
occurro, -ere 1598
oceanus, -i 28, 85, 657
ocellus, -i 1361
octavus, -a, -um 1584
octo 503
oculus, -i 98, 625, 735, 780, 946, 952, 1202, 1573
oda, -ae 861
odium, -ii 367
odor, -oris 966, 980, 1000
Offa 388
offero, -ferre 828

officium, -ii 1469
olim 146, 205, 743
Olympus, -i 8, 535, 562, 632, 862, 1244, 1258
omen, -inis 160
Omnipotens, -ntis 234, 475
omnipotens 579, 627
omnis, -e 108, 116, 120, 133, 152, 155, 162, 252, 256, 269, 293, 337, 352, 384, 411, 438, 496, 527, 554, 572, 618, 685, 746, 818, 831, 859, 863, 867, 870, 895, 900, 933, 967, 986, 1023, 1043, 1053, 1065, 1157, 1237, 1241, 1244, 1260, 1430, 1499, 1526, 1581
opes, -um 436, 1254, 1531
opimus, -a, -um 275, 659, 1096, 1229
oppono, -ere 539, 1332
opprimo, -ere 260
opto, -are 779, 1149
opus, -eris 189, 530, 1047, 1517
opusculum, -i 1306
ora, -ae 66, 236, 607, 640, 1466
orarium, -ii 735
oratio, -onis 864
orbis, -is 79, 194, 578, 613, 1073, 1082, 1537
ordo, -inis 164, 964, 1059, 1136, 1270, 1423, 1470, 1496, 1521, 1584
origo, -inis 132, 1208
orior, -iri 1415
ornamentum, -i 1222, 1266, 1488
ornatus, -us 1514
orno, -are 388, 600, 1040, 1221, 1229, 1302, 1483
oro, -are 384, 669, 722, 733, 1264
oroma, -atis 93
Orosius 1543
orphanus, -i 1402, 1577
ortus, -us 140, 628, 907, 958, 1443, 1629, 1633
os, oris 51, 137, 157, 317, 709, 713, 948, 992, 1111, 1142, 1235, 1405, 1645 (bis)
os, ossis 362, 364, 367, 399, 419, 444
ostendo, -ere 1107, 1611
Osthryda 358
ostrum, -i 1273
Osuuald(us) 235, 241, 257, 260, 265, 319, 355, 359, 383, 432, 481, 499
Osuui 304, 506, 508, 566
ovile, -is 255, 672, 1026, 1471

ovis, -is 1028
ovo, -are 421, 1114, 1204, 1455 1623

pabulum, -i 1473
paciscor, -sci 273
pactum, -i 106
paganus, -a, -um 313, 1035, 1050
palam 164
pallium, -ii 209, 1280
pallor, -oris 1142
palo, -are 546
Pan 747
pando, -ere 1115, 1414, 1448
panis, -is 694, 719
pannum, -i 341, 345
papa, -ae 1544
par 1047, 1363
paralysis, -is 325
parco, -ere 530, 1479
parcus, -a, -um 269, 783
parens, -entis 754, 820, 1252, 1286, 1293, 1419
paries, -etis 278
pario, -ire 474
pariter 591, 757, 935, 1113, 1116, 1656
Parnassus, -i 1439
paro, -are 54, 224, 372, 638, 1160, 1266, 1631
pars, -tis 131, 290, 425, 485, 492, 889, 996, 1073, 1157, 1472, 1569
Parthus, -i 183
particula, -ae 441
parumper 17, 1600
parvulus, -a, -um 1093
parvus, -a, -um 197, 238, 471, 539, 663, 867, 981, 1504, 1635; minor, -us 1488
paschalis, -c 194, 292, 1447
pasco, -ere 693
pascua, -orum 1030
passim 553
pastor, -oris 725, 1121, 1239, 1470, 1567, 1589
pastoralis, -e 1248, 1467
patefacio, -ere 765, 1316, 1449
pateo, -ere 188
pater, -ris 1, 14, 52, 72, 118, 132, 143, 327, 502, 623, 624, 709, 723, 732, 737, 750, 857, 1083, 1087, 1092, 1110, 1202, 1217, 1281, 1313, 1317, 1341, 1364, 1402, 1484,

saepio, -ire 1326
saepta, -orum 1093, 1239, 1525, 1566
saevus, -a, -um 39, 368, 406, 838, 1356
sagax 1303, 1405, 1422, 1482
salsus, -a, -um 57
salubris, -e 33
salus, -utis 2, 89, 149, 171, 212, 332, 340, 355, 376, 420, 436, 441, 581, 609, 637, 641, 716, 722, 724, 779, 1035, 1127, 1149, 1316, 1387, 1401
salutifer, -fera, -ferum 190, 202, 314, 1148
saluto, -are 1168, 1129
salvo, -are 13, 555, 587, 953, 993 .
sanctus, -i 9, 393, 397, 479, 706, 712, 740, 971, 1013, 1064, 1320, 1353, 1655, 1656
sanctus, -a, -um 133, 280, 301, 330, 339, 359, 360, 364, 377, 382, 396, 427, 499, 634, 646, 769, 1005, 1092, 1108, 1122, 1128, 1222, 1265, 1307, 1383, 1459, 1493, 1543, 1624; sanctissimus, -a, -um 265, 291
sanguineus, -a, -um 261, 1429
sanguis, -inis 159, 304, 354, 513, 548
sano, -are 329, 386, 705, 717, 720, 732, 734, 879, 1119, 1318
sanus, -a, -um 320, 395, 415, 453, 738, 773, 1116, 1174, 1385
sapiens 1397
sapientia, -ae 1
sapor, -oris 709
sarcofagus, -i 372
satago, -ere 661, 802
satis 556, 895, 1024, 1415, 1499
Saxones, -um 123, 482, 1050
Saxonia, -ae 583
saxum, -i 48
scabrigo, -inis 1102
scamma, -atis 315
scando, -ere 680, 935
sceleratus, -a, -um 71, 513
scelus, -eris 171, 467
sceptrum, -i 23 38, 41, 76, 115, 117, 274, 506, 507, 558, 576, 1274, 1286
scio, -ire 477, 814, 986, 1006, 1613
scisco, -ere 1154
scitum, -i 129

scolasticus, -i 462
scopulosus, -a, -um 1323
Scotus, -i 123, 462, 839, 1016
scribo, -ere 686, 807, 877, 1303, 1311, 1548, 1555, 1560, 1561, 1655
Scriptura, -ae 1308, 1448, 1481
scutum, -i 44, 1332
se, sui, sibi 14, 37, 55, 66 (bis), 68, 77, 89, 226, 269, 333, 339, 341, 371, 397 (bis), 404, 425, 434, 448, 452, 453, 465, 491, 501, 520, 532, 541, 555, 567, 594, 595, 605, 672, 701, 707, 710, 714, 795, 798, 799, 812, 821, 829 (bis), 833, 935 (bis), 869, 871, 961, 1009, 1019, 1099, 1141 (bis), 1171, 1176, 1183, 1241 (bis), 1250, 1258, 1329, 1407 (bis), 1451, 1457, 1464, 1524, 1537, 1593, 1627, 1648, 1652
secedo, -ere 39, 1133
secerno, -ere 858
secrete 809
secretus, -a, -um 667, 675, 1115, 1389, 1414, 1524, 1566
sector, -ari 1487
secundus, -a, -um 1404, 1571
securis, -is 128
securus, -a, -um 25, 1349, 1377
secus 257, 1639
sed 84, 117, 156, 235, 241, 349, 351, 370, 459, 464, 531, 535, 540, 552, 587, 607, 674, 748, 761, 796, 813, 822, 826, 832, 864, 870, 892, 898, 936, 963, 1006, 1011, 1019, 1024, 1047, 1052, 1056, 1057, 1059, 1127, 1167, 1182, 1198, 1219, 1233, 1253, 1344, 1349, 1352, 1355, 1368, 1381, 1383, 1405, 1464, 1480, 1561, 1576, 1603, 1621, 1624, 1628, 1631, 1634
sedeo, -ere 96, 1170, 1177
sedes, -is 37, 40, 80, 667, 971, 1211, 1396, 1533, 1632
Sedulius (Caelius) 1551
sedulus, -a, -um 212
seges, -etis 526
segnis, -e 70, 1304
semel 993, 1454
semen, -inis 82, 206, 610, 1012

tenuissimus, -a, -um 773, 978
ter 499, 503, 520, 521, 837, 1286
tergum, -i 261, 940, 954
termino, -are 103
terminus, -i 962
ternus, -a, -um 215, 499
terra, -ae 13, 24, 36, 72, 181, 340,
 374, 392, 398, 580, 590, 599,
 778, 868, 1214, 1243, 1254, 1258,
 1375, 1381, 1392, 1444, 1454,
 1457, 1594
terrenus, -a, -um 228, 564, 605, 694,
 740, 871, 1327, 1390
terreo, -ere 149, 241, 950, 1350
terrestris, -e 506
terribilis, -e 183
terror, -oris 26, 568, 937, 1276, 1478,
 1610
tertius, -a, -um 827
testifico, -are 164
testis, -is 1601
testudo, -inis 542
teter, -ra, -rum 141, 927
tetricus, -a, -um 144, 580
texo, -ere 1208, 1226
thalamus, -i 756
Thalia 1597
theoricus, -a, -um 1025
thesaurus, -i 1532
thorus, -i 759
timeo, -ere 128, 350
timidus, -a, -um 65
timor, -oris 466, 543, 772, 1338
titulus, -i 286, 323, 1222
Tonans 9, 75, 553, 671, 761, 852,
 1270, 1355
tormenta, -orum 177, 1057
torqueo, -ere 423, 1340, 1348
torrens, -entis 525
totidem 521
totus, -a, -um 79, 104, 129, 165, 190,
 316, 348, 365, 418, 433, 474, 491,
 683, 730, 741, 748, 767, 768,
 1113, 1132 (bis), 1240, 1292,
 1498, 1564
toxicus, -a, -um 665
trado, -ere 225, 575, 1249, 1416,
 1523, 1526
traduco, -ere 1641
traho, -ere 733, 854, 943
trames, -itis 1029, 1375, 1454
tranquillus, -a, -um 640
trans 62, 456, 838, 1011, 1034

transago, -agere 400, 1106
transeo, -ire 875, 1568
transilio, -ire 1187
transmitto, -ere 1538
transveho, -ere 1247
tremefacio, -ere 1338
tremor, -oris 1444
trepido, -are 466
trepidus, -a, -um 534, 930
tres, tria 588, 1496
tribunal, -alis 124
tribunus, -i 1460
tribuo, -ere 1257
triginta 1285, 1348, 1514
trinus, -a, -um 540
triumphus, -i 64, 76, 119, 249, 563,
 565, 751
trophaeum, -i 248
trucido, -are 1056
trudo, -ere 1595
trux, -cis 1356, 1403
tu 3, 6, 7, 61, 99, 101 (bis), 103, 104,
 106, 169, 170, 427, 430, 433, 438,
 440, 482, 487, 489, 637, 639 (bis),
 785, 896, 1002, 1319, 1320, 1321,
 1356, 1357, 1383, 1385, 1409,
 1590, 1591, 1597, 1654
tuba, -ae 1401
tueor, -eri 40, 1471
Tullius 1550
tum 492, 940
tumba, -ae 390, 777
tumeo, -ere 180
tumidus, -a, -um 85
tumor, -oris 445, 689, 1125
tumulo, -are 766, 1298
tumulus, -i 734
tunc 22, 41, 78, 113, 167, 192, 250,
 294, 314, 320, 343, 353, 366,
 639, 786, 819, 848, 922, 929,
 951, 954, 978, 1009, 1017, 1069,
 1098, 1100, 1150, 1160, 1181,
 1195, 1211, 1214, 1277, 1337,
 1343, 1350, 1358, 1427, 1607,
 1619
turba, -ae 190, 294, 1339
turbo, -are 38, 327, 1590
turma, -ae 242, 521, 971, 1005, 1328
turris, -is 19
tutamen, -inis 1121
tutator, -oris 267
tutor, -ari 532
tutus, -a, -um 545, 1324

GENERAL INDEX

This index refers to the Introduction and Commentary. References in Roman numerals are to the Introduction. Unless otherwise indicated, references in Arabic numerals are to the Commentary. Excluded from the General Index are extant manuscripts, which are indexed in the Select Bibliography (pp. xvii–xviii); Latin names and words, which are listed in the Index Nominum et Verborum (pp. 155–88), and some authors or works not discussed in the Introduction or Commentary, which appear in the Index of Quotations and Allusions (pp. 139–54).

Aachen, xxxvii, 30 ff.

abbas, use of, 1218; *and see* Index Nominum et Verborum

ablative, case, formation and use of, xcv, xcviii, 512, 557

accusative, case, use of, xciv, xcvii, xcviii

acrostic poems, 427 ff.

Adamnan, his *De Locis Sanctis* in Northumbria, 843–6

Addi, *gesith*, 1154

adjectives, use of, xciv, xcv, ci, 530, 651

adverbs, formation and use of, xcvi, xcvii, cix, 362–3

aenigmata, Anglo-Latin, lxxvii

Africa, texts from, 1537–40

agency, expression of, xcviii

Aidan, St., bishop of Lindisfarne, l, lii

Alcluith, British capital, 1273–6

Alcuin:

— and his poem on York, *passim*; reputation of and recent scholarship on, vii–viii, xxxiii–xxxv

— life of, xxxv–xxxviii; biographies of, xxxv; date and place of birth, xxxvi, 1635–6; possible noble descent, xxxvi, 754–5; friendship, teaching and patronage by Aelberht, xxxvi, 1438–9, 1450–3, 1454–9; miracle witnessed in youth, 1600 ff.; training at school of Aelberht, lxii–lxiii, lxiv, 1437, 1438–9, 1450–3; succeeds as master of school of York in 767, xxxvi; role in construction of basilica of Sancta Sophia, lx, 1515–17

— continental journeys of, xxxvi, xliii, 1393, 1454–9; meets Charlemagne in 781, moves to Charlemagne's court, influence there, xxxvii, 1436–7, 1441–5; prophecies concerning his move to court, xxxvii, 1393; return journeys of 786 and 793, xxxvii; teaching of, 1432–3, 1436–7, 1441–5; made abbot of St. Martin's in 796, xxxviii; death in 804, xxxviii

— sources for Alcuin's career, xxxviii–xxxix

— works of: astronomy, 1441–5; Bible and biblical exegesis, xxxviii, 1448–9, 1541, 1542, 1546; computus, 1447; *De Grammatica* of, 1550, 1555, 1556, 1557; *De Musica* attributed to, 1437; letters: editions of and research on, xxxiv, as a source for Alcuin's career, xxxviii–xxxix, as a source for Alcuin's view of Northumbrian history, xlvii, to Offa, lviii; antedating 790, xxxix, n. 1; antedating 794, xxxviii–xxxix; written 793–801 on the continent to York, xlii–xliii; *and see* Index of Quotations; liturgy, xxxiv; mathematical (ascribed), xxxiii, 1446; orthography, xxxiii, cx–cxiii, 557, 1555, 1556; philosophical-theological, xxxiii, 1448–9, 1542, 1546, 1548, 1550

— Poem on York, authorship of, cxiv, pp. 2–3a; autograph and autograph marginalia of, cx, cxi, cxiv, pp. 2–3a; scholarship on, vii–viii, xxxv; character and synopsis of, xxxix–xlvii; date

Alcuin (*cont.*)
of, xlii–xlvii; source for Alcuin's career, xxxv, xlii; source for Northumbrian history, xxxv, xlvii–lx; the school of York and Alcuin's reading and sources, lx–lxxv; its place in Anglo-Latin literature, lxxv–lxxviii; influence on Carolingian and Anglo-Latin poetry, lxxxviii–xciii; its form and previous literature, lxxviii–lxxxviii; language of, xciii–cx; orthography, cx–cxiii; textual history, cxiii–cxxix; *and see under* Bede, Gale, Mabillon, Reims, Ruinart, *and see* Index of Quotations
— poetry: (general), xxxiv–xxxv, xlii, 1438–9; *Carmen* ii, xxxvi, xxxix; *Carmen* iv, xxxvi, xxxix; *Carmen* lix, xliii; rhetorical works, xxxiii, 1434–5; *Vitae S. Willibrordi* (prose and metrical), xxxiii, xliii, lxxviii, lxxxv–lxxxviii
Aldfrith, king of Northumbria, liii, liv, 843–6
Aldhelm, bishop of Sherborne, xliv, lxxv; Alcuin's debts to and use of, lxvii n., lxviii–lxix, lxxiii, lxxv; *De Virginitate*, prose and metrical versions, lxxvii, lxxxii–lxxxiv, lxxxviii; *De Metris*, cviii n., 843–6; debts to Caelius Sedulius, lxxxii, to Alcimus Avitus and Prudentius, lxvii, to Prosper of Aquitaine, lxvii–lxviii, to Caelius Sedulius, Arator, Juvencus, lxix, slight knowledge of Paulinus of Nola, lxx, and of Lucan and Statius, lxxii, quotations from Phocas, 1556; use of alliteration, cv n., cvi, use of third strong caesura, cvii, use of written formulae, cvii, letter to Aldfrith, 843–6; opinion of secular poetry, 747–50, teaching of, 1432–3, works of at York, 1547; *and see* Index of Quotations
Alhred, king of Northumbria, xlvi
alliteration, use of, cv–cvi, cx
allusions, classical to Christian subjects, 8–9
altar, pagan, 168 ff.; at York, dedicated to St. Paul, 1488 ff.; in Sancta Sophia, 1507 ff., 1512
Altger, *Vita Liutgeri* of, 35–6, 1533–5

Altsige, abbot of York, letter of Lupus of Ferrières to, 1218
Ambrose, St., of Milan, works of at York, 1542
amulet, magical, 807
anaphora, ciii
anastrophe, 48
anchorites, xli, lvi–lvii, 1025, 1388 ff.
Anglade, Arnould d., cxx, cxxiii
Anglo-Latin literature, development of, vii, viii, lxix, lxxv–lxxviii, lxxxiv–lxxxv, xci; gaps in and Viking devastation, xlv, xci, cxxix, orthography of Anglo-Saxon place- and proper names, cxii–cxiii; surveys of, xxxv, lxxv
Anglo-Saxon Chronicle, 'Northern recension' of, xxxix
Anna, king of East Anglia, 753 ff.
'Annales', see under 'Poeta Saxo'
annominatio, ciii
antithesis, ciii
aphaeresis, cviii
apodosis, c
Apollo, 747–50
apostolicus, xcv, 651, 1280; *and see* Index Nominum et Verborum
apparatus, i, ii, and iii, purpose and organization of, cxxx
Arator, lxix, lxxiv; *and see* Index of Quotations
aristocracy, Carolingian, xxxvi
Aristotle, works of at York, 1548, 1550
art, English continental influence on, 1268
asceticism, lv; *and see under* anchorites
asyndeton, ciii
Athanasius, Evagrius's translation of, 1327 ff., 1543
athletae Christi, in Aldhelm, lxxxiii, lxxxviii
audience, of Alcuin's poem, xliii, xlvi–xlvii, lx–lxxv, 61
Augustine, archbishop of Canterbury, mission of, xxxvii
Augustine, St., of Hippo, works of at York, 1537–40, 1542; *and see* Index of Quotations
Avitus, Alcimus, lxvii, lxxiv, 1552; *and see* Index of Quotations

Ælberht, archbishop of York, Alcuin's description of, 1393; bibliophile